JEWISH AND CHRISTIAN TEXTS IN CONTEXTS AND RELATED STUDIES

Executive Editor
James H. Charlesworth

Editorial Board of Advisors
Motti Aviam, Michael Davis, Casey Elledge, Craig A. Evans,
Loren Johns, Amy-Jill Levine, Lee McDonald, Lidia Novakovic,
Gerbern Oegema, Henry Rietz, Brent Strawn

THE PROTEVANGELIUM OF JAMES

Greek Text, English Translation, Critical Introduction: Volume 1

George Themelis Zervos

LONDON • NEW YORK • OXFORD • NEW DELHI • SYDNEY

T&T CLARK
Bloomsbury Publishing Plc
50 Bedford Square, London, WC1B 3DP, UK
1385 Broadway, New York, NY 10018, USA
29 Earlsfort Terrace, Dublin 2, Ireland

BLOOMSBURY, T&T CLARK and the T&T Clark logo are trademarks
of Bloomsbury Publishing Plc

First published in Great Britain 2019
This paperback edition published in 2021

Copyright © George Themelis Zervos, 2019

George Themelis Zervos has asserted his right under the Copyright,
Designs and Patents Act, 1988, to be identified as Author of this work.

For legal purposes the Acknowledgments on pp. xiv–xv constitute an
extension of this copyright page.

All rights reserved. No part of this publication may be reproduced or transmitted
in any form or by any means, electronic or mechanical, including photocopying,
recording, or any information storage or retrieval system, without prior
permission in writing from the publishers.

Bloomsbury Publishing Plc does not have any control over, or responsibility for,
any third-party websites referred to or in this book. All internet addresses given
in this book were correct at the time of going to press. The author and publisher
regret any inconvenience caused if addresses have changed or sites have ceased
to exist, but can accept no responsibility for any such changes.

A catalogue record for this book is available from the British Library.

Library of Congress Cataloging-in-Publication Data
Names: Zervos, George, editor.
Title: The protevangelium of James: the Greek manuscript tradition /
edited by George Themelis Zervos.
Other titles: Protevangelium Jacobi. English.
Description: New York: 2019. | Includes bibliographical references and index.
Identifiers: LCCN 2019020099 (print) | LCCN 2019980422 (ebook) |
ISBN 9780567256546 (hardback) | ISBN 9780567689757 (epub) |
ISBN 9780567053169 (pdf)
Subjects: LCSH: Protevangelium Jacobi.
Classification: LCC BS2860.J2 A1 2019 (print) | LCC BS2860.J2 (ebook) |
DDC 229/.8–dc23
LC record available at https://lccn.loc.gov/2019020099
LC ebook record available at https://lccn.loc.gov/2019980422

ISBN: HB: 978-0-5672-5654-6
PB: 978-0-5677-0038-4
ePDF: 978-0-5670-5316-9
ePUB: 978-0-5676-8975-7

Series: Jewish and Christian Texts in Contexts and Related Studies, volume 17

Typeset by Integra Software Services Pvt. Ltd.

To find out more about our authors and books visit www.bloomsbury.com
and sign up for our newsletters.

CONTENTS

Preface	vii
Foreword *James H. Charlesworth*	ix
Acknowledgments	xiv
INTRODUCTION: THE GENERAL BACKGROUND	1
The Publication History of the Greek Text of the *ProtJac*	4
The History of Scholarly Investigation of the *ProtJac*	13
The Compositional Problem of the *ProtJac*	15
The Present Study	19
Chapter 1	
EVIDENCE OF REDACTION OF THE *PROTJAC*	23
The Joseph Council: *ProtJac* 8:03–9:12	23
The Veil Council: *ProtJac* 10:01–12:11	35
The Original *GenMar* Annunciation Story	39
Mary's Visit to Elizabeth	49
The Trial of Joseph and Mary: *ProtJac* 13:01–16:07	55
The Nativity Complex: *ProtJac* 17–21	77
The Journey to Bethlehem	84
Topographical and Archaeological Factors	89
The Midwife	92
The Birth	104
Doubting Salome	108
The Magi	113
The Zachariah Apocryphon	123
The Colophon	126
CONCLUSIONS: THE "AUTHORS" OF THE *PROTJAC*	129
The Redactor: The *Protevangelium Jacobi*	131
The Composer: The Composer-enhanced *GenMar*	148
Joseph in the ProtJac	151
The Author: The *Genesis Marias*	158

Appendices	171
Appendix 1: Mary's Evolving Virginity in Early Christianity	171
Appendix 2: The Apologetic Purpose of the *ProtJac*	174
The Evidence of Malcom Lowe	193
Appendix 3: The *ProtJac* and the New Testament Gospels	198
Appendix 4: The Kathisma Church	205
The Original Cave of the Nativity	209
Illustrations	219

PREFACE

This book was conceived the first time I opened Michel Testuz's diplomatic edition of Bodmer Papyrus V[1] (P.Bodm V) and saw at the beginning of the book the plate which contained a photograph of a leaf of this magnificent papyrus manuscript. Having labored in the Duke University papyrology room to piece together fragments of disintegrated papyri, I was impressed that an entire papyrus codex could have survived from antiquity in such a near perfect state of preservation, with all pages intact, all margins complete, and all letters legible. My interest in the papyrus itself gave way to the realization of the great importance of the document that it contained, the *Protevangelium Jacobi* (*ProtJac*). It became apparent to me that the *ProtJac* constituted a major extra-biblical source of early Christian beliefs. Long since cured of any "canonical myopia" in Professor J. H. Charlesworth's seminars on the Apocrypha and Pseudepigrapha at Duke, I soon recognized that the *ProtJac* could be dated to a time before there existed any concept of a New Testament canon in the collective mind of early Christianity.

The second major step in the progressive development of this book was taken when I discovered in the Duke library Boyd Lee Daniels's massive three-volume dissertation, *The Greek Manuscript Tradition of the Protevangelium Jacobi*.[2] During his doctoral studies at Duke thirty years earlier, Daniels had identified 138 Greek manuscripts containing the *ProtJac* in libraries all over the world. Working from microfilms and photographic copies of eighty-one of these documents, Daniels was able to present full collations of these Greek witnesses in his dissertation. The remaining texts were either lost, destroyed, or unavailable to him for study.[3] When I found the same materials used by Daniels still accessible in the Duke library, I undertook the task of adding as many photographic images as possible to the Duke collection of Greek manuscripts of the *ProtJac*.

My own doctoral research came to focus upon those manuscripts of the *ProtJac* that had not been collated by Daniels. I intended that my work would constitute a second major step—after that of Daniels—toward the ultimate goal of a definitive critical edition of the original text of this Apocryphon based upon all the extant manuscript witnesses. In my own dissertation I was able to examine and publish a total of forty-five new manuscripts fully collated in a format compatible with

---

1. *Papyrus Bodmer V: Nativité de Marie* (Cologny-Genève: Bibliotheca Bodmeriana, 1958).
2. Unpublished dissertation of Duke University, 1956.
3. Daniels was working during the Cold War so manuscripts from Soviet Bloc countries were difficult to obtain.

that of Daniels. I am now presenting in this book the combined variant readings from Daniels's and my own dissertations, based upon Daniels's original format, and now collated against my own transcription of the text of P.Bodm V. Exhaustive collations of 126 out of 169 known, extant Greek manuscripts of the *ProtJac* are available in Volume 2 of this book, easily linked to the text of P.Bodm V, so as to provide an easy reference for scholarly study of the text of the *ProtJac*. It is my hope that this work will facilitate the eventual production by future scholars of the elusive definitive critical edition of this most important New Testament Apocryphon.

In reading through the Greek text of the *ProtJac* literally hundreds of times while preparing my own collations and merging them with those of Daniels, I detected numerous instances of editorial activity in the *ProtJac* text. I then conducted an exhaustive redaction-critical analysis of the text of the *ProtJac* as presented in P.Bodm V. I believe that through this analysis I have been able to illuminate the multilevel compositional process that produced the text of the *ProtJac* as it exists today. I offer the results of my investigation in Volume 1 of this book as a critical introduction to the textual materials contained in Volume 2. In my opinion the extreme importance of this document as a witness to very early Christian teachings concerning Jesus's mother Mary and Jesus himself has long been ignored by scholars because it has been misrepresented by a scholarly consensus regarding its compositional history, authorship, and date. It is my hope that this study will shed new light on these issues and thus provide scholars with the opportunity to delve deeper into the mysteries hidden in the pages of this fascinating Christian Apocryphon.

FOREWORD
ARE WINDOWS INTO THE FIRST CENTURY CE PROVIDED BY THE PROTEVANGELIUM JACOBI?

James H. Charlesworth

Early Gospels, Epistles, and Apocalypses placed in the New Testament Apocrypha and Pseudepigrapha (NTAP) tend to fade from view even for experts on the New Testament and Early Church History. Some books in the NTAP predate or are contemporaneous with some books in the New Testament canon. Two excellent examples are the *Gospel of Thomas* and the *Protevangelium Jacobi* (the *ProtJac*), using the nomenclature of Guillaume Postel. The Apocryphon is also known as *The Infancy Gospel of James*. Most NT scholars concur that the *ProtJac* antedates, or is contemporaneous with, some compositions collected into the NT canon, notably 1 Peter and 2 Peter. The *ProtJac* should be perceived as an example of *sacra scriptura* since it was considered "scripture" by many early Christians and it antedates discussion of a closed canon.

Now, Professor George Zervos, who has devoted his life to this composite, perceives that some traditions in it antedate the final composition. The excavation of the Kathisma church (see Appendix 4) may prove the importance and antiquity of these traditions and perhaps the document. Surely, Christians in the Holy Land and elsewhere will find Zervos's labors fascinating. I am convinced that we should be open to the possibility that some edited traditions in the *ProtJac* take us back into the second half of the first century CE. Zervos and the recent excavations north of Bethlehem at the Kathisma church open our eyes to the early traditions codified in the *ProtJac*.

When I visited the site, I was impressed by the remains of the Kathisma church. Barely to the northeast of the church, I saw an ancient road leading from Jerusalem to Bethlehem and caves perhaps known to the Holy Family. Near the ruins of the early Byzantine church is a large pool for water. Most likely the water and place were chosen for baptisms. These archaeological treasures help us comprehend early Byzantine celebrations of Mary and warn us not to jettison as irrelevant the historical and theological claims in the *ProtJac*.

In my *Jesus of Nazareth: Imagining a Biography* I begin with "The Preteen Mary in the Temple." Too often NT scholars are overly influenced by the negative conclusions of the nineteenth-century Tübingen School. Experts can find historical gems even in *Kerygmata* and liturgies. Perhaps there is reliable history in the claims that Joachim and Anne lived near the Pool of Bethzatha. Do not archeological discoveries raise that presumption? If so, Mary would have known the dancing in the Temple and have heard the singing of Levites, the thunder of drums, and the blaring trumpets. The Temple defined not only worship in Jerusalem before 70 CE; it defined the culture and the preoccupation of many. Inebriation today is defined by a drink; in pre-70 Jerusalem it signified being intoxicated with the Creating Lord of History. That enthusiasm was stimulated by the smell of stimulating incense and joyous singing in the Temple.

Jesus's family was related to the priestly family that resided in Ain Karem. Zechariah was a distinguished and influential leader of the Temple cult and the father of Jesus's cousin, John the Baptizer. Maybe Jesus's family is one of the numerous groups who migrated northward to Galilee and to Nazareth, Migdal, Gamla, and other villages after the defeat of the Greeks by the Judean Hasmoneans in the second century BCE.

Scholars are now reexamining the early gospels that were not placed in the canon. The most important for understanding the early life of Mary are the *Gospel of Pseudo-Matthew*, the *Gospel of the Birth of Mary*, and especially the *Protoevangelium of James*. Most notably, in light of the most recent research, the latter composition preserves portions of a very early report about Mary and a description of the Temple that seems representative of the late first century CE.

In many early Christian apocryphal texts, Jews are slandered. None of these acids drip from the *ProtJac*. Note this positive appreciation of Judaism and the Temple:

Summon the undefiled virgins from the tribe of David.
And the servants went out and sought and found seven.
And the priest remembered the child Mary,
That she was of the tribe of David and undefiled to God.
And the servants went out and brought her.
And they brought them into the temple of the Lord. (*ProtJac* 10)

The early Semitic poetry (*parallelismus membrorum*) also reflects a pre-Greek Semitic source.

I find most striking the absence of anti-Jewish thoughts in this early gospel. These appear with increasing frequency in the apocryphal gospels. While the full narrative of the *ProtJac* seems late and misrepresentative of Mary's time, there are ancient traditions within it. The most important passage reflects life in the Temple before 70 CE (when the cult ceased due to Roman conquest).

According to these ancient traditions, Mary's parents were Joachim and Anna, who were descended from David. Their home was in Jerusalem, just north of the Temple and near the Sheep Gate and the Pool of Bethzatha. As a virgin, Mary, with her parents, could walk five minutes to the Temple gates and enter the services in the Temple.

With other virgins, Mary probably danced in the Temple. Her young feet tapped out the rhythm of the timbrel, harp, trumpet, and drum. Like other Jewish girls reared in a religious home, she had for years memorized David's psalmic exhortation found in Psalm 149.

Let Israel rejoice in their Maker;
Let the children of Zion be joyful in their King.
Let them praise His name with dancing;
Let them sing praises to Him with the timbrel and harp. (Ps 149:2-3; NKJV)

According to early Christian sources, Joachim and Anne loved Mary. They yearned for her to join the virgins in the Temple. They knew that the Temple cult demanded the highest morality and any sexual innuendoes were strictly taboo. Mary's parents recognized that the Temple cult was emphatically different from other temples throughout the Mediterranean world; in contrast to the Jerusalem cult, the "pagan" temples celebrated ritual prostitution.

Zervos was my graduate student at Duke University. I urged him to focus his dissertation on the *ProtJac*. He and I knew about four important Greek manuscripts of this work. I showed him how to discover other copies in the leading libraries of the world. He found over 100 and his dissertation showed their importance. Now, Zervos shares with the world his insights, creative reflections, and mastery of this extremely important early Christian composition. Wisely, he points out the seams left by the composer or the redactor. Certainly on target is Zervos's insight that the *ProtJac* antedates any consideration of a New Testament canon. Thus, it appeared before the "canon" and should not be categorized as outside of a canon. Later developments must not blind us to the origins of our *sacra scriptura*.

Many questions are raised by Zervos's research and publication. How early is the final work? Do some traditions in it take us back into the first century CE? Does it not, like the *Odes of Solomon*, awaken in us a deep admiration for the minds of the earliest Christians, perhaps converted Jews? Why is the author so fascinated with Mary, Jesus's mother? Are its traditions close to the Infancy Gospels preserved by Matthew and Luke?

The *ProtJac* is relegated today to the *Apocryphal New Testament*. That categorization misleads too many. The work was composed before the canon was defined and later "closed" in the West. Perhaps no one needs to clarify today that worldwide "Christianity" never canonized one "closed" New Testament. Different versions of the New Testament are used by the Protestants, Roman Catholics, Russian Orthodox, Greek Orthodox, Armenians, and Ethiopians.

Long before a book in the Jewish and Christian canon was composed, many Hebrews believed in a female consort to YHWH. Wisdom was later perceived to be a feminine deity. In Semitics "the Holy Spirit" is a feminine noun and often a feminine concept. In some early Christian communities the need for a feminine divine person to balance the "maleness" of Jesus Christ is fulfilled by some believers as Mary Magdalene. In many other circles, and those represented by the *ProtJac*, Mary was elevated as a divine being. The Roman Catholic Church in more recent times recognized the assumption of Mary. These reflections bring us back to the beginning of our Bible. "Adam" is not a male; Adam is both male and female. The female and male originated in Adam.

Before concluding my reflections, I wish to highlight Zervos's forty years of pursuing research on the *ProtJac*. He began his doctoral studies at Duke University, under my tutelage, as a deeply professing Eastern Orthodox Christian. He was then ordained as a priest of the Greek Orthodox Church. In his search for the earliest possible traditions of the "Virgin" Mary, he delved into the text of the *ProtJac*. He was surprised to discover even more significant mysteries hidden within its pages. As his research continued to focus on the *ProtJac*, he found the ancient gospel to be a multilayered composition. In summary, he was astounded to find that this composition may contain traditions about Mary and Jesus that reach back into the first century CE. He is even convinced that the *ProtJac* should be considered to be the original source of many influential Mary traditions; that is, they should not be limited to the canonical Matthew.

Zervos contemplates that the antiquity of the traditions in the *ProtJac* was hidden by the presuppositions and methodologies of the ancient and modern editors of the document and redactors of the *ProtJac*. Zervos argues that only an intensive redaction-critical analysis of the *ProtJac*, as represented in vol. 1 of his opus, allows an expert to peer through the layers of redaction and expose the original underlying texts or traditions.

Zervos also was surprised to discover that it was not only the earliest Marian traditions that were being exposed by his lengthy research but also those relating to Jesus himself. It was particularly revealing that the *ProtJac* was not written merely as an apologetic response to early calumnies against Mary's reputation and Jesus's legitimacy but as a rejection of the early Docetic Christological understanding of Jesus as a divine being who was not incarnate in a human body. The author, like the author of the Gospel of John, affirmed Jesus's full humanity. This revelation highlighted the great paradox of an enigmatic first-century Judean-Christian gospel that was written before the hostile environment that was created when Jews and Christians went their separate ways. Perhaps his insights are best articulated in the following excerpt from pp. 168–9, as he peers behind the Redactor to the Composer:

> The *GenMar* truly is "a riddle wrapped in a mystery inside an enigma." The "enigma" inside of which the mystery-wrapped "riddle" of the *GenMar* has been secreted is the *ProtJac*, which itself represents an anachronistic puzzle that defies conventional interpretations of the history of Mariology. If scholars have been perplexed by the *ProtJac*, dating by all accounts to the second century CE, whose principle purpose was to certify what eventually would become the full-blown Catholic dogma of the perpetual virginity of Mary, how much more would they be confounded by its source document, the apparently Jewish *GenMar*, which seems to promote the same objective and dates to a century earlier? The "mystery" inside of the *ProtJac* "enigma," in which the "riddle" of the *GenMar* is wrapped, is the CEGM which contains copious amounts of extraneous materials inserted by the Composer into the *GenMar* in pursuit of his own agenda. The Composer thus contributed an entire level of additional complexity to the overall *ProtJac* puzzle and further obscured the original character of the *GenMar*. It is my hope that this redaction-critical study of the *ProtJac* has provided insights that will form a basis for future scholarly

investigations towards the ultimate resolution of the many enigmas, mysteries, and riddles hidden in the pages of this extraordinarily important Apocryphon and its sources.

If Zervos has discovered the multilayers of this composition, he has achieved at least two unforeseen breakthroughs. First, historically, he shines a light into the second half of the first century CE when the Temple in Jerusalem was still (or imagined to be) the centralizing magnet for Jews. Second, theologically and Christologically, he grounds the beliefs of many Christians, uniting Christendom that has been too long divided between East and West. Too many savants have forgotten that the *ProtJac* was published in the 1564 edition of Martin Luther's *Small Catechism*. My heart is moved when I recall worshipping with Zervos and Archbishop Damianos and the Holy Council in St. Catherine's Monastery in the southern mountains of the Sinai.

With great enthusiasm, I recommend Zervos's book. He demonstrates why the ban in the *Decretum Gelasianum* was rightly dismissed and presents one of the most erudite studies ever published on this early composition. The *ProtJac* is a major contribution to the reception history of Jesus from Nazareth. Zervos's masterpiece is full of challenging insights. His work helps heal the schism that has too often separated Christianity into the West and the East. Many scholars will agree with me that Zervos helps us obtain a new perspective on the origins of Christianity.

A masterful monograph is a tome that helps us realize new questions and explore answers. Are windows into the first century of the Common Era provided by this early document known as the *Protevangelium of James*? Is it a composite document reflecting traditions that antedate the final gospel? Professor Zervos helps us answer these challenging and new questions.

May 30, 2019
JHC
Princeton

ACKNOWLEDGMENTS

First and foremost I would like to acknowledge the immense contribution of Boyd Lee Daniels to my investigation of the *ProtJac*. Boyd was kind enough in the last days of his life to grant me the rights to publish in this book the collations of the eighty-one Greek manuscripts in the format that he himself created to present his collations in his doctoral dissertation. I have always felt a loving solidarity with Boyd and his lovely wife Pat as I have carried forward the task that he initiated seven decades ago. I offer herein the fruits of our joint labors, our combined collations presented over against the text of P.Bodm V with a fresh translation. I have added my own critical introduction which I hope has revealed the immense significance of the document that we toiled over for so many years of our lives.

Many individuals and institutions over the span of four decades contributed to the completion of this book. Mr. Donn Michael Farris, who served as the Director of the Duke Divinity School Library from the 1950s to the 1980s, oversaw the long process of ordering and reordering photographs and microfilm copies of the manuscripts studied by both Boyd Daniels and me. Donn Michael and his decades-long assistant in the Duke Divinity Library, Harriet Leonard, were most generous and unflagging in their support. Numerous individuals in ancient monasteries and academic institutions in Greece were very helpful during a research expedition sponsored by Duke during which I was able to photograph previously unseen manuscripts of the *ProtJac* in that country.

Although heavily burdened with his own important research, Professor James H. Charlesworth was the primary source of guidance during my studies in the Duke Graduate Program in Religion. It was under his tutelage that I learned and practiced the critical methodologies that I applied to the Greek text of the *ProtJac* in order to produce the present volumes. I owe him an inestimable debt in this final fruition of my scholarly work. My association with Professor Charlesworth has continued in the following decades during which we often crossed paths in scholarly conferences where we presented papers on the related issues in our research. More recently Professor Charlesworth has afforded me the opportunity to speak in conferences that he organized and now to publish my life's work in his most prestigious scholarly series on Jewish and Christian texts with T&T Clark. I owe thanks as well to Professor Charlesworth for providing me with the excellent images contained on pp. 219–20, which he personally took and which illustrate so well the *ProtJac* Nativity story described in this book.

I also must acknowledge the generations of my students at UNCW who assisted me in the preparation of the combined collations of Daniels and myself. The list is too long to include here, but I would single out Daniel Rayburn-Reeves, Dr. Crystal Lynn Lubinsky, Daniel McClusky, Sophia Fuller, Richie Whatley, Jamie Brummitt,

Mark Reece, Laurence Maultsby, Justin Snider, Joseph Kunze, Sarah Bode, Mike Meyer, David Townsend, Mark Xanthos, Holly Jones, Chip Perry, and Lauren Love. Cody Covan proved to be an invaluable and exceptionally efficient assistant and proofreader. In the final stages of the completion of the second volume of this work, I was most fortunate to have had the invaluable assistance of one of the most brilliant students whom I have ever taught, Kelsey Noelle Waller.

Above all, I wish to express my appreciation to my family for their unwavering support throughout the long difficult years of study that led to the eventual accomplishment of my life's goals. Without the reinforcement provided by my parents, my sister, brother-in-law, and Aunt Lou, the completion of this work would have been impossible. My mother, Dolly, the epitome of traditional Greek Christian womanhood, was the most constant source of inspiration and encouragement in my life's path. It is to her that I lovingly dedicate these volumes.

INTRODUCTION: THE GENERAL BACKGROUND

It has been customary among the past editors of the *ProtJac*[1] to begin their comments on the history of this document with a reference to the French humanist Guillaume Postel. Postel is credited with *rediscovering* this ancient New Testament Apocryphon during his tour of the East in 1549–1551.[2] Even the artificial title, *Protevangelium*, was assigned by Postel himself in his own Latin translation of the Greek text of the *ProtJac*, which he had discovered. Postel's Latin translation was published by Theodore Bibliander in 1552.[3] It would be more appropriate to say that Postel reintroduced the *ProtJac* into Western Europe, thus effectively lifting a millennium-long ban on the Apocryphon that was imposed by a fifth-/sixth-century collection of papal decrees known as the *Decretum Gelasianum de libris recipiendis et non recipiendis*.[4] Although not known directly in the West, the *ProtJac* did exercise significant influence on Western Marian thought through several popular Latin versions that contained some major themes of this document.[5]

---

1. Also referred to as the Protevangelium of James, the Infancy Gospel of James, and the Proto-Gospel of James.

2. William J. Bouwsma, *Concordia Mundi: The Career and Thought of Guillaume Postel (1510–1581)*, Harvard Historical Monographs, vol. XXXIII (Cambridge, MA: Harvard University Press, 1957), 16.

3. *Proteuangelion sive de natalibus Iesu Christi, et ipsius matris Virginis Mariae, sermo historicus diui Jacobi minoris, consobrini et fratris Domini Iesu, apostoli primarii, et episcopi Christianorum primi Hierosolymis. Evangelica historia, quam scripsit beatus Marcus, Petri apostolorum principis discipulus et filius, primus episcopus Alexandriae. Vita Ioannis Marci euangelistae, collecta ex probatioribus autoribus, per Theodorum Bibliandrum* (Basel ex officina Ioannis Oporini, 1552). The Latin text of the *ProtJac* is found on pp. 24–50 of this edition.

4. Ernst von Dobschütz, *Das Decretum Gelasianum de libris recipiendis et non recipiendis: in kritischem Text* (*Texte und Untersuchungen*, 3 Reihe, 8 Bd Hft 4; [der ganzen Reihe] 38 Bd Heft 4; Leipzig: J. C. Hinrichs, 1912). For an overview of recent scholarly discussion on the historical and theological background of Pope Gelasius, see Samuel Cohen, *Heresy, Authority and the Bishops of Rome in the Fifth Century: Leo I (440–461) and Gelasius (492–496)* (Toronto: University of Toronto, 2014). Cohen discusses the *Decretum Gelasianum* specifically on pp. 139–41.

5. I.e., the Infancy Gospel of Thomas.

Although forgotten by Western Christianity, the *ProtJac* enjoyed great popularity in the eastern Byzantine world, as abundantly witnessed by the list in Volume 2 of 169 known Greek manuscript witnesses containing this Apocryphon, which date from the second through the nineteenth centuries. In addition to this voluminous Greek material, translations and paraphrases from the original Greek text of the *ProtJac* into Syriac, Coptic, Armenian, Ethiopic, Arabic, and Georgian further attest to the great popularity of this Apocryphon throughout the ancient and medieval Christian world.[6] This mass of primary manuscript evidence is unparalleled among the extra-biblical writings of the early Christian centuries and evinces a general acceptance of the *ProtJac* as an authoritative source of Christian teaching.

But the influence of this ancient infancy narrative goes far beyond its mere appearance in numerous manuscripts. The *ProtJac* was instrumental in the development of Marian doctrines that found expression in a series of ritualistic observances in the regular liturgical cycle of the Church regarding the life of the mother of Jesus. Feast days commemorating Saint Anne's conception of Mary, the birth of Mary, and Mary's presentation to the temple—with their associated iconographic and hymnological manifestations—bear the distinct imprint of the *ProtJac*. For example, one need only peruse the Greek hymns of the Byzantine vesper service in the November 21 *Feast of the Presentation of the Theotokos*[7] to find a number of examples of direct verbal dependence upon the Greek text of the *ProtJac*. Thus, because of its early incorporation into the dominant ancient ecclesiastical liturgical cycle, the *ProtJac* has exercised a widespread influence over the Eastern Christian faithful for centuries through the common means of popular catechism—religious festivals, hymnology, and iconography.

Such extensive ramifications could only have resulted from a work of the first magnitude of importance in the ancient Church. But the significance of the *ProtJac* within its own *Sitz im Leben* has yet to be understood. Scholars generally have been content to characterize the *ProtJac* as a unitary, monolithic document of the mid-to-late second century.[8] But my own decades-long research on the *ProtJac* has

---

6. The versions of the *ProtJac* text have yet to be fully explored.

7. The text of these hymns can be found in the November volume of any edition of the Byzantine *Menaia*—the monthly service books of the Byzantine office. These original Greek texts are still in use in the Greek Orthodox Church today and have been translated into the local languages of other Orthodox Churches, which grew out of the Byzantine ecclesiastical tradition. For a thorough, lavishly documented, study of the manuscript tradition of the Byzantine *Menaia*, see Roman Krivko, "A Typology of Byzantine Office Menaia of the Ninth-Fourteenth Centuries," *Scrinium* VII, no. 2 (2011), *Ars Christiana*, 1–68.

8. See the discussion by George T. Zervos, "Dating the Protevangelium of James: The Justin Martyr Connection," *SBLSP*, no. 33 (1994), 415–34.

convinced me that the importance of this early Christian Apocryphon supersedes previous assumptions in regard to its antiquity and its influence upon developing Christian dogma. I have been led to conclude that the *ProtJac* is a primary source of information about the origins and development of Christian perceptions of the persons of Mary of Nazareth and her son, Jesus.

THE PUBLICATION HISTORY OF THE GREEK TEXT OF THE *PROTJAC*

The Greek text of the *ProtJac* first appeared in print at Basel, Switzerland, in 1564, where it was published by Michael Neander in his 1564 edition of Martin Luther's *Small Catechism*.[9] Neander, a philologist and former student of Luther and Philipp Melanchthon at the University of Wittenberg, may thus be credited with bringing the *ProtJac* to the attention of Renaissance scholars and Protestant reformers. Neander presented his Greek text of the *ProtJac* on facing pages opposite Postel's Latin translation as it appeared in Bibliander's 1552 edition.[10] Neander followed Bibliander's division of the text into paragraphs usually consisting of several verses punctuated with periods, commas, and semicolons, but Neander did not enumerate the paragraph or verse divisions.[11] In 1569 J. J. Grynaeus reprinted Neander's Greek and Latin texts in parallel columns in a new Basel edition.[12]

In 1702, J. A. Fabricius published an annotated version of Neander's Greek text of the *ProtJac* beside Postel's Latin translation in his compendium of apocryphal documents of the New Testament, the *Codex Apocryphus Novi Testamenti*.[13] Fabricius included an introduction to the *ProtJac* containing the principle references to this document from the ancient and contemporary Christian literature. Fabricius generally followed the verse divisions designated by commas, semicolons, and periods from the earlier editions of the *ProtJac*. However, he abandoned the segmentation of the text into paragraphs and created the twenty-five-chapter division, which became the standard in all subsequent editions. Two

---

9. *Katechesis Marteinou tou Loutherou, he mikra kaloumene hellenikolatinike. Catechesis Martini Lutheri parua, Graecolatina, postremum recognita. Ad eam uero accesserunt Sententiae aliquot Patrum selectiores Graecolatinae: Narrationes item Apocryphae de Christo, Maria, etc. cognatione ac familia Christi, extra Biblia: sed tamen apud veteres probatos autores, Patres, Historicos, Philologos, et multos alios Scriptores Graecos repertae. Omnia Graecolatina, descripta, exposita et edita studio et opera Michaelis Neandri Sorauiensis* (Basel: Ioannem Oporinum, 1564), 356–92. This text was republished by Neander in 1567.

10. See n. 3. Neander occasionally emended the text, apparently from one or more Greek MSS that differed slightly from that of Postel.

11. Neander also sparingly made adjustments to the chapter divisions of Bibliander's text, e.g., combining smaller segments into larger paragraphs, cf. ibid., 381, 387.

12. Johann J. Grynaeus, *Monumenta S. Patrum Orthodoxographa, hoc est Theologiae sacrosanctae ac synceriosis fidei Doctores, numero circiter LXXXV*, vol. 1 (Basileae: Ex officina Henricpetrina, 1569), 71–84.

13. Johann A. Fabricius, *Codex Apocryphus Novi Testamenti, Collectus, Castigatus, Testimoniisque, Censuris et Animadversionibus illustratus a Johanne Alberto Fabricio* (Hamburgi: Sumtib. Benjam. Schiller, 1702), 39–126. A second edition of Fabricius's work appeared in 1719, *Codex Apocryphus Novi Testamenti, Collectus, Castigatus, Testimoniisque, Censuris et Animadversionibus illustratus a Johanne Alberto Fabricio. Editio secunda* (Hamburgi: Sumptu Viduae Benjam. Schilleri et Joh. Christoph. Kisneri, 1719), 39–126.

less popular publications of the Greek text in 1726 and 1798 by Jeremiah Jones[14] were followed by the first rudimentary attempt at a critical edition of the text by A. Birch in 1804.[15] Birch used the Fabricius text as a base and supplied variants from two Vatican MSS, Vat. gr. 455 and 654. Birch also retained the verse divisions of the previous editions but modified the punctuation in conformity with that used in the publications of standard Greek classical texts.

Critical study of the Greek text of the *ProtJac* was put on a more solid foundation by J. C. Thilo in 1832.[16] Thilo used the tenth-century Parisian Greek MS 1454 as a base text. His critical apparatus contained witnesses from nine other MSS, including Fabricius's text; the two Vatican MSS edited by Birch; Parisian gr. MSS 1174, 1176, 1190, 1215, and 1468; as well as Vienna MS Theol. gr. 123. On facing pages opposite his new Greek text, Thilo reproduced Postel's Latin translation, which had been used by his predecessors. Thilo included an introduction and substantial critical notes and comparisons with other apocryphal and canonical documents. A less significant critical study of the Greek text of the *ProtJac* was published by C. A. Suckow in 1840.[17] Suckow used Venetian MS gr. II 42 as his base text and cited variants from other already known MSS. His edition also included an introduction and critical notes.

In 1853, Constantine Tischendorf published the first edition of his textual work on the Greek text of the *ProtJac*. In his *Evangelia Apocrypha*[18] Tischendorf presented a Greek text and critical apparatus, which contained readings from

---

14. *A New and Full Method of settling the canonical authority of the New Testament; herein All the antient Testimonies concerning this Argument are produced; the several Apocryphal Books, which have been thought canonical by any writers, collected, with an English Translation of each of them; together with a particular Proof that none of them were ever admitted into the Canon, and a full Answer to those, who have endeavored to recommend them as such*, 2 vols (London: J. Clark and R. Hett, 1726–1727). The second edition of Jones's work is entitled *A New and Full Method of Settling the Canonical Authority of the New Testament. To which is subjoined a Vindication of the Former Part of St. Matthew's Gospel, from Mr. Whiston's Charge of Dislocations*, 3 vols (Oxford: Clarendon Press, 1798).

15. Andreas Birch, *Auctarium Codicis Apocryphi N. T. Fabriciani, continens plura inedita, alia ad fidem codd. mss. emendatius expressa. Congessit, disposuit, edidit Andreas Birch, Fasciculus primus* (Copenhagen: Arntzen et Hartier, 1804), 195–242.

16. Ioannis C. Thilo, *Codex Apocryphus Novi Testamenti, e libris editis et manuscriptis, maxime Gallicanis, Germanicis et Italicis, collectus, recensitus notisque et prolegomenis illustratus, opera et studio Ioannis Caroli Thilo. Tomus Primus* (Leipzig: Sumptibus Frid. Christ. Guilielmi Vogel, 1832), 159–273.

17. Carolus A. Suckow, *Protevangelium Jacobi ex cod. MS. Venetiano descripsit prolegomenis, varietate lectionum, notis criticis instructum edidit Carol. Adolph. Suckow* (Breslau: apud Grassium, Barthium et Socium, 1840).

18. Constantinus Tischendorf, *Evangelia Apocrypha, adhibitis plurimus codicibus Graecis et Latinis maximam partem nunc primum consultis atque ineditorum copia insignibus* (Leipzig: Avenarius et Mendelssohn, 1853), 1–49.

seventeen MSS of the *ProtJac* plus the evidence from the editions of Neander and Postel. From Birch's edition, Tischendorf collated Vatican MSS 455 and 654, and Vienna Theol. gr. 123. From Thilo's edition, he collated completely Paris MSS 1215, 1454, 1468, and 1190 and partially Paris MSS 1174 and 1176, which Thilo had presented incompletely in his edition.[19] To these witnesses Tischendorf added the complete Venetian MSS II 42 and 363, and the now lost Dresden MS A187. He also included collations of the beginning and end of Milan MSS A63 and C92, and of Venice MS VII 40, as well as the extant sections of the fragmentary MSS Paris Coislin 152 and Venice XI 200.

In 1876, two years after Tischendorf's death, a second edition of his *Evangelia Apocrypha* appeared. This *editio altera*[20] contained a revision of the Greek text and critical apparatus of the *ProtJac* from the 1853 edition. The 1876 text formed the basis of almost all subsequent critical editions of the Greek version of the *ProtJac*. The *editio altera* text was essentially reproduced by the later critical editors of the *ProtJac* Greek text, some of whom added a selection of variants from other sources. The 1876 Greek text also served as the foundation for virtually every translation of the *ProtJac* until the mid-1950s. Tischendorf retained Fabricius's original, and by now standard, twenty-five-chapter division of the text, but he also contributed his own, also now standard, system of enumeration to the verses within the chapters, which he punctuated according to the classical system.[21]

The only additional Greek textual evidence for the *ProtJac* to appear for half a century after Tischendorf's 1876 edition were three publications of ancient fragments preserved on papyrus and vellum. In 1896 B. P. Grenfell published fragments of a quire of a fifth- or sixth-century vellum MS containing parts of the *ProtJac*.[22] Grenfell collated this text against Tischendorf's and noted the many differences between them. In 1912 E. Pistelli published five fourth-century papyrus fragments containing parts of the *ProtJac*, which originated in Aschmunen, Egypt.[23] And in 1928, H. Schöne published a transcription of the underlying text

---

19. Paris MSS 1174 and 1176 are fully collated in the present edition.

20. Constantinus de Tischendorf, *Evangelia Apocrypha, adhibitis plurimus codicibus Graecis et Latinis maximam partem nunc primum consultis atque ineditorum copia insignibus. Editio altera* (Leipzig: Hermann Mendelssohn, 1876), 1–50.

21. Although this writer finds Tischendorf's verse enumeration to be imprecise and inadequate, it will be noted in the text of the present edition to facilitate comparisons with the editions of the past. In the present edition the text of the *ProtJac* will follow the verse enumeration established by Daniels with a few minor adjustments made necessary by the merging of Daniels's collations with my own.

22. Bernard P. Grenfell, ed., *An Alexandrian Erotic Fragment and Other Greek Papyri Chiefly Ptolemaic* (Oxford: Clarendon Press, 1896), 13–19.

23. Ermenegildo Pistelli, *Papiri Greci e Latini, Pubblicazioni della Società Italiana per la ricerca dei Papiri greci e latini in Egitto* (Firenze: Tipografia Enrico Ariani, 1912), I, 9–15. Pistelli's fragments were republished by Carl Wessely, "Les plus anciens monuments du Christianisme écrits sur Papyrus. II," in *Patrologia Orientalis*, XVIII, 3 (Paris: Firmin-Didot, 1985).

of a ninth-century, vellum, palimpsest MS, which also preserved portions of the *ProtJac*.[24]

G. Rauschen published selected chapters (1, 4, 5, 7–11) of the Greek *ProtJac* in 1905 and the entire text in 1914.[25] He presented Tischendorf's text but included readings from Grenfell's sixth-century Bodleian fragments. É. Amann republished the text of the *editio altera* in 1910 and added readings from the Coptic, Syriac, and Ethiopic versions.[26] The following year C. Michel also reproduced the Tischendorf text,[27] and in 1940 P. Vannutelli presented the same text together with Syriac and Ethiopic readings as well as the witness of the Grenfell papyrus.[28] The 1876 text was used by G. Bonaccorsi in 1948[29] and by A. de Santos Otero in 1956, who also noted principle variants and versions.[30]

In the same year that de Santos's publication appeared, Boyd Lee Daniels completed his doctoral dissertation at Duke University on the Greek text of the *ProtJac* in which he presented exhaustive collations of eighty-one Greek MSS and bibliographical information on fifty-seven more to which he had been unable to obtain access or which had been lost or destroyed since antiquity. The scholarly community remained largely unaware of Daniels's massive, 1,033-page, three-volume dissertation. For several decades after the completion of Daniels's work, not a single scholar had even taken this invaluable resource under consideration, and it received only a single footnote in reference to its inaccessibility.[31]

---

24. Hermann Schöne, "Palimpsestblätter des Protevangelium Iacobi in Cesena," in *Westfälische Studien; Beiträge zur Geschichte der Wissenschaft, Kunst, und Literatur in Westfalen, Alois Bömer zum 60 Geburtstag gewidmet*, eds. H. Degering and W. Menn (Leipzig: Verlag Karl W. Hiersemann, 1928), 263–76.

25. Gerhard Rauschen, *Florilegium Patristicum, Fasciculus Tertius: Monumenta Minora Saeculi Secundi. Editio altera emendata* (Bonn: Sumptibus Petri Hanstein, 1914), 57–84.

26. Émile Amann, *Le Protévangile de Jacques et ses remaniements latins*, in *Documents pour servir à l'étude des origines Chrétiennes: Les Apocryphes du Nouveau Testament, publiés sous la direction de J. Bousquet et E. Amann* (Paris: Letouzey et Ané, 1910).

27. Charles Michel, *Évangiles apocryphes, Vol. I: Protévangile de Jacques, Pseudo-Matthieu, Évangile de Thomas* (Paris: Libraire Alphonse Picard et Fils, 1911). Michel's work is found in volumes 13 and 18 in the series *Textes et Documents pour l'Étude historique du Christianisme*, eds. H. Hemmer and P. Lejay.

28. Primus Vannutelli, ed. *Protevangelium Jacobi Synoptice* (Roma: Scuola Tipografica Italo-Orientale, 1940).

29. Giuseppe Bonaccorsi, *Vangeli apocrifi*, vol. 1 (Firenze: Libreria editrice fiorentina, 1948), 58–109.

30. Aurelio de Santos Otero, *Los Evangelios Apocrifos: colección de textos griegos y latinos, versión crítica* (Madrid: Biblioteca de Autores Cristianos, 1956), 135–88.

31. H. R. Smid, *Protevangelium Jacobi: A Commentary*, trans. G. E. van Baaren-Pape (Assen, the Netherlands: VanGorcum & Comp. N. V., 1965), 5, n. 24.

But even if the work of Daniels had come to the attention of his contemporaries, its significance probably would have been overshadowed by the sensational recovery of the pristine P.Bodm V, which contained the complete text of the *ProtJac* on forty-nine almost perfectly preserved papyrus leaves dating at least to the third century CE. Testuz, Curator at the Bodmer Library, published a diplomatic transcription of P.Bodm V in 1958 with a discussion of the far-reaching implications of this papyrus text for the question of the unity and composition of the *ProtJac*.[32] Testuz originally dated P.Bodm V to the third century, thus making it the oldest extant witness to the *ProtJac* text.

In correspondence with Testuz, Émile de Strycker, a Flemish Jesuit scholar, took up the study of the *ProtJac* text in the late 1950s and by 1961 would publish a critical edition of the *ProtJac*, which would supplant Tischendorf's *Evangelia Apocrypha* as the premier Greek text of this document.[33] De Strycker's request to study the original papyrus at the Bodmer library was denied, but he managed to obtain a complete set of photographs of P.Bodm V through the "active obligeance" of Testuz.[34] De Strycker presented his own corrected transcription of P.Bodm V as the base text, confronted by the readings from Tischendorf's MSS and collations of the three additional ancient witnesses: PSI 6; P.Grenfell II 8; Schöne's palimpsest;[35]

32. Testuz, *Nativité*.

33. *La Forme la plus ancienne du Protévangile de Jacques: Recherches sur le Papyrus Bodmer 5, avec une édition critique du texte grec et une traduction annotée*, Subsidia Hagiographa, No. 33 (Bruxelles: Société des Bollandistes, 1961).

34. Ibid., 24, "Nous avons exprimé à la Direction de la Bibliothèque Bodmer le désir d'examiner personnellement le papyrus à Cologny. Elle n'a pas estimé pouvoir accéder à notre demande. Mais grâce à l'active obligeance de M. Testuz, la Bibliothèque nous a envoyé un jeu complet d'excellentes photographies, d'un format identique à l'original." De Strycker claimed that he examined the photographs of the papyrus and communicated to Testuz his suggested corrections to Testuz's original transcription of the text of P.Bodm V. To my knowledge Testuz and de Strycker were the only two scholars who had direct access to the papyrus text itself, either physically or through photographic images, for a half century after its discovery and initial publication. In 1977 the eminent papyrologist, Eric Turner, complained that he was denied access to the original papyrus, although he "visited the Bodmer Library more than once," *The Typology of the Early Codex* (University of Pennsylvania Press, 1977), 79-80. The present writer also has experienced similar difficulty as repeated requests over two decades to the Bodmer Library for access to P.Bodm V went unanswered. Photographic images of P.Bodm V were finally published in 2000, but these were so small and of such low resolution as to render them practically useless for close scholarly study of the papyrus itself, Martin Bircher, *Bibliotheca Bodmeriana. La collection des papyrus Bodmer* (Munich: K. G. Saur, 2000).

35. The significance of the three most ancient witnesses—P.Bodm V, PSI 6, and P.Grenfell II 8—toward isolating the original *ProtJac* text is diminished somewhat by the fact of their common Egyptian provenance. These papyri—which together constitute the

the Syriac, Armenian, Georgian, Ethiopic, Sahidic Coptic, and Latin versions; and paraphrases of the *ProtJac* text.³⁶

With the inclusion of the readings from Tischendorf's *Evangelia Apocrypha*, the four ancient documents on papyrus and parchment, and the versions and paraphrases, *La Forme* became the most complete presentation of the witnesses to the *ProtJac* text, which had already been published. But de Strycker was premature in labeling his work as "the most ancient form of the *Protevangelium of James*." Scholars familiar with the textual issues surrounding the *ProtJac*, the present writer included, have concluded that de Strycker did not achieve his stated objective of determining the most ancient form of the *ProtJac*.³⁷ H. R. Smid, who published a Greek text of the *ProtJac* four years after *La Forme*, purposely did not reproduce de Strycker's critical text in his own edition.³⁸ Instead, he printed Tischendorf's favorite MS, Paris 1454, beside P.Bodm V in parallel columns.³⁹ Smid was aware of the extensive textual work of Daniels on the *ProtJac* and criticized de Strycker for ignoring the great majority of the extant Greek witnesses:

entire body of extant pre-seventh-century MS material of the *ProtJac*—having originated in Egypt, could therefore in all probability lean toward an Egyptian form of the most ancient *ProtJac* text. De Strycker's suggestion of an Egyptian provenance for the *ProtJac* would, no doubt, mitigate this issue in his estimation.

36. *La Forme*, 30–45. The readings from the versions of the *ProtJac* text are included in the critical apparatus of *La Forme*; the text of the Armenian versions translated into Latin by Hans Quecke is presented in an appendix on pp. 439–73 of de Strycker's book. For a more recent edition of the Armenian versions, see Terian, *The Armenian Gospel of the Infancy: With Three Early Versions of the Protevangelium of James* (Oxford and New York: Oxford University Press, 2008).

37. Ibid., 19, "Tel est donc le but du présent volume: déterminer par une étude comparative du papyrus Bodmer et de l'ensemble de la tradition, telle qu'elle est connue aujourd 'hui, quelle est la forme la plus ancienne du *Protévangile de Jacques*."

38. *Protevangelium*, 1, "It seemed preferable not to give the text as established in the last critical edition of the P.J., i.e., the edition by É. de Strycker"; cf. above p. 7, n. 31.

39. More recently Ronald F. Hock reproduced de Strycker's text but with attention to Tischendorf's readings as well, *The Infancy Gospels of James and Thomas: With Introduction, Notes, and Original Text Featuring the New Scholars Version Translation* (Santa Rosa, CA: Polebridge Press, 1995), 30. Hock introduced innovations in his edition that serve to confuse serious research on the text of the *ProtJac*. He has minimized the importance of the crucial witness of P.Bodm V and imposed his own arbitrary system of verse division and enumeration that will cause difficulty to readers desiring to reference both Tischendorf's and de Strycker's important editions. Ultimately, Hock's work represents a running commentary on the printed editions of P.Bodm V and Tischendorf and adds little to the ongoing quest for the original text of the *ProtJac*.

The author [de Strycker] does not use the about 100 MSS which are to be found in many different libraries dispersed over many different countries. Those were studied by B. L. Daniels, who collected all the MSS which were available to him ... [de Strycker] did not look into the rest of the material. That is the great objection to his procedure. In order to reconstruct the earliest text it is necessary to examine all the extant manuscripts and impermissible to leave some eighty manuscripts out of the account. The results S. has achieved may be termed very good, but it is not "la forme la plus ancienne" of the text, at least the method he uses arouses some doubt about this.[40]

De Strycker, however, was aware of the existence of other Greek MSS containing the *ProtJac*, but since it would have taken so long to locate and study all these witnesses he chose to base his determination of the original text of the *ProtJac* in *La Forme* upon a limited number of MSS.[41] De Strycker did accept in principle that *"L'idéal serait d'examiner directement tous les témoins existants"*[42] and in a 1964 article repeated this assertion, but he expressed doubts that a study of the newer MSS would yield any benefits other than more information concerning the history of the text of the *ProtJac* from the ninth to the sixteenth centuries.[43] He thus, as of 1964, persisted in believing that the limitation of his study to the already published textual materials had enabled him to discern the main lines of the history of the MS tradition.

Aside from his exclusion of the great bulk of the textual data in producing his critical text of the *ProtJac*, de Strycker also has been criticized for demonstrating an excessive reliance on the work of Tischendorf. De Strycker's dependence on Tischendorf hardly inspires confidence, considering that in his own edition the German scholar himself actually collated just two complete MSS of the *ProtJac* and that the earliest of these was only of the thirteenth century.[44] Tischendorf's

---

40. Ibid., 5-6. Cf. Édouard Cothenet, "Protévangile de Jacques," in *DBSup* 8 (Paris: Letouzey & Ané), col. 1376, "la simple confrontation de Bodmer V avec l'édition de Tischendorf ne pouvait donner de résultats satisfaisants."

41. *La Forme*, 19.

42. Ibid.

43. "Le Protévangile de Jacques: Problémes critiques et exégétiques," in *Studia Evangelica*, ed. F. L. Cross (Berlin: Akademie Verlag, 1964), 348-9; "En principe, il sera nécessaire d'examiner en détail les mss. grecs, mais nous savons déjà qu'ils ne pourrant plus guère ameliorer un texte établi à l'aide de nombreux témoins antérieurs en date," 349.

44. The same criticism that Daniels levels against Tischendorf applies just as well to de Strycker: "The extent of his apparatus is not as great as the number seventeen would make it appear." Daniels goes on to point out that "Tischendorf really had only ten complete witnesses to the text of the Protev., and he had to rely on the work of others for seven of these," *Tradition*, 24. Daniels points out that neither MS Vatic. gr. 455 nor Venet. Marc. gr. 818 should be considered as containing the whole *ProtJac* text intact. In both cases an older, partial text was completed by a later scribe.

remaining six complete MSS came directly from Thilo and Birch; the oldest of these was of the tenth century. Thus, when scrutinized carefully, the witnesses that de Strycker received from Tischendorf do not warrant the appellation "the older MSS," by which de Strycker commonly refers to them. Ironically, Tischendorf's readings, upon which de Strycker was so dependent in his own critical edition, derive from MSS falling within the identical chronological range (the ninth to the sixteenth centuries) as the about 100 similar MSS, which de Strycker marginalized—because of their lateness—in his attempt to establish the most ancient text of the *ProtJac*.[45]

Regardless of his questionable earlier presuppositions, de Strycker did eventually move toward the goal of including all the extant MSS of the *ProtJac* of which he was aware, in a future major critical edition of its text. In his 1968 book, *De Griekse Handschriften van het Protevangelie van Jacobus*, de Strycker wrote that in 1961—the year of the publication of *La Forme*—P. Halkin had given him a list of 121 Greek MSS containing the *ProtJac*, then later added fifteen more to that number.[46] De Strycker examined these MSS, with the exception of seven, which were included in catalogs but which had been lost or destroyed; nineteen more witnesses were inaccessible to him.[47] De Strycker stated, prophetically, that he wrote *De Griekse* in 1968 as a guideline for any potential successor to him in case he himself would be unable to complete his final definitive publication of the *ProtJac* text presenting all the available MSS and their mutual relationships.[48]

It is evident in *De Griekse* that de Strycker's views on his methodology were evolving as a result of his study of the newer *ProtJac* texts.[49] He initially planned to establish the original text of the *ProtJac* from the MSS already published by Tischendorf and subsequently to analyze the newer MSS in order to identify their place in the overall MS tradition. He then hoped to choose the best examples of each group and from these twenty to thirty witnesses to create a critical edition while disregarding the rest of the MSS.[50] However, his original plan had proved ineffective as de Strycker realized that the MS evidence was much more complex

---

45. Cf. especially *Le Protévangile*, 348–9, where de Strycker refers to Tischendorf's MSS of the tenth century and later as "les formes les plus anciennes du texte," while relegating the "proche de la centaine" witnesses to the category of "témoins récents."

46. Émile de Strycker, *De Griekse Handschriften van het Protevangelie van Jacobus* (Brussels: Paleis der Academiën, 1968), 10.

47. Ibid., 11, 15. Of these "ongeveer 140 handschriften," de Strycker examined 121 MSS apart from the three pre-seventh-century witnesses (P.Bodm V, PSI 6, P.Grenfell II 8), "buiten de drie getuigen van voor de VIIde eeuw, hebben wij 121 handschriften onderzocht."

48. Ibid., 15, n. 39.

49. Ibid., 14, n. 37. At one point de Strycker indicates an awareness of certain deficiencies in Tischendorf's collations, stating that errors or incompleteness misled de Strycker in his original attempt to establish family relationships among the MSS.

50. Ibid., 14–15.

than he had originally anticipated.[51] Consequently, he determined to obtain the most complete picture possible of the entire MS tradition of the *ProtJac* before proceeding with any definitive publication.[52] In any event, de Strycker held that his study of the later Byzantine MSS (eighth or ninth century or later) confirmed in large part his 1961 text that was based on "twelve older" MSS,[53] stating that he changed his original text in only ten places as a result of his study of the "later" witnesses.[54]

As de Strycker himself had foreseen, he did not live long enough to produce his definitive critical edition of the Greek text of the *ProtJac* based upon the entire MS tradition arranged according to their family relationships. In spite of its flawed theoretical basis, the edition of the *ProtJac*, which has come to be recognized as the "received" text of our document, is that which perhaps inaccurately claims the title *La Forme la plus ancienne du Protévangile de Jacques*. In the final analysis we may characterize de Strycker's 1961 critical edition as a meticulous investigation of textual materials most of which (Tischendorf's witnesses) were overvalued.[55] In allying himself so completely to Tischendorf's readings of his MSS, de Strycker severely limited the compass of his work with the result that it remains primarily a commentary on P.Bodm V. The present edition represents an attempt to make as much of the Greek manuscript tradition of the *ProtJac* as fully and readily accessible to scholars as possible for further in-depth investigations into this most important New Testament Apocryphon.

---

51. Ibid., 15, 23–4, de Strycker found that chronologically later MSS of the *ProtJac* often preserved old and reliable readings and that sometimes scribes themselves intentionally revised their texts by choosing preferred readings from among several MSS or by simply correcting or improving a single text according to their liking. At one point de Strycker states that the Byzantine MSS can hide surprises. As an example he cites Sinai 491, which contains a short text in chapter 21 of the *ProtJac* and which he describes as having ramifications of preserving an old reliable reading.

52. In 1980 de Strycker published an updated, but shorter and less comprehensive, article containing a list of 149 Greek MSS of the *ProtJac*—123 of which he had studied and classified according to the principle families and their subdivisions, "Die griechischen Handschriften des Protevangeliums Iacobi," in *Griechische Kodikologie und Textüberlieferung, herausgegeben von Dieter Harlfinger* (Darmstadt: Wissenschaftliche Buchgesellschaft, 1980), 577–612. Even in 1980, de Strycker was still unacquainted with Daniels's work, although he had essentially reduplicated Daniels's efforts toward compiling a comprehensive list of the known MSS containing the *ProtJac*.

53. See n. 43.

54. *De Griekse*, 22.

55. See Daniels's judicious review of *La Forme* in *JBL* 80 (1961), 399.

THE HISTORY OF SCHOLARLY INVESTIGATION OF THE *PROTJAC*

With the discovery of P.Bodm V, scholarly interest in the *ProtJac* began to intensify, thus necessitating a new critical edition of its original text. The 1876 Tischendorf text was still considered to be the best available and formed the basis for most later editions of the Greek text of the *ProtJac* and its translations.[56] The need for an updated critical edition was filled by de Strycker, whose book by default has attained ascendancy as the "received" Greek text of the *ProtJac*.[57] But the preeminence accorded to *La Forme* through its elevated status vis-à-vis the *ProtJac* text also lent more credence to de Strycker's own concomitant opinions expressed in *La Forme* on the historical-critical issues of the authorship, date, provenance, purpose, and composition of this Apocryphon. This has led to the perpetuation of certain misconceptions on the part of de Strycker as regards the *ProtJac* and P.Bodm V, which have exerted a significant influence on the study of our document by most later scholars.

Unfortunately the *ProtJac* appears to have fallen victim to a potential flaw in the process by which scholars seek answers to the critical questions surrounding this, or any, written text. This process should necessarily be more complex in the case of documents that are not single-author, unitary compositions—but were composed out of discrete preexistent sources or have undergone significant redaction or revision.[58] This flaw in the analytical process may arise when more advanced historical-critical interpretive methodologies[59] are applied to a document before the foundational methodologies[60] are successfully completed. In such instances researchers would proceed to formulate theories on the critical issues pertaining to their document based on the dubious foundations of a deficient text and fallacious perceptions of its compositional makeup.

In the case of the *ProtJac*, as we have seen, the most foundational critical procedure of establishing a definitive text was in effect stillborn at its inception with *La Forme* and has yet to achieve fruition over a half century later. But even more far-reaching in their influence over the ensuing scholarly investigation of the

---

56. See above, pp. 6–7.
57. *La Forme*.
58. Examples of such texts abound in the biblical literature, as viewed from the historical-critical perspective. Each of the sources of such composite documents—both preexisting texts and any substantial redactions or revisions—has its own individual author, date, provenance, and purpose and should be evaluated as such. This holds true especially for a very theologically and dogmatically relevant document such as the *ProtJac*, which has suffered through a long history of redaction, revision, and correction from its origins in the earliest Christian times, throughout antiquity and the middle ages, and even into modernity with the work of de Strycker.
59. E.g., literary, rhetorical, sociological, feminist criticism.
60. E.g., text, redaction, form criticism.

ProtJac were de Strycker's conclusions published in *La Forme* regarding the critical questions of the authorship, date, provenance, and purpose of this Apocryphon. These conclusions were founded upon de Strycker's assumptions regarding the compositional nature of the *ProtJac*, that is, that it was a unitary composition by a single author writing in the latter part of the second century CE. Following de Stryker, most scholars have viewed the *ProtJac* through this prism. Thus it appears that in the case of the *ProtJac* the above mentioned "potential flaw" in the scholarly evaluative process has been fully realized as an essentially "manufactured" scholarly consensus that has been created and perpetuated concerning this most important early Christian apocryphal Gospel.

THE COMPOSITIONAL PROBLEM OF THE *PROTJAC*

The prevailing consensus view of the *ProtJac* as a unitary, one-author composition did not always exist but may be attributed to de Strycker who was primarily responsible for turning the attention of the scholarly world away from previous theories that held the *ProtJac* to be a compilation of several preexisting sources.[61] Before the publication of de Strycker's *La Forme*, the interpretation of the composition of the *ProtJac* that held sway among scholars was the three-document hypothesis of the great German scholar Adolf Harnack.[62] According to Harnack, the *ProtJac* consists of three originally independent parts (*"drei zusammengearbeitete Theile"*): (1) chapters 1–17, the Γέννησις Μαρίας ("Nativity of Mary"),[63] a history of the conception, birth, and life of Mary, (2) chapters 18–20, the *Apocryphum Josephi*, regarding the nativity of Jesus and the virginity of Mary *"in partu et post partum,"* and (3) chapters 22–24, the *Apocryphum Zachariae*.[64] Harnack was unclear as to the position of chapters 21 and 25 in his overall scheme, but he held that all three parts of the *ProtJac* were combined before the middle of the fourth century.[65]

Harnack's three-document hypothesis was accepted along its general lines, but opinions varied on the dates of the individual source documents and the time of their incorporation into the *ProtJac*. Harnack himself placed the Γέννησις Μαρίας in the early third century on the basis of his identification of chapters 1–17 of the *ProtJac* as the Βίβλος Ἰακώβου ("book of James") that was mentioned by Origen as one of two documents that described the brothers of Jesus as the sons of Joseph

---

61. See de Strycker's overview of the history of scholarly discussion on the compositional unity of the *ProtJac* in *La Forme*, 6–13; cf. 392–404, for de Strycker's own contribution to the discussion.

62. *Die Chronologie der altchristlichen Literatur bis Eusebius*, vol. 2 (Leipzig: J. C. Hinrichs, 1904), 598–603. Cf. de Strycker, *La Forme*, 11, "*Cette prise de position de Harnack eut une influence décisive. Depuis lors, c'est à peine si une voix isolée s'est élevée pour défendre l'unité du Protévangile. Un bon nombre d'auteurs se rallia à la these des trois documents.*" Cf. n. 5 for bibliography.

63. It is to Harnack's credit that, even laboring under the limited evidence that was available in 1904 when there were no known MSS of the *ProtJac* dating before the ninth century, he identified a document named the Γέννησις Μαρίας as chapters 1–17 of the *ProtJac*. Harnack anticipated by a half century the remarkable discovery of a complete text of the *ProtJac* preserved on the very early papyrus P.Bodm V bearing the title Γένεσις Μαρίας, Ἀποκάλυψις Ἰακώβ (Genesis of Mary, Apocalypse of James).

64. *Chronologie*, 600, "*1) die Geschichte der Empfängniss, Geburt und des Lebens der Maria bis zu dem Moment, wo die kanonischen Texte einsetzen. 2) Geschichte der Geburt Jesu, erzählt von Joseph, also ein Apocryphum Josephi, 3) ein Apocryphum Zachariae.*"

65. Ibid., 602–3, "*Die Zusammenarbeitung der Stücke ist vor der Mitte des 4. Jahrh. erfolgt.*" Cf. de Strycker, *La Forme*, 11.

from a former wife.[66] Harnack assigned—with reservations in both cases—the *Apocryphum Josephi*[67] and the *Apocryphum Zachariae* to the second century.[68]

Amann led a group of scholars who also viewed the *ProtJac* as consisting of three originally separate documents, two of which, the *Apocryphum Mariae* and the *Apocryphum Josephi*, were merged together closely in the late second century as a unified work. To this compilation of the original two documents was added the *Apocryphum Zachariae* in the late fourth or early fifth century.[69] Charles Michel agreed essentially with Amann[70] but followed P. Peeters in placing the addition of the *Apocryphum Zachariae* "a little before the sixth century."[71] Speculation on a later date for the composition of the *ProtJac* and the addition of the *Apocryphum Zachariae* was ended in 1906 by the publication of PSI 6, a fragmentary fourth-century papyrus containing material from chapters 13–22 of the *ProtJac*.[72] The presence of all three of the hypothetical source documents of the *ProtJac* in PSI 6 established the *terminus ante quem* for the final composition of the *ProtJac* in the fourth century thus refuting the position of Amann, Michel, and Peeters that the *Apocryphum Zachariae* was added between the late fourth and the late fifth centuries.

Harnack's three-document hypothesis was also embraced by Testuz, the first editor of P.Bodm V. Testuz identified certain distinctive peculiarities of the

---

66. Ibid., 601, "*die βίβλος Ἰακώβου, die Origenes gekannt hat, wesentlich identisch gewesen ist mit Protev. Jacobi c. 1-17*," Comm. Matt. 25.26 τοὺς δὲ ἀδελφοὺς Ἰησοῦ φασί τινες εἶναι ἐκ παραδόσεως ὁρμώμενοι τοῦ ἐπιγεγραμμένου κατὰ Πέτρον εὐαγγέλιον ἢ τῆς βίβλου Ἰακώβου υἱοὺς Ἰωσὴφ ἐκ προτέρας γυναικὸς συνῳκηκυίας αὐτῷ πρὸ τῆς Μαρίας.

67. Ibid., 602, "*So muss es dahingestellt bleiben, ob der Abschnitt 18-20, wie er vorliegt, dem 2. Jahrh. Angehört.*"

68. Ibid., 600, "*Das 3. Stück reicht in seinen Grundlagen auch bis in das 2. Jahrh.*" Harnack seems to distinguish between the original form of the *Apocryphum Zachariae*, which he dates to the second century and what he believed to be a later form of the Zachariah story that became chapters 22–24 of the present form of the *ProtJac* in the fourth century.

69. *Protévangile*, 99–100, "*Il est impossible de soutenir l'unité fondamentale du Protévangile actuel; la légende de Zacharie est certainement un appendice qui n'a été ajouté à l'ouvrage qu'à une date assez récente (fin du IVe ou commencement du Ve siècle). Mais d'autre part la distinction que fait Harnack entre l'Apocryphum Mariae et l'Apocryphum Josephi est d'un ordre tout à fait différent. Il s'agit moins ici de deux documents juxtaposés à une date tardive, que de deux sources utilisées simultanément, par un auteur qui écrivait vers le milieu ou vers la fin du IIe siècle, et qu'on peut appeler en toute vérité l'auteur du Protévangile de Jacques.*"

70. Charles Michel and Paul Peeters, *Évangiles Apocryphes*, vol. 13 of *Textes et Documents pour l'Étude Historique du Christianisme*, eds. H. Hemmer and P. Lejay (Paris: Libraire Alphonse Picard et Fils, 1911), vii–xvii.

71. Ibid., xvii, "*L'Apocryphum Zachariae, sous la forme que lui donne le Protévangile, doit être postérieur au IIe siècle, et, ajouterons-nous avec le P. Peeters, de peu antérieur au VIe siècle.*"

72. Pistelli, *Papiri*, see above, p. 6, n. 23.

Introduction: The General Background   17

papyrus text that distinguish the second section from the first[73] and understood these to signify that the *ProtJac* underwent an elaboration after the writing of P.Bodm V[74] in the third century.[75] In a final *résumé* of his compositional theory of the *ProtJac*, Testuz wrote that (1) the first and third sections of the *ProtJac*, the *Nativité de Marie* and the *Apocryphum Zachariae*, were redacted at the end of the second century; (2) the second section, the *Apocryphum Josephi*, was constituted from two separate episodes, the journey to Bethlehem and the birth of Jesus, by the beginning of the third century; (3) the first two sections were joined together shortly afterward to form a more developed version of the *Apocryphum Zachariae* around the middle of the third century; and (4) the final elements were added in the late third or early fourth century after P.Bodm V was written and the *Apocryphum Zachariae* received further embellishment.[76]

Upon entering this debate, de Strycker correctly affirmed that the discovery of the PSI 6 fragments constituted material proof of the unity of the *ProtJac* in the early fourth century and that the complete text of P.Bodm V confirmed this conclusion.[77] Ultimately, he rejected in toto the composite character of the *ProtJac* on the basis of the manuscript evidence from the fourth century and following and presented a series of mostly subjective arguments as further support of his claim of its original redactional unity.[78] Citing the "unanimous and uninterrupted tradition since the first half of the fourth century," as well as other witnesses dating

---

73. *Nativité*, 12–26.

74. Ibid., 20, "*indiquons comment il se présente dans les manuscrits tardifs et les textes imprimés, après l'élaboration subie dans les siècles suivant l'exécution de notre copie.*"

75. Ibid., 10. Testuz's third-century date for P.Bodm V was based upon his own paleographic assessment of the papyrus and comparison with a previous study of the related P.Bodm. XX by Victor Martin. "*On peut cependant penser que notre manuscript a été exécuté dans le courante du III*ᵉ *siécle; c'est une évaluation qui paraît prudente, et que confirment les indices fournis par l'orthographe, la grammaire, et la parenté de cette écriture avec celle de l'Evangile de Jean édité par le Professeur V. Martin que l'on date des environs de l'an 200 de notre ère.*"

76. Ibid., 26.

77. *La Forme*, 12–13, "*la preuve matérielle que l'unité du Protévangile est plus ancienne ... Devant l'existence de ce document, il devenait impossible de faire descendre la rédaction définitive de l'oeuvre, et en particulier l'intégration de l'histoire de Zacharie, jusqu'à la fin du V*ᵉ *siècle.*" Cf. ibid., 13–18, for P.Bodm. V. It should be noted that PSI 6 and P.Bodm. V do not affect the basic premise of the three-document theory. As early as they may seem, the fourth-century date of PSI 6 and P.Bodm V (according to de Strycker) is still two full centuries removed from the actual time of the composition of the *ProtJac*. These papyri necessitated an adjustment in the dating of the various component parts of the *ProtJac* but added nothing to our knowledge of the extent of its text before the fourth century.

78. Ibid., 392–404; especially 403–4: "*La théorie des trois documents est dépourvue de tout fondement dans le domaine de la critique tant externe qu'interne. Elle ne peut rendre compte ni des liens intimes et multiples qui existent entre les différents épisodes ni de l'unité de conception, de langue et de style qui se manifeste dans toute le Protévangile. Elle doit donc être rejetée comme arbitraire.*"

from the early fourth century through the Byzantine middle ages, de Strycker stated categorically that "the redactional unity of the *ProtJac* is certain."[79] De Strycker, however, failed to offer any evidence from before the fourth century to justify his *argumentum ex silentio*. It is precisely in this silent period of the first three centuries of Christian history that Christian redactors appear to have been most active, as abundantly witnessed inter alia by the Synoptic Gospels with their numerous associated redactional issues and by the composite nature of the Gospel of John.[80]

Many of de Strycker's arguments represent his own subjective judgments and carry with them no corroborating evidence. He asserted, for example, that since the *ProtJac* was used by later writers in its entirety there is no evidence of the continued existence of its various sources after they were joined together.[81] But it is not at all unusual in the redactional process by which ancient Christian works were formed, for the sources making up these works to disappear after their incorporation into the context within which they are preserved. De Strycker's argument is refuted by conspicuous examples from the early Christian literature such as the Sayings Source Q, which disappeared within decades of its integration into Matthew and Luke. Likewise, the Signs Source, which forms the framework of the Gospel of John, left no independent traces after its incorporation into the fourth Gospel.

De Strycker also argued that the *Apocryphum Zachariae* (*ProtJac* 22–24)[82] is too small to have been an independent work and that there is no known larger "*Apocryphe de l'Enfance*" of which it originally could have formed part.[83] But this phenomenon also occurs regularly in the canonical Christian documents.

---

79. Ibid., 397, "*l'unité redactionnelle du Protévangile est certaine, attestée qu'elle est par une tradition unanime et ininterrompue depuis la première moitié du IVe siècle.*" But see ibid., 399, where he accepts in principle the partial composite nature of the *ProtJac* by admitting that the "vision of Joseph" found in *ProtJac* 18–20 "*est une pièce rapportee et que l'auteur l'a introduite sans changement notable dans uncontexte auquel, primitivement, elle n'appartenait pas.*"

80. The earliest Christian papyri provide evidence also of the ongoing revision of the New Testament texts in the early centuries. Examples of composite Christian scriptural documents are cited within this context, but the same also holds true for many Hebrew biblical documents, e.g., the Documentary Hypothesis of the Torah, and the prophets Isaiah, Daniel, and Zechariah.

81. Ibid., 12–13, "*Sans doute, il n'y a pas lieu de nier la réalité de disparates dans le Protévangile. Mais ils ne prouvent pas que cette oeuvre résulte de la mise bout à bout de documents pratiquement complets qui auraient encore continué à circuler comme tels pendant des siècles. De l'existence de ces documents, nous n'avons aucun attestation positive.*"

82. See above, p. 15, n. 64.

83. *La Forme*, 400, "*Son ampleur est nettement insuffisante pour un ouvrage indépendent. Et s'il faisait partie d'un Apocryphe de l'Enfance plus vaste, en connaît-on un, pour cette période, qui convienne mieux que le Protévangile de Jacques?*"

A prominent example is the composite infancy narrative found in the first two chapters of the canonical Gospel of Luke in which smaller, individual, preexisting literary units of unknown origin are strung together into a larger story. And the Gospel of John may again be cited as an example in this discussion. In the same manner, there are no remnants of any of the various preexisting sources that were interwoven together within the framework of the Signs Source to produce the fourth canonical Gospel, for example, the hymn to the Logos, the Baptist materials, the discourse materials, and chapter 21.

De Strycker based much of his argumentation for the compositional unity of the *ProtJac* upon his study of various formal literary characteristics that he supposed were shared in common by all three parts of the document.[84] Among these are what he perceived as the simple character of the narrative text; aspects of the literary technique of the author; and similarities in language, style, and composition.[85] But the force of these literary observations is mitigated by de Strycker's own strict adherence to the unity of the *ProtJac* to the exclusion of any redactional process in its creation. Many of these elements that de Strycker views as links between the parts of the *ProtJac* may be explained by the strong possibility that its text has developed through a series of stages at the hands of one or more redactors during the "silent" centuries before the earliest extant textual evidence.[86] Later editors would have striven to obscure the discrepancies between the sources, as in the case of Luke and Matthew, who rigorously revised the text of Mark as they incorporated the first Gospel into their own compositions. Early Christian redactors and later editors were so effective that centuries of intense scholarly study were required to unravel their work.

The Present Study

The present study is based upon the premise that the *ProtJac* was not the unitary composition of a single author dating to the second half of the second century CE but rather was a composite work largely composed of a very early document whose original title, the *Genesis Marias* (*GenMar*), may be preserved in the oldest copy of the *ProtJac*, P.Bodm V. The individual who wrote the *GenMar* will be designated as the Author. The *GenMar*, which was written as early as the first century CE,

---

84. Ibid., 401–3, "*plusieurs caractéristiques formelles se constatent à travers tout le Protévangile et en conferment l'unite.*"

85. De Strycker also cites the central idea of the purity of Mary as a unifying element among the several parts of the *ProtJac*, but that argument is weakened by the vagueness of his description of Mary's "purity" in comparison to the highly specific terminology used by scholars to denote this aspect of the *ProtJac*, i.e., *virginitas ante partum, in partu*, and *post-partum*.

86. E.g., p. 16 above, Amann's suggestion that the first two parts of the *ProtJac* were joined together very closely in the late second century before this union was integrated into the final form of the text.

seems to have undergone substantial augmentation, already in the first century, by a subsequent writer to whom we shall refer as the Composer. In this second phase of the composition of the *ProtJac* a large amount of new material, which featured the person of Joseph, was integrated into the *GenMar* text. This Joseph material was thought by earlier scholars to have constituted a discrete individual document, which they labeled as the *Apocryphum Josephi*.[87] However, in this study the secondary Joseph materials will be considered to have been written ad hoc by the later Composer and interpolated into the *GenMar* in a second stage of the progressive composition of the *ProtJac*. The document consisting of the *GenMar*, augmented with the Joseph materials, will be referred to as the Composer-enhanced *GenMar* (CEGM).

In the second century CE, the CEGM underwent significant modification at the hands of a third individual who strove to convert what he must have considered to be a heretical document into one that exhibited his own orthodox leanings. This individual, to whom we shall refer as the Redactor, carried out the third major phase of the composition of the *ProtJac* by interpolating materials into the text of the CEGM. Some of these he apparently derived from the canonical texts of Luke, Matthew, and John. But the Redactor also inserted dialogues, prayers, and extended narratives into his source document, which he either created himself or derived from additional written sources. He employed editorial devices to accommodate his interpolations into the CEGM text.[88] Furthermore, the Redactor attached at the end of his heavily edited source document two chapters of material that featured Zachariah, Elizabeth, and their son John the Baptist. This material had been labeled by earlier scholars as the *Apocryphum Zachariae*.[89] Thus the Redactor was ultimately responsible for creating the final form of the *ProtJac* as it is known today.

The major second-century redaction of the CEGM was followed by additional, more minor, revision at the hands of generations of copyists and scribes, continuing from late antiquity throughout the medieval period and into modern times. Many of these later scribal revisions were dogmatically oriented and included the modification of the original text as well as the insertion of foreign material of the editors' own creation. Even modern critical editions of the text of the *ProtJac*, most notably that of de Strycker, further muddled its textual history by imposing yet another stratum of revisions based on subjective conjectures by the editors. All of this editorial activity by so many disparate voices essentially confused the

---

87. See pp. 15–17 above. In short, I agree with certain elements of the compositional theories of the early scholars but differ as to the date of each of the segments of the *ProtJac*.

88. As will be noted often in the presentation of the evidence of redaction below, the Redactor was not successful in concealing his editorial handiwork. On the contrary, his attempts to smooth over the transition points between his own interpolations and his source document were often heavy-handed and careless.

89. See pp. 15–17 above, and the discussion below in "The Redactor: *The Protevangelium Jacobi*," pp. 131–47.

critical issues of the authorship, date, provenance, purpose, and composition of the *ProtJac* and, even more so, of its original source document, the *GenMar*. The fortuitous discovery of P.Bodm V, with its witness to the complete text of the *ProtJac*, dated within a century of its final composition, allows us to leap back over the centuries-long revisionist history of our Apocryphon and to view its text in the most pristine possible state.

Once having recognized the presence of the work of generations of writers, composers, redactors, and subsequent scribes and editors throughout a time span of almost two millennia to produce the text of the *ProtJac* as it exists today, the researcher is confronted with the complicated task of determining the parameters of the original source document, the *GenMar*, and the extent of the major revisions of the *GenMar* by the first-century Composer and the second-century Redactor, as well as the subsequent lesser revisions by later scribes and editors. It is only after this foundational work of identifying and isolating these elements has been accomplished that one can set about appropriately to ascertain the *Sitz im Leben* of each of the actors who played a role in the creation of today's *ProtJac*. Through the present redaction-critical investigation of the text of the *ProtJac* as preserved in P.Bodm V, I hope to have contributed toward the realization of this foundational work.

Chapter 1

EVIDENCE OF REDACTION OF THE *PROTJAC*

THE JOSEPH COUNCIL: *PROTJAC* 8:03-9:12

In accordance with the theory of the composition of the *ProtJac* upon which the present study is based, the unredacted Veil Council, now contained in *ProtJac* 10-12, was the original continuation of the *GenMar*, which now occupies the initial chapters of the *ProtJac* 1:01-8:02. The Joseph Council, now *ProtJac* 8:03-9:12, was interpolated by the Composer into the original text of the *GenMar*. The first indication that the Joseph Council may constitute a distinct block of material that was inserted by the Composer into the *GenMar* before the Veil Council is the similarity between the statements that introduce each of these two successive priestly councils respectively that now occur in the present form of the *ProtJac*:

Joseph Council
ProtJac 8:03b συμβουλιον εγενετο των ιερεων λεγοντων
there was a council of the priests saying
Veil Council
ProtJac 10:01 εγενετο δε συμβουλιον των ιερεων λεγοντων
and there was a council of the priests saying.[1]

Both statements contain the same five identical words, although in a different order. In *ProtJac* 8:03b συμβουλιον εγενετο των ιερεων λεγοντων ("there was a council of the priests saying") is the main clause of a larger sentence that is introduced by a subordinate clause in the form of a genitive absolute phrase γενομενης δε δωδεκαετους ("she becoming twelve years old").[2] This verse serves as the transitional link between the preceding chapters of the *GenMar* and the beginning of the Joseph Council in *ProtJac* 8:03 within the context of the redactional enhancement of the *GenMar* by the Composer's interpolation of the Joseph

---

1. Underlining and italics will be used in the quotations of the Greek text of the *ProtJac* to illustrate the presence of redactional activity.
2. The feminine genitive form of the Greek participle γενομενης contains the implication that "She," Mary, had become twelve years old, thus obviating the need for a feminine pronoun to refer to her.

Council before the Veil Council. In that setting the genitive absolute γενομενης δε δωδεκαετους was introduced by the Composer[3] to facilitate the abrupt transition from ProtJac 8:02, which briefly describes Mary's life in the temple from the age of three, to ProtJac 8:03, where Mary is now a physically mature twelve years old, thus obliging the priests to hold the Joseph Council to resolve the issue of her new impure status vis-à-vis the purity laws regarding menstruant women in the temple[4]:

ProtJac 8:03 γενομενης δε δωδεκαετους
συμβουλιον εγενετο των ιερεων λεγοντων
    She becoming twelve years old
    there was a council of the priests saying:
04 ιδου μαρια γεγονε δωδεκαετης εν τω ναω κυριου·
    "Behold, Mary has become twelve years old in the temple of the Lord,
τι ουν αυτην ποιησωμεν,
μηπως μιανη το αγιασμα κυριου του θεου ημων.
    what will we do with her
    so that she will not defile the holy place of the Lord our God?"

The Composer's interpolation of the Joseph Council before the Veil Council interrupts the natural flow of the *GenMar* narrative and creates a problem by distancing Mary from participating directly in the preparation of the new temple veil. There must now be an entire two-chapter-long process by the priests to remove Mary from the temple and a special dispensation to return her to the temple from Joseph's home to help prepare the new veil. This is accomplished by an editorial adjustment to the now detached Veil Council in *ProtJac* 10:02-05.[5] As opposed to the sudden leap over nine years of Mary's life in the first verse of the Joseph Council in *ProtJac* 8:03, the initial verse of the Veil Council in *ProtJac* 10:01 does not mention Mary's age, which is irrelevant to her participation in preparing the new veil: εγενετο δε συμβουλιον των ιερεων λεγοντων· ποιησωμεν καταπετασμα τω ναω κυριου ("And there was a council of the priests saying, 'Let us make a veil for the temple of the Lord'"). *ProtJac* 10:01 represents an unobtrusive, and thus probably original, continuation of the preceding narrative of Mary's life in the temple ending in *GenMar* 8:02.

The duplication of the initial verses in the Joseph and Veil Councils is an example, on a larger scale, of the standard editorial modus operandi of the Composer that occurs also on two occasions later in the Veil Council in which

---

3. The Redactor was responsible for inserting the contradictory editorial statement of Mary's age of sixteen at the end of the Veil Council in *ProtJac* 12:11 ην δε ετων δεκαεξ οτε ταυτα τα μυστηρια εγινετο αυτη ("And she was sixteen years old when those mysterious events happened to her"); cf. p. 54; 150–1; 165–6, n. 141.

4. Cf. the classical biblical passage in Lev. 15:19-31.

5. See below, pp. 35–7.

the Composer modified *GenMar* texts to reflect Mary's location at "home" as opposed to her being in the temple.[6] Since the primary purpose of the Joseph Council was to relocate Mary from the temple to Joseph's home, it stands to reason that the Composer would implement the same editorial strategy in this larger scenario as well. In the account of the gathering of virgins to spin the threads in *ProtJac* 10:02-05 and 10:09-11:05,[7] the Composer revised the *GenMar* narrative by duplicating and modifying elements of the relevant verses and then inserting his own materials into these scenarios to create his versions of the original texts now reflecting Mary's location at "home." In the case of the introductory verses of the two priestly councils, the Composer duplicated the entire initial sentence of the Veil Council in 10:01, rearranged the words of its text, and then inserted his revised version at the beginning of his own new creation, the Joseph Council.

A number of irregularities within the text of the Joseph Council indicate the presence of editorial activity, which suggests that the Composer found it difficult to integrate his new Joseph material into the existing *GenMar* text as he constructed the final form of his narrative. The first anomaly in the Joseph Council follows immediately after the initial introductory verses in *ProtJac* 8:03-04. A disconnect in the continuity of the text occurs between *ProtJac* 8:03-04, in which the priests as a group are in dialogue among themselves, and the following verse *ProtJac* 8:05, in which the priests are addressing a single individual who has appeared unexpectedly: και ειπαν αυτω οι ιερεις ("and the priests said to him"). There was no previous reference to this individual priest in the preceding text but he is soon recognized as the high priest when the priests as a group describe him as standing at the altar of the Lord and propose that he enter the Holy of Holies to pray about Mary:

ProtJac 8:03 γενομενης δε δωδεκαετους
συμβουλιον εγενετο των ιερεων λεγοντων
    She becoming twelve years old
    there was a council of the priests saying:
04 ιδου μαρια γεγονε δωδεκαετης εν τω ναω κυριου·
    "Behold, Mary has become twelve years old in the temple of the Lord,
τι ουν αυτην ποιησωμεν,
μηπως μιανη το αγιασμα κυριου του θεου ημων
    what will we do with her
    so that she will not defile the holy place of the Lord our God?"
05 και ειπαν αυτω οι ιερεις· συ εστης επι το θυσιαστηριον κυριου,
    And the priests said to him, "you stood at the altar of the Lord,
και εισελθε και προσευξε περι αυτης,
    enter also and pray about her

---

6. This first major instance of the modus operandi of the Composer precedes and serves as the prototype of several minor examples that occurred later in the CEGM.

7. See below, pp. 35-9, also two instances in "The Trial of Joseph and Mary," pp. 65-9.

και ο εαν φανερωση σοι κυριος ο θεος τουτο ποιησωμεν
   and that which the Lord God reveals to you, this we will do."
06 και <u>εισηλθεν ο ιερευς</u> λαβων τον δωδεκακωδωνα
εις τα αγια των αγιων,
   And <u>the priest entered</u>, taking the vestment with twelve bells,
   into the Holy of Holies
και ηυξατο περι αυτης
   and prayed about her

This break in the continuity of the narrative suggests the possible existence of an original element between *ProtJac* 8:04 and 8:05 that somehow dropped out of the text and which may have contained information about the high priest who now appears abruptly in *ProtJac* 8:05. This is only the first example of a number of such anomalies that occur in the first verses of the Joseph Council, which, when viewed collectively, suggest the presence of redactional activity. In *ProtJac* 8:06 the high priest took up the vestment with twelve bells,[8] entered into the Holy of Holies, and prayed about Mary. In *ProtJac* 8:07 the high priest received an answer to his prayer from an angel who appeared and addressed him as Zachariah:

ProtJac 8:07 και ιδου αγγελος κυριου εστη λεγων· ζαχαρια, ζαχαρια,
   and behold an angel of the Lord stood saying, 'Zachariah, Zachariah,
εξελθε και εκκλησιασον τους χηρευοντας του λαου
   go out and call together the widowers of the people
08 και ω εαν επιδειξη κυριος ο θεος σημειον, τουτω εσται γυνη
   and to whom the Lord God will show a sign, to him she will be a wife.

Angels appear in all three layers of the *ProtJac*, whether written by the *GenMar* Author (*ProtJac* 4:01, 4:05, 4:06, 8:02), the Redactor (*ProtJac* 11:06, 11:09, 14:05, 12:07, 20:07, 20:11, 21:15, 22:06), or, possibly, the Composer (*ProtJac* 8:07). If the angel's appearance in *ProtJac* 8:07 is a genuine element of the Joseph Council, this would be the only instance of an angel appearing in the materials in the *ProtJac* that may be ascribed to the Composer,[9] as opposed to three cases in the *GenMar* and eight in the Redactor's interpolations. However, there are several exceptional elements in the text of *ProtJac* 8:07 that distinguish this verse from its context and may serve as clues to its special role in the narrative.

---

8. Exod. 28:31-5 describes a liturgical vestment worn by the high priest in the Jerusalem temple, the ephod, that had golden bells and pomegranates hanging from it.

9. Angels are mentioned in the Composer's Trial story in *ProtJac* 13:09 and 14:11 but do not actually appear. Both of these verses essentially replicate the text of the original *GenMar* in *ProtJac* 8:02 with respect to Mary being fed by the hand of angels in the Holy of Holies.

The first distinguishing element in 8:07 is the naming of the high priest by the angel as Zachariah in 8:07; this is a distinctive feature of the editorial activity of the Redactor who was responsible for inserting the Zachariah materials into the *ProtJac*.[10] Second, the designation of the men called to the temple as prospective husbands[11] for Mary as χηρευοντας ("widowers") only occurs in *ProtJac* 8:07 within the Joseph Council. The only other references to widowers or widows in the *ProtJac* are in the *GenMar* text at *ProtJac* 2:02 and 4:13 where Anna refers to herself as a widow. Finally, the verb εκκλησιασον ("call out") in the angel's order to gather the "widowers," here in its imperative form, is an odd choice by the writer and occurs only here in the *ProtJac*. The nominal form of εκκλησιασον, ἐκκλησία ("church"), occurs only in Matthew among the canonical Gospels.[12] The idiosyncratic nature of the angel's message is perpetuated in *ProtJac* 8:08, the only verse in the *ProtJac* in which Mary is explicitly said to be Joseph's wife.[13]

The presence of three *hapax legomena* and the clue to the Redactor's influence reveal the angel's message in *ProtJac* 8:07-08 to be a crux for understanding the composition of the Joseph Council. *ProtJac* 8:07 is so thoroughly enmeshed in its present context of the angelic visitation to the high priest that it is difficult to argue for the possibility that it might be an interpolation. It would be more realistic to assume that the scenario of the high priest praying for guidance in the temple may have been an original part of the *GenMar* and that the high priest did receive an answer to his prayer. But the idiosyncratic elements in *ProtJac* 8:07— the only appearance of an angel in the Composer's work, the exclusive Zachariah connection to the Redactor, the Matthean word for "church," and the unique reference to widowers—strongly suggest that the original *GenMar* verse must have been heavily edited, but by whom?

The one individual who is associated with most of the exceptional elements in *ProtJac* 8:07-08 is the Redactor. The Redactor will be shown to have interpolated angelic appearances into the Composer-enhanced Annunciation story in *ProtJac* 11:06, 09; in Joseph's dream vision in *ProtJac* 14:05; in the Nativity story in *ProtJac* 20:07, 11; and in his Zachariah Apocryphon in *ProtJac* 21:15, 22:06.[14] The Redactor is responsible also for all the references to Zachariah in the

---

10. These include the Zachariah Apocryphon in *ProtJac* 22-24, the reference to the death of Zachariah in the Veil Council in *ProtJac* 10:08, and the present text of *ProtJac* 8:07.

11. See the discussion below, pp. 30-4, on the contradictions in the Joseph Council regarding the role of the individual who will remove Mary from the temple. In *ProtJac* 8:07-08 he is described as her husband but in *ProtJac* 9 he will be assigned as her custodian or guardian.

12. Mt. 16:18 and 18:17, both within texts interpolated by Matthew into his source document, Mark.

13. See *ProtJac* 17:03 below where Joseph specifically refuses to refer to Mary as his wife.

14. Of the numerous appearances of angels that have been interpolated by the Redactor into the *ProtJac*, some are taken from the canonical Gospels while others are not. The angel's appearance to the high priest in *ProtJac* 8:07-08 was not canonical in origin; the same holds

ProtJac including his insertion of *ProtJac* 10:08 into the Veil Council[15] and the Zachariah Apocryphon in its entirety in *ProtJac* 22–24 at the end of the CEGM. Furthermore, the Redactor is linked to the verb εκκλησιασον in *ProtJac* 8:07 through his familiarity with the Gospel of Matthew, having interpolated texts from Matthew into Joseph's angelic dream vision in *ProtJac* 14[16] and into the Magi story in *ProtJac* 21–22.[17]

The connection of the Redactor to three of the four distinctive elements in *ProtJac* 8:07 is evident, but the fourth element, the χηρευοντας ("widowers"), is more complicated. Although the Redactor would not have been averse to Mary being in the custody of an elderly widower, the "widowers" element is particularly prominent in the Composer's materials. The author of the *ProtJac* is named in chapter 25 as Ἰάκωβος, in modern biblical parlance James, and appears ostensibly in the *ProtJac* as an adult son of an elderly Joseph by a prior wife. The Composer never mentions Joseph's first wife in his materials but refers to his sons several times. Joseph is depicted as a widower when he considers registering Mary as his wife in the census in the Nativity story in *ProtJac* 17:02-03: εγω απογραψομαι τους υιους μου. πως αυτην απογραψομαι; γυναικα εμην; επαισχυνομαι αλλα θυγατερα; οιδαν οι υιοι ισραηλ οτι ουκ εστιν θυγατηρ μου ("I will register my sons. How will I register her? As my wife? I am ashamed. As my daughter? The sons of Israel know that she is not my daughter").

Joseph first speaks of his sons in his response to the priest's assignment of Mary into his custody in *ProtJac* 9:06: υιους εχω και πρεσβυτης ειμι, αυτη νεανις ("I have sons and am an old man, she is young"). The Composer positions Joseph's sons, including James, to be eyewitnesses to the Nativity. In *ProtJac* 17:05 one of Joseph's sons, ostensibly James, leads the donkey that carries Mary on the journey to Bethlehem: και εστρωσεν τον ονον και εκαθισεν αυτην και ειλκεν ο υιος αυτου ("and [Joseph] saddled the donkey and sat her [upon it], and his son led"). On their way to Bethlehem in *ProtJac* 18:01 Joseph leaves Mary in a cave and goes out to seek a Hebrew midwife, giving Mary over to the care of his sons (παρεστησεν αυτην τους υιους αυτου). Joseph's sons, and especially James, are present at the very site of the cave at the moment when Mary gives birth. The Composer has thus situated James in a position that enables him to observe the Nativity firsthand and to record his eyewitness report in the *ProtJac*.

---

true for later angelic appearances to Salome in *ProtJac* 20:04, 07, and 10-11. The angelic appearances in the Annunciation story in *ProtJac* 11:06-12 are from Luke, cf. pp. 44–9 below; the dream vision of Joseph in *ProtJac* 14:05-08 is from Mt. 1:20, cf. pp. 60–5 below.

15. See below, pp. 37–8.
16. See below, pp. 60–5.
17. See below, pp. 113–22. The Redactor has taken substantial material from the Nativity story in Mt. 1:18-25 and especially from the Magi story in Mt. 2:1-12.

Joseph as a widower is such a fundamental component of the Composer's entire narrative that he may have been responsible for that element of *ProtJac* 8:07 but with the acquiescence of the Redactor in allowing it to remain in the text.[18] Unfortunately, the hand of the Redactor rests so heavily on this important verse that any vestiges of an original *GenMar* text are no longer discernible. It would be more fruitful to theorize concerning the original agent of the message to the high priest by the *GenMar* Author in *ProtJac* 8:07. An angelic visitation suits the agenda of the Redactor, but not that of the Composer. Might we postulate that in the original unredacted *GenMar* the answer to the prayer of the high priest was not conveyed by an angel but may have been communicated directly to the high priest, liturgically vested in his official capacity seeking guidance through prayer in the Holy of Holies, by the same voice—as will be seen below—that addressed Mary in the original *GenMar* Annunciation story, the Voice of God, widely known in Jewish sources as the *Bath Kol*?[19]

The verses following the angel's message to the high priest in *ProtJac* 8:07-08 contain additional irregularities. In *ProtJac* 8:09 the narrative leaps from the words of the angel to the rambling statement εξηλθαν οι κηρυκες καθ ολου της περιχωρου της ιουδαιας, και ηχησεν σαλπιγξ κυριου, και ιδου εδραμον απαντες ("the heralds went out throughout the environs of Judea and the trumpet of the Lord sounded and behold everyone ran"). The priests gave no order for the heralds to go out and it is not articulated that the unspecified απαντες ("everyone") are widowers.[20] The disorder in the text worsens in *ProtJac* 9:01a where Joseph is injected into the story brusquely as an afterthought and with an action unrelated to the context. Joseph throws a hammer and goes out to join the unspecified "everyone" who were left running in the preceding verse: ιωσηφ δε ριψας το σκεπαρνον εξηλθεν αυτος εις συναντησιν αυτων ("and Joseph, having thrown the hammer, came out himself to meet them"). With this extemporaneous statement the Composer first introduces the central character of his story, Joseph, into the *GenMar* and adds the unrelated detail that he was involved in construction.[21]

---

18. See above, pp. 27-8; the only references to widowers or widows in the *GenMar* are at *ProtJac* 2:02 and 4:13 where Anna refers to herself as a widow.

19. See the analysis below in "The Veil Council," pp. 39-44. Such a scenario would have been anathema to both the Composer and the Redactor. The Composer created and interpolated the entire Joseph Council into the *GenMar* precisely to distance the Annunciation from the temple. The Redactor also put forth prodigious efforts to suppress the same scenario in the *GenMar* Annunciation story by means of the modus operandi that he employs in *ProtJac* 8:07, the interpolation of an angelic visitation with a different message.

20. In view of the questionable origin of the reference to "widowers" above it cannot be assumed that the απαντες are in fact "widowers."

21. See the discussion below on the implications of this reference to Joseph's hammer with respect to the description of Jesus as a carpenter's (i.e., Joseph's) son in Mt. 13:55, as opposed to Mk 6:3 where Jesus himself is said to be "the carpenter, the son of Mary." Joseph is mentioned nowhere in Mark but is a central figure in Matthew.

The erratic storyline continues in *ProtJac* 9:01b: και συναχθεντες ομου απηλθαν προς τον ιερεα, λαβοντες τας ραβδους αυτων ("and coming together they all went out towards the priest, having taken their staffs").[22] The Composer seems to have added the subordinate participle phrase "having taken their staffs" as another afterthought[23] whose secondary nature is perceptible within the sequence of events in 8:09–9:01. The heralds went out, the trumpet sounded, "everyone" was running, Joseph threw the hammer and went out to meet them, and gathering together they went out toward the priest. Only after all these events with "everyone," now including Joseph as an afterthought, on their way to the priest does the Composer first insert the detail retroactively that they had taken their staffs. The staffs will play a central role in the narrative from this point in the quest by the priests to obtain a sign from God revealing the person who will take Mary into his care.

After retroactively inserting the staff motif into *ProtJac* 9:01 the Composer progressively clarified the intentions of the high priest regarding the staffs in 9:02-03. In 9:02 the priest received the staffs from the candidates, entered into the sanctuary and prayed. But it is only in 9:03 that the Composer finally discloses that the staffs were the means by which the sign would be obtained: τελεσας δε την ευχην ελαβεν τας ραβδους και εξηλθεν και εδωκεν αυτοις και σημειον ουκ ην εν αυταις ("and finishing the prayer, he took the staffs and went out and gave [them] to them [the widowers], and there was no sign in them [the staffs]").[24] After stating in 9:03 that the high priest had returned all their staffs to the widowers without a sign, in 9:04 the Composer reintroduces Joseph from his first appearance in 9:01a. Joseph now takes the last staff and receives the sign: την δε εσχατην ραβδον ελαβεν ο ιωσηφ και ιδου περιστερα εξηλθεν απο της ραβδου και επεσταθη επι την κεφαλην του ιωσηφ ("and Joseph took the last staff and behold a dove came out of the staff and stood upon Joseph's head"). Thus again in 9:04, as before in 901a, Joseph is inserted belatedly into a scene as an afterthought after the action of the scene has been completed.

The examination of the text of the Joseph Council thus far has revealed discontinuity and inconsistencies in *ProtJac* 8:03-9:04 as opposed to the succeeding text in *ProtJac* 9:05-12, which appears to be more homogeneous and relatively free of such internal incongruities. Within the parameters of our compositional theory,

---

22. Although the aorist form of the participle occurs several times in this passage, I have rendered only λαβοντες with the extended translation "having taken their staffs" to emphasize the awkwardness of the Composer's insertion of the staffs retroactively at the end of the preceding sequence of events.

23. The repeated presence of actions expressed retroactively as afterthoughts in the Composer's narrative suggests that he is redacting his source, the *GenMar*, in a careless, haphazard manner and did not return later to revise his work. The Composer's use of the "afterthought" motif seems to be a regular element of his modus operandi. See below and on pp. 35–6, 67–9, 125, and 131.

24. The deficiency of the editorial process in these verses extends to the clarity of expression as well.

the problems in the first segment of the Joseph Council suggest that the Composer struggled to integrate his Joseph materials into his source text, the *GenMar*. Naturally, this would result in a text that appears fragmented and haphazard in its composition at the point of contact between the *GenMar* and the Composer's new materials in *ProtJac* 8:03–9:04. The tantalizing hints of an original *GenMar* account of Mary's departure from the temple do not offer adequate substance to prove its existence, much less to allow a reconstruction. It must suffice here to offer an analysis of the confusion surrounding the two most essential elements in the Joseph Council: the manner with which an appropriate person was chosen to receive Mary and the nature of her relationship to him. This confusion is revealed in a systematic presentation of the incongruities between the fragmented verses in *ProtJac* 8:03–9:04 and the block of more homogeneous text that follows them in *ProtJac* 9:05-12.

From a comparison of the two distinct sections in *ProtJac* 8:03-9:12, a pattern emerges of two parallel, intermingled stories that coexist in the Joseph Council, each with its own method of identifying the person who will take Mary from the temple, and describing the nature of their relationship:

ProtJac 8:03–9:04, the fragmented section:

- in 8:08 the angel instructs the high priest: "to whom the Lord God will show a sign, to him she will be a wife"
- only in 8:03–9:04 is Mary the γυνη ("wife") of the yet unnamed person who will be selected to receive her[25]
- only in 8:08 is this person to be revealed by a divine σημειον ("sign")
- the "sign" motif is repeated in 9:03
- the "sign" motif becomes related to ραβδους ("staffs") in 9:01-04
- a "staff" is revealed to be the vehicle by which the "sign" is given in 9:04
- only in 9:01a and 9:04 does Joseph appear within 8:03–9:04 where he was intercalated into the text by the Composer as an afterthought
- in 9:01a and 9:04 "staffs" accompany Joseph also as afterthoughts.

ProtJac 9:05-12, the homogeneous section:

- in 9:05 the priest informs Joseph: "you have been appointed by lot to receive the virgin of the Lord in custody for him"
- only in 9:05-12 does Joseph receive Mary εις τηρησιν αυτω "in custody for him [the Lord]"
- only here has Joseph κεκληρωσαι been chosen ("by lot")
- Joseph's status as Mary's "custodian" is repeated in 9:10
- There are no "signs" or "staffs" in 9:05-12

25. Later in the Midwife story in *ProtJac* 19:04, Joseph refers to Mary as his μεμνηστευμένη ("betrothed").

A story of priests deciding to remove Mary from the temple after the completion of their veil project would not be inappropriate for the *GenMar*. In view of Mary's special status in the *GenMar* it would be natural for them to seek instructions from God in the temple as to how to proceed. And they would be expected to do so through the mediation of their high priest, given the previous occurrences of priests and high priests in *ProtJac* 4–9. A prayer delivered by the official, liturgically vested high priest in the Holy of Holies hypothetically could have elicited a direct response from God himself via his *Bath Kol*.[26] It must be remembered that in the original *GenMar* Veil Council—before the Composer's interpolation of the Joseph Council—Mary has just conceived by the Annunciation of the *Bath Kol* and is now pregnant with the divine child.[27] Under these circumstances God himself would be expected to continue to be involved actively in Mary's situation, as he was previously in the *GenMar* Annunciation story.

Any preexisting *GenMar* text in *ProtJac* 8:03–9:12 was obscured and largely supplanted by the radical editorial revisions of the Composer and the Redactor who in two successive phases imposed their respective agendas on the original storyline. The primary enhancement of the *GenMar* was effected by the Composer who first began to insinuate Joseph into the fragmented section of the Joseph Council in *ProtJac* 8:03–9:04. The Composer intercalated Joseph's first appearances in *ProtJac* 9:01a and 9:04 in tandem with the "staffs" motif as the priest's method of discerning the divine will. He then augmented the story with his own Joseph materials in *ProtJac* 9:05-12. The Redactor later interpolated at *ProtJac* 8:07 his particular version of the divine response to the prayer of the high priest as a message mediated in an angelic visitation, thus effectively suppressing the original divine response in the *GenMar*.[28] Consequently, the highly problematic text created successively, and collectively, by the Composer and the Redactor represents a most daunting, and perhaps insurmountable, challenge to any attempt to determine which of the conflicting elements in the text should be attributed to the Author of the *GenMar*, the Composer, or the Redactor, respectively.

Although this systematic examination of *ProtJac* 8:03–9:04 has not produced definitive conclusions concerning the authorship of specific parts of the story, a summary of the results of our analysis is in order with respect to the two central elements, the method of choosing the person who will receive Mary and the nature of their relationship. Both references to a "sign" as the means to designate the chosen individual occur in the fragmented early section in *ProtJac* 8:08 and 9:03. The first of these was in the angel's message to the priest, which would associate it with the Redactor.[29] But it is also stated in *ProtJac* 8:08 that Mary would be the "wife" of the designee, which seems contrary to the Redactor's motivation to promote

---

26. See above, p. 29, n. 19. This part of the text would have been suppressed by the Redactor.

27. See the analysis below in "The Original *GenMar* Annunciation Story," pp. 39–49.

28. It is also possible that the Composer is at work here.

29. See pp. 26–8 above on the strong link between the Redactor and *ProtJac* 8:07-08.

the perpetual virginity of Mary.[30] The second reference to the "sign" in *ProtJac* 9:03 is part of the larger passage *ProtJac* 9:01-04 that contains the intercalation of Joseph and the "staffs," which fall within the purview of the Composer.[31] But later in *ProtJac* 19 the Composer will refer to Mary as Joseph's betrothed thus reflecting a possible connection to the "wife" reference in *ProtJac* 8:08.

The same priest who sought a "sign" to designate a "widower" to be Mary's husband in the fragmented section in *ProtJac* 8:07-08 now informs Joseph in the homogenous section in *ProtJac* 9:05 that he has been chosen "by lot" to take the "virgin of the Lord" "into his custody for the Lord."[32] Although this lottery occurs in a section written by the Composer, a parallel lottery was held by the priests in the *GenMar* Author's Veil Council making the lottery element attributable either to the Author or to the Composer.[33] But this parallel may not be as significant as it first seems. The lottery concept is represented by a different Greek word in each of the two texts, κεκλήρωσαι from κληρόω in the Joseph Council in *ProtJac* 9:05 and λάχετε from λαγχάνω in the Veil Council in *ProtJac* 10:06-07. In conclusion, the manner of selecting the person who will receive Mary is inextricably intertwined with the problem of the nature of the relationship between them. And the confusion surrounding these two elements is compounded by the broader problem of their being embedded within two discrete divisions of the Joseph Council, *ProtJac* 8:07–9:04 and 9:05-12.

Leaving behind the virtually insoluble difficulties of the disorderly and fragmented early section of the Joseph Council and moving forward, one is struck by the smoothly flowing narrative of the succeeding Joseph materials written by the Composer in *ProtJac* 9:05-12. The later section of the Joseph Council is not without

---

30. See the discussion of the Nativity story below, pp. 92-7, where the Redactor eliminates elements from his interpolated texts from Matthew that specifically refer to Mary as Joseph's wife and imply that Joseph and Mary will eventually have marital relations after the birth of Jesus. See also the Redactor's interpolated "Doubting Salome" episode in the Nativity story whose purpose was to promote the perpetual virginity of Mary, pp. 108–13. See also pp. 165–7 below regarding the possibility that the original Author of the *GenMar* also promoted the postpartum virginity of Mary.

31. The likelihood that the "staffs" motif was part of the original *GenMar* story is diminished by its apparent secondary nature and its limitation only to the passage *ProtJac* 9:01-04.

32. These contradictions in the Composer's Joseph Council will have significant, far-reaching ramifications in later chapters of the *ProtJac*. See the discussion below on the Composer's conception of the evolving relationship between Joseph and Mary.

33. The lottery in *ProtJac* 10:05-07 was held to determine which colored threads would be spun by the virgins, pp. 37–8 below. The description of this event in the *ProtJac* specifically as being "by lot" is important as a parallel to a reference in the *Asc. Isa*, an early Old Testament pseudepigraphon containing Christian elements. See G. T. Zervos, "Seeking the Source of the Marian Myth: Have We Found the Missing Link?" in *Which Mary? The Marys of Early Christian Tradition*, ed. F. Stanley Jones, Society of Biblical Literature Symposium Series 19 (Atlanta, GA: Society of Biblical Literature, 2002), 107–20, especially 118.

its own incongruities, but these are explicable within the context of the Composer's objectives. At first Joseph responds negatively to his assignment as Mary's custodian in *ProtJac* 9:06: και αντειπεν ο ιωσηφ λεγων υιους εχω και πρεσβυτης ειμι, αυτη νεανις μηπως εσομαι περιγελος τοις υιοις ισραηλ ("and Joseph resisted saying, 'I have sons and am old, she is young, perhaps I will be ridiculed by the sons of Israel'"). This response appears to be inconsistent with Joseph's specific role as a "custodian" of the "virgin of the Lord" "for the Lord" in *ProtJac* 9:05. Joseph would not be ridiculed as an elderly "custodian" or "guardian" of a young virgin, but he could be ridiculed as an elderly husband of a very young wife as specified in *ProtJac* 8:08.

This apparent incongruity suggests that the Composer may have viewed the relationship between Joseph and Mary as evolving. Mary could have been assigned initially to Joseph as her "custodian" "for the Lord" to ensure her virginal status only until the delivery of her divine child. After the birth of the child they could have been married. This interpretation finds support in the Nativity story in *ProtJac* 19 where Joseph describes Mary to a midwife as his "betrothed."[34] In *ProtJac* 9:07-09 the priest must pressure Joseph to accept Mary by reminding him of ancient Israelites who were destroyed for speaking against the will of God.[35] In *ProtJac* 9:10 Joseph relents and consents to his assignment: και φοβηθεις ιωσηφ παρελαβεν αυτην εις τηρησιν αυτω ("and being afraid, Joseph received Mary in custody for him [the Lord]").[36] With Mary now in his "custody," it remains only for Joseph to remove her from the temple in *ProtJac* 9:11, thus accomplishing the Composer's primary purpose in the Joseph Council: και ειπεν αυτη μαρια, παρελαβον σε εκ ναου κυριου ("and he said to her, 'Mary, I took you out of the temple of the Lord'").

Immediately after declaring to Mary in *ProtJac* 9:11 that he had taken her out of the temple, in *ProtJac* 9:12 Joseph informs her: και νυν καταλειπω σε εν τω οικω μου, απερχομαι γαρ οικοδομησαι τας οικοδομας, και ηξω προς σε· κυριος σε διαφυλαξει ("and now I leave you in my home for I am going to build the buildings and I will return to you. The Lord will guard you"). Initially it seems odd that Joseph's first act as Mary's "custodian" is to take her to his home and leave. But Joseph's immediate departure after leaving Mary at home accentuates another objective of the Composer, to eliminate any doubt that Joseph and Mary may have had marital relations before her conception in the ensuing Annunciation in the Veil Council. It was the Composer himself who established the sequence of events in his enhanced version of the *GenMar*. He purposefully created and inserted the Joseph Council before the Veil Council precisely to set the stage for the Annunciation to take place outside of the temple at Joseph's home. Having achieved that in *ProtJac* 9:11-12, he has brought the Joseph Council to its conclusion and prepared the way for the immediately ensuing Veil Council in *ProtJac* 10-12. In *ProtJac* 9:12 he has provided the link to his own subsequent Joseph materials beginning in *ProtJac* 13:01.

34. See below, pp. 92-8.
35. Cf. the story of Korah, Dathan, and Abiram in Num. 16.
36. Following *ProtJac* 9:05 Joseph's status as Mary's custodian is restated in *ProtJac* 9:10.

THE VEIL COUNCIL: *PROTJAC* 10:01-12:11

Although the Veil Council follows the Joseph Council in the present form of the *ProtJac*, evidence will be presented below showing that the unredacted Veil Council, centering on the original Annunciation story in the temple, was a direct continuation of the *GenMar*, which now occupies the initial chapters of the *ProtJac* through 8:02. In accordance with the compositional theory upon which the present study is based, the evidence indicates that the Joseph Council, now in *ProtJac* 8:03-9:12, and the bulk of the texts of the Trial of Mary and Joseph in *ProtJac* 13-16 and the Nativity story in *ProtJac* 17-20 were added by the Composer in his substantial expansion of the original *GenMar*. Joseph appears suddenly in the Composer's new material and takes the stage as a central figure in this second major phase in the compositional development of the *ProtJac*, even overshadowing Mary who exclusively occupied center stage in the *GenMar*. The Redactor then superimposed his own editorial embellishments over the Composer-enhanced text of the *GenMar* in the third major phase of the composition of the *ProtJac*. In the original *GenMar*, before the Composer's interpolation of the Joseph Council, the Veil Council would have been the next event in Mary's life in the temple where she was still living when she participated in the weaving of the temple veil.

The Composer's insertion of the Joseph Council into the *GenMar* narrative before the Veil Council had the effect of relocating Mary from the temple to Joseph's home. It now became necessary for the Composer to adjust the *GenMar* Veil Council narrative to accommodate this inconsistency that he had brought about in Mary's location in *ProtJac* 10:02 when the priest called for the "undefiled virgins of the tribe of David" to be summoned to the temple to weave a new veil. The Composer addressed this incongruity by inserting *ProtJac* 10:04 into the *GenMar* Veil Council text in which, as an afterthought, the priest remembered Mary who was also an undefiled virgin and now residing at Joseph's home. The servants now went out a second time, on this occasion to Joseph's home, to bring Mary to the temple so that she could play her role in weaving the veil and receive the Annunciation.

The discontinuity in the sequence of the events depicted in *ProtJac* 10:02-05 betrays the apparent redactional activity present in this passage especially with respect to the two successive departures of the servants from the temple, first to find and return the seven virgins in *ProtJac* 10:03 and second to bring Mary to the temple from Joseph's home in *ProtJac* 10:04. It is significant that the same verb απηλθασιν ("went out") occurs in both verses, the second instance most likely copied by the Composer from the first. This is an example of what appears to be a typical technique in the modus operandi of the Composer in creating his interpolations. He duplicates one or more words from the original text of the *GenMar* into which he intends to insert his text, in this case απηλθασιν. He then constructs his own secondary narrative around this word and introduces it into the existing *GenMar* context at his desired location.[37] In the text below, the Composer's insertion of *ProtJac* 10:04 is indented, and απηλθασιν is underlined to emphasize the secondary nature of its repetitive occurrence:

ProtJac 10:01 εγενετο δε συμβουλιον των ιερεων λεγοντων·
    And there was a council of the priests, saying,
ποιησωμεν καταπετασμα τω ναω κυριου.
    "Let us make a veil for the temple of the Lord."
02 και ειπεν ο ιερευς·
    And the priest said,
καλεσατε τας παρθενους τας αμιαντους απο της φυλης του δαυιδ.
    "Summon the undefiled virgins from the tribe of David."
03 και <u>απηλθασιν</u> οι υπηρεται και εξεζητησαν και ευρησαν επτα.
    And the servants <u>went out</u> and sought and found seven.
    04 και εμνησθη ο ιερευς της παιδος μαριας,
        And the priest remembered the child Mary,
    οτι ην της φυλης του δαυιδ, και αμιαντος τω θεω.
        that she was of the tribe of David and undefiled to God.
    και <u>απηλθασιν</u> οι υπηρεται και ηγαγαν αυτην.
        And the servants <u>went out</u> and brought her.
05 και εισηγαγαν αυτας εν τω ναω κυριου·
    And they brought them into the temple of the Lord.

In *ProtJac* 10:01 the council of priests decides to create a new veil for the temple: "and there was a council of the priests (ιερεων) saying, 'let us make a veil for the temple of the Lord.'" In *ProtJac* 10:02 a single, as yet unidentified, priest (ιερευς)[38] orders that the undefiled virgins of the tribe of David be summoned: "and the priest said, 'summon the undefiled virgins from the tribe of David.'" In *ProtJac* 10:03 "the servants went out (απηλθασιν) and sought and found seven." In the original *GenMar* text, *ProtJac* 10:03 was followed directly by what is now *ProtJac* 10:05 in the CEGM: "and they brought them into the temple of the Lord." These two verses in succession originally formed the smoothly flowing sentence: και απηλθασιν οι υπηρεται και εξεζητησαν και ευρησαν επτα και εισηγαγαν αυτας εν τω ναω κυριου ("the servants went out and sought and found seven (virgins) and brought them into the temple of the Lord").[39]

---

37. See below, pp. 37–9, where he follows the same procedure with the word λαβουσα. This modus operandi of the Composer seems to be present on a larger scale in his interpolation of the entire Joseph Council into the *GenMar*.

38. This priest will be named below as Zachariah in an interpolation by the Redactor at *ProtJac* 10:08.

39. This is a classic example exhibiting the principle indicators of redactional activity in a text. When the interpolated material, *ProtJac* 10:04, is excised from its present redacted context, *ProtJac* 10:03-05, it leaves a smooth transition in the original unredacted text,

Evidence of Redaction of the ProtJac 37

It is into the middle of this formerly continuous text that the Composer inserted his own ad hoc creation, now *ProtJac* 10:04: και εμνησθη ο ιερευς της παιδος μαριας οτι ην της φυλης του δαυιδ, και αμιαντος τω θεω. και απηλθασιν οι υπηρεται και ηγαγαν αυτην ("and the priest remembered the child Mary that she was of the tribe of David and undefiled to God, and the servants went out [απηλθασιν] and brought her"). This editorial adjustment by the Composer represents an attempt to resolve the problem he had fostered by inserting the Joseph Council into the *GenMar* before the Veil Council, an original *GenMar* story in which Mary was still living in the temple. As a result of the Composer's insertion of the Joseph Council before the Veil Council, Mary was now not living in the temple but residing at Joseph's home, hence the need for the Composer to create and insert a scenario into the Veil Council accounting for Mary's presence in the temple at the time of the preparation of the new veil by the virgins.

The inconsistency between his interpolated verse, *ProtJac* 10:04, and the preceding and succeeding texts, now *ProtJac* 10:03 and 10:05, betrays the Composer's redactional activity. The servants could not have known of the priest's sudden remembrance of the undefiled Mary, nor could they have gone out a second time (απηλθασιν) from the temple to bring her back, as stated in *ProtJac* 10:04, because they had not yet returned to the temple from their first mission that was initiated in the preceding verse. In *ProtJac* 10:03 the servants were still in the process of seeking and finding the seven virgins—but they had not yet completed their task by returning them to the temple; this has now been delayed until *ProtJac* 10:05. The Composer has created a disjointed scenario in which the servants departed (απηλθασιν) from the temple a second time to bring Mary to the temple in *ProtJac* 10:04 before they had returned to the temple after their first departure (απηλθασιν) in *ProtJac* 10:03 on their first assignment to bring in the original seven virgins.

Immediately after the return of the servants to the temple with the seven virgins they had found, the priest who had summoned the virgins to the temple to weave the veil—who remains unnamed in the *GenMar*[40]—calls for a lottery to determine which of the virgins will weave which of the threads needed to create the new veil (λαχετε μοι ωδε τις νησει). *ProtJac* 10:06 lists these threads as "gold, flax, linen, silk, hyacinth, red, and true purple."[41] In the original *GenMar* text, that is now divided into two parts in *ProtJac* 10:07a

---

ProtJac 10:03 and 10:05. The case for redaction here is made even stronger when the interpolated material contains irregularities between the original unredacted context and the new context that was brought about by the interpolation. These indicators are manifestly evident in *ProtJac* 10:03-05.

40. See below where the Redactor imposes his identification of this individual as Zachariah on the text of the CEGM.

41. Cf. the discussion in Smid, *Protevangelium*, 76–80, τον χρυσον και τον αμιαντον και την βυσσον και το σιρικον και το υακινθινον και το κοκκινον και την αληθινην πορφυραν.

and 10:09, Mary receives the purple and red threads as her lot[42] and then begins to spin the red thread. Between these verses in the *ProtJac* occur two successive redactional elements, one each by the Composer and the Redactor, which exhibit their respective distinguishing motivations and modi operandi. The Composer inserted *ProtJac* 10:07b into his source, the *GenMar*, and the Redactor subsequently inserted *ProtJac* 10:08 into his own source, the *GenMar*, which has now been enhanced by the Composer. In the text below, the interpolations of the Composer and the Redactor are indented to highlight their intrusive, secondary nature, and the instances of λαβουσα and το κοκκινον are underscored to illustrate the editorial techniques implemented by the Composer and the Redactor:

> *ProtJac* 10:07a και ελαχεν μαριαμ την αληθινην πορφυραν και <u>το κοκκινον</u>
> And Mary obtained by lot the true purple and red [threads],
> 07b και <u>λαβουσα</u> εποιει εν τω οικω αυτης.
> And taking them she was working on them in her house.
> 08 τω δε καιρω εκεινω ζαχαριας εσιγησεν,
> at that time Zachariah became silent;
> εγενετο αντι αυτου σαμουηλ, μεχρι οτε ελαλησεν ζαχαριας.
> his place was taken by Samuel, until Zachariah spoke.
> 09 μαρια δε <u>λαβουσα</u> <u>το κοκκινον</u> εκλωθεν.
> And Mary, taking the red [thread], was spinning.

In *ProtJac* 10:07a Mary has obtained by lot the true purple and red threads. Disregarding the interpolated materials in *ProtJac* 10:07b-08, the narrative moves seamlessly from *ProtJac* 10:07a—where Mary has received the red thread (το κοκκινον)—directly to *ProtJac* 10:09 where again the focus is on the red thread (το κοκκινον). Mary takes up and begins spinning the red thread: μαρια δε λαβουσα το κοκκινον εκλωθεν ("And taking the red, Mary was spinning"). Into this previously continuous text the Composer has inserted *ProtJac* 10:07b in which Mary takes the purple and red threads to her house to spin them: και λαβουσα εποιει εν τω οικω αυτης ("and taking them she was working on them in her house"). The prepositional phrase εν τω οικω αυτης ("in her house") represents another editorial adjustment to the original Veil Council by the Composer to accommodate his previous relocation of Mary out of the temple to Joseph's house in the Joseph Council in *ProtJac* 9.[43]

The Composer's subtle augmentation of *ProtJac* 10:07 with 10:07b betrays the presence of his standard modus operandi. The original *GenMar* text is preserved in *ProtJac* 10:07 and 10:09. In *ProtJac* 10:07 Mary has the purple and

---

42. These colors will come to be highly symbolic as the narrative moves forward quickly to the all-important Annunciation story below.
43. See above, pp. 24–5.

red threads, and in *ProtJac* 10:09 she takes up (λαβουσα) and spins the red thread. As he did before with the verb ἀπήλθασιν vis-à-vis the movements of the temple servants in *ProtJac* 10:04,⁴⁴ here again the Composer replicates a verb, λαβουσα, from its original context in the *GenMar* in what is now *ProtJac* 10:09 (μαρια δε λαβουσα το κοκκινον), where Mary was spinning the red thread in the temple. On the basis of this duplicate verb, he manufactures his own scenario in which Mary is now spinning the red thread εν τω οικω αυτης ("in her house") and inserts it before the original verse in *ProtJac* 10:09 to show that Mary is spinning the red thread at home. This is the second occasion in the *GenMar* Veil Council in which the Composer is compelled to show that Mary is no longer in the temple, but at home, in order to accommodate his major insertion of the Joseph Council into the *GenMar* by which he relocated Mary from the temple to Joseph's home.

This insertion of *ProtJac* 10:07b by the Composer into the original text of the *GenMar* is followed immediately in *ProtJac* 10:08 by a second, and even more egregious, intrusive element by the Redactor into the now CEGM. This is the first of two interpolations by the Redactor of materials taken from the Gospel of Luke by which he intends to identify the unnamed priest in the *GenMar* as Zachariah, the father of John the Baptist⁴⁵: τω δε καιρω εκεινω ζαχαριας εσιγησεν, εγενετο αντι αυτου σαμουηλ, μεχρι οτε ελαλησεν ζαχαριας ("at that time Zachariah became silent, his place was taken by Samuel, until Zachariah spoke"). *ProtJac* 10:08 breaks the continuity of the narrative in the CEGM text—*ProtJac* 10:07 and 10:09—and is completely alien to the context in which it now resides, that is, Mary's obtaining and spinning thread for the temple veil. The Redactor derived this Zachariah material in *ProtJac* 10:08 from the account of the silence and renewed speech of Zachariah in Lk. 1:5-22 and 59-64. These interpolations of textual materials from the canonical Gospels, especially Luke, into the Composer-enhanced text of the *GenMar* constitute a principle identifying characteristic of the Redactor's work.⁴⁶

The Original GenMar *Annunciation Story*

With Mary left spinning the red thread after a series of redactions in *ProtJac* 10, the stage is set for one of the central episodes in the *ProtJac*, the Annunciation story. In this narrative one finds more clear evidence of layers of editorial revisions by the Composer and the Redactor by which they transformed the original *GenMar* Annunciation story into its present highly redacted version. In *ProtJac* 11:01 Mary picks up a pitcher

---

44. See above, pp. 35-7.

45. Lk. 3:2. These two interpolations in *ProtJac* 8:07 and 10:08 should be viewed in concert with the Redactor's attachment of the Zachariah Apocryphon in what is now *ProtJac* 22-24. The Redactor will include references to the death of Zachariah, originating in Lk. 11:51 and Mt. 23:35, and in the Zachariah Apocryphon in *ProtJac* 22-24.

46. See the discussion in "The Redactor: *The Protevangelium Jacobi*," pp. 131-47.

and goes out (εξηλθεν) to fill it with water.⁴⁷ What follows in *ProtJac* 11:02-03 appears to be the original Annunciation in the *GenMar* to Mary by an unknown voice. The actual words spoken by the voice in 11:02, however, seem to have been suppressed by the later Redactor and replaced with text gleaned from Lk. 1:28, 42:

11:01 και ελαβεν την καλπην και εξηλθεν γεμισαι υδωρ·
And she picked up the pitcher and went out to fill it with water.
11:02 και ιδου αυτη φωνη λεγουσα·
χαιρε κεχαριτωμενη συ εν γυναιξιν
And behold a Voice saying to her:
Greetings, you have received grace[48] among women,
11:03 και περιεβλεπεν τα δεξια και τα αριστερα μαρια, ποθεν αυτη ειη η φωνη
And Mary looked to the right and left from where that voice might be.
11:04 και συντρομος γενομενη εισηει εις τον ναον[49]
And becoming frightened she entered into the temple
και αναπαυσασα την καλπην,
and putting down the pitcher,
11:05 ελαβεν την πορφυραν και εκαθισεν επι τω θρονω και ηλκεν την πορφυραν.
she took up the purple and sat on the throne and spun the purple.

At this point in the story there is no indication of where Mary is spinning the red thread, whether in the temple or, as the Composer would have it, at home. In the Composer-enhanced text of *ProtJac* 11:04 Mary became frightened by the unknown voice (συντρομος γενομενη) and "entered into her house" (εισηει εις τον οικον αυτης). Given the Composer's persistent record of editorial revisions designed to show Mary at home during the events in the Veil Council, it seems likely that he also would have altered the text of *ProtJac* 11:04 for the same purpose.[50] In

47. Biblical and rabbinical sources describe a large bronze "molten sea" and smaller bronze "lavers" located in the court outside the temple that contained water for ritualistic purposes, 1 Kgs 7:23-39; 2 Kgs 16:17, 25:13; 1 Chron. 18:8; 2 Chron. 4:6, *Midrash Tadshe*. In the scene depicted in the *ProtJac*, Mary would have exited the temple proper to fill her pitcher with water from one of these lavers. It is there that she would have heard the voice of the Annunciation and then reentered the temple building to resume spinning the thread.

48. The Greek perfect middle participle κεχαριτωμενη is here rendered as a direct verbal action from the unknown voice, the *Bath Kol* (see above pp. 29, 32) to Mary, as opposed to its adjectival sense in Lk. 1:28, which has elicited circumlocutions in various English translations of the "hail, Mary," e.g., "full of grace" (RSVCE), "you who are highly favored" (NIV), "favored one" (RSV, NRSV, NASB). *ProtJac* 11:02 could be interpreted as Mary receiving a tangible benefit of grace or favor. See the discussion below, pp. 40-9, regarding the attempts by the Composer and the Redactor to mitigate this possibility.

49. εις τον οικον αυτης ("into her house") in the Composer-enhanced version.

50. This is now the third occasion in the Veil Council that the Composer is adjusting the text of the *GenMar* to accommodate his relocation of Mary from the temple to Joseph's house in the Joseph Council in *ProtJac* 9. In *ProtJac* 10:04 the Composer required the temple servants to go out of the temple a second time to retrieve Mary from her home before they

the original *GenMar* text Mary would have sought to reenter the temple where she had been spinning the red thread before she ventured out to fill her pitcher with water. It would have been a simple task for the Composer to substitute the phrase εις τον οικον αυτης ("entered into her house") for what in the original text must have been εις τον ναον ("into the temple"). Such a rudimentary editorial revision did not require the fabrication of a parallel scenario as in previous instances of the Composer's modus operandi.

The Composer's manipulation of the text of *ProtJac* 11:04 is further exposed in *ProtJac* 11:05 where Mary sits on a mysterious throne to weave the purple thread: ελαβεν την πορφυραν και εκαθισεν επι τω θρονω και ηλκεν την πορφυραν ("she took the purple and sat on the throne and spun the purple"). Was there a throne in Mary's house on which she sat when she returned after hearing the anonymous voice, put down her water pitcher, picked up the purple thread, then sat on the throne and began to spin the purple thread? Or is the throne in *ProtJac* 11:05 in reality the throne of God in the Holy of Holies in the temple,[51] where Mary has continuously resided for nine years? That this is the case is strongly supported by the identification of the anonymous voice that Mary had just heard when she was outside of the Holy of Holies drawing water. This voice in all probability would have been the *Bath Kol*, the "daughter of a voice," as it was widely known in Jewish tradition.

The existence of the almost personified, hypostasized Voice of God[52] is widely attested in the Hebrew Scriptures and the New Testament[53] and occurs throughout the literature of the late and post-second temple periods in the pseudepigrapha, targums, and the Hellenistic Jewish and rabbinical writings.[54]

---

had returned to the temple from their first venture out in search of virgins to weave the temple veil. In his second interpolation in *ProtJac* 10:07b the Composer attempted to show that Mary was working on the threads "in her house" before she actually began spinning the red thread in the temple in *ProtJac* 10:09. See the detailed discussion above.

51. The concept of the Jerusalem temple being the earthly house and throne of God is ubiquitous in Jewish tradition and is well represented in the Hebrew Scriptures. On the significance of this for the *ProtJac*, see the discussion in G. T. Zervos, "An Early Non-Canonical Annunciation Story," in *SBL Seminar Papers*, 1997 SBLSP 36 (Atlanta, GA: Scholars Press), 677–9.

52. J. H. Charlesworth, "The Jewish Roots of Christology: The Discovery of the Hypostatic Voice," *SJT* 39 (1986), 19–41; Azzan Yadin, "Kol as Hypostasis in the Hebrew Bible," *JBL* 122 (2003), 601–26.

53. Cf. e.g., Gen. 1; 3:9-11; 15:4; Exod. 4; Dan. 4:28; Mt. 3:17, 17:5; Mk 1:11, 9:7; Lk. 3:22, 9:35; Jn 12:28; Acts 9:4, 7; 10:13, 15.

54. See the numerous examples cited by Peter Kuhn, *Offenbarungsstimmen im Antiken Judentum: Untersuchungen zur Bat Qol und verwandten Phänomenen*, TSAJ 20 (Tübingen: Mohr-Siebeck, 1989); cf. the example well attested in the Tosefta, the Jerusalem Talmud, and Josephus of a direct communication from the *Bath Kol* to the high priest John Hyrcanus announcing a Jewish Victory against the Syrians, Zervos, "Non-Canonical," 681.

A most germane parallel to the Annunciation of Mary in the Jerusalem temple by the *Bath Kol* is found in the celebrated vision of the post-Babylonian captivity temple recorded in chapter 43 of the prophet Ezekiel.[55] The prophet is being given a tour of the future temple by an angelic guide and is taken into the inner court where he sees the "glory of the Lord" fill "the house."[56] In the LXX translation of Ezek. 43:6-7 the prophet hears a φωνή ἐκ τοῦ οἴκου λαλοῦντος πρός με ("a voice out of the house speaking to me"). This φωνή ("voice") points out to Ezekiel in the temple the place of his θρόνος "throne" (τὸν τόπον τοῦ θρόνου μου) and the place of the soles of his feet, that is, his footstool (τὸν τόπον τοῦ ἴχνους τῶν ποδῶν μου).

> Ezek. 43:6a καὶ ἔστην καὶ ἰδοὺ φωνή ἐκ τοῦ οἴκου λαλοῦντος πρός με ...
> And I stood and behold, a voice out of the house speaking to me ...
> 43:7 καὶ εἶπεν πρός με ἑώρακας υἱὲ ἀνθρώπου
> and it said to me, "do you see, son of man,
> τὸν τόπον τοῦ θρόνου μου καὶ τὸν τόπον τοῦ ἴχνους τῶν ποδῶν μου
> the place of my throne and the place of the soles of my feet,
> ἐν οἷς κατασκηνώσει τὸ ὄνομά μου ἐν μέσῳ οἴκου Ἰσραὴλ τὸν αἰῶνα;
> In which my name will dwell in the midst of the house of Israel forever?"

The resemblance of the temple setting and the introductory vocabulary in Ezek. 43:6 and *ProtJac* 11:02 lead to the inescapable conclusion that the unidentified voice of the *GenMar* is in fact the *Bath Kol* so widely acknowledged to be present in the classical vision of Ezekiel:

> *ProtJac* 11:02 <u>και ιδου</u> αυτη <u>φωνη λεγουσα</u>
> <u>And behold</u>, <u>a voice</u> <u>saying</u> to her
> Ezek. 43:6 <u>καὶ ἰδοὺ</u> φωνή ἐκ τοῦ οἴκου <u>λαλοῦντος</u> πρός με
> <u>And behold a voice</u> out of the house <u>speaking</u> to me.

In the original *GenMar* Mary was in the temple spinning the red thread when she went out to the courtyard and filled her pitcher from one of the lavers of water. It is there outside the temple that she heard the unidentified voice, leaving the impression that the voice would have originated from inside the temple. The similarities between Ezek. 43 and *ProtJac* 11 are so striking that we must entertain the possibility that the Author of the *GenMar* was inspired by Ezekiel's vision. The likelihood of direct influence increases with the speculation that the Author of the *GenMar* may have been connected to Saducean circles in Jerusalem, especially in view of the fact that Ezekiel himself was a Zadokite (Sadducean)

---

55. Ibid., 678-9.
56. Ezek. 43:5. Symbolically the glory of God is returning to the future rebuilt temple after it had left the original temple of Solomon before its destruction by the Babylonians in 587 BCE.

priest and that the Sadducees were a later outgrowth of the ancient Zadokite priesthood.[57]

The only element in the *GenMar* Annunciation narrative that remains to be clarified is the identity of the Agent of Mary's conception. That Agent can be none other than the *Bath Kol*, the Voice of God. After hearing the unidentified voice speaking to her, Mary is now pregnant. At this point Mary is unaware of this and only comes to realize that she is pregnant when her womb begins to swell at the end of the Veil Council in *ProtJac* 12:09: και ημερα αφ ημερας η γαστηρ αυτης ωγκουτο ("and day by day her womb swelled").[58] We cannot know if there was any hint of conception in the original statement of the *Bath Kol* to Mary that seems to have been suppressed by the Redactor, and her reaction of fear shows that she had no understanding of what had happened to her.[59] When Joseph returns from his construction work in *ProtJac* 13 and confronts her about her pregnancy, Mary cries bitterly and declares her innocence. In response to Joseph's pointed question in *ProtJac* 13:11: ποθεν ουν τουτο εστιν εν τη γαστρι σου; ("from where then is this in your womb?") Mary vows truthfully in *ProtJac* 13:12: ζη κυριος ο θεος μου καθοτι ου γινωσκω ποθεν εστιν εμοι ("As the Lord my God lives, I do not know from where it is in me").

Once purged of the foreign editorial and redactional elements that were imposed upon the original *GenMar* Annunciation story, a rational, coherent narrative emerges that could very well have originated in an early Jewish-Christian environment and that shows no influence from, or knowledge of, the canonical Annunciation stories of Luke and Matthew. If this reconstruction of the *GenMar* Annunciation in the temple by the *Bath Kol* is valid, then the remaining details of the narrative fall logically into place. This pure, undefiled twelve-year-old virgin puts down the red thread,[60] which is symbolic of her first menstruation; goes out to the court to draw

---

57. The basic understanding of the Sadducean presence in Judaism continues to be a matter of intense debate among scholars. Consequently it is difficult to draw any conclusions about a relationship between the *GenMar* Author and the Sadducees beyond his favorable attitude toward the temple and its priesthood, and the portrait presented in the *GenMar* of Mary's family being wealthy and circulating in the highest priestly circles of the Jerusalem temple.

58. *ProtJac* 12:09-11 constitutes a redactional transition marking the end of a large interpolation of texts from Luke by the Redactor in *ProtJac* 11:06–12:09, including events of the Annunciation and Mary's visit to Elizabeth. See also "The Joseph Council," pp. 23–34.

59. This lack of information imparted to Mary by the *Bath Kol* is part of a consistent motif of secrecy in the *GenMar*. The child conceived and born by Mary is never identified.

60. There is no specific reference in *ProtJac* 10:09–11:05 to Mary putting down the red thread before going out to draw water. However, this element of the original story may have been preserved in an obviously dislocated verse in *ProtJac* 12:04 in the Redactor's interpolated account of the Lukan visit of Mary to Elizabeth where Elizabeth puts, or throws, down "the red" when she hears Mary's greeting and goes to open her door for her; see below, pp. 49–50.

water from a laver, which represents her ritual purification; is then impregnated directly by the Voice of God, the *Bath Kol*;[61] and is now worthy to reenter the temple, sit upon God's royal throne in the Holy of Holies, and spin the true purple thread, which is symbolic of the divine, royal child whom she now bears.

Our redaction-critical analysis of the *ProtJac* Veil Council has revealed the existence of a concerted series of systematic revisions of the underlying *GenMar* text by the Composer whose primary purpose was to alter the Annunciation to Mary in the Jerusalem temple. The Composer transformed the *GenMar* Annunciation story into one that was compatible with his substantial expansion of the entire *GenMar* with his own secondary materials centered on the figure of Joseph. But the redactional manipulation of the *GenMar* Annunciation story has only just begun as the Redactor, who has already inserted texts foreshadowing his larger interpolation of the Zachariah Apocryphon later in the narrative, will now contribute his own layer of even more radical augmentation of the Annunciation over and above the enhancements already enacted by the Composer. If the Composer's objective was to distance Mary from the *Bath Kol* as the Agent of the Annunciation in the temple, then the Redactor's purpose was to distance her from direct contact with the *Bath Kol* as the Agent of the Conception.

The Redactor accomplished his purpose by further modifying the *GenMar* Annunciation story, which was now embedded in the Composer-enhanced Veil Council in *ProtJac* 11, by his interpolation of canonical materials taken from Lk. 1:26-45 into *ProtJac* 11:06-12 and 12:03-11. These materials consist of two successive angelic appearances to Mary and the visit of Mary to Elizabeth. Once these Lukan interpolations are excised from the Annunciation story, one is left with the coherent narrative of the original *GenMar* story following *ProtJac* 10:09, where Mary is spinning the red thread in the temple, and concluding in *ProtJac* 12:01-02 with Mary returning her completed work to the priest and receiving his blessing:

> *ProtJac* 10:09 μαρια δε λαβουσα το κοκκινον εκλωθεν.
> And Mary, taking up the red, was spinning.
> 11:01 και ελαβεν την καλπην και εξηλθεν γεμισαι υδωρ·
> And she picked up the pitcher and went out to fill it with water.
> 02 και ιδου αυτη φωνη λεγουσα·
> χαιρε κεχαριτωμενη συ εν γυναιξιν.
> and behold a voice saying to her:
> "Greetings, you have received grace among women."
> 03 και περιεβλεπεν τα δεξια και τα αριστερα μαρια, ποθεν αυτη ειη η φωνη.
> And Mary looked right and left, from where that voice might be.
> 04 και συντρομος γενομενη εισηει εις τον ναον[62]
> And becoming frightened she entered into the temple

---

61. See the discussion on the *Bath Kol* within the overall perspective of the *GenMar* in "The Author: *The Genesis Marias*," pp. 158-60.

62. "Entered into her house" ("εις τον οικον αυτης") in the Composer-enhanced version.

και αναπαυσασα την καλπην,
and putting down the pitcher,
05 ελαβεν την πορφυραν και εκαθισεν επι τω θρονω και ηλκεν την πορφυραν.
she took up the purple and sat on the throne and spun the purple.
12 01 και εποιησεν την πορφυραν και το κοκκινον, και ανηνεγκεν τω ιερει.
And she prepared the purple and the red and brought them to the priest.
και λαβων ο ιερευς ευλογησεν αυτην και ειπεν·
And, taking them, the priest blessed her and said:
02 μαρια, εμεγαλυνεν σε κυριος ο θεος το ονομα σου,
"Mary, the Lord God blessed you, your name,
και εση ευλογημενη εν πασαις ταις γενεαις της γης.
And you will be blessed in all the generations of the earth."

The Redactor's interpolation of the two angelic appearances to Mary into the *GenMar* Annunciation story in *ProtJac* 11:06-12 is one of the most perplexing passages in the *ProtJac*, but one that is most illustrative of his purpose and methodology. The text of the interpolation is replete with borrowings from canonical Luke, some verbatim and some less so:

ProtJac 11:06 και ιδου εστη αγγελος ενωπιον λεγων·
And behold, an angel stood before her saying,
07 μη φοβου, μαρια· ευρες γαρ χαριν ενωπιον του παντων δεσποτου,
"Do not fear, Mary, for you have found favor before the master of all.
συνλημψη εκ λογου αυτου.
You will conceive through his Logos."
08 η δε ακουσασα μαρια διεκριθη εν εαυτη λεγουσα·
And Mary, hearing, considered in herself, saying,
εγω συνλημψομαι απο κυριου θεου ζωντος, ως πασα γυνη γεννα;
"Will I conceive from the living Lord God, as every woman gives birth?"
09 και ιδου αγγελος εστη αυτη λεγων αυτη·
And behold, an angel stood with her, saying to her,
ουχ ουτως μαρια· δυναμις γαρ θεου επισκιασει σοι.
"Not thus, Mary, for the power of God will overshadow you,
10 διο και το γεννωμενον αγιον κληθησεται υιος υψιστου.
therefore the holy one born will be called the son of the Most High.
11 και καλεσης το ονομα αυτου ιησουν·
And you will call his name Jesus,
αυτος γαρ σωσει λαον αυτου εκ των αμαρτιων αυτων.
for he will save his people from their sins."
12 και ειπε μαρια· ιδου η δουλη κυριου κατενωπιον αυτου·
And Mary said, "behold, the maid-servant of the Lord before him,
γενοιτο μοι κατα το ρημα σου.
let it be done to me according to your word."

The Redactor interpolated these dialogues between Mary and the angels to correct what he saw as a theological problem in the Annunciation story of the CEGM: the direct Conception of Mary by the Voice of God, the *Bath Kol*. To this end one can observe three distinct objectives: (1) to change the Agent of the Annunciation in the original *GenMar* story from the unmediated *Bath Kol* to one more in agreement with canonical sensitivities, the mediating archangel Gabriel, (2) to change the Agent of the Conception from the *Bath Kol* itself to the more indirect Lukan δυναμις ... θεου ("power of God"), and (3) to identify the mysterious unnamed child whom Mary conceives and bears in the CEGM as ιησους ("Jesus") the υιος υψιστου ("Son of the Most High"). A close inspection of this interpolation reveals several strategies that the Redactor implemented to accomplish his ultimate purpose of detaching the Conception of Mary from direct contact with the *Bath Kol*.

The Redactor's principle strategy was to present the Conception within the framework of a conversation between Mary and a mediating angel as opposed to a direct interaction between her and the *Bath Kol*. He also appears to have suppressed the original declaration of the voice to Mary in the *GenMar*, leading us to suspect that he must have found that statement contrary to his purpose. In lieu of whatever must have been the original utterance of the *Bath Kol*, the Redactor substituted two of the words spoken by the mediating archangel Gabriel to Mary in Lk. 1:28: Χαῖρε, κεχαριτωμένη, ὁ κύριος μετὰ σοῦ ("Greetings, you who have received grace, the Lord is with you"). It is highly pertinent to our discussion that the Redactor omitted the second part of Gabriel's statement in Lk. 1:28: ὁ κύριος μετὰ σοῦ ("the Lord is with you"), thus advancing his prime objective of suppressing any hint of direct contact between Mary and God. The Redactor replaced "the Lord is with you" from Lk. 1:28 with the words of Elizabeth to Mary in Lk. 1:42: σὺ ἐν γυναιξίν ("you among women"), thus completing the benign statement of the angel to Mary in *ProtJac* 11:02: "Greetings, you have received grace among women."

The Redactor apparently desired to mitigate any possibility that even his own contrived version of the words of the voice to Mary might be interpreted as implying direct contact. In the declaration of the first angel to Mary in *ProtJac* 11:06-07, the Redactor provided a clarification of the meaning of the word κεχαριτωμενη spoken by the voice in v. 11:02. The angel declared to Mary that she has found χαριν ("grace"), a noun form of the participle κεχαριτωμενη, which in the context of the Redactor's interpolation in *ProtJac* 11:02 might be seen as conveying an active verbal sense of Mary receiving a tangible benefit of grace.[63] And this χαριν is specifically described by the Redactor as being spatially separate from God: ενωπιον του παντων δεσποτου ("before the master of all"). Thus, through the agency of the first angel, the Redactor weakens the sense of an active causal transference of the tangible benefit of grace between the voice and Mary and replaces it with a more passive, physically detached relationship in which

---

63. See above, p. 40, n. 48.

Mary "finds" a nominal grace "before" God but does not "receive" tangible grace directly from God via his *Bath Kol*.

The Redactor further detaches Mary's conception from the Annunciation of the *Bath Kol* by transposing her conception chronologically into the future in three separate statements in his interpolation. In *ProtJac* 11:07b the angel tells Mary that she "will conceive" (συνλημψη) using the future tense of the verb. In *ProtJac* 11:08 after hearing the angel's words Mary questions in her mind how she "will conceive" (συνλημψομαι), again in the future tense. Mary's question in her mind elicits the response in the second angelic appearance in *ProtJac* 11:09 in which the angel reaffirms that Mary has not yet conceived but will do so in the future when the "power of God" (δυναμις ... θεου) "will overshadow" her (επισκιασει in the future tense). Thus the entire dialogue with the Redactor's angels positions Mary's conception as a future event after the *Bath Kol* Annunciation, and therefore not having been accomplished in the temple directly by the *Bath Kol*.[64] By these various strategies, the Redactor has effectively eliminated the Conception of Mary's child from her previous interaction with the *Bath Kol* in the temple in *ProtJac* 11:02.

But the Redactor's most masterful stratagem is the manner in which he seeks to obscure Mary's Conception by the *Bath Kol* in the *GenMar* by changing the agent of the Conception from the *Bath Kol* to the overshadowing δυναμις ... θεου ("power of God"). And it is in this context that the Redactor clearly betrays his understanding that our interpretation of the direct Conception of Mary by the *Bath Kol* in the *GenMar* is accurate. Initially the Redactor seems to confirm the Conception by the voice in his angel's statement in *ProtJac* 11:07b: συνλημψη εκ λογου αυτου ("you will conceive by his [God's] logos"). The idea of Mary's Conception by God's "word" (εκ λογου αυτου) in Greek has an affinity with the idea of conception "by God's Voice," the Hebrew *Bath Kol*, in that God's Voice produced words that were the direct agent of Mary's Conception.[65] Thus the Redactor is at least aware of the serious implications of the direct impregnation of Mary by the *Bath Kol* for second-century orthodox Christianity of which he was a fervent proponent.

---

64. The actual time of Mary's conception is not specified in the account of Luke as well but is also projected into the future in Lk. 1:31 with the verb συλλήμψη and in Lk. 1:35 with the verbs ἐπελεύσεται and ἐπισκιάσει all of which are in the future tense. Perhaps it was Luke's intention also to distance Mary's conception from the Annunciation by the archangel Gabriel, which had occurred previously in Lk. 1:28. See the discussion below in "The Redactor: *The Protevangelium Jacobi*," pp. 131–47, regarding the possibility that the Redactor was a member of the "School" of Justin Martyr in the mid-second century CE where the Nativity materials in Lk. 1–2 may have been added to an earlier form of Luke that began with Lk. 3:1.

65. Compare the creation story in Gen. 1 where God does not directly create the elements of the cosmos himself. He does so by calling them into existence by his voice, or *Bath Kol*, e.g., "And God said, 'Let there be light', and there was light." He thus called the cosmos into existence by means of his spoken word or λόγος.

The next verse in the Redactor's interpolation further supports our contention that he did indeed recognize that the Annunciation by the *Bath Kol* in the CEGM signified the actual physical impregnation of Mary by the Voice of God. In *ProtJac* 11:08 Mary herself understood the angel's declaration that she will conceive ἐκ λόγου αὐτοῦ "by his [God's] word" to mean physical impregnation by God. The Redactor placed the question in Mary's mind: εγω συνλημψομαι απο κυριου θεου ζωντος, ως πασα γυνη γεννα; ("will I conceive from the living Lord God, as every woman gives birth?"). Although it is the Redactor's ultimate intention to refute this interpretation, he has now twice affirmed its validity in the very scenario that he himself created for its refutation. The Redactor invalidated Mary's thought question in *ProtJac* 11:08 by introducing his second angel, who appears immediately in v. 11:09 obviously for the purpose of responding specifically to Mary's thought question with an emphatic denial: ουχ ουτως μαρια ("not thus, Mary"). The second angel proceeds to correct Mary's perception of a direct physical impregnation by God by informing her that she would conceive by the overshadowing "power of God" (δυναμις γαρ θεου επισκιασει σοι). The very vehemence of the Redactor's multifaceted attempts to conceal the Conception of Mary by the *Bath Kol* arguably confirms our interpretation that Mary's child was thus conceived in the original *GenMar*.

By his interpolation of the double angelic visitation into the Annunciation story of the CEGM, the Redactor has fulfilled his primary purpose of exchanging the Agent of the Conception of Mary's child from the *Bath Kol* for the second-century orthodox version presented in the canonical Gospels. Although the Redactor has fashioned the scenario of his angelic visitations to fit the context of *ProtJac* 11:06-12, the origin of the angels' messages to Mary from the Annunciation narrative in Lk. 1:26-38 is obvious, as is clear from the following parallel presentation of the relevant texts:

ProtJac 11:07a <u>μη φοβου μαρια ευρες γαρ χαριν</u> ενωπιον του παντων δεσποτου
Lk. 1:30b <u>μὴ φοβοῦ, Μαριάμ, εὗρες γὰρ χάριν</u> παρὰ τῷ Θεῷ

ProtJac 11:07b <u>συνλημψη</u> εκ λογου αυτου
Lk. 1:31a <u>Συλλήμψῃ</u> ἐν γαστρὶ

ProtJac 11:09b <u>δυναμις</u> γαρ θεου <u>επισκιασει σοι</u>
Lk. 1:35a <u>δύναμις</u> Ὑψίστου <u>ἐπισκιάσει σοι</u>

ProtJac 11:10 <u>διο και το γεννωμενον αγιον κληθησεται υιος</u> υψιστου
Lk. 1:35b <u>διὸ καὶ τὸ γεννώμενον ἅγιον κληθήσεται υἱὸς</u> Θεοῦ

ProtJac 11:11a <u>και καλεσης το ονομα αυτου ιησουν</u>
Lk. 1:31b <u>καὶ καλέσεις τὸ ὄνομα αὐτοῦ Ἰησοῦν</u>
Mt. 1:21a <u>καὶ καλέσεις τὸ ὄνομα αὐτοῦ Ἰησοῦν</u>[66]

---

66. The great antiquity of the *ProtJac* text represents a significant witness to the Greek text of the canonical Gospels. Cf. n. 64 above regarding connections between the texts of the Redactor's interpolations and those of the writings of Justin Martyr in the mid-second century CE.

ProtJac 11:11b αυτος γαρ σωσει λαον αυτου εκ των αμαρτιων αυτων
Mt. 1:21b αὐτὸς γὰρ σώσει τὸν λαὸν αὐτοῦ ἀπὸ τῶν ἁμαρτιῶν αὐτῶν

ProtJac 11:12a και ειπε μαρια ιδου η δουλη κυριου κατενωπιον αυτου
Lk. 1:38a εἶπεν δὲ Μαριάμ, ἰδοῦ ἡ δούλη Κυρίου

ProtJac 11:12b γενοιτο μοι κατα το ρημα σου
Lk. 1:38a γένοιτό μοι κατὰ τὸ ῥῆμά σου

Mary's Visit to Elizabeth

In Luke's Annunciation story the appearance of the archangel Gabriel to Mary in Lk. 1:26-38 was followed immediately by Mary's visit to her relative Elizabeth, the mother of John the Baptist, in Lk. 1:39-56. The Redactor follows Luke's pattern by dividing his interpolation into two sections, the double angelic appearance to Mary in *ProtJac* 11:06-12 and Mary's visit to Elizabeth in *ProtJac* 12:03-09a. The Redactor inserted *ProtJac* 11:06-12 into the *GenMar* Annunciation narrative, which begins in *ProtJac* 10:09 with Mary spinning the red thread in the temple and concludes in *ProtJac* 12:01-02 with Mary returning her completed work of spun threads to the priest and receiving his blessing. The Redactor inserted his version of Luke's Elizabeth episode after the priest's blessing to Mary in *ProtJac* 12:03-09a. *ProtJac* 12:09b-11 brings the Veil Council to a close.

The heavy-handed editorial activity of the Redactor, which was so manifest in his major interpolation into the Annunciation story, continues even more visibly in his abbreviated version of the ensuing visit of Mary to Elizabeth, which consists of insertions of Lukan texts interspersed with his own created material. After "receiving joy" (χαραν λαβουσα) from the blessing of the priest in *ProtJac* 12:03a, Mary απηει προς την συγγενιδα αυτης ελισαβεδ ("departed to her relative Elizabeth").[67] In *ProtJac* 12:03b Mary knocks on Elizabeth's door, and in *ProtJac* 12:04 Elizabeth hears the sound, runs to the door and opens it to Mary. Within *ProtJac* 12:04 the Redactor carelessly has embedded an element that is foreign to the Elizabeth story and that betrays the connection of his present redactional activity to his earlier interpolation into the *GenMar* text beginning after *ProtJac* 10:09 where Mary was still spinning the red thread in the temple before her exit to the temple court to draw water.

In the succession of events from *ProtJac* 10:09, where Mary is spinning the red thread in the temple, through 11:01-05 where she exits to draw water, hears the *Bath Kol*, and reenters the temple to spin the purple thread, it is never stated in the redacted text of the *ProtJac* that Mary actually put down the red thread. Apparently, in the process of interpolating his materials into the Annunciation

---

67. Cf. Lk. 1:39-40. Mary's visit to Elizabeth in Luke seems to have been prompted by the archangel Gabriel's statement to Mary in Lk. 1:36 that her relative Elizabeth is now six months pregnant with her own child. Note that the characterization of Elizabeth as Mary's συγγενίς in Luke is reflected in the same word συγγενίδα in the *ProtJac*.

text, the Redactor detached that element from its appropriate place in the original *GenMar* story and injected it into the Elizabeth narrative at precisely the point at which Elizabeth is running to her door to open it to Mary. As the redacted text of *ProtJac* 12:04 now reads, it is Elizabeth who ερριψεν το κοκκινον ("threw down the red")[68] when she heard Mary's knock at her door and ran to open it. This of course raises the question: why would Elizabeth be holding red thread when it was Mary who was spinning red thread in the temple before the Annunciation scenario even unfolded and well before her visit to Elizabeth?

The more drastic action of the verb "throwing" (ερριψεν) the red thread, as opposed to Mary simply putting it down, suggests that in its original location in the *GenMar* Mary may have carried the red thread, which she was spinning at that time, out to the courtyard with the pitcher to draw water. If this were the case, it would lend support to the interpretation of the red thread as being symbolic of the twelve-year-old Mary's first menstruation[69] from which she would have required purification by the waters in the lavers in the courtyard of the temple. Upon being startled and frightened by the *Bath Kol* Mary more applicably would have "thrown," rather than merely "put" down, the red thread before reentering the temple. The displacement of the element of Mary throwing the red thread is not the only telltale trace of the Redactor's editorial work that he leaves behind in the Elizabeth story.

In *ProtJac* 12:03-04 the Redactor condenses the longer narrative in Lk. 1:39-42 in which Mary travels from Nazareth to a town of Judah and is received with joy and extended blessings by Elizabeth. In the Redactor's version Mary receives joy from the blessing of the priest and goes to Elizabeth, who upon hearing May's knock ran to the door and opened it:

ProtJac 12:03 χαραν λαβουσα μαρια απηει προς την συγγενιδα αυτης ελισαβεδ
    receiving joy Mary departed to her relative Elizabeth
και εκρουσεν προς την θυραν.
    and knocked on the door.
12:04 και ακουσασα η ελισαβεδ ερριψεν το κοκκινον
    And hearing, Elizabeth threw down the red [thread]
και εδραμεν προς την θυραν και ηνοιξεν αυτη
    and ran to the door and opened it to her

The Redactor follows his summary of Lk. 1:39-42 with the more straightforward text in *ProtJac* 12:05-06 most of which he borrows from Lk. 1:43-4:

---

68. The nominal characterization of το κοκκινον ("the red") in *ProtJac* 12:04 agrees with the previous references to the threads simply by their color; for example, το κοκκινον again in *ProtJac* 10:09, την πορφυραν και το κοκκινον ("the purple and the red") in *ProtJac* 12:01, την αληθινην πορφυραν και το κοκκινον ("the true purple and the red") in *ProtJac* 10:07; cf. all the colors of threads listed in *ProtJac* 12:06.

69. See above, pp. 43-4.

Evidence of Redaction of the ProtJac   51

ProtJac 12:05b ποθεν μοι ινα η μητηρ του κυριου ελθη προς εμε[70];
 "Whence [is it] to me that the mother of the Lord comes to me?
Lk. 1:43 πόθεν μοι τοῦτο ἵνα ἔλθῃ ἡ μήτηρ τοῦ Κυρίου μου πρὸς ἐμὲ;
 Whence [is] this to me that the mother of My Lord comes to me?
ProtJac 12:06 ιδου γαρ το εν εμοι εσκιρτησεν και ευλογησεν σε
 For behold, that which is in me sprung about and blessed you
Lk. 1:44 ἰδοὺ γὰρ ... ἐσκίρτησεν ἐν ἀγαλλιάσει τὸ βρέφος ἐν τῇ κοιλίᾳ μου
 For behold, [the child in my womb] sprung about in exultation

In *ProtJac* 12:07 the Redactor must again implement a blatant correction of the text to explain the incongruity he had created with his interpolated angelic Annunciation materials into the *GenMar*. At this point in the unredacted *GenMar* story Mary still does not know the identity of the voice that spoke to her in the temple, still does not understand the meaning of the words she heard, and is unaware that she is pregnant. She is also no doubt perplexed by the blessing pronounced upon her in *ProtJac* 12:02 by the priest to whom she returned the threads she had spun: εμεγαλυνεν σε κυριος ο θεος το ονομα σου, και εση ευλογημενη εν πασαις ταις γενεαις της γης ("the Lord God has magnified your name, and you will be blessed in all the generations of the earth"). The blessing of this priest seems disproportionate for the mere work of spinning the red and purple threads for the temple veil. This priest remains unidentified in the *GenMar* but may be the high priest who called for the gathering of the virgins and the lottery to disseminate the threads.

The scene of Mary returning her completed work of the spun purple and red threads and being blessed by the priest in *ProtJac* 12:01-02 represents a significant crossroads in the process of delineating the parameters of the original *GenMar*. This passage is followed immediately by the Redactor's interpolated visit of Mary to Elizabeth in *ProtJac* 12:03-11 and subsequently by the Composer's extensive Joseph-related materials beginning in *ProtJac* 13. One possibility is that the original *GenMar* narrative ended at this point and did not record any response by Mary to the priest's blessing. Alternatively, an original response by Mary to the priest's blessing did exist but was heavily revised by the Redactor and incorporated into his following interpolation of the visit of Mary to Elizabeth. The extensive recasting of the exchange between the priest and Mary by the Redactor has rendered its text very difficult to recover, but in such a passage, the priest's blessing in *ProtJac* 12:02 would have been followed immediately by Mary's response of wonderment to his blessing in what is now *ProtJac* 12:08:

και ανεστεναξεν εις τον ουρανον και ειπεν·
 and she sighed to heaven and said,
τις ειμι εγω, οτι ιδου πασαι αι γυναικες της γης μακαριουσιν με;
 "Who am I that, behold, all the women of the earth will bless me?"

---

70. In *ProtJac* 12:05a και ευλογησεν αυτην και ειπεν ("and she blessed her and said") the Redactor summarizes the extended blessing of Mary and her child by Elizabeth in Lk. 1:42 εὐλογημένη σὺ ἐν γυναιξὶν καὶ εὐλογημένος ὁ καρπὸς τῆς κοιλίας σοῦ ("blessed are you among women and blessed is the fruit of your womb"). He most likely does this so as not to

It is appropriate for Mary to wonder at the excessive blessing given to her by the priest if she is still ignorant of the true nature of the events that have just transpired in the temple and especially if she is still unaware of her pregnancy. But with the Redactor's interpolation of an astounding angelic appearance to Mary after these events in which the angel reveals to her their great significance, the Redactor must now accommodate the problem of Mary's surprise at the priest's blessing in view of the angelic appearances. He therefore inserts *ProtJac* 12:07 into his own interpolated text: η δε μαρια επελαθετο των μυστηριων ων ελαλησεν γαβριηλ ο αγγελος ("but Mary had forgotten the mysteries which the angel Gabriel spoke to her"). The Redactor here compounds his creation of a transparent and ineffective explanation for Mary's wonderment at the priest's blessing; he betrays his dependence on Luke by naming the angel as Gabriel, which he had not done even in his own interpolated angelic visitation in *ProtJac* 11:06-12.

Had there existed in the Redactor's source document any original response by Mary to the priest's blessing, it would have been necessary for him to adjust the text of this response in *ProtJac* 12:08 to accommodate his insertion of the visit to Elizabeth in *ProtJac* 12:03-07. In its present redacted setting in *ProtJac* 12:08, Mary is responding with wonder, not to the priest's blessing, which occurred in *ProtJac* 12:02 before the interpolated vv. 12:03-07, but to the blessing she now received from Elizabeth in v. 12:05.[71] Thus Mary wonders in *ProtJac* 12:08 why πασαι αι γυναικες της γης μακαριουσιν με ("all the women of the earth will bless me"). The Redactor has again left incongruities in his revised text that betray his activity. First, γυναικες ("women") in the plural: Mary has just been blessed, not by all the women of the earth, but by one woman, Elizabeth. Second, μακαριουσιν ("will bless") in the future tense and in the plural: Elizabeth's blessing contained no suggestion that Mary would be blessed by all the women of the earth in the future. Both of these discrepancies in the present text of Mary's response to Elizabeth's blessing in *ProtJac* 12:05 would have been appropriate in any original response by Mary to the priest's blessing in v. 12:02, thus further revealing the Redactor's editorial activity.

Traces of the Redactor's handiwork may perhaps be visible also in the priest's blessing in *ProtJac* 12:02 that Mary would be ευλογημενη εν πασαις ταις γενεαις της γης ("blessed by all the generations of the earth"). This text has affinities with Mary's exclamation in Lk. 1:48: ἀπὸ τοῦ νῦν μακαριοῦσίν με πᾶσαι αἱ γενεαί ("from now all the generations will bless me"). Mary's response in *ProtJac* 12:08 would have been an appropriate expression of wonderment at why all the future generations of the earth would bless her for simply spinning thread for the temple veil. It would have been a simple matter for the Redactor to have substituted γυναικες ("women") in Mary's response to Elizabeth's blessing for γενεαι in her response to the priest's blessing in the *GenMar* in *ProtJac* 12:02. Likewise the Redactor would have replaced ευλογησουσιν in Mary's response to the priest's blessing to match

duplicate the words spoken to Mary by the unknown voice in the temple in *ProtJac* 11:02: χαιρε κεχαριτωμενη συ εν γυναιξιν ("Greetings, you have received grace among women"), which derive from the same context in Lk. 1:42-3 as *ProtJac* 12:05a; cf. pp. 39–40 above.

71. Mary herself did not hear the blessing from Elizabeth's unborn child but was informed of it by Elizabeth in *ProtJac* 12:06.

the priest's ευλογημενη with μακαριουσιν from Lk. 1:48. Without the intervening Elizabeth material in *ProtJac* 12:03-07, Mary's return of her completed spun thread to the priest, the priest's blessing to her, and her response to his blessing would have constituted a coherent seamless narrative, which included *ProtJac* 12:01-02 and 08:

ProtJac 12:01 και εποιησεν την πορφυραν και το κοκκινον,
   And she completed the purple and the red
και ανηνεγκεν τω ιερει.
   and she brought [them] to the priest,
και λαβων ο ιερευς ευλογησεν αυτην και ειπεν·
   and taking them, the priest blessed her and said,
12:02 μαρια, εμεγαλυνεν σε κυριος ο θεος το ονομα σου,
   "Mary, the Lord God has blessed you, your name,
και εση ευλογημενη εν πασαις ταις γενεαις της γης
   and you will be blessed by all the generations of the earth"
12:08 και ανεστεναξεν εις τον ουρανον και ειπεν·
   And she sighed to heaven and said,
τις ειμι εγω, οτι ιδου πασαι αι γενεαι της γης ευλογησουσιν με[72];
   "Who am I that, behold, all the generations of the earth will bless me?"

The Redactor completed his insertion of Elizabeth materials into the Veil Council with *ProtJac* 12:09a: και εποιησεν τρεις μηνας προς την ελισαβεδ ("and she remained three months with Elizabeth"), which he derived from Lk. 1:56: ἔμεινεν δὲ Μαριὰμ σὺν αὐτῇ ὡς μῆνας τρεῖς ("and Mary stayed with her for three months"). *ProtJac* 12:09b-10 was original to the *GenMar* and followed immediately after Mary's response to the priest's blessing in *ProtJac* 12:02. The Composer inserted in *ProtJac* 12:10a—now for the fourth time in the Veil Council—a phrase locating Mary at home instead of in the temple:

ProtJac 12:09b και ημερα αφ ημερας η γαστηρ αυτης ωγκουτο.
   And day by day her womb swelled.
10 φοβηθεισα η μαρια ηλθεν <u>εν τω οικω αυτης</u>,
   Becoming frightened, Mary went <u>into her house</u>,
και εκρυβεν αυτην απο των υιων ισραηλ.
   And hid herself from the sons of Israel.

As a result of her Conception in the *GenMar* Annunciation story, Mary's womb began to swell in *ProtJac* 12:09b: ημερα αφ ημερας η γαστηρ αυτης ωγκουτο ("day by day Mary's womb was swelling"). Still ignorant of her pregnancy, Mary was frightened by the swelling of her womb and—in the original *GenMar* text in *ProtJac* 12:10—went into the temple and hid herself from the sons of Israel:

---

72. To correct the Redactor's revision of this text, γενεαι has been substituted for γυναικες, and ευλογησουσιν for μακαριουσιν.

φοβηθεισα η μαρια ηλθεν εν τω ναω, και εκρυβεν αυτην απο των υιων ισραηλ ("Becoming frightened, Mary went into her house. And hid herself from the sons of Israel"). The Composer substituted εν τω οικω αυτης ("in her house") in this text for the original *GenMar* reading εν τω ναω ("in the temple"), thus once again locating Mary at home instead of in the temple.

The text above that was reclaimed by a redaction-critical analysis of *ProtJac* 12 (12:01-2, 08, 09b-10) represents the end of the more easily recoverable text of the *GenMar*. However, the image of Mary hiding in the temple with her womb swelling would appear to point toward a continuation of the narrative, as an increasingly pregnant Mary would presuppose an eventual Nativity. The Composer-enhanced Veil Council ends in *ProtJac* 12:11 with an editorial insertion that gives Mary's age as sixteen years: ην δε ετων δεκαεξ οτε ταυτα τα μυστηρια εγινετο αυτη ("and Mary was sixteen years old when these mysteries happened to her"). *ProtJac* 12:11 represents a fault line between the Veil Council and the resumption of the Composer's Joseph materials that will carry the narrative forward to the discovery of Mary's pregnancy, her and Joseph's trial and exoneration, and the Nativity Complex. It seems prudent, at first sight, to assign *ProtJac* 12:11 to the Composer, although it will be shown below that there are good reasons to attribute this verse to the Redactor instead.[73] Any vestiges of a continuation of the *GenMar* beyond *ProtJac* 12:09b-10 would be difficult to discern in the midst of the extensive Joseph-related texts that the Composer adds to the Veil Council beginning in *ProtJac* 13.

---

73. Cf. pp. 150; 165–6, n. 141; 200–1, n. 132.

THE TRIAL OF JOSEPH AND MARY: *PROTJAC* 13:01-16:07

The process by which the Composer augmented the *GenMar* narrative with his own Joseph materials may be observed in the series of apparently contrived editorial seams in the text by which he linked together the various building blocks of material that he employed in his construction of the enhanced *GenMar*.[74] The Joseph Council proper, itself a discrete textual unit that he inserted before the Veil Council at *ProtJac* 8:03, began with the abrupt statement that Mary is now twelve years old and then continued to an equally abrupt intermediate stopping point at *ProtJac* 9:12 at which Joseph leaves Mary at his home and departs immediately for his construction work. In the text actually written by the Composer the departure of Joseph in *ProtJac* 9:12 is followed directly in *ProtJac* 13:01 by his return from his work to find Mary pregnant. Mary's impregnation is explained in the intervening chapters *ProtJac* 10-12, the Veil Council, which the Composer had detached from its original location after *ProtJac* 8:01-02 and enhanced with his own editorial revisions. Thus the Composer apparently penned his Joseph narrative purposefully with the strategy in mind to embed the Veil Council[75] between the editorial seams that he himself created in *ProtJac* 9:12 and 13:01.[76]

The aftereffects of the confusion in the text of the Joseph Council regarding Mary's status vis-à-vis her custodian or future husband will continue to be felt throughout the remainder of the *ProtJac* in the Joseph materials that were created and introduced by the Composer. One major theme in these narratives is the atmosphere of guilt that surrounds the fact that Mary has become pregnant while she was in Joseph's custody. In *ProtJac* 13:01-02 when Joseph returns from his work and finds Mary six months pregnant he justifiably becomes very distraught, strikes himself on his face, throws himself down on sackcloth, and weeps bitterly. In *ProtJac* 13:03-06 Joseph enunciates a poetic lamentation in which he bewails his failure to protect the virgin of the Lord and compares his misfortune with that suffered by Adam when the serpent found Eve alone and deceived and defiled her.[77] In this section of the narrative the assumed guilt is only on Mary, not Joseph, and is not tied to the issue of whether Joseph was her betrothed or her custodian.

In *ProtJac* 13:07-12 Joseph confronts Mary about her pregnancy and questions her as to why she defiled herself. In *ProtJac* 13:09 he describes Mary as η

---

74. This CEGM was the text to which the later second-century Redactor added his own layer of editorial enhancements.

75. The original *GenMar* Veil Council now includes redactional elements from both the Composer and the Redactor.

76. It is significant that the qualitative homogeneity of the texts that the Composer himself wrote overlaps both of the editorial seams he created to facilitate his insertion of his enhanced Veil Council into his own Joseph materials.

77. For the important parallels in the ancient Jewish and Christian literature, which may help to determine the date and location of the Redactor, see the discussion in "The Composer: The Composer-enhanced *GenMar*," pp. 141-3.

ανατραφεισα εις τα αγια των αγιων και τροφην λαμβανουσα εκ χειρος αγγελου ("she who was nurtured in the Holy of Holies and received food from the hand of an angel"). This verse contains an illuminating editorial association with *ProtJac* 8:02. The Composer would have regarded *ProtJac* 8:02 as a major transitional seam between the chapters of the *GenMar* ending with Mary's parents leaving her at the temple in *ProtJac* 8:01 and his own insertion of the Joseph Council beginning at *ProtJac* 8:03 with Mary's sudden leap forward in age from three to twelve years. The Composer essentially replicated the *GenMar* verse *ProtJac* 8:02 in *ProtJac* 13:09 but added an element that betrays this verse and the entire section *ProtJac* 13:07-12 as being his own handiwork.

The element in question is the reference to the Holy of Holies (τα αγια των αγιων), which is found only three times in the entire *ProtJac*. All three cases occur in the Composer's own Joseph materials: in *ProtJac* 8:06 where the high priest enters the Holy of Holies seeking God's will about Mary's removal from the temple, in the present verse *ProtJac* 13:09, and below in *ProtJac* 15:11 where the high priest is interrogating Mary about her pregnancy in a scenario that essentially reproduces the previous text of the interrogation of Mary by Joseph. The Composer has replaced the *GenMar* description of Mary as being εν ναω κυριου ("in the temple of the Lord") in *ProtJac* 8:02 with his own specific reference in *ProtJac* 13:09b to her being εις τα αγια των αγιων ("in the Holy of Holies"). The Composer modified the image of Mary in the *GenMar* from her being nourished in the temple with food from the hand of an angel to his version of her being raised or nurtured[78] in the Holy of Holies, also receiving food from the hand of an angel.

ProtJac 8:02—*GenMar*
   ην δε μαρια <u>εν ναω κυριου</u> ωσει περιστερα νεμομενη
      And Mary was <u>in the temple of the Lord</u> being nourished as a dove
   <u>ελαμβανε τροφην εκ χειρος αγγελου</u>
      <u>she was receiving food from the hand of an angel</u>
ProtJac 13:09b—CEGM
   η ανατραφεισα <u>εις τα αγια των αγιων</u>
      you who were nurtured <u>in the Holy of Holies</u>
   και <u>τροφην λαμβανουσα εκ χειρος αγγελου</u>
      and <u>receiving food from the hand of an angel</u>

The following verses *ProtJac* 13:10-12 provide us with significant evidence that supports our compositional theory regarding the redactional process that formed the *ProtJac*. Joseph poses harsh questions to Mary in *ProtJac* 13:08, επελαθου κυριου του θεου σου; ("have you forgotten the Lord your God?") and in *ProtJac* 13:09, τι εταπεινωσας την ψυχην σου ("why have you humbled your soul?"). Mary weeps bitterly (<u>εκλαυσεν πικρως</u>) in *ProtJac* 13:10 and affirms that she is clean and

---

78. The verb ἀνατρέφω could also carry the meaning of being nourished or fed.

knows no man (καθαρα ειμι εγω και ανδρα ου γινωσκω). In *ProtJac* 13:11 Joseph asks her, ποθεν ουν τουτο εστιν εν τη γαστρι σου; ("from where then is this in your womb?"). In *ProtJac* 13:12 Mary answers honestly with a sacred vow ζη κυριος ο θεος μου καθοτι ου γινωσκω ποθεν εστιν εμοι ("as the Lord my God lives, I do not know from where it is in me").[79] The dialogue between Joseph and Mary in *ProtJac* 13:10-12 is replicated later in the Composer's Trial story in *ProtJac* 15:10-12 where Mary is interrogated by the high priest. In *ProtJac* 15:12 Mary again weeps bitterly (εκλαυσεν πικρως) and responds to the high priest with most of the same words as she did to Joseph ζη κυριος ο θεος καθοτι καθαρα ειμι ενωπιον αυτου και ανδρα ου γινωσκω ("as the Lord God lives, I am clean and know no man").[80]

Mary is confused about her pregnancy in *ProtJac* 13:10-12 and 15:10-12 because these texts were written by the Composer in the second phase of the redactional development of the *ProtJac* in which Mary had not been made aware of her conception by the unknown voice in the temple.[81] The Composer created these interrogations of Mary by Joseph in *ProtJac* 13:10-12 and by the high priest in *ProtJac* 15:10-12 in accordance with his current state of knowledge of the Annunciation story in the Veil Council, *ProtJac* 10:01-07; 10:09–11:05; 12:01-02, 08, and 10, which he himself had enhanced from its original form in the *GenMar*.[82] Mary's fervent assertion in *ProtJac* 13:12 that she does not know from where the fetus in her womb originated verifies that the Composer knew the Annunciation story as it existed before the Redactor added his own materials to the Composer-enhanced Annunciation story subsequently in the third phase of the compositional development of the *ProtJac*.[83]

The Redactor caused this conflict between the Composer's version of Mary in *ProtJac* 13:12 and 15:12, where Mary did not know how she became pregnant, and his own version of Mary in *ProtJac* 11, where in the interim Mary had learned of her pregnancy by the angelic visitation that he had interpolated into the Composer's text in *ProtJac* 11:06-12. In *ProtJac* 11:07 the Redactor's angel declares to Mary, "You will conceive through his [God's] Logos." That Mary fully comprehends the angel's announcement is confirmed in *ProtJac* 11:08 where she contemplates, "Will I conceive from the living Lord God, as every woman gives birth?" The angel responds to her in *ProtJac* 11:09b-10 with more details: "Not thus Mary, for the power of God will overshadow you therefore the holy one

---

79. Mary received no information about her conception from the unknown voice that spoke to her in the temple in "The Original *GenMar* Annunciation Story," pp. 39–44.

80. Identical words in Mary's dialogues with Joseph and the high priest are underscored. In *ProtJac* 15:10-12 Mary responded appropriately to the high priest's specific question τι τουτο εποιησας; ("why have you done this?") by saying that she was clean and knew no man. The high priest did not inquire about the origin of her unborn child. Hence Mary made no assertion that she did not know the origins of her unborn child.

81. See above, p. 43.

82. See below in "The Composer: The Composer-enhanced *GenMar*," pp. 148–50.

83. See above, pp. 44–5.

born will be called the son of the Most High."[84] In *ProtJac* 11:12 Mary accepts the angel's message and submits to his directions: "let it be done to me according to your word." Thus the Redactor's "phase three" Mary in *ProtJac* 11:06-12 is fully aware that she is pregnant and cognizant of how she became so, as opposed to the Composer's "phase two" Mary in *ProtJac* 13:10-12 and 15:10-12 who is unaware of the circumstances surrounding her pregnancy because the interpolation of the Redactor has not yet taken place.

The Redactor's insertion of the angel's informative message to Mary in *ProtJac* 11:06-12 produced a similar anomaly in another scenario that will shed further light on the issue of Mary's forgetfulness concerning her pregnancy. In the Redactor's Elizabeth story, which he fashioned under the influence of Luke[85] and interpolated into *ProtJac* 12, Mary again fails to understand a message that is communicated to her. In *ProtJac* 12:05-06, after the angelic appearance in the preceding chapter, Mary visited Elizabeth and received blessings from her and her unborn fetus: "And she [Elizabeth] blessed her and said: 'whence [is it] to me that the mother of the Lord comes to me? For behold, that which is in me sprung about and blessed you.'"[86] Mary's response to these blessings in *ProtJac* 12:08 indicates that she did not understand them within the context of the Redactor's newly created Elizabeth story: "who am I that behold all the women of the earth will bless me?"[87]

The solution to the problem of Mary's confusion in *ProtJac* 12:08 lies in the context within which this verse originated. *ProtJac* 12:08 was not created by the Redactor as part of his Elizabeth story but was a component in the Author's "phase one" *GenMar* Veil Council and was preserved in the Composer's "phase two" enhanced version of the *GenMar* before the Redactor interpolated his angelic appearances and his Elizabeth story into the text.[88] Mary misunderstood Elizabeth's blessing because in the two earlier phases of the *ProtJac* she was not responding to a blessing from Elizabeth but to a blessing from a priest in *ProtJac* 12:01-02: "the Lord God has magnified you, your name, and you will be blessed in all the generations of the earth."[89] Mary was perplexed by the priest's blessing because in its original setting in the *GenMar* Annunciation: (1) the unknown voice of the Annunciation in the temple had given her no information about her conception, (2) her womb had not yet begun to swell as it would afterward in *ProtJac* 12:09b, and (3) the Redactor's angelic communications to Mary had not yet been invented and interpolated into the text.

In "phase three" of the composition of the *ProtJac* the Redactor modified the preexisting verse *ProtJac* 12:08 to reflect its new context and incorporated it

---

84. See the entire Greek text of the Redactor's interpolation above, pp. 44–5.
85. See above, pp. 49–54.
86. The Redactor derived this text essentially from Lk. 1:43-4.
87. See above, pp. 50–1, for the Greek texts.
88. The Redactor would have known *ProtJac* 12:08 only from the Composer's "phase two" version of the text.
89. See above, pp. 50–3.

into his interpolated Elizabeth story as Mary's response to Elizabeth's blessing in *ProtJac* 12:06.[90] He altered the source of the blessing from the priest in *ProtJac* 12:01 to Elizabeth and her child in *ProtJac* 12:04-06 and changed the agent of the blessing from "all the generations of the earth" in *ProtJac* 12:02 to "all the women of the earth" in *ProtJac* 12:08. However, the Redactor retained Mary's bewilderment in the *GenMar* text by leaving her response to the blessing of the priest unchanged ("who am I?") but relocating it to her response to Elizabeth in his interpolation. Just as Mary was perplexed by the priest's original blessing in the *GenMar* so is she also by Elizabeth's blessing in the Redactor's new setting, but for a different reason. With respect to the subsequent interrogations of Mary by Joseph in *ProtJac* 13:10-12 and by the high priest in *ProtJac* 15:10-12, Mary is confused about her pregnancy in these later scenarios for the same reason that she was confused by the blessings of the priest and Elizabeth above. In *ProtJac* 13 and 15 Mary is participating in "phase three" level scenarios within the fully redacted *ProtJac* but possesses information that was available to her only in the Composer's "phase two" scenario in *ProtJac* 12, hence Mary's persistent perplexity regarding her pregnancy.

The Redactor appears to have realized that he must rationalize the inconsistency that he was creating in his Elizabeth story between the "phase two" Mary in *ProtJac* 12:08, who was unaware that she was pregnant, and the "phase three" Mary who, owing to his interpolation in *ProtJac* 11:06-12, had been informed of her pregnancy and its cause by the angel. The Redactor preempted the impending contradiction by implanting his contrived rationalization of Mary's ignorance directly before his problematic modified version of Mary's response to her blessings in *ProtJac* 12:08. He inserted an explanatory comment in *ProtJac* 12:07: η δε μαρια επελαθετο των μυστηριων ων ελαησεν γαβριηλ ο αγγελος ("but Mary forgot the mysteries which Gabriel the angel spoke"). With this transparent, heavy-handed subterfuge, the Redactor attempted to minimize the negative effects that this inconsistency in his interpolations would have for the coherence of his "phase three" revision of his source document, the CEGM.[91]

The Redactor must have become aware of the inconsistency that he was creating at the actual time that he was in the process of composing his texts of the angelic appearances and the Elizabeth story and was interpolating them into his source document. Accordingly he corrected the problem that he was creating as he was creating it. But evidently the Redactor was unaware that he had caused identical problems with the "phase two" interrogations of Mary by Joseph and the high

---

90. In its original *GenMar* context Mary would have responded to the priest's blessing by saying "who am I that, behold, all the generations of the earth will bless me?" In the Redactor's revised context Mary responds to Elizabeth's blessing by saying "who am I that, behold, all the women of the earth will bless me?"

91. The Redactor's characteristically obvious and clumsy manipulations of his source texts are easily discernible and distinguishable as opposed to the sometimes more subtle enhancements and revisions by the Composer.

priest that were embedded within the Composer's Joseph materials in *ProtJac* 13 and 15. As the Redactor was copying the Composer's Trial narrative in *ProtJac* 13–16, the problems of *ProtJac* 11–12 receded into the background and he failed to recognize the inconsistency that he was causing in Mary's "phase two" response to her interrogators in *ProtJac* 13:10-12 and 15:10-12. Thus, thanks to the editorial ineptitude of the Redactor, our three-phase compositional theory of the *ProtJac* appears to have been corroborated once more by this elucidation of the problem of Mary's unwittingness regarding her pregnancy in the Redactor's "phase three" Elizabeth story and in the two separate interrogations of Mary in the Composer's "phase two" Trial story.

In the Composer's Trial story in *ProtJac* 13–16, only chapter 14 contains obvious evidence of redaction. The private dialogue between Joseph and Mary in *ProtJac* 13 and their public trial in the temple in *ProtJac* 15–16 are composed mostly of Joseph materials written by the Composer, but chapters 15–16 also contain well-hidden traces of redactional activity.[92] Among these narratives *ProtJac* 14 alone contains canonical influences, displaying significant parallels with the account of the Nativity in the Gospel of Matthew 1:18-25. *ProtJac* 14:04-08 contains texts that appear to have been taken directly, some verbatim, from the Matthean account. The critical question to be addressed is whether these Matthean elements were included in the text by the Composer or by the Redactor. We must resist prejudging this issue, given that the Composer's Joseph materials have shown no relation to the canonical Joseph stories, whereas it has been demonstrated on several occasions that one of the principal distinguishing characteristics of the Redactor is precisely his interpolation of canonical materials into the CEGM.[93] This question should be answered by an analysis of the relevant texts.

In *ProtJac* 13 Joseph conducted an intense interrogation of Mary following his discovery of her pregnancy. Mary proclaimed her innocence and swore a sacred oath denying any sexual misdeed. Joseph was frightened by Mary's oath "and became calm towards her" (ηρεμησεν εξ αυτης) in *ProtJac* 14:01a. In *ProtJac* 14:01b-04a Joseph considered what to do about Mary: τι ουν αυτη ποιησω; ("what then shall I do with her?"). It is at this point, *ProtJac* 14:04b, that the text begins to display close parallels with the Nativity story in Mt. 1:18-25. The similarities between the two passages, including a number of verbatim equivalents, warrant the conclusion that the text of Joseph's angelic visitation in the *ProtJac* was derived directly from Matthew. In *ProtJac* 14:04b as in Mt. 1:19 Joseph decided not to expose Mary to disgrace. In the ensuing storyline after Joseph's decision, the literal correspondence between the text of *ProtJac* 14:04b-08 and Mt. 1:19-21, 24 is obvious:

---

92. See below, pp. 65–76.

93. See above, pp. 48–9, where the Redactor has taken texts from Luke, and at one point from Matthew, and below, pp. 111–13, where he seems to introduce material from the Gospel of John into the *GenMar* Nativity story; also pp. 113–22, the *ProtJac* Magi story, which exhibits close affinities with the parallel story in Mt. 2.

Joseph resolves to put Mary away secretly:

ProtJac 14:04b λαθρα αυτην απολυσω απ εμου
    in secret I will release her from me
Mt. 1:19 ἐβουλήθη λάθρᾳ ἀπολῦσαι αὐτήν
    he planned in secret to release her

Joseph experiences a dream vision of an angel bearing a message to him:

ProtJac 14:05 και ιδου αγγελος κυριου φαινεται αυτω κατ ονειρον λεγων:
    Behold an angel of the Lord appears to him in a dream, saying:
Mt. 1:20 ἰδοὺ ἄγγελος κυρίου κατ' ὄναρ ἐφάνη αὐτῷ λέγων:
    Behold an angel of the Lord in a dream appeared to him, saying:

The angel instructs Joseph not to fear Mary,

ProtJac 14:06a μη φοβηθης την παιδα ταυτην
    "Do not fear this maiden,
Mt. 1:20a μὴ φοβηθῇς παραλαβεῖν Μαρίαν τὴν γυναῖκά σου,
    "Do not be afraid to receive your wife Mary,

for that which is in her is from the Holy Spirit.

ProtJac 14:06b το γαρ εν εαυτη ον εκ πνευματος εστιν αγιου.[94]
    for that which is in herself is from the Holy Spirit.
Mt. 1:20b τὸ γὰρ ἐν αὐτῇ γεννηθὲν ἐκ πνεύματός ἐστιν ἁγίου.
    for that born in her is from the Holy Spirit.

Mary will bear a son who is to be called Jesus

ProtJac 14:07a τεξεται δε σοι υιον και καλεσης το ονομα εαυτου ιησουν
    she will bear you a son and you will call his own name Jesus[95]
Mt. 1:21a τέξεται δὲ υἱόν καὶ καλέσεις τὸ ὄνομα αὐτοῦ Ἰησοῦν,
    she will bear a son and you will call his name Jesus

who will save his people from their sins.

ProtJac 14:07b αυτος γαρ σωσει τον λαον αυτου εκ των αμαρτηματων αυτων.
    for he will save his people from their sins."
Mt. 1:21b αὐτὸς γὰρ σώσει τὸν λαὸν αὐτοῦ ἀπὸ τῶν ἁμαρτιῶν αὐτῶν.
    for he will save his people from their sins."

Joseph awoke and took Mary into his care:

ProtJac 14:08 και ανεστη ιωσηφ απο του υπνου ... και εφυλασσε την παιδα
    And Joseph arose from sleep ... and took custody of the maiden.
Mt. 1:24 ἐγερθεὶς δὲ ὁ Ἰωσὴφ ἀπὸ τοῦ ὕπνου ... παρέλαβεν τὴν γυναῖκα αὐτοῦ
    And awaking from sleep ... Joseph received his wife.

---

94. Cf. *ProtJac* 19:06.

95. The angel's statement that Mary will bear a son σοι ("to you"), i.e., to Joseph, within the context of the *ProtJac* does not mean that the child will be Joseph's son, but that it will be born while Mary is in Joseph's care.

The actual texts of Joseph's dream vision in the *ProtJac* that were derived directly from the account in Matthew are indeed noteworthy. But even more significant for our investigation are the elements of Matthew's story that were omitted, apparently deliberately, by whomever these canonical materials were inserted into *ProtJac* 14. These omissions will further clarify the issue of whether Joseph's dream vision was an original component of the CEGM or was another instance of an interpolation of a canonical text by the Redactor. Both references to Mary as Joseph's γυναῖκα ("wife") in Mt. 1:20 and 24 were replaced in *ProtJac* 14:06 and 08 with the term παιδα, which could mean "young girl" or "maiden."[96] On the one hand this would serve the purpose of the Redactor who was intent upon presenting Mary as a perpetual virgin before, and even after, giving birth.[97] But the Composer also may have preferred Joseph to have been Mary's custodian rather than her husband, at least temporarily.[98]

The interpolator of the Matthean angelic dream vision of Joseph into the *ProtJac* also omitted two important verses in Mt. 1:18 and 25 that imply that Mary was a virgin only up to the point at which she gave birth to Jesus. Mt. 1:18 states that Mary μνηστευθείσης ... τῷ Ἰωσήφ ... εὑρέθη ἐν γαστρὶ ἔχουσα ἐκ πνεύματος ἁγίου ("being betrothed ... to Joseph ... she was found to be pregnant by the Holy Spirit"). This all occurred πρὶν ἢ συνελθεῖν αὐτοὺς ("before they came together"), that is, ostensibly before Mary and Joseph had marital relations, thus implying that they eventually did have marital relations. Likewise after Joseph received the angel's instructions in his dream vision to accept Mary as his wife in Mt. 1:20 (παραλαβεῖν Μαρίαν τὴν γυναῖκά σου), in Mt. 1:24-5 he παρέλαβεν τὴν γυναῖκα αὐτοῦ καὶ οὐκ ἐγίνωσκεν αὐτὴν ἕως οὗ ἔτεκεν υἱόν ("received his wife and did not know her until she gave birth to a son"). Again this verse suggests as well that Joseph did indeed "know" Mary in the biblical sense after she gave birth to Jesus. This second occurrence of the same theme in such close proximity in Matthew's Nativity story seems to verify that the author of the canonical Gospel of Matthew recognized Mary to have been a virgin only temporarily, before the birth of Jesus.[99]

The inference in Mt. 1:20 and 25 that Mary's virginal status existed only before the birth of Jesus unambiguously conflicts with a major goal of the Redactor, to substantiate Mary's *virginitas post-partum* or virginity after giving birth.[100] But the concept of postpartum virginity occurs nowhere in

---

96. The Author of the *GenMar* refers to Mary as παιδα at her one-year birthday party in *ProtJac* 6:07, 08, and 11, and at her Trial in 16:04. All other references to her as παιδα are in the Redactor's interpolated texts: *ProtJac* 14:06, 08; 19:06; and 22:02.

97. On the Redactor's intention to promote the postpartum virginity of Mary, see the discussion below on his insertion of the Doubting Salome episode into the Nativity story in *ProtJac* 19-20.

98. *ProtJac* 9:05, 10. See above, pp. 33-4.

99. See "Appendix 1: Mary's Evolving Virginity in Early Christianity," pp. 171-3.

100. See "Doubting Salome," pp. 108-13.

the Composer's materials. On the contrary, ample evidence affirms our theory stated above that the Composer thought of the relationship of Joseph and Mary as evolving from Joseph's initial status as Mary's "custodian" "for the Lord" and after the birth of her child as her husband.[101] Mary was first described as the future wife of Joseph in the angel's message to Zachariah in *ProtJac* 8:07-08, but in *ProtJac* 9:05 and 9:10 the same priest assigned Joseph to be Mary's "custodian" for the Lord. Although the Trial story seems to be based on Joseph being Mary's custodian, Joseph is accused of having "stolen" (εκλεψεν) Mary's (*ProtJac* 15:06) and his own (*ProtJac* 15:15) marriage (γαμους).[102] In the Nativity story in *ProtJac* 17:03 Joseph considers registering Mary as his wife (γυναικα εμην) and later in *ProtJac* 19:01 tells the midwife that she is his "betrothed" (μεμνηστευμενη μοι).

The internal evidence in the Matthean insertions points toward the Redactor, rather than the Composer, as their interpolator. This conclusion finds further support in the traces left in their present setting in *ProtJac* 14 of the manner by which the Matthew texts were introduced into the CEGM. *ProtJac* 14:01a appears to be the natural conclusion to the heated exchange between Mary and Joseph in *ProtJac* 13. The intensity of the quarrel reached its climax in *ProtJac* 13:12 when Mary invoked the name of the Lord God (Yahweh God) in an oath proclaiming her innocence (ζη κυριος ο θεος μου). At that point in *ProtJac* 14:01a Joseph's anger subsided and his attitude toward her became peaceful. Excising the angelic visitation to Joseph in 14:01b-08 from the text, the action seems to flow naturally from the resolution of the preceding argument in *ProtJac* 14:01a to the next successive event in the storyline, the appearance of the scribe Annas at Joseph's home in *ProtJac* 15:01 to inquire about Joseph's absence from a meeting. Annas sees Mary's swollen womb and reports Joseph to the priests, thus precipitating the remainder of the Trial narrative in *ProtJac* 15–16.

ProtJac 14:01a και εφοβηθη ο ιωσηφ σφοδρα,
    και ηρεμησεν εξ αυτης,
    and Joseph was exceedingly frightened
    and became calm towards her
ProtJac 15:01 ηλθεν δε αννας ο γραμματευς προς αυτον και ειπεν αυτω
    and Annas the scribe came to him and said to him,
ιωσηφ διατι ουκ εφανης τη συνοδω ημων;
    "Joseph, why did you not appear at our meeting?"

---

101. See the discussion above, pp. 32-4.

102. By this act Joseph's seed (σπέρμα) will not be blessed, again implying a full marriage scenario with Mary. Cf. Smid, *Protevangelium*, 106, 110 for gamoklopia as adultery. Regarding the possibly related issue of Jewish couples cohabitating before marriage, see Tal Ilan, "Premarital Cohabitation in Ancient Judea: The Evidence of the Babatha Archive and the Mishnah (Ketubbot 1.4)," *HTR* 86 (1993), 247-64.

The Matthean materials interrupt the original sequence of the narrative in *ProtJac* 14:01a and continue to the end of chapter 14.¹⁰³ An intermediary passage occurs between *ProtJac* 14:01b and the close parallels with Matthew that begin at *ProtJac* 14:04b. *ProtJac* 14:01b-04a represents an expansion of Mt. 1:19 in which Joseph has made his decision to put Mary away in secret (ἐβουλήθη λάθρᾳ ἀπολῦσαι αὐτήν) immediately after she was found pregnant in Mt. 1:18 (εὑρέθη ἐν γαστρὶ ἔχουσα).¹⁰⁴ But in *ProtJac* 14:01b-04a Joseph engages in an internal dialogue considering what he should do about Mary (διαλογιζομενος αυτην τι ποιησει). Joseph pondered two options. In *ProtJac* 14:02 he considered the risk that if he hid her sin he would violate the law of the Lord (εαν αυτης κρυψω το αμαρτημα ευρεθησομαι μαχομενος τω νομω κυριου).¹⁰⁵ In *ProtJac* 14:03 he thought of exposing her but feared that if her child was of "angelic" origin he would be guilty of betraying innocent blood to a judgment of death (και εαν αυτην φανερωσω ... φοβουμαι μηπως αγγελικον εστιν το εν εαυτη και ευρεθησομαι παραδιδους αθωον αιμα εις κριμα του θανατου).

Having come to the same decision in both Mt. 1:19 and ultimately in *ProtJac* 14:04b to put Mary away secretly, Joseph then experiences his dream vision of the angel carrying the same message in both texts.¹⁰⁶ The angel's message consists of the close, partially verbatim, parallels between *ProtJac* 14:04b-08 and Mt. 1:19-21, 24. It seems clear that the Redactor derived the texts of his angelic message (*ProtJac* 14:04b-08) from the parallel passage in Mt. 1:19-21, 24. But given that the transitional passage *ProtJac* 14:01b-04a is an expansion of Mt. 19 and contains no close parallels with the text of Matthew, must it be presumed that this passage also was written by the Redactor as he was inserting the more direct Matthean parallels into the text? Could the transitional passage have been an original component of the CEGM?

One indication that *ProtJac* 14:01b-04a is a discrete text that may have been created ad hoc by the Redactor is the presence of the verb ποιεῖν in both its opening and closing verses. In *ProtJac* 14:01b the passage begins with Joseph "dialoguing" (διαλογιζομενος) with himself regarding what he should do with Mary (αυτην τι ποιησει) and concludes with him asking himself the same question (τι ουν αυτη ποιησω). The occurrence of the verb ποιεῖν at the beginning and end of its text leaves the impression of a circular or chiastic composition of this passage. A more significant clue connecting the transitional passage to the Redactor lies in Joseph's fear of exposing Mary to the sons of Israel in *ProtJac* 14:03. Joseph was afraid that if he exposed Mary, perhaps the child in her womb was αγγελικον, "angelic"

---

103. See above, pp. 60–1.

104. After Joseph has already decided to put Mary away in Mt. 19, Matthew inserts retroactively in v. 1:20a that "he was reflecting on these things" (ταῦτα δὲ αὐτοῦ ἐνθυμηθέντος) when the angelic dream vision occurred.

105. Cf. the marriage laws in Deut. 22:13-30 according to which Mary would be guilty of a capital offense and would be stoned to death.

106. See the comparison of the parallel texts above on p. 61.

Evidence of Redaction of the ProtJac 65

or originating from an angel. The word αγγελικον ties the entire passage to the angelic dream vision of Joseph and provides a valuable connection to the Redactor as being the author of the transitional passage as well as the interpolator of the Matthean parallels into the CEGM. We may conclude therefore that *ProtJac* 14 in its entirety constitutes an interpolation of canonical Gospel materials by the Redactor into the Composer-enhanced text of the *GenMar*.

Whereas *ProtJac* 13–14 were found to be comprised exclusively of materials attributable to the Composer and the Redactor, *ProtJac* 15–16 consist of the Composer's Joseph materials but do seem to contain certain irregularities that may betray redactional activity. In *ProtJac* 15:01-08 the scribe Annas finds Mary at Joseph's home with her swollen womb and reports his discovery to the temple priests who send servants to bring Mary to the temple. This section of text appears to have been written by the Composer as is suggested first by the recurrent theme in the Composer's work of servants being sent by the temple priests to Mary's home to bring her to the temple.[107] Another indication that the Composer wrote this passage is the phrase εμιανεν αυτην ("he defiled her") in Annas's account to the high priest of Joseph's transgression in *ProtJac* 15:06:

την παρθενον ην ιωσηφ παρελαβεν εκ ναου κυριου,
the virgin which Joseph received from the temple of the Lord,
<u>εμιανεν αυτην</u> και εκλεψεν τους γαμους αυτης,
he defiled her and stole her marriage[108]
και ουκ εφανερωσεν τοις υιοις ισραηλ
and did not reveal this to the sons of Israel.

The same phrase appears verbatim in the Composer's text of Joseph's lament at finding Mary pregnant when he returned home in *ProtJac* 13:01-06. In 13:06 Joseph expressed his suspicion that Mary had been defiled as Eve had been defiled by the serpent in the Genesis story: ο οφις ... εξηπατησεν αυτην και <u>εμιανεν αυτην</u> ("the serpent ... deceived her and defiled her").[109]

Although the account of the discovery of Mary's pregnancy by the temple priests in *ProtJac* 15:01-08 is most likely a homogeneous creation of the Composer, the subsequent text contains certain irregularities that suggest the possible presence of original elements from the *GenMar* that have been obscured by the Composer's redaction. Traces of an interrogation of Mary by the high priest from the original

---

107. Cf. the Composer's redaction of the *GenMar* story of the weaving of the temple veil, pp. 35-9. The Composer adjusted the text to accommodate the fact that he had removed Mary from the temple previously in his interpolated Joseph Council in *ProtJac* 9.

108. Cf. Smid, *Protevangelium*, 110-11; this phrase could be interpreted as an act of adultery (*Sibylline Oracles* ii 52; v. 429) or of a secret marriage, which also would have been viewed as illicit. The same accusatory phrase is repeated by the high priest directly to Joseph in *ProtJac* 15:15.

109. This is the important Eve/Mary typology that is paralleled in Justin's *Dial.* 100.5. See the discussion below in "The Redactor: *The Protevangelium Jacobi*," pp. 141-3.

GenMar, but without Joseph present, may be preserved in *ProtJac* 15:09-12. But this potential element from the *GenMar* has been so thoroughly embedded in the Composer's scenario of a joint Trial of both Mary and Joseph that it is difficult to isolate. The text of *ProtJac* 15:09-14 is presented below with a following commentary to highlight the irregularities that occur in the text as the narrative moves from the high priest's interrogation of Mary to that of Joseph:

> *ProtJac* 15:09 και απηλθον οι υπηρεται και ευρον αυτην καθως ειπεν,
> And the servants went out and found her as he [Annas] said,
> και απηγαγον αυτην εις το ιερον, και εστη εις το κριτηριον.
> And they led her to the sanctuary, and she stood in the place of judgment.
> 10 και ειπεν αυτη ο αρχιερευς, μαρια, τι τουτο εποιησας;
> And the high priest said to her, Mary, "what is this that you have done?
> τι εταπεινωσας την ψυχην σου; επελαθου κυριου του θεου σου;
> Why have you humbled your soul? Have you forgotten the Lord your God?
> 11 η ανατραφεισα εις τα αγια των αγιων
> You who have been raised in the Holy of Holies,
> και λαβουσα τροφην εκ χειρος αγγελων
> and received food from the hand of angels,
> συ η ακουσασα τον υμνον αυτων
> you who have heard their hymns,
> και χορευσασα ενωπιον αυτων, τι τουτο εποιησας;
> and have danced before them, what is this that you have done?"
> 12 η δε εκλαυσε πικρως λεγουσα ζη κυριος ο θεος
> But she cried bitterly, saying, "as the Lord God lives,
> καθοτι καθαρα ειμι ενωπιον αυτου και ανδρα ου γινωσκω.
> I am clean before him and know no man."
> 13 και ειπεν ο αρχιερευς ιωσηφ οτι τουτο ειπεν.
> And the high priest said to Joseph that she said this.
> 14 ειπεν δε ιωσηφ ζη κυριος ο χριστος αυτου
> And Joseph said, "as the Lord his Christ lives,
> καθοτι καθαρος ειμι εγω εξ αυτης.
> I am clean from her."

In *ProtJac* 15:09 temple servants are sent out to bring Mary to the temple where she is questioned by the high priest. The distinctive nature of this verse within this context is evident in the terminology used to describe where Mary was taken: απηγαγον αυτην εις το ιερον ("they led her to the sanctuary").[110] This is one of only two occurrences of the term ιερον in the *ProtJac*; it is translated as "sanctuary" to distinguish it from ναὸς, which normally denotes the "temple." It is relevant

---

110. The text further clarifies the location: και εστη εις το κριτηριον ("and she stood in the place of judgment"). This is the only appearance of the κριτηριον (place of judgment) in the *ProtJac*, which is to be expected as the only scenario involving a trial.

to our purpose that ιερον occurs in *ProtJac* 15:09, in the passage suspected of being a remnant of the original *GenMar*, only three verses after ναός was used by the Composer in *ProtJac* 15:06,[111] within the text that he wrote to introduce the interrogation of Mary. ναός occurs again in *ProtJac* 16:01, in the passage containing the interrogation of Joseph by the high priest (*ProtJac* 15:13–16:01), which was also created by the Composer. Thus, apparently there is inconsistency in the terms used for the temple between the proposed *GenMar* account of Mary's interrogation and the larger narrative matrix of the Trial of Joseph and Mary that was created by the Composer, and within which he embedded the *GenMar* story.

The only other incidence of ιερον, in *ProtJac* 9:02, also occurs in a very confused textual setting in which original *GenMar* material has been so well integrated by the Composer into his new enhanced matrix, that it is nearly imperceptible.[112] Remarkably, it is within this problematic passage in the Joseph Council (*ProtJac* 8:07–9:04) that the Composer first introduces into his work the protagonist of the CEGM, Joseph.[113] Joseph makes his debut in this passage as the one who was selected to remove Mary from the temple and thus to fulfill a major objective of the Composer. Our analysis of *ProtJac* 8:07–9:04 revealed the existence of two parallel stories intermingled with each other, each with its own method by which the priests identified the person who would receive Mary from the temple, and each presenting in its own way the nature of the relationship between Joseph and Mary.[114] The presence of so many irregularities in the two passages in the *ProtJac* in which the term ιερον occurs lends credence to our suspicion that original *GenMar* material has survived in both of these texts. And in both scenarios we can discern the hand of the Composer as he was augmenting his source document, the *GenMar*, with extensive interpolations of Joseph material that were accompanied by editorial adjustments to accommodate his intrusions into the text.

This inconsistency in the terms used to designate the temple in *ProtJac* 15 constitutes only one piece of evidence in the cumulative argument supporting the existence of an original account in the *GenMar* of an interrogation of Mary alone by the high priest. Once Mary was brought into the sanctuary, the high priest asked her in *ProtJac* 15:10: τι τουτο εποιησας; τι εταπεινωσας την ψυχην σου; επελαθου κυριου του θεου σου; ("What is this that you have done? Why have you humbled your soul? Have you forgotten the Lord your God?"). Mary responds in *ProtJac* 15:12 by swearing an oath to the Lord God (ζη κυριος ο θεος) that she is innocent before God and knows no man (ανδρα ου γινωσκω). But there are significant indications of redactional activity by the Composer within the matrix

---

111. See the Greek text above, p. 66.

112. See "The Joseph Council," pp. 25–32. Because of the many inconsistencies and discontinuity present in this text, our analysis found that attributing any of its various conflicting elements to the *GenMar* was a most daunting, and perhaps insurmountable, challenge.

113. Ibid., pp. 29–30.

114. Ibid., pp. 31–2.

of these verses in *ProtJac* 15:10-12. The continuity between the high priest's initial questions and Mary's direct response is interrupted by an extension of the high priest's questions in *ProtJac* 15:11 that consists of four clauses, each initiated by an aorist participle: "having been raised" (ανατραφεισα), "having received" (λαβουσα), "having heard" (ακουσασα), and "having danced" (χορευσασα). Also, these clauses are framed by two occurrences of the phrase τι τουτο εποιησας; ("what is this that you have done?"). The text of *ProtJac* 15:10-12 is presented below with v. 15:11 indented to highlight its intrusive nature; the significant repetition of the phrase τι τουτο εποιησας; is underlined:

ProtJac 15:10 και ειπεν αυτη ο αρχιερευς, μαρια,
And the high priest said to her, Mary,
<u>τι τουτο εποιησας;</u>
"<u>what is this that you have done?</u>
τι εταπεινωσας την ψυχην σου; επελαθου κυριου του θεου σου;
Why have you humbled your soul? Have you forgotten the Lord your God?
11 η ανατραφεισα εις τα αγια των αγιων
You who have been raised in the Holy of Holies,
και λαβουσα τροφην εκ χειρος αγγελων
and received food from the hand of angels,
συ η ακουσασα τον υμνον αυτων
you who have heard their hymns,
και χορευσασα ενωπιον αυτων,
and have danced before them,
<u>τι τουτο εποιησας;</u>
<u>what is this that you have done?</u>"
12 η δε εκλαυσε πικρως λεγουσα ζη κυριος ο θεος
But she cried bitterly, saying, "as the Lord God lives,
καθοτι καθαρα ειμι ενωπιον αυτου και ανδρα ου γινωσκω.
I am clean before him and know no man."

The series of four participial clauses in *ProtJac* 15:11 has been attached awkwardly after the high priest's questions in v. 15:10, thus creating an abnormally lengthy separation between his questions and Mary's response in v. 15:12. The secondary character of *ProtJac* 5:11 is evident also from its unnatural position after the high priest had already finished asking his questions in v. 15:10. It is noteworthy that these four clauses in this interrogation scenario exhibit certain aspects of the modus operandi implemented by the Composer in previous instances of his interpolations into the *GenMar* text.[115] *ProtJac* 15:11 appears to have been inserted by the Composer into 15:10-12 as an afterthought, as was the case with *ProtJac* 10:04 and 10:07b in the Veil Council and with *ProtJac* 8:08–9:01 and 9:04 in the Joseph Council. Another feature of the Composer's modus operandi appears in

---

115. See "The Joseph Council," pp. 24-5; also "The Veil Council," pp. 35-9.

the repetition of the phrase τι τουτο εποιησας ("what is this that you have done?") at the beginning of the series of questions of the high priest to Mary in *ProtJac* 15:10 and following the fourth and last participial clause in 15:11. The Composer typically duplicates words from the *GenMar* text at the point at which he intends to insert his own material. He then interpolates his material into the *GenMar* text at that point and attaches his duplicated words at the end of his insertion, as he seems to have done in the present case as well.

A particularly interesting feature of the high priest's interrogation of Mary and Joseph in *ProtJac* 15:09-14 is that it closely parallels Joseph's interrogation of Mary in *ProtJac* 13:07-12. Both interrogations follow the same order and share much verbatim vocabulary: τι τουτο εποιησας in 15:10, 11 and 13:08; τι εταπεινωσας την ψυχην σου in 15:10 and 13:09; επελαθου κυριου του θεου σου in 15:10 and 13:08; η ανατραφεισα εις τα αγια των αγιων in 15:11 and 13:09 (cf. 19:06); η δε εκλαυσε πικρως λεγουσα in 15:12 and 13:10; ζη κυριος ο θεος in 15:12 and 13:12; καθοτι καθαρα ειμι εγω ... και ανδρα ου γινωσκω in 15:12 and 13:10. The Composer seems to have adopted a basic sequential dialogue of Mary being questioned and responding to those questions and has adapted this dialogue to the individual scenarios of her being questioned alone by Joseph in chapter 13 and jointly with Joseph by the high priest in chapter 15. If, in fact, *ProtJac* 15:09-12 contain a remnant of an original interrogation of Mary by the high priest in the *GenMar*, then this interrogation could have constituted the basic dialogue that the Composer found in his source and enhanced with his own Joseph materials to create the present scenarios in *ProtJac* 13:07-12 and 15:09-14, respectively.

With respect to isolating the original *GenMar* story of the interrogation of Mary by the high priest, the question arises regarding which of the two parallel interrogation scenarios may preserve the original story more faithfully. Subtle differences between the texts of the two scenarios may provide answers to that question. The Composer would have had to adjust the *GenMar* scene of the high priest's interrogation of Mary in *ProtJac* 13:07-12 by substituting Joseph as the interrogator instead of the high priest, thus possibly generating inconsistencies in the text. Conversely, no adjustment of the scene in *ProtJac* 15:09-14 would have been necessary since the high priest was the interrogator, thus allowing a more seamless integration of the *GenMar* text. Both scenes begin with the same three questions, verbatim, being asked of Mary by Joseph in *ProtJac* 13:08-09 and by the high priest in *ProtJac* 15:10. The only difference is in the order of the second and third questions, which is reversed in the two scenarios:

ProtJac 13:08-09—Joseph as the interrogator
08 τι τουτο εποιησας;   "What is this that you have done?"
επελαθου κυριου του θεου σου;   "Have you forgotten the Lord your God?"
09 τι εταπεινωσας την ψυχην σου;   "Why have you humbled your soul?"

ProtJac 15:10—the high priest as the interrogator
τι τουτο εποιησας;   "What is this that you have done?"
τι εταπεινωσας την ψυχην σου;   "Why have you humbled your soul?"
επελαθου κυριου του θεου σου;   "Have you forgotten the Lord your God?"

This seemingly trivial detail is not insignificant. Mary's response in *ProtJac* 15:12 directly answers only the high priest's third and final question in 15:10 and does not address the first two questions. The emphasis in the *ProtJac* 15:10-12 scenario is theological, that in sinning Mary forgot God:

ProtJac 15:10—the high priest's third and final question
επελαθου κυριου του θεου σου;   "Have you forgotten the Lord your God?"
15:12—Mary's response
η δε εκλαυσε πικρως λεγουσα   But she cried bitterly, saying,
ζη κυριος ο θεος   "as the Lord God lives,
καθοτι καθαρα ειμι ενωπιον αυτου   I am clean before him [the Lord God]
και ανδρα ου γινωσκω   and know no man."

In contrast to Mary's unitary response to the high priest in *ProtJac* 15:12, her response to Joseph is divided into two components, in *ProtJac* 13:10 and 13:12, which are separated by a fourth question asked by Joseph in 13:11. Her response in *ProtJac* 13:10 is directed toward the moral charge of humbling her soul with an illicit pregnancy, which was the last of the three initial questions asked of her in the Joseph scenario in *ProtJac* 13:09. In *ProtJac* 13:10 Mary responds to this moral charge by denying that she has had sexual contact with a man:

ProtJac 13:09—Joseph's third and last of the initial three questions
τι εταπεινωσας την ψυχην σου   "Why have you humbled your soul?"
13:10—Mary's response
η δε εκλαυσεν πικρως, λεγουσα   But she cried bitterly, saying,
καθοτι καθαρα ειμι εγω   "I am clean
και ανδρα ου γινωσκω.   and know no man."

Thus, in both of these question-answer scenarios in *ProtJac* 15:10-12 and 13:09-10, the Composer forms Mary's responses specifically toward the third, and last, of the initial questions asked of her in each scenario, respectively. Therefore, the Composer's reversal of the order of the second and third of the initial questions asked of Mary in the high priest and Joseph scenarios, respectively, must have been intentional. Obviously, the Composer paid close attention to detail in constructing his parallel question-answer scenarios in *ProtJac* 13 and 15.

In *ProtJac* 13:11, after Mary's response in 13:10, Joseph asks her a fourth question that was not in the parallel high priest scenario. How did Mary become pregnant if she had no sexual contact? In *ProtJac* 13:12 Mary responds to this question with an oath denying any knowledge of how she became pregnant:

ProtJac 13:11—Joseph's fourth question after the three initial questions in 13:08-09
και ειπεν αυτη ιωσηφ   And Joseph said to her,
ποθεν ουν τουτο εστιν εν τη γαστρι σου; From where then is this in your womb?

13:12—Mary's response
η δε ειπεν
ζη κυριος ο θεος μου
καθοτι ου γινωσκω ποθεν εστιν εμοι

And she said,
"As the Lord my God lives,
I do not know from where is this in me."

A comparative analysis of Mary's responses to the questions posed to her in the high priest and Joseph scenarios may assist in resolving the problem of which of the two scenarios preserves the original *GenMar* text more faithfully. The issue is whether Mary's single response in the high priest scenario in *ProtJac* 15:12 was genuine or whether the two separate answers in her divided two-part response to Joseph in *ProtJac* 13:10 and 13:12 were conflated by the Composer to form the single answer in *ProtJac* 15:12. Fortunately, the Composer left behind a clue that reveals the division of Mary's response in *ProtJac* 13:10-12 to have been a contrived editorial revision. In dividing Mary's response to Joseph into two parts, the Composer detached Mary's invocation of the Lord God, ζη κυριος ο θεος μου ("as the Lord my God lives"), from its original setting in *ProtJac* 13:10 and placed it in 13:12. The Composer's editorial action is exposed by the double occurrence of the word καθοτι in both verses.[116] When the Composer detached Mary's invocation of God from *ProtJac* 13:10, he failed to delete the καθοτι that originally followed the invocation and introduced the actual statement of the oath as καθοτι does in *ProtJac* 13:12 and 15:12, 14. Without the invocation, *ProtJac* 13:10 is an incomplete sentence: "She cried bitterly saying, 'inasmuch as I am clean and know no man.'"[117]

In view of this analysis, we must conclude that the version of Mary's response to the high priest's interrogation contained in *ProtJac* 15:12 is more authentic than the form of her response to Joseph's questions in *ProtJac* 13:10-12 and thus may approximate more closely an original interrogation by the high priest in the *GenMar*. Furthermore, we found that the Composer purposely reversed the order of the last two of the three identical initial questions asked of Mary by the high priest and Joseph in their respective scenarios so that the final question in each scenario would correspond to the nature of Mary's response.[118] Given the

---

116. This may perhaps represent another instance, although a less effective one, of the Composer's modus operandi of duplicating words in his process of interpolating his own materials into his source text; see above, pp. 35–9.

117. The Composer's editorial error has caused confusion in the entry for καθότι in *A Greek-English Lexicon of the New Testament and Other Early Christian Literature*, third edition, rev. and ed. Frederick William Danker (Chicago and London: The University of Chicago Press, 2000), 493; definition 3 cites *ProtJac* 13:12 and 15:12 as examples of the proper use of καθότι, "of an oath," but definition 4 is devoted entirely to the Composer's version of *ProtJac* 13:10 and appears to be unaware of the defective nature of this verse; καθότι is described as "of dir. speech, *in this matter* (an approximation, but best left untransl.)."

118. The Composer crafted Mary's response in *ProtJac* 13:10, καθαρα ειμι εγω και ανδρα ου γινωσκω, to match Joseph's third question in *ProtJac* 13:09, τι εταπεινωσας την ψυχην σου, which accused Mary of an immoral pregnancy.

relative authenticity of Mary's theological dialogue with the high priest in *ProtJac* 15:10-12, the order of the questions in 15:10 and Mary's response in 15:12 may preserve the true nature of an interrogation scene of the high priest and Mary in the original *GenMar*. The contrast between the moral-ethical character of the Composer's Joseph scenario in chapter 13 and the theological scenario with the high priest in chapter 15, which may reflect the original *GenMar* scenario, may contribute to our further comprehension of the character and *Sitz im Leben* of the Composer and of the Author of the *GenMar*.

More insights into what may have been the original form of Mary's interrogation by the high priest in the *GenMar* may be gained by an analysis of the differences between the participial clauses that follow the initial three questions asked of Mary by the high priest and by Joseph in the two scenarios. The series of four clauses in *ProtJac* 15:11 display all the characteristics of an interpolation by the Composer into the *GenMar* text.[119] This set of clauses is uniform in structure, all having been constructed around an aorist participle. In contrast, the interrogation scenario by Joseph in *ProtJac* 13:09 contains only two clauses, the first of which is a verbatim match for the first clause in *ProtJac* 15:11: η ανατραφεισα εις τα αγια των αγιων ("you who have been raised in the Holy of Holies"). But the second clause in *ProtJac* 13:09, although containing the same basic vocabulary as its counterpart in *ProtJac* 15:11, presents the words in a different form.

At this point it would be instructive to introduce another piece of evidence that may help to resolve the dilemma of which of the two sets of participial clauses before us is more original and consequently may contain authentic *GenMar* material. The content of the first two clauses in both scenarios seems to have originated in *ProtJac* 8:02, which not only represents the last verse of the initial chapters of the Author's *GenMar* text but also sits astride the critical juncture at which the Composer began to interpolate his Joseph materials, beginning with the Joseph Council in *ProtJac* 8:03.[120] It would be useful to add the witness of *ProtJac* 8:02 in a comparison of the second participial clauses in the two interrogation scenarios to assist in determining which is more faithful to their ostensible common source:

ProtJac 15:10—the high priest's second participial clause
και <u>λαβουσα</u> τροφην εκ χειρος <u>αγγελων</u>
and <u>having received</u> food from <u>the hand of angels</u>

ProtJac 13:09—Joseph's second participial clause
και τροφην <u>λαμβανουσα</u> εκ χειρος <u>αγγελου</u>;
and <u>receiving</u> food from <u>the hand of an angel</u>

ProtJac 8:02—the original *GenMar* witness to the second participial clause
<u>ελαμβανε</u> τροφην εκ χειρος <u>αγγελου</u>
Mary <u>was receiving</u> food from <u>the hand of an angel</u>.

---

119. See pp. 68–9 above on *ProtJac* 15:11 representing a classic example of the Composer's standard modus operandi in interpolating his materials into the *GenMar* text.
120. See "The Joseph Council," pp. 23–34.

The participle λαβουσα, literally "having received," in the high priest's second clause in *ProtJac* 15:11 is in the aorist (past) tense and in that respect matches the form of the other three clauses in the same verse. In contrast, the participle λαμβανουσα in the analogous position in the Joseph scenario is in the present tense. In *ProtJac* 8:02 the verb ελαμβανε ("was receiving") is in the imperfect indicative active tense, thus differing from both interrogation scenarios and being of no assistance in determining the authenticity of one or the other.

However, the witness of *ProtJac* 8:02 is useful in resolving the discrepancy in the number of angels from whom Mary is receiving food in these three sources. In the Joseph scene in *ProtJac* 13:09 Mary is fed by a single "angel" (αγγελου) as opposed to plural "angels" (αγγελων) in the high priest scene in *ProtJac* 15:11. The *GenMar* text in *ProtJac* 8:02 also contains a single "angel," thus validating the Joseph scenario against that of the high priest and raising the prospect that the Composer may have altered the text in *ProtJac* 15:11. Furthermore, in changing the number of the angels who fed Mary from one to a plurality in *ProtJac* 15:11, the Composer created a grammatical conflict in the text of the prepositional phrase εκ χειρος αγγελων ("from the hand of angels") that verifies its secondary nature. In the common text shared by all three of our sources, Mary is fed by a single hand: εκ χειρος ("from the hand"). And in the text of the prepositional phrase shared by both *ProtJac* 8:02 and 13:09 verbatim, εκ χειρος αγγελου ("from the hand of an angel"), this single "hand" appropriately belongs to a single angel. But in the Composer's revised text in *ProtJac* 15:11, Mary is fed by the single hand of multiple angels: εκ χειρος αγγελων ("from the hand of angels"). The negligence of the Composer in not synchronizing the number of angels with the number of hands that are feeding Mary betrays his alteration of the text of *ProtJac* 15:11 and affirms the authenticity of the parallel clause in *ProtJac* 13:09.[121]

The first two participial clauses in both interrogation scenarios contain content derived from the text of the *GenMar* and, therefore, may have constituted an original part of a *GenMar* interrogation story. However, the third and fourth clauses in the high priest interrogation scenario in *ProtJac* 15:11 show no affinity with any part of the *ProtJac* narrative: συ η ακουσασα τον υμνον αυτων και χορευσασα ενωπιον αυτων ("you who have heard their [the angels'] hymn and

---

121. The Composer's editorial carelessness here is reminiscent of his previous mistake (see p. 71 above) where he excised Mary's invocation of God (ζη κυριος ο θεος μου) from its original position in Joseph's first question to her in *ProtJac* 13:10 and inserted it into her answer to Joseph's second question in v. 13:12. In so doing he left in *ProtJac* 13:10 the first καθοτι that originally introduced the text of Mary's oath after her invocation of God, thus leaving this verse as an incomplete sentence. We are grateful for these random blunders of both the Composer and the Redactor that are so helpful in permitting us to identify their redactional activity and to determine the authentic underlying texts.

have danced before them").[122] Given that the high priest interrogation scenario in 15:10-12 may preserve elements of an original *GenMar* story, one might speculate that an original dialogue between the high priest and Mary in the *GenMar* may have contained references to Mary hearing the hymns of the angels and dancing before them. But other evidence suggests that the final two prepositional clauses in *ProtJac* 15:11 are secondary additions by the Composer, although this evidence provides no information on their place of origin from where the Composer derived them.

Apart from the fact that the third and fourth clauses in *ProtJac* 15:11 do not occur in the parallel scenario in *ProtJac* 13:09, the third clause in 15:11 begins with the personal pronoun συ, which constitutes a grammatical break from the first two clauses. The three questions of the high priest in *ProtJac* 15:10 and the first two participial clauses in 15:11 represent an independent grammatical unit that coincides with its counterpart in *ProtJac* 13:07-09. The last two clauses with the Composer's duplicate τι τουτο εποιησας; ("what is this that you have done?") form a new sentence: "You who have heard the hymn of the angels and danced before them, what is this that you have done?" This sentence stands apart as a self-contained text that has the features of an interpolation by the Composer according to his typical modus operandi. This exegesis would account for the discrepancy in the number of the angels who fed Mary in the two scenarios. The Composer must have changed the single angel (αγγελου) to the plural (αγγελων) to conform to his interpolated last two clauses, both of which show Mary as interacting with multiple angels: "hearing their hymn and dancing before them". He also may have modified the present participle λαμβανουσα to the aorist form λαβουσα to be in agreement with ανατραφεισα and his interpolated ακουσασα and χορευσασα and thus to bring his set of four aorist participles in *ProtJac* 15:11 into harmony with each other.

The text of the interrogation of Mary and Joseph in *ProtJac* 15:09-17 represents a double-edged sword in our search for remnants of the original text of the *GenMar* beyond its initial chapters now in *ProtJac* 1:01-8:02 and whatever parts of the *GenMar* that we were able to identify in the highly redacted Veil Council in *ProtJac* 10–12. We have found significant evidence of redaction by the Composer in chapter 15 but also identified in *ProtJac* 15:09-12 what may be the vestiges of an original account of an interrogation of Mary alone by the high priest of the temple after her pregnancy was discovered. These conclusions appear to be confirmed by the immediately following account of Joseph's interrogation by the high priest in *ProtJac* 15:13-17, which also appears to be an interpolation into the text. Peculiarities emerge when, after interrogating Mary in *ProtJac* 15:09-12, the high priest suddenly speaks to Joseph in 15:13, although nowhere in the text up

---

122. There is a scene in *ProtJac* 7:12, which presents Mary as dancing, but there she is dancing on the steps of the temple at her dedication to the temple by her parents at the age of three. There is no apparent connection between v. 7:12 and the reference to Mary dancing before the angels in *ProtJac* 15:11.

to this point is it stated that Joseph was brought to the temple. In *ProtJac* 15:01-12 the scribe Annas visited Joseph at his home and discovered Mary to be pregnant. He then returned to the temple and reported what he saw to the high priest. In *ProtJac* 15:09 it is specified that servants went out and brought Mary alone to the temple—with no mention of Joseph—where the high priest interrogated her in *ProtJac* 15:10-12.

Remarkably, after completing his interrogation of Mary, the high priest abruptly addresses Joseph in *ProtJac* 15:13 and has to inform him of what Mary said as if Joseph was not present at Mary's interrogation: και ειπεν ο αρχιερευς ιωσηφ οτι τουτο ειπεν ("and the high priest said to Joseph that she said this"). The text of Joseph's response to the high priest in *ProtJac* 15:14 resembles Mary's oath in 15:12 but with the surprising substitution of the words "his Christ" (ο χριστος αυτου), for God (ο θεος) in Mary's oath, the only occurrence of the word "Christ" in the entire *ProtJac*: ζη κυριος ο χριστος αυτου καθοτι καθαρος ειμι εγω εξ αυτης ("as the Lord his Christ lives, I am clean from her").[123] The high priest's retort in *ProtJac* 15:15-16 to Joseph's response reiterates most of the text of Annas's report of Joseph's sin to the high priest in 15:06. Thus, Joseph's interrogation by the high priest in *ProtJac* 15:13-17 is comprised of reworked repetitions of previous texts. It seems to have been contrived by the Composer to camouflage the presence of an interrogation of Mary alone by the high priest as would have appeared in the original *GenMar*. The Composer interpolated this Joseph scene in *ProtJac* 15:13-17 immediately after Mary's scene in 15:10-12 to foster the impression of a joint interrogation of Mary and Joseph by the high priest.[124]

More indications of redaction occur at the end of the Trial story in *ProtJac* 16:06-07, which serves as the critical transitional seam between the Trial story and the Nativity Complex. Several elements with idiosyncratic characteristics—as was the case with the *hapax legomenon* ο χριστος previously in *ProtJac* 15:14— seem to converge at this juncture in the CEGM and attest cumulatively that the Composer is at work redacting his source document. The high priest exonerates Mary in *ProtJac* 16:06 with the words ουδε εγω κρινω υμας ("neither do I judge you"), which represent a significant parallel with the story of the woman caught in adultery in Jn 8:11.[125] The *Pericope Adulterae* is renowned among scholars as an early, originally independent story that was joined to the Gospel of John centuries after the composition of the Gospel. Another idiosyncratic element in *ProtJac* 16:07 is the first of the three instances in the *ProtJac* of the unique spelling

---

123. The presence of an extraneous element such as the *hapax legomenon* ο χριστος that is so inapposite to the context of this verse and to the entire *ProtJac* is a strong indicator of redactional activity in this passage.

124. See the analysis above of Mary's responses to her interrogations by Joseph in chapter 13 and the high priest in chapter 15, pp. 67–74.

125. Cf. Zervos, "Caught in the Act: Mary and the Adulteress," *Apocrypha* 15 (2004), 57–114. See the discussion below on the possible connection between *ProtJac* 16:06 and the *Pericope Adulterae* in Jn 7:53-8:11.

of Mary's name as Mariamme (μαριαμμη); these occur only in P.Bodm V in the Greek manuscript tradition of the *ProtJac*.[126] Interestingly, their presence overlaps a redactional seam between two major sections of the document. The first instance of Μαριάμμη occurs in the last verse of the Trial story in *ProtJac* 16:07, and the second and third are found in the Nativity story in *ProtJac* 17:09 and 11.

There is much to commend the proposition that the Composer's narrative of the Trial of Joseph and Mary preserves elements of an original *GenMar* story that reported the individual interrogation of Mary by the high priest, separate from any presence of Joseph. The Composer's redacted story of Mary's trial begins in *ProtJac* 15:09 with servants being sent by the priests to her home to bring her to the temple and ends in *ProtJac* 16:07 with Joseph taking Mariamme back to his house: και παρελαβεν ιωσηφ την μαριαμμην και απηει εν τω οικω αυτου ("And Joseph took Mariamme and went into his house"). This replicates the scenario in the Veil Council in *ProtJac* 10:01-05 in which the Composer was concerned also to show that Mary was living at home and not in the temple, as she was in the *GenMar*.[127] There also he inserted material into the *GenMar* text describing servants being dispatched by the temple priests to Mary's home to bring her to the temple to weave the veil. In both contexts the Composer found it necessary to adjust the *GenMar* to be consistent with his premature removal of Mary from the temple by his interpolation of the Joseph Council in *ProtJac* 9.[128] The survival of such major elements from the *GenMar* may be discerned in the Composer's persistent application of his redactional modus operandi throughout his systematic enhancement of the *GenMar* to create his own document amplified with his perspectives.

---

126. See Stephen J. Shoemaker, "Rethinking the 'Gnostic Mary': Mary of Nazareth and Mary of Magdala in Early Christian Tradition," *JECS* 9 (2001), 555–96; Stephen J. Shoemaker, "A Case of Mistaken Identity? Naming the Gnostic Mary," in *Which Mary? The Marys of Early Christian Tradition*, ed. F. Stanley Jones (Leiden: Brill, 2003), 5–30; see especially François Bovon's very informative article in the same volume, "Mary Magdalene in the Acts of Philip," 75–89. In *ProtJac* 8:07 Mary is named Μαριάμ (Mariam).

127. Cf. pp. 35–7.

128. See "The Joseph Council," pp. 23–34.

THE NATIVITY COMPLEX: *PROTJAC* 17-21

In the following discussion of the final section of the *ProtJac* 17:01-24:11 we will refer to the Nativity story as the Nativity Complex in view of the fact that it consists of components from diverse origins within the scope of the redactional development of the *ProtJac*. Belonging to the CEGM are elements of the stories narrating the Journey to the Cave of the Nativity in *ProtJac* 17:01-18:01, the Midwife episode in 18:02-19:07, and the birth of the divine child in the cave in 19:08-20:11. Substantial interpolations by the Redactor are encompassed within the Nativity Complex as well, including parts of the Journey story, the Midwife episode, and the Birth story. The Doubting Salome story in *ProtJac* 19:13-20:11, the Matthew-inspired Magi story in 21:01-22:02, and the Zachariah materials in 22:03-24:11 were attached by the Redactor to the end of the CEGM directly following its Birth story. Since the content of the Zachariah materials is entirely unrelated to the preceding narratives, they were thought by early scholars to constitute a separate preexisting document, the *Apocryphum Zachariae*.[129] The *ProtJac* concludes with a colophon in chapter 25 that identifies the author of this "history" as James who was, no doubt, one of Jesus's brothers named in Mk 6:3.

The Nativity Complex presents potential redactional issues already in its initiatory verse, *ProtJac* 17:01, which functions as a transitional seam between the Trial story and the Nativity Complex. The origin of this verse is complicated by the presence within it of a canonical element (a reference to Augustus as Aostos) and by its position between the three distinctive incidences of Mary's name written as Mariamme.[130] The first instance of Mariamme occurred immediately before *ProtJac* 17:01 in the final verse of the Trial story in v. 16:07. The remaining two cases in *ProtJac* 17:09 and 17:11, together with v. 17:01, are found in the text of the Journey of Mary and Joseph to the Cave of the Nativity in *ProtJac* 17:01-18:01. Redactional activity is strongly indicated by the collective presence of all these complicating elements within a limited section of the text, *ProtJac* 16:07-18:01, which extends over and includes several seams that connect smaller literary units in the narrative. The first case of Mariamme in *ProtJac* 16:07 and the adjoining Aostos[131] reference in v. 17:01 occur at a strategic junction between two major components of the CEGM, the Trial narrative and the Nativity Complex. The second and third incidences of Mariamme in *ProtJac* 17:09 and 17:11 are found respectively in each of two redactional subdivisions of the Journey story.

---

129. See above, pp. 15-19.

130. It is highly significant for the redactional analysis of the *ProtJac* that the three occurrences of Mariamme are found only in the text of P.Bodm V. Mary's name is written normally as Μαρία or Μαριάμ in all the other Greek MSS; cf. p. 85 below.

131. The idiosyncratic spelling of the name of king Ναόστου in P.Bodm V caused considerable consternation among the later copyists of the *ProtJac* who felt compelled to correct this name to conform to the Καίσαρος Αὐγούστου in Lk. 2:1. See the discussion below on pp. 86-7.

The Journey of Mary and Joseph to the Cave of the Nativity, the Midwife story, and the Birth story all occur within the framework of a scenario in which a king Aostos has called for a registration of the residents of Bethlehem in *ProtJac* 17:01: κελευσις δε εγενετο απο του αοστου του βασιλεως απογραψασθαι οσοι εισιν εν βηθλεεμ της ιουδαιας ("there was a call from Aostos the king for all who are in Bethlehem of Judea to be registered"). A researcher is faced here with a strong temptation to assume that the census motif and the journey to Bethlehem in the *ProtJac* Nativity Complex derive from the parallel Nativity story in Lk. 2:1-7. And most scholars have readily adopted that assumption, largely under the influence of the long-standing perception that the "canonical" Gospel traditions generally are more authoritative and historically trustworthy than those of the "non-canonical" documents, most of which are deemed to be secondary to, and largely dependent upon, their canonical prototypes.[132] That perception may hold true for many of the "apocryphal" New Testament writings, but not for the *ProtJac*.

Our extensive redaction-critical examination of the text of the *ProtJac* up to this point has revealed three individuals at work in the production of this document. Only the Redactor, who was the last of the three chronologically, has consistently exhibited knowledge of the canonical Gospels. On the contrary, the narratives of the earlier writers, the Author of the *GenMar* and the Composer, show no direct influence from the canonicals and regularly contradict elements that are contained within their canonical parallels. Apart from the Redactor's obvious interpolations of canonical texts, the stories in the CEGM could have been composed on the basis of traditions circulating among the early followers of Jesus, as was the case also with the canonical writings. The results of our investigation into the composition of the *ProtJac* thus far mandate that we continue to apply the same critical methodology in our analysis of the Nativity Complex as well.

With respect to the occurrence of the registration, or census, motif as the backdrop of the Nativity stories in both *ProtJac* 17:01–22:02 and Lk. 2:1-7, rather than dismiss the *ProtJac* text outright as being secondary to, and necessarily dependent upon, Luke we should first make note of the problems associated with Luke's Nativity story that raise doubts regarding its authenticity. The Nativity story occurs in the first two chapters of Luke whose existence as an original part of the earliest form of the Gospel is seriously disputed. According to the Proto-Luke hypothesis the Gospel of Luke originally began in what is now Lk. 3:1; Lk. 1–2 were added in the second century within the context of the polemics between "orthodox" and Marcionite Christianity. The Proto-Luke hypothesis will form an essential part of our final assessment of the *Sitze im Leben* of the individual authors of the disparate materials now contained in the *ProtJac*, especially that of the Redactor.[133]

132. See the discussion regarding scholars expressing these opinions with respect to the *ProtJac* in "Appendix 3: The *ProtJac* and the New Testament Gospels," pp. 198–204.

133. See the discussion regarding the Redactor's usage of Luke's problematic Nativity materials vis-à-vis the *ProtJac* in "The Redactor: *The Protevangelium Jacobi*," pp. 131–47. Cf. Joseph B. Tyson in *Marcion and Luke-Acts: A Defining Struggle* (Columbia: University of South Carolina Press, 2006), 90–100.

The legitimacy of Luke's Nativity story is further compromised by its position within the larger setting of the Synoptic Problem, a major issue in New Testament scholarship concerning the literary relationship between the Synoptic Gospels Matthew, Mark, and Luke. Most scholars identify Mark as the earliest of the three Synoptics and the source upon which both Matthew and Luke based their Gospels. Since Mark begins with the Baptism of Jesus as an adult, Matthew felt compelled to preface his Gospel with two opening chapters of information about Jesus's origins, including the Nativity story.[134] Luke also begins with two chapters of background information on Jesus including his own Nativity story; these are the disputed chapters mentioned above. But a comparison of Matthew's original story with the secondary version in Luke reveals substantial variance between the two accounts.[135] The Nativity stories in Matthew and Luke seem to be based upon a common set of preexisting oral traditions but differ so fundamentally in their distinctive materials that they constitute two independent narratives. The same could be said as well of the Nativity story in the CEGM.

But in addition to its dubious legitimacy within the disputed matrix of Lk. 1–2 and its inferiority in comparison to the parallel account in Matthew, Luke's Nativity story has its own internal difficulties. Most scholars view as unhistorical the depiction in Lk. 2:1 of a universal census of "all the world," that is, of the entire Roman Empire, in the time of Augustus: Ἐγένετο δὲ ἐν ταῖς ἡμέραις ἐκείναις ἐξῆλθεν δόγμα παρὰ Καίσαρος Αὐγούστου ἀπογράφεσθαι πᾶσαν τὴν οἰκουμένην ("and it happened in those days an order came out from Caesar Augustus for all the world to be registered"). Additionally, the identification in Lk. 2:2 of this imaginary universal census as the actual historical census of the province of Syria under Quirinius in 6 CE has also been dismissed: αὕτη ἀπογραφὴ πρώτη ἐγένετο ἡγεμονεύοντος τῆς Συρίας Κυρηνίου ("this was the first registration with Quirinius ruling Syria"). The reference to the existence of a census by Quirinius in Lk. 2:2 was accurate but that census had no association with the birth of Jesus of Nazareth.

The problems in Lk. 2:1-2, appropriately described as "the still vexed question of the census under Quirinius"[136] have been widely debated by scholars for centuries

---

134. It must be noted that there is no mention of the birth of Jesus in the earliest strata of Christian writings, i.e., Paul, Q, Mark, and whatever earlier elements are preserved in later documents such as the Gospels of John and Thomas, all of which may be dated before Matthew. Thus Matthew has been considered to be the first to record the Nativity traditions of Jesus. However, the present study makes it clear that that distinction actually belongs to the *GenMar*.

135. Matthew contains the visit of the Magi to the infant Jesus, Herod's massacre of the Bethlehem infants, and the flight of Joseph, Mary, and Jesus to Egypt and their subsequent return to Nazareth. Luke has extensive materials on the Annunciation and birth of John the Baptist, Mary's visit to Elizabeth, angels and shepherds observing Jesus's birth, the circumcision and presentation of Jesus in the temple, and the story of the twelve-year-old Jesus in the temple. Cf. also n. 154 below.

136. C. F. Evans, "Tertullian's References to Sentius Saturninus and the Lukan Census," *JTS*, new series, 24 (1973), 24–39.

and need not be deliberated here. These issues will be discussed within the context of the supposed connection between Luke's census and the one occurring in *ProtJac* 17. The five major arguments against Luke's version are summarized in Emil Shürer's classic work *The History of the Jewish People in the Age of Jesus Christ*:[137]

1. "History does not otherwise record a general imperial census in the time of Augustus."
2. "Under a Roman census, Joseph would not have been obliged to travel to Bethlehem, and Mary would not have been required to accompany him there."
3. "A Roman census could not have been carried out in Palestine during the time of king Herod."
4. "Josephus knows nothing of a Roman census in Palestine during the reign of Herod; he refers rather to the census of A.D. 6/7 as something new and unprecedented."
5. "The census held under Quirinius could not have taken place in the time of Herod, for Quirinius was never governor of Syria during Herod's lifetime."

In contrast to Luke's universal, empire-wide census by order (δόγμα) of Caesar Augustus the *ProtJac* registration is limited to Bethlehem of Judea and came about as the result of a "call" (κελευσις) from a certain "king Aostos" (απο του αοστου του βασιλεως).[138]

It is exceedingly difficult to reconcile the localized registration in Bethlehem in *ProtJac* 17:01 with the universal census described in Lk. 2:1-2 and I am not aware of any attempt to do so in the scholarly literature. The account in the *ProtJac* is inevitably subordinated to Luke and regarded as being dependent upon the assumedly superior canonical version. But Luke's story hardly constitutes an authoritative standard against which the Birth story of the *ProtJac* should be judged, especially in view of the questionable standing of the Lukan story in general vis-à-vis (1) the disputed status of Lk. 1–2 within the Gospel as a whole, (2) its inferiority in comparison to Matthew's parallel account, and (3) its own internal historical inaccuracies as regards a universal registration under Augustus and the timing of the Quirinian census.[139] Given the repudiation of a universal census and the disassociation of Quirinius's census from Jesus's birth, the possibility should not be excluded without reservation that a limited local census may have occurred in the area of Judea around the time of the birth of Jesus.

Scholars who have engaged in exhaustive studies of demographics in the Roman Empire note that the plentiful papyrus records found in Egypt document the use

---

137. Schürer presents the classical argumentation on this matter in his *The History of the Jewish People in the Age of Jesus Christ*, ed. and rev. by Géza Vermès, Fergus Millar, Matthew Black, vol. I (Edinburgh: T. & T. Clark, 1973), 399–427; for an excellent recent treatment cf. Edward Dąbrowa, "The Date of the Census of Quirinius and the Chronology of the Governors of the Province of Syria," *ZPE* 178 (2011), 137–42.

138. Corrected from τουναοστουτου βασιλεως in P.Bodm V.

139. See the preceding discussion.

of censuses as a regular process of the Roman fiscal system in that province.[140] But the absence of primary documentary evidence from the other provinces of the empire does not exclude the systematic execution of censuses as part of the standard operating procedure of the fiscal system in every province.[141] The Romans characteristically are considered to have been meticulous archivists who kept exhaustive records of their administrative transactions mostly on the standard writing material of the time which was made from the organic papyrus plant. Given that ancient papyrus documents have survived almost exclusively in Egypt due to the extreme dryness of its climate,[142] the absence of original documentation of censuses in the other provinces of the empire should not be attributed to their not having occurred. These documents were lost because the organic papyrus material upon which they were written deteriorated over time due to the humidity in the atmosphere of the geographic regions in which they were housed.

It happens that the census of Quirinius in 6 CE is particularly well documented, not only in Luke and Josephus[143] but also in an inscription according to which the *censitor* Q. Aemilius Secundus at the behest of his administrative superior P. Sulpicius Quirinius—our Quirinius—conducted a local census in Apamea, another city in the province of Syria.[144] This limited census in Apamea was directed by a local official as part of the larger census of the entire Province of Syria that was attributed correctly by Luke to Quirinius in 6 CE. Also encompassed within this Syrian census was the formerly semi-independent client state of Judea, which had been joined administratively to the Province of Syria. This had occurred in 6 CE when Augustus deposed the Judean king Herod Archelaus and converted Judea into a Roman Prefecture. Judea would be governed henceforth by a Roman prefect, the first of whom was Coponius.[145]

The unusually well-documented case of the Syrian census of Quirinius attests that details of the census practices in the Roman Empire emerge rarely

140. Cf. Roger S. Bagnall and Bruce W. Frier, *The Demography of Roman Egypt* (Cambridge: Cambridge University Press, 2006); Claude Nicolet, *Space, Geography, and Politics in the Early Roman Empire* (Ann Arbor: University of Michigan Press, 1991).

141. Nicolet, *Space,* 136. Cf. David Kennedy in "Demography, the Population of Syria and the Census of Q. Aemilius Secundus," *Levant* 38 (2006), 109–24, "the almost total absence of documentation from virtually every province is not because the census was not regular outside Egypt. Rather, the nature of the fiscal system everywhere, despite variation in detail, necessitated a register of property and people and would require constant updating. In short, there is every reason to suppose that censuses were a regular feature of life in every province and that that is supported by occasional anecdotal evidence and career inscription references to censitors."

142. The survival of the Dead Sea Scrolls likewise is due to the dry climate of that geographical area in Israel. Ancient papyrus documents also were preserved in Pompeii in a very fragile and brittle state, having been carbonized during the eruption of Mount Vesuvius in 79 CE.

143. The census of Quirinius is mentioned by Josephus in *A.J.* 17.13.355, 18.1.1-6.

144. Kennedy, "Demography," 113–15.

145. Josephus *A.J.*, 18.1.1-2.

and erratically but also demonstrates that such practices were more regular, systematic, and extensive than the paucity of the evidence suggests. Another instance of evidence that came to light by accident was the discovery among the Dead Sea Scrolls of an archive of papyrus documents dating to the early part of the second century CE that belonged to Babatha, a Jewish woman who originally resided in Arabia but had relocated to Judea and died during the Bar Kochba revolt.[146] Babatha's papyri contain references to a census conducted in Arabia in 127 CE and illustrate how census documents were written.[147] The connection of the Quirinian census to the birth of Jesus has been rejected. But the example of the very extraordinariness of the discoveries of the Secundus inscription and of the Babatha archive justifies the *argumentum ex silentio* that the census mentioned in *ProtJac* 17:01 may preserve an echo of a local census involving the area of Judea that may have occurred around the time of the Nativity but of which no historical traces have survived.

The prospect of an author of a New Testament Gospel committing an error in dating the historical census of Quirinius to the time of Jesus's birth has so "vexed" traditional sensibilities that for centuries conservative scholars have expended considerable efforts in attempts to justify this error and thus to rehabilitate Luke's tarnished image of infallibility.[148] It is beyond the scope of this study to review the

---

146. Babatha's documents were published in Naphtali Lewis, Yigael Yadin, and Jonas C. Greenfield, *Ḥevrah la-ḥakirat Erets-Yiśra'el ve-'atiḳoteha* (*The Documents from the Bar Kokhba Period in the Cave of Letters*), Judean Desert Studies Series (Jerusalem: Israel Exploration Society, 1989).

147. Babatha's papers also illuminate the process by which new provinces were added to the Roman Empire. Arabia had become a province officially in 106 CE but its first census only occurred in 127 CE. In comparison it seems that the Syrian-Judean census of 6 CE occurred shortly after the attachment of Judea to the province of Syria. Cf. H. M. Cotton, "Ἡ νέα ἐπαρχεία 'Αραία: The New Province of Arabia in the Papyri from the Judaean Desert," *ZPE* 116 (1997), 206–8. Cotton has published an entire series of articles in *ZPE* related to the Babatha Archive.

148. Daniel R. Schwartz, "On Quirinius, John the Baptist, the Benedictus, Melchizedek, Qumran and Ephesus," *RevQ* 13 (1988), 635, "There has been no dearth of scholarly ingenuity applied to saving Luke's chronology, usually either in attempts to show a Roman census under Herod could be plausible or to translate Luke 2, 2 in such a way as to avoid the difficulty. Nevertheless, it seems fair to say that the scholarly consensus today [1988], shared even by many conservative Christian scholars, is that Luke is wrong," cf. conservative Bible scholar Luke Timothy Johnson: "Luke's attempt at synchronism is not entirely successful, as endless technical discussions have made clear. Herod died in 4 B.C.E., and Augustus was emperor from 27 B.C.E. to 14 C.E. So far so good. But Quirinius was governor in Syria from 6-7 C.E., and the gap can't be filled. Luke simply has the facts wrong," *The Gospel of Luke* (Collegeville, MI: Liturgical Press, 1991), 49. With respect to the dangers in earlier times of questioning the inerrancy of scripture, Stephen C. Carlson described an interesting account of the Renaissance

great variety of inventive approaches employed by these scholars toward this end.[149] In any case they have failed to achieve their principal objective of confirming Luke's designation of Quirinius's census as that which took place when Jesus was born. However, an unintended consequence of their labors was to marshal significant evidence, albeit largely circumstantial, that supports the possible existence of local registrations, unrelated to that of Quirinius, which included Judea around the time of Jesus's birth. And in so doing they have provided significant support for the registration described in the *ProtJac*.

One of the most successful of these approaches maintains the likelihood that Herod the Great, as the Roman client king of Judea, would have conducted his own censuses modeled after those of the Roman administration for taxation purposes. Brook W. R. Pearson carefully lays out a strong case for the "possibility that there was indeed a Roman-style process of census or taxation in Herod's kingdom."[150] Basing his argument on the abundant information on Herod's rule in the works of Josephus, Pearson asserts that to understand Josephus's witness to Herod necessitates the assumption of the existence of a Herodian census: "Josephus records a great deal of indirect evidence that a careful and detailed system of census and taxation existed under Herod."[151] Much of this evidence occurs in Josephus's description of the official documents presented to Augustus in the aftermath of Herod's death in 5/4 BCE, including Herod's will and accounts of Herod's money as well as the financial accounts and annual revenue of the kingdom found by Caesar's Legate Sabinus in the royal precincts in Jerusalem.[152] Pearson appropriately considers this to be strong evidence that Herod kept careful and accurate records of taxation and enrollment.[153]

---

scholar Francisco Sánchez de las Brozas having been reported by his students to the Inquisition for questioning whether Jesus was born in a stable or in a private home, "The Accommodations of Joseph and Mary in Bethlehem: Κατάλυμα in Luke 2.7," *NTS* 56 (2010), 326–8.

149. For a helpful catalog of approaches to this problem that focus on Luke's text, see Stanley Porter, "The Reasons for the Lukan Census," in *Paul, Luke and the Graeco-Roman World: Essays in Honour of Alexander J. M. Wedderburn*, eds. A. J. M. Wedderburn and Alf Christophersen (London/New York: Sheffield Academic Press, 2002), 165–88.

150. "The Lucan Censuses, Revisited," *CBQ* 61 (1999), 264.

151. Ibid., 265.

152. Josephus *A.J.* 17.9.221-223, 228-229. Josephus states in *A.J.* 17.9.222 that Σαβῖνος ἐπὶ Ἱεροσολύμων χωρήσας παραλαμβάνει τὰ βασίλεια ("Sabinus went to Jerusalem and took control of the royal precincts").

153. "Lucan Censuses," 266, n. 12, "This is strong evidence that the records of taxation and enrollment kept by Herod's administration were careful and accurate, since a 'foreign' administration was able to make use of them almost immediately after taking possession of the kingdom. It must also be remembered that after Herod's death, Sabinus, the Syrian legate, came to the area to take possession of what was Caesar's property—which amounted to the entire estate of Herod the Great (A.J. 17.9.3 §§221–23)! Keeping accurate records for Caesar must, then, have been part of Herod's duties as king."

Pearson's study reveals the possible existence of local Judean registrations as described in *ProtJac* 17:01 that may have occurred toward the end of the reign of Herod around the time of the birth of Jesus of Nazareth. This corroborates our understanding of the *GenMar* as an authentic early Christian interpretation of the origin and nature of Mary's divine child that was independent of the canonical Gospel traditions. Pearson's evidence also validates our observation that the *ProtJac* census story was presumed too readily in the past to have been an expansion of the Lukan prototype. Both *ProtJac* 17 and Lk. 1–2 include the generic themes of an official call for a census and a journey to Bethlehem. These most likely originated within a preexisting set of oral traditions relating to the Nativity that were in circulation among some of the earliest communities of the Jesus movement.[154] But apart from these fundamental themes the two stories diverge significantly in such essential elements as the point of origin of the journey and the location of the Nativity itself.

The Journey to Bethlehem

In Lk. 2:4 Joseph and Mary leave from Nazareth in the Galilee and travel to Bethlehem in Judea where Jesus is born in Lk. 2:6-7.[155] In *ProtJac* 17 it is not stated where their journey begins, but Joseph and Mary appear to reside in Jerusalem as implied by their proximity to the temple in the Trial story in *ProtJac* 15. We must assume therefore that they depart from Jerusalem on their short journey of about six miles to the nearby town of Bethlehem. Following the announcement of the registration in *ProtJac* 17:01, Joseph engages in an internal dialogue in 17:02-04 considering how to register his family.[156] He will register his sons (εγω απογραψομαι τους υιους μου) but wonders what to do about Mary: ταυτην δε την παιδα τι ποιησω; ("what will I do with this maiden?"). He questions whether he

---

154. Matthew's Nativity story differs significantly from that of Luke and the *ProtJac*, containing neither a census nor a journey to Bethlehem. Jesus appears to have been born in Bethlehem, ostensibly in Joseph's house (οἰκίαν) where he was found by the Magi according to Mt. 2:11. After their flight to Egypt in Mt. 2:14 and the death of Herod the Great in 2:19, Joseph and Mary with the infant Jesus returned to the land of Israel in 2:21. They did not remain in Bethlehem in Joseph's home for fear of Herod Archelaus but finally settled in Nazareth in Mt. 2:23.

155. Lk. 2:4: Ἀνέβη δὲ καὶ Ἰωσὴφ ἀπὸ τῆς Γαλιλαίας ἐκ πόλεως Ναζαρὲθ εἰς τὴν Ἰουδαίαν εἰς πόλιν Δαυὶδ ἥτις καλεῖται Βηθλέεμ; Lk. 2:6-7: ἐγένετο δὲ ἐν τῷ εἶναι αὐτοὺς ἐκεῖ … ἔτεκεν τὸν υἱὸν αὐτῆς τὸν πρωτότοκον. Luke emphasizes Joseph's Davidic descent in v. 2:4 by specifying that Bethlehem is the "city of David" (πόλιν Δαυὶδ) after having affirmed in the preceding v. 2:3 that the travelers would be registered "each one to his own city" (καὶ ἐπορεύοντο πάντες ἀπογράφεσθαι, ἕκαστος εἰς τὴν ἑαυτοῦ πόλιν). Thus Joseph traveled to "his own city," the "city of David," to be registered.

156. In his internal dialogue in *ProtJac* 14:04 Joseph does not leave it up to the Lord. Both internal dialogues begin with και ειπεν Ιωσηφ and both introduce possible interpolations.

should register her as his wife: πως αυτην απογραψομαι; γυναικα εμην; ("how shall I register her? As my wife?") but is embarrassed to do so (επαισχυνομαι). He also decides against registering Mary as his daughter (αλλα θυγατερα;) because the sons of Israel know that she is not his daughter. In ProtJac 17:04 he finally leaves it up to the Lord to decide (αυτη η ημερα κυριου ποιησει ως βουλεται).

The journey toward Bethlehem ensues in ProtJac 17:05–18:02 with Mary sitting on a donkey that is being led by one of Joseph's sons. The journey itself is divided into two separate scenes, the first of which occurs in ProtJac 17:05-10 as they near "the third mile" (ενηγγισεν επι μιλιον τριτον).[157] The second scene follows in ProtJac 17:11–18:02 as they come to the "middle of the way" (αναμεσον της οδου). In the first scene Joseph turns to look at Mary twice. At first she appears sad, prompting Joseph to think that the child is causing her distress. He turns again and sees her laughing. He asks Mary[158] why he sees her face sometimes sad and sometimes laughing. She responds that she sees two nations with her eyes, one crying and mourning, and the other being happy and rejoicing. In the second scene Mary[159] asks Joseph to take her down from the donkey because the child is pressuring her to come out. Joseph takes her down and settles her in a cave there to cover her "nakedness" (ἀσχημοσύνη).[160]

Before addressing the substantial redactional activity in the following Midwife episode and the Birth story, we will present the remaining evidence of redaction in the text of the Journey narrative, which serves as a transition from the Trial to the Nativity. The Journey story, which begins with the announcement of the registration in ProtJac 17:01, consists of three segments: the inner dialogue of Joseph in 17:02-04, the first part of the journey proper from 17:05-10 up to "the third mile," and the second part in the "middle of the way" in 17:11–18:02, which ends with Mary situated in the cave and Joseph departing to find a Hebrew midwife in nearby Bethlehem. Both of the scenes in the Journey proper are introduced, respectively, by geographical references that are not completely compatible with each other. Each of the scenes also contains an incidence of Mary's name written as Mariamme. The incompatible geographical details in ProtJac 17:06 and 17:11, when viewed collectively with the canonical reference to Augustus as Aostos in ProtJac 17:01 and the occurrences of the distinctive name Mariamme in ProtJac 16:07, 17:09, and 17:11, constitute significant evidence of redactional activity in the Journey story and provide valuable clues to its composition.

The incongruence between the geographical details in ProtJac 17:06 and 17:11 suggests that the scenes they introduce in the narrative, ProtJac 17:06-10 and

---

157. The term μιλιον represents the Roman mile.

158. This is the second of the three occurrences of the spelling of Mary's name as Mariamme in the ProtJac. See above, pp. 75-7.

159. This is the third and final occurrence of the form Mariamme in the P.Bodm V text of the ProtJac.

160. The Hebrew עֶרְוָה "nakedness," shameful or indecent exposure, is regularly rendered in the LXX by the Greek word ἀσχημοσύνη, cf. Exod. 20:26; Lev. 18:6-18.

17:11-18:02, respectively, are two originally distinct elements that were joined together at some point to form the Journey proper. Given the redactional process that has occurred in the construction of previous sections of the *ProtJac* text, we would be justified in suspecting that one of the two scenes in the Journey may have preexisted as an original part of the text of the CEGM, while the other was introduced into the text subsequently by the Redactor. The first scene is immediately suspect as a later insertion because it interrupts the storyline of the narrative from *ProtJac* 17:05—where Joseph saddled the donkey, sat Mary upon it, and began the journey—to 17:11 when they arrived "in the middle of the road" where Mary felt the pressure of her impending delivery of her child and asked Joseph to take her down from the donkey. This original storyline continues in *ProtJac* 17:12-18:02 in which Joseph takes Mary down from the donkey, places her in the cave with his sons, and leaves to find a midwife.

When the first scene is excised from the text, the remaining narrative, which previously was our second scene, constitutes a coherent, self-contained story. We may now consider this second scene to have been part of the original CEGM story of the Journey. Our former first scene, which by redaction-critical methodology has been exposed as an intrusion into the original story, displays characteristics that have been associated with the Redactor. This realization allows a new perspective on the conflicting geographical details in *ProtJac* 17:06 and 17:09. The "middle of the way" in the original CEGM story now, without the Redactor's interpolation, is understandable as being halfway between the destination of the journey, Bethlehem, and the point of origin in the original story, which was Jerusalem. But the question arises: why would the Redactor qualify the original location halfway between Jerusalem and Bethlehem in his source by inserting before it his own scene in *ProtJac* 17:06-10 that takes place specifically at "the third mile" before Bethlehem?

We will explore below several potential motives that may have led the Redactor to modify the original Journey narrative in the CEGM. These motives may be clarified by factors related to the archaeological and topographical setting of the road between Jerusalem and Bethlehem. But before examining the remarkable new archaeological evidence[161] that may illuminate the Redactor's motivation for his interpolation of Mary's vision of the two nations in *ProtJac* 17:06-10, we will complete our examination of the evidence of redaction in the Journey story. Having established that the scene in *ProtJac* 17:06-10 is most likely another characteristic interpolation by the Redactor, we find that the preceding verses as well bear marks of his work. We may now further extend the Redactor's editorial work earlier in the Journey story to include the Aostos reference in *ProtJac* 17:01 and Joseph's internal dialogue in 17:02-04.

The puzzling reading τουναοστουτου βασιλεως in P.Bodm V has been emended readily by the later scribes who copied the *ProtJac* and by modern

---

161. This evidence will be examined in more detail in "Appendix 4: The Kathisma Church," pp. 205–20.

scholars to conform to the correctly spelled Lukan version of Καίσαρος Αὐγούστου. De Strycker cited examples of similar variations of the name of Augustus among the Greek papyri found in Egypt, such as Ἄουστος, Ἄγουστος, and Ἄγοστος.¹⁶² The authenticity of the P.Bodm V text is supported by the confusion that it caused among the later manuscript copies of the ProtJac. Many of these preserve the reading βασιλεως ("king") as Αὐγούστου βασιλέως ("Augustus the king") from P.Bodm V, while others retained the word order in the papyrus as Αὐγούστου Καίσαρος; both of these readings are in contrast to the Καίσαρος Αὐγούστου of Luke. In view of the redactional activity that has been detected in ProtJac 17, Aostos, or Naostos, may be a corruption by the Redactor of the name of a local king in the original text, under the influence of canonical Luke.¹⁶³ It would be reasonable to assume that to be the case since it is difficult to imagine any literate person in the Roman world of the second century CE not knowing Augustus.

An element in the ensuing internal dialogue of Joseph in ProtJac 17:02-04 that points to the influence of the Redactor is the reference to Mary as την παιδα ("the maiden") in 17:02. The same words were also used to describe Mary by the angel who appeared to Joseph in his dream vision in the Trial story in ProtJac 14:06 and 14:08. This dream vision was identified also as being an interpolation by the Redactor into the CEGM.¹⁶⁴ Joseph asks himself in ProtJac 17:02 regarding how to register Mary for the census: ταυτην δε την παιδα τι ποιησω; ("what will I do with this maiden?"). This is reminiscent of the scenario in ProtJac 14:02-04 in which Joseph is engaged in a similar internal dialogue after returning home and finding Mary pregnant. In that scenario he is considering whether to hide Mary's pregnancy or expose her to public shame and in ProtJac 14:04 asks himself the same question as in 17:02: τι ουν αυτη ποιησω; ("what will I do with her?").

The obvious similarities in these two parallel scenarios may reveal the Redactor's modus operandi in implementing his larger interpolations. In both cases the Redactor prefixes one of his interpolated texts with an internal dialogue by Joseph. The dialogue in ProtJac 14:01-04, regarding what he should do about the pregnant Mary, introduces the insertion of the Matthean angelic dream vision in ProtJac 14:05-08. In ProtJac 17:02-04 Joseph's internal dialogue regarding how he will register Mary in the census is followed by the interpolation of Mary's vision of the two nations in the Journey to Bethlehem. All these considerations, both internal and external, lend support to the conclusion that the first scene of the Journey to Bethlehem in ProtJac 17:06-10 at "the third Mile" in fact represents another case of an interpolation by the Redactor into the CEGM. The Redactor adjusted the name of the king to Aostos in the introductory verse ProtJac 17:01

162. La Forme, 309–10.
163. See the preceding discussion, pp. 77–84.
164. See the discussion of Joseph's dream vision on pp. 60-2 above which was taken from Mt. 1:20-4.

then inserted Joseph's internal dialogue followed by the story of Mary's vision of the two nations. The Redactor's possible motivations for doing so will be discussed below.

With the Redactor's secondary augmentations now removed from the text we can more clearly discern the original narrative of the CEGM. In *ProtJac* 17:01 an unknown local king, possibly Herod, called for a registration of the residents of a limited area, which included Judea and thus Bethlehem. In *ProtJac* 17:05 Joseph saddled a donkey and sat Mary upon it. One of Joseph's sons, probably James, led the donkey, and an unknown person named Samuel followed along. In *ProtJac* 17:11 at the "middle of the way" Mary felt her child pressing her to be born and asked Joseph to take her down from the donkey, which he did. Joseph found a cave there in which he left Mary with his sons and departed to seek a Hebrew midwife in the area around Bethlehem. It was in this cave that Mary's divine child would be born.

The Composer's story is readily distinguished from the Redactor's insertions both by its independence from any canonical influences and by the fact that it contains elements that directly contradict the Nativity stories of Matthew and Luke. Mary's child is not born in Bethlehem as in both of the canonical Gospels, and he is not born in a house as in Matthew.[165] The child is born in a cave in "the middle of the way" between Jerusalem and Bethlehem, three miles outside of Bethlehem. Mary is attended in the cave by Joseph's sons, one of whom is unnamed, but who is probably James. The plural "sons" (υἱοὺς) presupposes the existence of more than one son, and since the only other person present was the otherwise unknown Samuel, we may assume that this Samuel was also a son of Joseph. Apparently Joseph has only two sons in the original narrative, which contradicts the canonical version of Jesus's family in Mk 6:3, and its parallel in Mt. 13:55, in which four brothers of Jesus are named: James, Joses,[166] Judas, and Simon.[167] All of these elements collectively confirm that the original Journey story, at least partially preserved in *ProtJac* 17:01, 05, 11-12, and 18:01-02, was part of a narrative written by someone who had no knowledge of the canonical Gospel texts. The same may be said of the CEGM, and the *GenMar* itself, in their entirety.

---

165. Although Luke's version agrees with Matthew that Jesus was born in Bethlehem, Luke is vague as to the specific location of the Nativity. Lk. 2:7 states only that Mary put Jesus in a manger because there was no place for them in "the shelter" but gives no further information on what or where that shelter was: ἀνέκλινεν αὐτὸν ἐν φάτνῃ, διότι οὐκ ἦν αὐτοῖς τόπος ἐν τῷ καταλύματι.

166. In Matthew's version the second son is named Joseph instead of Joses.

167. In Mk 6:3 Jesus is identified by his neighbors in Nazareth as "the son of Mary" and the brother of James, Joses, Judas, and Simon. Mark does not mention a father for Jesus or for his brothers. In Mt. 13:55 the neighbors describe Jesus as "the carpenter's son" whose mother is "called Mary." Both texts contain the perceptions of Jesus's neighbors and are vague as to the actual parentage of the four "brothers" of Jesus.

Topographical and Archaeological Factors

Having presented the evidence of redaction in the *ProtJac* narrative of the Journey to the Cave, we may ask what may have motivated the Redactor to augment the original story in the CEGM with his own scene of Mary's vision at "the third mile" before Bethlehem. First, the Redactor may have been concerned about the lack of clarity in his sources regarding the point of origin of the journey. It is not clear in the Composer's document that Jerusalem was the location of Joseph's home and thus the point from which Joseph and Mary began their journey.[168] It is equally obscure in the Gospel of Matthew that Joseph's home was in Bethlehem, which would have precluded the need for a journey to the place of registration.[169] Thus the Redactor may have followed his only source that gave a precise point of origin of the journey, Nazareth, in Lk. 2:4.[170] And since it would have been nonsensical for Joseph and Mary to have stopped "in the middle of the way" on a seventy-mile journey from Nazareth to Bethlehem—and for the Nativity therefore to have taken place in the mountains of Samaria—the Redactor would have felt compelled to qualify the original stopping point in the CEGM story by specifying that it occurred much closer to Bethlehem, at "the third mile," that is, three miles from the town.

To follow that line of reasoning leads to another question: why would the Redactor, who has augmented his source document so liberally by inserting texts from Matthew and Luke, have allowed in this case the all-important Nativity to occur outside of Bethlehem in contrast to both Matthew and Luke, who present Jesus's birth as occurring in Bethlehem? Insights regarding this question may be derived from the events that transpired at the Redactor's three-mile scene in *ProtJac* 17:05-10. Joseph turns to Mary twice and observes her first being sad and then as laughing. He asks her why she appears alternately sad and laughing to which she responds that she sees "two nations," one "crying" and "mourning," and the other "being happy" and "rejoicing." The verbiage in this dialogue between Mary and Joseph suggests that the Redactor may have intended to modify the original "middle of the way" scene in order to associate it with an archaeological site nearby that represents an important and well-known Old Testament tradition, the Tomb of Rachel.

By placing his "third mile" scene before the "middle of the way" the Redactor actually established "the third mile" as a new reference point in the journey where Mary had her vision of the two nations. In the Redactor's new scenario, the journey continued from "the third mile" and reached its conclusion at the "middle of the way" where the Nativity took place. The Redactor's "third mile" became a point from which the distance could be recalculated to the "middle of the way," which originally represented the actual stopping point of the entire journey at

---

168. See above, p. 84.

169. ibid., n. 154.

170. Ἀνέβη δὲ καὶ Ἰωσὴφ ἀπὸ τῆς Γαλιλαίας ἐκ πόλεως Ναζαρὲθ εἰς τὴν Ἰουδαίαν εἰς πόλιν Δαυὶδ ἥτις καλεῖται Βηθλέεμ.

the Cave of the Nativity in the CEGM. The "middle of the way" is no longer halfway between Jerusalem and Bethlehem, but halfway between "the third mile" and Bethlehem, and thus in closer proximity to Bethlehem. The Redactor's new location for the Nativity was one-and-a-half miles outside of Bethlehem and thus nearer, first to the canonical location of Jesus's birth in Bethlehem and second to one of the most revered shrines of ancient Israel, the tomb of Rachel, which was on the northern outskirts of Bethlehem on the road to Jerusalem. An ancient tradition recorded in the book of Genesis[171] states that Rachel died in childbirth and was buried at the location of this tomb as she and Jacob traveled toward Bethlehem. She died giving birth to Benjamin who was Jacob's twelfth son and his second by Rachel.

The text of Gen. 35:16-20 may further illuminate the Redactor's possible motivation for associating the location of the *ProtJac* Nativity more closely with the tomb of Rachel:

Gen. 35:16 Then they [Jacob and Rachel] journeyed from Bethel.
And when there was but a little distance to go to Ephrath,
Rachel labored in childbirth, and she had hard labor.
17 Now it came to pass, when she was in hard labor that the midwife said to her,
"Do not fear; you will have this son also."
18 And so it was, as her soul was departing (for she died),
that she called his name Ben-Oni; but his father called him Benjamin.
19 So Rachel died and was buried on the way to Ephrath (that is, Bethlehem).
20 And Jacob set a pillar on her grave,
which is the pillar of Rachel's grave to this day.[172]

The shrine of Rachel's tomb was well known among the local Judeans before the advent of Christianity and would have been familiar to the earliest followers of Jesus. By associating his augmented Journey story with Rachel's tomb, the Redactor may have intended to highlight the noteworthy parallels between *ProtJac* 17:06-10 and Gen. 35:16-20. Particularly relevant are the "hard labor" that Rachel suffered and the name of her child that she uttered as she died. Ben-Oni, literally "son of my sorrow," speaks to *ProtJac* 17:06b-07 in which Joseph first turned to Mary and observed her sadness and thought that the child in her was causing her distress (και εστραφη ιωσηφ, και ειδεν αυτην στυγνην, και ελεγεν ισως το εν αυτη χειμαζει αυτην). The parallel with Rachel also extends to Mary's vision of two nations in *ProtJac* 17:6-10. According to the Jewish tradition recorded in Gen. 25:19-26, Rachel's husband Jacob was one of two twins who struggled with each other in the womb of their mother, the matriarch Rebekah. Rebekah prayed to God about her

---

171. Gen. 35:16-20. The story of Rachel's death follows immediately after a passage of central importance in the Bible, Gen. 35:9-15, in which God appears to Jacob in Bethel, changes his name to Israel, and renews his former promises to Abraham of multitudes of descendants of kings and mighty nations who will possess the land of Israel.

172. NKJV translation.

difficult pregnancy. The similarities between God's response to Rebekah's prayer and Mary's response to Joseph's inquiry about her facial expressions are notable:

Gen. 25:23—God's response to Rebekah's prayer:
"Two nations are in your womb.
Two peoples shall be separated from your body;
one people shall be stronger than the other,
And the older shall serve the younger."[173]
ProtJac 17:10—Mary's response to Joseph's inquiry:
"I see two nations with my eyes,
one crying and mourning,
and the other being happy and rejoicing."

But the Redactor also may have intended to draw a significant parallel with a text in the canonical Gospel of Matthew, which he must have borne in mind as he would soon interpolate elements from the Magi story of Matthew into the CEGM.[174] The Redactor will interpolate Mt. 2:12 and 2:16 almost verbatim into ProtJac 21:15–22:01. These verses relate the anger of Herod when he realized that the Magi would not return to report to him on the whereabouts of the newly born king of the Jews. Herod would order the slaughter of the children in Bethlehem aged two years and less. But the Redactor will not include the succeeding verses, Mt. 2:17-18, in his own version of Matthew's Magi story. Mt. 2:17 introduces the prophecy in Jer. 31:15 whose LXX version is quoted in Mt. 2:18: "A voice was heard in Rama, weeping, and much mourning, Rachel crying for her children, and she did not want to be comforted, because they are not" (Φωνὴ ἐν Ῥαμὰ ἠκούσθη, κλαυθμὸς καὶ ὀδυρμὸς πολύς· Ῥαχὴλ κλαίουσα τὰ τέκνα αὐτῆς, καὶ οὐκ ἤθελεν παρακληθῆναι ὅτι οὐκ εἰσίν). The Redactor may have not deemed it necessary to include Jeremiah's prophecy in his own Magi story later in the ProtJac because he had already associated Rachel's mourning with Mary's sadness in the scene he had inserted earlier into the Journey story in ProtJac 17:06b-07.

The connection between the redacted ProtJac Journey story, Rachel's tomb, and the original location of the Cave of the Nativity in the "middle of the way" between Jerusalem and Bethlehem will be further illuminated by a fortuitous archaeological discovery in 1992. A construction crew unearthed previously unknown ancient ruins on the road from Jerusalem to Bethlehem midway between the two cities. Subsequent archeological excavations from 1993 to 2000 uncovered and identified these ruins as the foundation of an ancient church known as the Kathisma ("seat"), which was built in the fifth century on the site where later tradition held that Mary rested on her journey toward Bethlehem. The location of the Kathisma church was lost after the expulsion of the Crusaders from Palestine in the twelfth century, but its existence was well known during the Byzantine era and in pilgrim accounts in

---

173. NKJV translation.
174. See the discussion below, pp. 113–22.

the Middle Ages. We will address the significant issue of the Kathisma church and its implications for the Nativity Story in the *ProtJac* and its source documents in Appendix 4 below.[175]

The Midwife[176]

Beginning with *ProtJac* 18:02, significant factors emerge that enhance our ability to distinguish the original elements of the text of the Composer from those that seem to represent the modifications of the Redactor. The Redactor's continued egregious revision of his source document is now cast into high relief by the appearance of major disagreements in the Greek manuscript tradition in *ProtJac* 18-21. In these chapters, many of the later MSS of the *ProtJac* contain a lengthier text that includes materials that do not occur in P.Bodm V.[177] These deviations in the manuscript tradition ultimately will facilitate our understanding of this problematic section of the *ProtJac*. The following analysis of the redactional evidence in the Nativity story proper, which includes the Midwife story and the Birth story in *ProtJac* 18:01-20:11, will take into account the entire Greek manuscript tradition of the *ProtJac* including both P.Bodm V and the later MSS.[178] The Midwife story contained in *ProtJac* 18:01-19:07 will be discussed first, followed by the treatment of the Birth story in *ProtJac* 19:08-22:02, which includes the Redactor's interpolated Doubting Salome and Matthean Magi stories. These major interpolations by the Redactor, together with the Zachariah Apocryphon, will bring to an end the Nativity Complex and the narrative of the *ProtJac* as a whole.

In *ProtJac* 18:01-02 the Journey of Joseph and Mary to Bethlehem has ended three miles outside of the town, where Joseph has left Mary in the cave with his

---

175. "Appendix 4: "The Kathisma Church," pp. 205-20.

176. The following section is a revision of my previous publication, "Christmas with Salome," in *A Feminist Companion to Mariology*, vol. 10, ed. A.-J. Levine (London; New York: T&T Clark/Continuum, 2005), 77-98. In the Midwife and Birth stories, the text of the CEGM is preserved in the MSS, while the Redactor's abbreviated version is preserved in P.Bodm V.

177. These include, according to the Tischendorf/de Strycker text enumeration: the "I, Joseph" passage in XVIII, 2; the extended dialogue between Joseph and the midwife in XIX, 1b; the two prayers of Salome in XX, 2 and 4a; and the extended dialogue between Herod and the Magi in XXI, 2b. These discrepancies do not continue into the Zachariah Apocryphon, which follows immediately from *ProtJac* 22:03-24:11. Testuz speaks about the discrepancies in terms of a shorter and a longer text without passing judgment on which may be more authentic, but de Strycker describes the papyrus, incorrectly, as a hasty and unintelligent abridgment of the text: "la rédaction du papyrus Bodmer est le résultat d'un abrégement hâtif et inintelligent." De Strycker, *La Forme*, 377-92, opines that the text contained in P.Bodm V represents an abridgment of what he considers to be the original *ProtJac* text as represented in the later MSS; cf. Smid, *Protevangelium*, 131.

178. The detailed textual evidence will be presented in Vol. 2 of this work.

sons and departs to seek a Hebrew midwife in the environs of Bethlehem. The text of the ensuing Midwife episode is brief in P.Bodm V, in contrast to many later MSS, which contain, first, a long monologue by Joseph—the "I, Joseph" passage— in *ProtJac* 18:03-12, and, second, a longer version of the dialogue between Joseph and the midwife. I believe that the longer version of the dialogue in *ProtJac* 19:01- 07 represents the original text in the CEGM, and the shorter version, according to P.Bodm V in *ProtJac* 19:01, 04, and 06-07, represents the Redactor's abridgment of the Composer's original text. Both versions of the text of the Midwife episode are presented below. The Composer's text, as preserved in later MSS of the *ProtJac*, will be presented first, followed by the Redactor's abridgment from P.Bodm V. *ProtJac* 18:01-02 will be prefixed to both versions below; these verses constitute the original transitional text between the Journey to the Cave and the Midwife episode, as preserved by both the Composer and the Redactor.

The original version of the Midwife episode according to the CEGM, as preserved in the later MSS in *ProtJac* 19:01-07:

ProtJac 18:01 και ευρεν εκει σπηλαιον και εισηγαγεν αυτην,
And he found a cave there and led her [Mary] in,
18:02 και παρεστησεν αυτην τους υιους αυτου,
και εξηλθεν ζητησαι μαιαν εβραιαν
εν χωρα βηθλεεμ.
and he placed her with his sons,
and he exited [the cave] to seek a Hebrew midwife
in the country of Bethlehem.[179]

19:01a και ιδου γυνη καταβαινουσα απο της ορεινης,
And behold, a woman descending from the hills,
19:01b και λεγει αυτω ανθρωπε που πορευη;
and she says to him, "Man, where are you going?"
19:02a και ειπεν μαιαν ζητω εβραιαν.
And he said, "I am seeking a Hebrew midwife."
19:02b και αποκριθεισα λεγει αυτω εξ ισραηλ ει;
And answering, she says to him, "Are you of Israel?"
19:03a ειπεν δε αυτη ναι.
And he said to her, "Yes."
19:03b η δε ειπεν και τις εστιν η γεννωσα εν τω σπηλαιω;
And she said, "And who is she who is giving birth in the cave?"
19:04a και ειπεν αυτη η μεμνηστευμενη μοι.
And he said to her, "My betrothed."

---

179. *ProtJac* 18:03-12, which contains the "I, Joseph" monologue in later MSS, is not included here. The MSS of the *ProtJac* are divided into three substantial groups with respect to their witness to the "I, Joseph" passage: those that, like P.Bodm V, do not contain the passage and those that preserve it in a first person and a third person form, respectively. This confusion among the Greek MSS of the *ProtJac* attests to the secondary nature of this passage.

19:04b και ειπεν αυτω ουκ εστι σου γυνη[180];
And she said to him, "She is not your wife?"
19:05a και ειπεν ιωσηφ ουκ εστι μου γυνη.
And Joseph said, "She is not my wife.
19:05b μαριαμ εστιν η ανατραφεισα εν τω ναω κυριου
Mariam is she who was raised in the temple of the Lord,
19:05c και εκληρωσαμην αυτην γυναικα.
and I obtained her by lot as a wife.
19:06a και ουκ εστιν μου γυνη,
And she is not my wife,
19:06b αλλα συλληψιν εχει εκ πνευματος αγιου.
but she has a conception from the Holy Spirit."
19:07a και ειπεν αυτω η μαια τουτο αληθες;
And the midwife said to him, "Is this true?"
19:07b και ειπεν αυτη ιωσηφ δευρο και ιδε.
And Joseph said to her, "Come and see."
19:07c και απηει μετ αυτου η μαια.
And the midwife went with him.

The Redactor's abbreviated version of the Midwife episode as preserved in P.Bodm V in *ProtJac* 19:01, 04, 06-07:

ProtJac 18:01-02
18:01 και ευρεν εκει σπηλαιον και εισηγαγεν αυτην,
And he found a cave there and led her [Mary] in,
18:02 και παρεστησεν αυτην τους υιους αυτου,
και εξηλθεν ζητησαι μαιαν εβραιαν
εν χωρα βηθλεεμ.
and he placed her with his sons,
and he exited [the cave][181] to seek a Hebrew midwife
in the country of Bethlehem.
19:01 και ευρων ηνεγκεν απο ορεινης καταβαινουσαν[182]
And having found, he brought from the hill country [her] descending.
19:04 και ειπεν ιωσηφ τη μαια οτι μαρια εστιν η μεμνηστευμενη μοι
And Joseph said to the midwife that "Mary is my betrothed,[183]

---

180. The underlined verses were eliminated by the Redactor in his abbreviated version of this text because they suggest that Mary may have been Joseph's wife; see below.

181. See the discussion below, pp. 98–9, concerning the specific translation of the verb ἐξῆλθεν as "exited [the cave]."

182. *ProtJac* 19:01-03 contain extended dialogue between Joseph and the midwife in later MSS.

183. *ProtJac* 19:04 and 19:06 together constitute a continuous text and represent the Redactor's substitution for the original text *ProtJac* 19:01b-07 preserved in some later MSS. The underlined statement of Joseph to the midwife indicating that Mary was his

19:06 αλλα συλλημμα εχει εκ πνευματος αγιου,
ανατραφεισα εν ναω κυριου.
but she has a conception of the holy spirit,
having been raised in the temple of the Lord."
19:07 και απηει μετ αυτου η μαια.[184]
And the midwife went with him.

The primary purpose of this revision by the Redactor—in accordance with his consistent strategy throughout the *ProtJac*—was to promote the perpetual virginity of Mary and to eliminate any hints in the text that Mary was Joseph's wife and thus may have had marital relations with him at some point. In this instance the Redactor preserved in P.Bodm V 19:04 and 19:06 the elements of Joseph's lengthier assertion in *ProtJac* 19:04-06 in the later MSS that Mary was his betrothed—and therefore not his wife—and that she was raised in the Jerusalem temple and has conceived from the Holy Spirit. For the same purpose the Redactor eliminated several statements from his source document that center on the issue of whether or not Mary was Joseph's wife. These are underlined in the Composer's full text above and designated as *ProtJac* 19:04b-05a: και ειπεν αυτω ουκ εστι σου γυνη; και ειπεν ιωσηφ ουκ εστι μου γυνη (And she said to him, "She is not your wife?" And Joseph said, "She is not my wife"); and *ProtJac* 19:05c και εκληρωσαμην αυτην γυναικα και ουκ εστιν μου γυνη ("and I obtained her by lot as a wife, and she is not my wife").

The Composer's text of *ProtJac* 19:01-07 in the later MSS is grammatically coherent and follows smoothly after *ProtJac* 18:01-02, where Joseph has taken Mary into the cave and then exited the cave in search of a Hebrew midwife. On the contrary, the Redactor's text following *ProtJac* 18:02 seems confused and inarticulate. The Redactor has compacted the appearance of the midwife in *ProtJac* 19:01a and her initial dialogue with Joseph in *ProtJac* 19:01b-03b into a single verse, P.Bodm V 19:01: και ευρων ηνεγκεν απο ορεινης καταβαινουσαν ("And having found, he brought from the hills [her] descending"). The Redactor's verse contains no expressed subject, as he has omitted the subject γυνη ("woman") from the Composer's text. In its present position immediately following *ProtJac* 18:02, it seems that the Redactor intended the subject of P.Bodm V 19:01 to be the midwife whom Joseph was seeking in the preceding verse: και εξηλθεν ζητησαι μαιαν εβραιαν εν χωρα βηθλεεμ ("he exited [the cave] to seek a Hebrew midwife in the country of Bethlehem"). P.Bodm V 19:01 oddly contains three verb forms that seem to refer to the midwife mentioned in *ProtJac* 18:02: the aorist verb ηνεγκεν ("brought") and two participles, ευρων ("having found") and καταβαινουσαν ("[her] descending"). These verbs are underlined in the text below to distinguish their use in the Composer's original coherent version as opposed to the Redactor's confused version:

"betrothed" should be viewed in connection with the Redactor's elimination of the texts above suggesting that Mary was Joseph's wife, cf. n. 180.

184. *ProtJac* 19:07 contains additional extended dialogue between Joseph and the midwife in later MSS.

ProtJac 18:01-02
18:01 και ευρεν εκει σπηλαιον και εισηγαγεν αυτην,
    And he found a cave there and led her [Mary] in,
18:02 και παρεστησεν αυτην τους υιους αυτου,
και εξηλθεν ζητησαι μαιαν εβραιαν
εν χωρα βηθλεεμ.
    and he placed her with his sons,
    and he exited [the cave] to seek a Hebrew midwife
    in the country of Bethlehem.

The Composer's original coherent version:
ProtJac 19:01a και ιδου γυνη <u>καταβαινουσα</u> απο της ορεινης,
    And behold, a woman <u>descending</u> from the hills,

The Redactor's revised confused version:
P.Bodm V 19:01 και <u>ευρων</u> <u>ηνεγκεν</u> απο ορεινης <u>καταβαινουσαν</u>
    And <u>having found</u>, he <u>brought</u> from the hills [her] <u>descending</u>.

In P.Bodm V 19:01 the Redactor has taken the prepositional phrase καταβαινουσα απο της ορεινης ("descending from the hills") from *ProtJac* 19:01a and rearranged the order of its words to απο ορεινης καταβαινουσαν ("from the hills [her] descending"). He also changed the nominative case of the participle καταβαινουσα to the accusative καταβαινουσαν, ostensibly to agree with the unexpressed feminine direct object of his interpolated verbs ευρων ("having found") and ηνεγκεν ("brought"). But even beyond the individual grammatical irregularities that we have noted in P.Bodm V 19:01, this creation of the Redactor is incoherent in toto. In essence, Joseph has found a midwife and brought her from the hills. But the participle καταβαινουσαν is feminine singular, meaning that the midwife is "coming down" from the hills alone, without the accompaniment of Joseph, who in this same verse ηνεγκεν ("brought") her down. In contrast, the Composer's text in *ProtJac* 19:01a is entirely intelligible. The participle καταβαινουσα is in the nominative case and appropriately refers to the subject of the sentence, a γυνη ("woman"), also in the nominative case, who encounters Joseph and begins a dialogue with him.

The grammatical awkwardness of P.Bodm V 19:01 is compounded further by the evident syntactical problem brought about by the Redactor's omission of most of the ensuing dialogue between Joseph and the midwife in his source, *ProtJac* 19:01b-03b. The Redactor's text leaps from P.Bodm V 19:01 to 19:04 where he belatedly identifies the unexpressed subject of P.Bodm V 19:01 as the midwife.[185] The Redactor appears to have added the reference to the midwife in P.Bodm V 19:04 as an afterthought. He may have realized his failure to clarify the subject of P.Bodm V 19:01 and sought to do so subsequently. The texts of both the Redactor (P.Bodm V 19:01, 04) and the Composer (*ProtJac* 19:01b-03a in the MSS) are presented

---

185. The "woman" who enters the scene in the Composer's document in *ProtJac* 19:01a and interacts with Joseph is not identified as a midwife until *ProtJac* 19:07.

together below to illustrate the complication that the Redactor introduced into his version of the Midwife story by his omission of the dialogue in *ProtJac* 19:01b-03b. The text of the Composer is indented to distinguish it from that of the Redactor, and the Redactor's immediately connected texts are underlined for emphasis:

ProtJac 18:01-02
18:01 και ευρεν εκει σπηλαιον και εισηγαγεν αυτην,
    And he found a cave there and led her [Mary] in,
18:02 και παρεστησεν αυτην τους υιους αυτου, [186]
και εξηλθεν ζητησαι μαιαν εβραιαν
εν χωρα βηθλεεμ.
    and he placed her with his sons,
    and he exited [the cave] to seek a Hebrew midwife
    in the country of Bethlehem.

P.Bodm V 19:01—Redactor's text followed directly by P.Bodm V 19:04 below:
<u>και ευρων ηνεγκεν απο ορεινης καταβαινουσαν,</u>[187]
<u>And having found, he brought from the hills [her] descending.</u>

    The Composer's dialogue omitted by the Redactor:
    ProtJac 19:01b και λεγει αυτω ανθρωπε που πορευη;
        And she said to him, "Man, where are you going?"
    19:02a και ειπεν μαιαν ζητω εβραιαν.
        And he said, "I am seeking a Hebrew midwife."
    19:02b και αποκριθεισα λεγει αυτω εξ ισραηλ ει;
        And answering, she said to him, "Are you of Israel?"
    19:03a ειπεν δε αυτη ναι.
        And he said to her, "Yes."
    19:03b η δε ειπεν και τις εστιν η γεννωσα εν τω σπηλαιω;
        And she said, "And who is she who is giving birth in the cave?"

P.Bodm V 19:04—Redactor's text directly following P.Bodm V 19:01 above:
<u>και ειπεν ιωσηφ τη μαια οτι μαρια εστιν η μεμνηστευμενη μοι</u>
<u>And Joseph said to the midwife that "Mary is my betrothed."</u>[188]

In the absence of the intervening dialogue of the Composer's text in *ProtJac* 19:01b-03b, the Redactor's verse P.Bodm V 19:04 constitutes a nonsequitur in which Joseph is responding to a question by the midwife that was not asked in the Redactor's text because the Redactor omitted her question, along with the entire dialogue in *ProtJac* 19:01b-03b. However, this question was asked by the midwife in the Composer's text in *ProtJac* 19:03b: και τις εστιν η γεννωσα εν τω σπηλαιω;

186. Παρέστησεν Mary in *ProtJac* 18:02 parallels ἔστησεν the midwife in 18:08.
187. Καταβαίνουσαν in *ProtJac* 19:01 contradicts και απηει in 19:07.
188. P.Bodm V 19:04 and 19:06 together constitute a continuous text and represent the Redactor's substitution for the original text preserved in some later MSS.

("And who is she who is giving birth in the cave?").[189] This is precisely the question that was required to elicit the response by Joseph in the Composer's text in *ProtJac* 19:04a: η μεμνηστευμενη μοι ("my betrothed") and which also has been preserved by the Redactor in P.Bodm V 19:04: μαρια εστιν η μεμνηστευμενη μοι ("Mary is my betrothed"). Thus *ProtJac* 19:03b affords us a valuable clue in our effort to determine the process by which the Redactor modified the Composer's midwife story to produce his version that is now contained in P.Bodm V 19:01, 04, and 06-07. But *ProtJac* 19:03b will provide yet another important piece of the complex redactional puzzle that is the Midwife episode.

ProtJac 19:03b initially appears to be inconsistent with respect to the continuity of the action from *ProtJac* 18:01-02 to the ensuing corresponding verses of both the Redactor, P.Bodm V 19:01, and the Composer, *ProtJac* 19:01a. In *ProtJac* 19:03b the midwife has asked Joseph: τις εστιν η γεννωσα εν τω σπηλαιω; ("who is the woman giving birth in the cave?"). But there is no indication in the preceding texts—either in the Redactor's verse P.Bodm V 19:01 or in the Composer's dialogue in *ProtJac* 19:01a-03a—that the midwife was told that there was a woman giving birth in a cave. This inconsistency can be resolved within the context of the original, pre-redactional version of the Midwife episode in *ProtJac* 18:02-19:07. The midwife's inexplicable knowledge that there was a woman giving birth in a cave in *ProtJac* 19:03b is intelligible only if the Composer's verse *ProtJac* 19:01a, which describes the midwife coming down from the hills (καταβαινουσα απο της ορεινης), follows immediately after *ProtJac* 18:01-02 where Joseph has taken Mary into the cave and then exited the cave to seek a Hebrew midwife.

The key word in an accurate interpretation of the sequence of events in the Composer's continuous text in *ProtJac* 18:01-19:01a is εξηλθεν ("came out"). In the Redactor's scenario, in which his interpolated verse P.Bodm V 19:01 follows *ProtJac* 18:02, εξηλθεν signifies generally that Joseph "went out" from the cave into the country of Bethlehem seeking a midwife. He found a midwife in the hills around Bethlehem and brought her, "from the hills [her] descending" (απο ορεινης καταβαινουσαν) to the cave. But in the Composer's original continuous text in *ProtJac* 18:01-19:01a, the aorist verb εξηλθεν in 18:02 should be translated specifically as "exited" and understood as a continuation of the similarly aorist verb εισηγαγεν ("led into") in *ProtJac* 18:01. These two verbs should be viewed together as describing the successive actions by which Joseph led, or took, Mary into the cave and then "exited" the cave after he had placed Mary there with his sons. According to this more precise interpretation, which seems to convey the Composer's original intent, Joseph was "exiting" from the cave when he encountered the midwife, who, at that time, was descending from the nearby hills to the north of Bethlehem.

---

189. The initial καὶ in the opening phrase of this verse, καὶ τίς ἐστιν ("And who is"), confirms that the midwife's question was a continuation of a previous dialogue just as is the case in *ProtJac* 19:01b-03b.

The original continuous text of the CEGM in *ProtJac* 18:01–19:01a is presented below. It is clear in this passage that a woman, soon to be revealed as the midwife, appears as Joseph is exiting the cave in which he has just placed Mary with his sons:[190]

ProtJac 18:01 και ευρεν εκει σπηλαιον και εισηγαγεν,
And he found a cave there and led her [Mary] in,
18:02 και παρεστησεν αυτην τους υιους αυτου,
και εξηλθεν ζητησαι μαιαν εβραιαν
εν χωρα βηθλεεμ.
and he placed her with his sons,
and he exited [the cave] to seek a Hebrew midwife
in the country of Bethlehem.
19:01a και ιδου γυνη καταβαινουσα απο της ορεινης.
And behold, a woman descending from the hills.

This scenario would resolve the apparent inconsistency of the midwife's awareness of a woman giving birth in the cave in *ProtJac* 19:03b, vis-à-vis her preceding dialogue with Joseph in *ProtJac* 19:01b–03a. The midwife would have been cognizant of the cave in her question to Joseph in *ProtJac* 19:03b—without having been told about it—if she actually saw Joseph as he was exiting the cave in which he had just left Mary. It follows also, therefore, that the dialogue between Joseph and the midwife in *ProtJac* 19:01b–03a took place within view of the cave out of which Joseph had just exited and encountered the midwife coming down from the nearby hills north of Bethlehem. The midwife initiated her dialogue with Joseph immediately upon meeting him outside of the cave. Her first question to Joseph in *ProtJac* 19:01b was ανθρωπε που πορευη; ("Man, where are you going?"), to which Joseph replied in *ProtJac* 19:02a: μαιαν ζητω εβραιαν ("I am seeking a Hebrew midwife"). Thus, the midwife has now been informed by Joseph that he is seeking a Hebrew midwife. And, being in view of the cave out of which Joseph has just "exited," the midwife would logically assume that there is a woman giving birth in the cave. It would be entirely consistent, therefore, for the midwife to ask Joseph in 19:03b: τις εστιν η γεννωσα εν τω σπηλαιω; ("who is she who is giving birth in the cave?").

---

190. This interpretation requires that the text of the Redactor's source document did not contain the disputed "I, Joseph" passage that is present in a number of later MSS of the *ProtJac* 18:03-12; cf. nn. 177, 179 above. Neither the Composer's verse *ProtJac* 19:01a nor the Redactor's corresponding verse P.Bodm V 19:01 would have been so closely tied syntactically to *ProtJac* 18:02 if either of these verses had been separated from *ProtJac* 18:02 by ten full verses of the "I, Joseph" passage. The Redactor's verse especially would have been incomprehensible in isolation, stating succinctly that Joseph found and brought some unidentified person who was descending from the hills. It is unlikely that the Redactor would have excised the "I, Joseph" passage from his source document.

Joseph's answer to the midwife's question in the Composer's version of the dialogue in *ProtJac* 19:01b-07b contains more details that the Redactor did not preserve in his summary in P.Bodm V 19:04, 06. In the Composer's text, Joseph's assertion to the midwife that the woman in the cave is his "betrothed" in *ProtJac* 19:04a is followed by a terse exchange between Joseph and the midwife in *ProtJac* 19:04b-05a concerning whether the woman is his wife. The midwife asks in *ProtJac* 04b ουκ εστι σου γυνη; ("she is not your wife?"); Joseph answers in 05a ουκ εστι μου γυνη ("she is not my wife"). Joseph feels constrained to convince the midwife that Mary's child is not his. He describes the circumstances of Mary's supernatural conception and again denies that she is his wife in *ProtJac* 05b-06b: μαριαμ εστιν η ανατραφεισα εν τω ναω κυριου και εκληρωσαμην αυτην γυναικα. και ουκ εστιν μου γυνη, αλλα συλληψιν εχει εκ πνευματος αγιου ("Mary was raised in the temple of the Lord and I obtained her by lot as a wife. And she is not my wife, but she has a conception from the Holy Spirit"). The canonical element of Mary's conception by the Holy Spirit would not have been original to the CEGM but must have been introduced by the Redactor. This information would exonerate both Joseph and Mary of any sexual transgression.

A comparison of the Redactor's text in P.Bodm V 19:04, 06 with the Composer's parallel text in *ProtJac* 19:01b-06b reveals the process by which the Redactor rearranged and condensed the Composer's lengthier dialogue between Joseph and the midwife to produce his abbreviated, and censored, version. The Redactor had before him the entire dialogue of the Composer and employed various editorial techniques to create an abridgment of the original, lengthier account. He substituted *ProtJac* 19:04 and 19:06 for the entire text of the Composer's dialogue in *ProtJac* 19:01b-07. *ProtJac* 19:04 and 19:06 together, without the intervening verses, *ProtJac* 04a-05b in the Composer's text, represent a continuous quotation and appear as a single verse in the Redactor's P.Bodm V text. This quotation is not presented as a response to a question by the midwife but rather contains a brief monologue by Joseph to the midwife after he found her in the Bethlehem hills and was coming down with her to the cave. In P.Bodm V 19:04 the Redactor preserved two details that were essential to the story: (1) from *ProtJac* 19:07, that the woman to whom Joseph was speaking was a midwife, and (2) from *ProtJac* 19:05b, that the name of the woman giving birth in the cave was Μαριάμ.[191]

P.Bodm V 19:04 και ειπεν ιωσηφ τη μαια οτι
μαρια εστιν η μεμνηστευμενη μοι,
    And Joseph said to the midwife that
    "Mary is my betrothed,
P.Bodm V 19:06 αλλα συλλημμα εχει εκ πνευματος αγιου,
ανατραφεισα εν ναω κυριου.
    but she has a conception of the holy spirit,
    having been raised in the temple of the Lord."

---

191. Mary's name is given as Μαριάμ in most of the later MSS.

The Redactor's editorial process is exhibited also in the manner by which he created his own version of Joseph's response to the midwife's question in the Composer's text in *ProtJac* 19:03b: "And who is she who is giving birth in the cave?" He appropriated ανατραφεισα εν τω ναω κυριου from the Composer's text in *ProtJac* 19:05b and prefixed to it the canonical element of the conception by the Holy Spirit from *ProtJac* 19:06b to create his text in P.Bodm V 19:06: αλλα συλλημμα εχει εκ πνευματος αγιου, ανατραφεισα εν ναω κυριου ("but she has a conception from the Holy Spirit, having been raised in the temple of the Lord"). In the Composer's text, the past participle ανατραφεισα functions naturally as an adjective, describing Mary as she who was raised in the temple. But in the Redactor's rewrite of the Composer's narrative, ανατραφεισα has the appearance of having been appended as an afterthought that seems unrelated to his statement of Mary's conception by the Holy Spirit. The Redactor's reversal of the order of these two phrases makes Mary's presence in the temple secondary to her conception and further distances the conception from being associated with the temple. The awkwardness of the Redactor's version in P.Bodm V 19:06 reveals it to be a clumsy, secondary revision of the Composer's original text.

Given the Redactor's penchant for avoiding any suggestion that Joseph and Mary were married, it may seem odd at first that in P.Bodm V 19:04, the Redactor retained from *ProtJac* 19:04a the Composer's description of Mary as Joseph's "betrothed" (μεμνηστευμενη). But this single exception by the Redactor may perhaps be understood as a measured response by Joseph to a veritable interrogation by the midwife regarding his relationship to Mary. The Redactor had to explain the relationship of the elderly Joseph to a pregnant woman in the face of the pointed queries by the midwife in the Composer's text in *ProtJac* 19:04-06 concerning whether or not Mary was his wife. By describing Mary as Joseph's betrothed, the Redactor was providing her with an alibi against the harsh penalties that might accrue to unwed mothers in Judea at that time.[192] Also, the Redactor may have felt justified in portraying Mary as Joseph's betrothed because of his proclivity toward the canonical Gospels. He has interpolated passages from Matthew into the Trial story in *ProtJac* 14:05-08[193] and will do so again shortly in the Magi story in *ProtJac* 21:01–22:02. The Redactor is well aware that Mary is presented as Joseph's betrothed in Mt. 1:18: μνηστευθείσης τῆς μητρὸς αὐτοῦ Μαρίας τῷ Ἰωσήφ ("his [Jesus's] mother Mary having been betrothed to Joseph").

A better understanding of the Redactor's overall editorial strategy may perhaps provide further insights into the apparent inconsistency regarding the

---

192. Cf. Jane Schaberg, *The Illegitimacy of Jesus* (San Francisco: Harper and Row, 1987), 46–51; Deut. 22:22-4 prescribes the death penalty for adulteresses in certain circumstances. It was more appropriate for the Redactor to have shown Mary as Joseph's betrothed, as in the Composer's text, than to have presented Joseph as lying to the midwife about the identity of the pregnant young girl in the cave.

193. See above, pp. 60–1.

relationship of Joseph and Mary in the Composer's text. The irregularities in the Midwife story are remarkably similar to those that we encountered previously in the even more complex redactional scenario in *ProtJac* 8–9. These two parallel scenarios, separated by ten chapters in the *ProtJac* text, demonstrate the Redactor's consistent pattern of introducing confusion into the CEGM as he moved through the document, systematically revising each successive section in the same way and for the same purpose. The analogous problems in both scenarios stem from the Redactor's persistent objective in the *ProtJac* to eliminate any indications in his source that Mary was anything other than a perpetual virgin. Hence, the same redactional process is evident here in the Midwife story as was the case formerly in the Joseph Council. And the same incongruities and contradictions are evident as well. The Midwife story contains two apparent contextually paradoxical elements, one each in the Composer's and the Redactor's parallel texts:

In *ProtJac* 19:05c, the Composer states that Joseph "obtained Mary by lot as a wife"
   in a context within which Joseph denies twice that Mary is his wife (*ProtJac* 19:05a, 06a).[194]

In P.Bodm V 19:04, the Redactor refers to Mary as Joseph's "betrothed"
   in a context from which he expunges three references in the Composer's text to Mary as Joseph's wife (*ProtJac* 19:04b, 05a, 06a).

The earlier redactional scenario, which contained similar inconsistencies regarding the relationship between Joseph and Mary, occurred in the Joseph Council, *ProtJac* 8:03–9:12, in which the priests of the temple were deciding how the twelve-year-old Mary would be removed from the temple and to whom she would be assigned.[195] Within that context, the contradiction regarded whether Mary was Joseph's wife or his ward. In *ProtJac* 9:05, which occurs within a section of homogeneous text that was attributed to the Composer, *ProtJac* 9:05-12, the high priest informed Joseph that he had obtained the "virgin of the Lord," Mary, "by lot" to keep in custody for the Lord (συ κεκληρωσαι την παρθενον κυριου παραλαβαι εις τηρησιν αυτω). This conflicted with a previous statement that occurred in the more compositionally fragmented section in *ProtJac* 8:03–9:04. *ProtJac* 8:07-08 proved to be particularly problematic with respect to their redactional nature, and it is in these verses that the high priest is told by an angel to expect a sign that would designate the person to whom Mary would be given as a "wife" (γυνη). The successive layers of redaction that were imposed on the *GenMar* by the Composer and the Redactor made it difficult to arrive at a definitive resolution

---

194. This incongruity in the Composer's text may be mitigated at least partially by the fact that it is not actually stated in *ProtJac* 19:05c that Mary is presently Joseph's wife, but only that "he obtained her by lot as a wife." There has been no indication in the *ProtJac* up to this point that Joseph and Mary were actually married.

195. See the discussion above in "The Joseph Council," pp. 30–4.

of the confusion in the Joseph Council regarding the relationship between Joseph and Mary.¹⁹⁶

It is noteworthy that the notion that Joseph obtained Mary "by lot" is found in both the Midwife and Joseph Council stories and that it seems at first to contradict other elements in each respective scenario. In the Composer's text in *ProtJac* 19:05c Joseph "obtained Mary by lot as a wife" between two verses, *ProtJac* 19:05a and 06a, in which Joseph denied that Mary was his wife. In the Composer's text in *ProtJac* 9:05, Joseph was told that he "obtained" Mary also "by lot" but not as a "wife." Instead he would be the custodian of Mary, "the virgin of the Lord" (την παρθενον κυριου), for the Lord (εις τηρησιν αυτω). *ProtJac* 9:05 seems to be in direct conflict with *ProtJac* 8:08 in which Joseph was designated by a sign as he who would take Mary as his "wife." However, *ProtJac* 8:08, in its present form, is most likely a product of the editorial activity of the Redactor and does not in its entirety reflect the original underlying text that would have been present in the CEGM.¹⁹⁷

It seems clear that the Redactor's ongoing, systematic, radical revision of the Composer's document contributed significantly to the confusion over the marital status of Joseph and Mary in both the Joseph Council and the Midwife story. However, the Composer's stance on this issue also may have been nuanced. In our discussion of the Joseph Council, a reasonable explanation was offered to account for the apparent inconsistency in the Composer's materials in the *ProtJac* with respect to the relationship of Joseph and Mary.¹⁹⁸ This theory would apply to the seeming incongruity in the Joseph Council between the images of Mary as both Joseph's wife and his ward. And it would explain the ostensible inconsistency in the Midwife story in which Joseph "obtained Mary by lot as a wife," while concurrently denying twice that Mary was his wife. The Composer may have had an evolving concept of the relationship between Joseph and Mary. Initially, Mary could have been Joseph's ward, or even his "betrothed," with the understanding that this status in their relationship would continue until the time when Mary's divine pregnancy would be brought to term with the delivery of her child. Joseph and Mary could then be married appropriately afterward.

---

196. Ibid., see the discussion on the very complicated redactional process by which, successively, the Composer created and the Redactor revised the Joseph Council.

197. See the detailed analysis of the authorship of the highly problematic passage *ProtJac* 8:07-08, which is critical for understanding the inconsistencies that are shared in common by both the Joseph Council and the present Midwife story regarding the relationship between Joseph and Mary, "The Joseph Council," pp. 26-9.

198. See pp. 29-34 in "The Joseph Council." The "evolving" relationship between Joseph and Mary in the Composer's writings is in essential agreement with what I have described in a previous publication as the first phase in the progressive development of the understanding of Mary's virginal status in early Christian literature, Zervos, "Christmas," 77-80, summarized below in "Appendix 1: Mary's Evolving Virginity in Early Christianity," pp. 171-3.

The Birth

The Hebrew midwife, with whom Joseph interacted outside the Cave of the Nativity in *ProtJac* 19:01-07, has functioned heretofore as the link between the Journey to the Cave and the Nativity; she will now continue to play a central role in the Birth story itself. *ProtJac* 19:07 serves as a transition from the dialogue between Joseph and the midwife in *ProtJac* 19:01-06 to the Birth story in *ProtJac* 19:08–20:11. In *ProtJac* 19:07 the midwife asks Joseph if it is true (τουτο αληθες;) that Mary was "raised in the temple of the Lord" and has a "conception from the Holy Spirit." Joseph replies, "come and see" (δευρο και ιδε), and the midwife then "went with him" (και απηει μετ αυτου η μαια). In *ProtJac* 19:08 Joseph and the midwife have moved from the location of their initial encounter at some distance from—but within sight of—the cave and are now standing "in the place of the cave" (εστησαν εν τω τοπω του σπηλαιου).[199] The odd expression "in the place of the cave" suggests that Joseph and the midwife are not actually inside the cave but are standing near the cave as the ensuing events of the birth occur. Inconsistencies regarding the vantage point vis-à-vis the cave, from which the midwife participated in the events of the birth narrative, are among the indicators of the presence of redactional activity in the text of this central event in the *ProtJac*.

The text of the redacted Birth story that is preserved in *ProtJac* 19:08-20:11 exhibits considerable disarray, which has been caused by the Redactor's interpolation of his Doubting Salome episode into the original *GenMar* Birth story, which itself had been enhanced by the Composer. A redaction-critical analysis of the text of the Birth story exposes the editorial activity of the Redactor and enables us to isolate certain elements of the underlying text. But the successive radical revisions of the *GenMar* by the Redactor and the Composer, respectively, hamper attempts to reconstitute, in its entirety, the original Birth narrative. Incongruences in the storyline begin to occur immediately after the appearance of Joseph and the midwife "in the place of the cave" in *ProtJac* 19:08. But aside from an apparent interpolation by the Redactor in *ProtJac* 19:09, it seems that the original account of the birth of the divine child is preserved in *ProtJac* 19:08-12. The Redactor integrated his Doubting Salome episode into the ending of the Birth story beginning with *ProtJac* 19:13.[200] The text of the Birth story of the

---

199. Ἐστησαν ("they stood") is the reading in the majority of MSS and reflects the original scenario in the CEGM in which Joseph and the midwife have engaged in a lengthy dialogue after they encountered each other at a distance from the cave and have now moved to the "place of the cave." The reading ἔστησεν in P.Bodm V reflects the Redactor's abbreviated scenario in which Joseph "found" the midwife in the hill country of Bethlehem and, in a brief statement in P.Bodm V 19:04 and 06, informed her of Mary's identity and justified her pregnancy. In the Redactor's muddled sequence of events (see discussion above), Joseph brought the midwife descending from the hill country and stood her (ἔστησεν) "at the place of the cave."

200. The text and analysis of the Doubting Salome story will be presented below.

GenMar[201] in *ProtJac* 19:08-12 is presented here with v. 19:09 indented to highlight its secondary nature:

ProtJac 19:08 και εστησαν εν τω τοπω του σπηλαιου,
    And they stood at the place of the cave,
και νεφελη σκοτεινη επισκιαζουσα το σπηλαιον.
    And a dark cloud [was] overshadowing the cave.
19:09 και ειπεν η μαια εμεγαλυνθη η ψυχη μου σημερον,
    And the midwife said, "my soul was magnified today,
οτι ειδον οι οφθαλμοι μου παραδοξα σημερον,
    for my eyes have seen strange things today,
οτι σωτηρια τω ισραηλ γεγενηται.
    for salvation has come to Israel."
19:10 και παραχρημα η νεφελη υπεστελλετο του σπηλαιου,
    And immediately the cloud receded from the cave,
και εφανη φως μεγα εν τω σπηλαιω, ωστε τους οφθαλμους μη φερειν.
    and a great light appeared in the cave, so that the eyes could not bear it.
19:11 και προς ολιγον το φως εκεινο υπεστελλετο εως εφανη βρεφος
    And for a little while that light receded until a child appeared
και ηλθεν και ελαβε μασθον εκ της μητρος αυτου μαριας.
    and it came and took a breast from its mother Mary.
19:12 και ανεβοησεν η μαια ως μεγαλη η σημερον ημερα,
    And the midwife cried out, "today is a great day,
οτι ειδον το καινον θεαμα τουτο.
    for I saw this new spectacle."

The secondary character of the midwife's exclamation in *ProtJac* 19:09 is attested first by an internal characteristic that distinguishes it from the narrative material in which it has been embedded and which identifies it as a probable creation of the Redactor. This verse contains terminology that bears a striking resemblance to passages in the canonical Gospel of Luke, which accords with the Redactor's consistent propensity to include canonical materials in the texts that he interpolates into the Composer's document.[202] The words εμεγαλυνθη η ψυχη μου σημερον ("my soul was magnified today") in *ProtJac* 19:09 closely parallel Mary's song in Lk.1:46: μεγαλύνει ἡ ψυχή μου τὸν κύριον ("my soul magnifies the Lord"). And the phrase οτι ειδον οι οφθαλμοι μου παραδοξα σημερον, οτι σωτηρια τω ισραηλ γεγενηται ("for my eyes saw strange things today, for salvation has come to

---

201. See the discussion regarding the original *GenMar* Birth story in "The Author: *The Genesis Marias*," pp. 158-69.

202. Cf., e.g., the numerous examples cited in the Annunciation story of the Veil Council (*ProtJac* 11), in Joseph's angelic dream vision in the Trial story (*ProtJac* 14), and in the Matthean Magi story (*ProtJac* 21-22).

Israel") seems to have been influenced by the song of Symeon in Lk. 2:30: ὅτι εἶδον οἱ ὀφθαλμοί μου τὸ σωτήριόν σου ("for my eyes have seen your salvation").[203] In addition to this linguistic evidence, the redactional nature of *ProtJac* 19:09 is strongly indicated by its disruptive influence in the narrative context in which it now occurs.

The midwife's interpolated exclamation of wonder in *ProtJac* 19:09 noticeably interrupts the continuity of the sequence of events that transpired in the original Birth story as related in *ProtJac* 19:08-11. *ProtJac* 19:08 describes a "dark cloud overshadowing" the cave when Joseph and the midwife arrived at "the place of the cave." In *ProtJac* 19:10, without the interpolated v. 19:09, the cloud "immediately" upon their arrival "receded from the cave." The Redactor simply inserted the midwife's exclamation into the middle of a verse of the original Birth story that described the cloud at the midwife's arrival and its immediate withdrawal thereafter. What are now *ProtJac* 19:08 and 19:10 originally constituted two parts of that verse and, when reunified as a single continuous text, appropriately state: και νεφελη σκοτεινη επισκιαζουσα το σπηλαιον και παραχρημα η νεφελη υπεστελλετο του σπηλαιου ("and a dark cloud [was] covering the cave and immediately the cloud receded from the cave"). But the implanted exclamation causes another anomaly in the text. The cloud was already present overshadowing the cave when the midwife arrived outside the cave and spoke her interpolated exclamation of wonder. It is precisely at this point that the cloud withdrew immediately. The immediacy with which the cloud withdrew after the midwife's exclamation—in the redacted version—gives the impression that its withdrawal was predicated upon the completion of her exclamation. In reality the withdrawal of the cloud would have been more appropriate after her arrival at the cave rather than after her exclamation.

The Redactor's placement of the midwife's words after her arrival at the cloud-covered cave is even more egregiously anomalous because nothing has occurred yet that would warrant an exclamation of such force: "my soul was magnified today, for my eyes saw strange things today, for salvation has come to Israel." As of *ProtJac* 19:09 the midwife has only seen the cave covered by a dark cloud. Even greater "strange things" will now transpire in *ProtJac* 19:10-11, after her exclamation of wonder at the sight of the dark cloud covering the cave. In *ProtJac* 19:10 the dark cloud withdrew and a "great light" appeared in the cave. In *ProtJac* 19:11 the light receded gradually until the divine child appeared who immediately after being born was able to come and take his mother's breast:

---

203. See also the crowd's response to Jesus's healing of the paralytic in Lk. 5:26, εἴδομεν παράδοξα σήμερον ("we have seen strange things today"). The linguistic connections in *ProtJac* 19:09 with the hymns contained in the Lukan Nativity story raise the intriguing possibility of a common *Sitz im Leben* in a pre-Gospel Jewish-Christian environment. See the discussion in "The Redactor: *The Protevangelium Jacobi*," pp. 135-6.

και ηλθεν και ελαβε μασθον εκ της μητρος αυτου μαριας ("and it came and took a breast from its mother Mary").²⁰⁴ It is clear that the midwife's exclamation in its present position in *ProtJac* 19:09 is premature and more logically would follow all of the "strange things" that would occur in *ProtJac* 19:10-11. However, there was a good reason for the Redactor to add such an obviously superfluous and discordant element into the text. Apparently he was confronted by an editorial dilemma that would have caused him to insert his exclamation so early in the story.

The original Birth story, into which the Redactor interpolated the Midwife's exclamation of wonder in *ProtJac* 19:09, already contained such an exclamation by the midwife in 19:12: και ανεβοησεν η μαια, ως μεγαλη η σημερον ημερα, οτι ειδον το καινον θεαμα τουτο ("And the midwife cried out, 'today is a great day, for I saw this new spectacle'"). And this original shout of joy appropriately followed this new spectacle in *ProtJac* 19:10-11: the "dark cloud," the "great light," and the remarkable child. The Redactor must have been aware of the redundancy that he was creating in the text and may have sought to diminish the repetitiveness of the midwife's two exclamations by separating them as much as possible. He inserted the first exclamation in *ProtJac* 19:09, immediately following the midwife's arrival in *ProtJac* 19:08, and at the beginning of the series of events that were concluded by her now redundant second exclamation. By sacrificing the contextual harmony of the first exclamation, the Redactor mitigated the redundancy issue, which he himself had caused. But his interpolation of the midwife's first exclamation in *ProtJac* 19:09 also served to de-emphasize the midwife's original, but now second, exclamation in *ProtJac* 19:12, thus facilitating his attachment of the Doubting Salome story to the original Birth story as the culminating event of his complete, redacted Birth narrative.

The Redactor has prepared the way for the climactic event of his revised Birth story—and of the entire finished *ProtJac*—by interweaving the beginning of the Doubting Salome material to the ending of the Birth story of the *GenMar*. He replicated the key phrase καινον θεαμα ("new spectacle") from the midwife's original, but now second, exclamation of wonder in *ProtJac* 19:12 and inserted it into his introduction of Salome into the narrative in *ProtJac* 19:13-14. According to the Redactor's account in *ProtJac* 19:13, the midwife came out of the cave and encountered Salome. In *ProtJac* 19:14 the midwife announced to Salome that she had seen a "new spectacle": καινον σοι θεαμα εχω εξηγησασθαι ("I have a new spectacle to describe to you"). But whereas the "new spectacle" in the midwife's exclamation of wonder in the original Birth story consisted of the "dark cloud," the "great light," and the appearance of the divine child; the Redactor, in his Doubting Salome story, has transformed the "new spectacle" into the virgin birth: παρθενος

---

204. This verse implies that Mary's divine child appeared at a more advanced stage of infancy in which it was able to make its way to its mother's breast. See the discussion on the Docetic nature of the Annunciation and Nativity stories in the *GenMar*, "The Author: The Genesis Marias," pp. 161-8.

εγεννησεν α ου χωρει η φυσις αυτης ("a virgin gave birth to something that her nature does not allow"). It only remains for Salome to enter the cave and verify the postpartum, and therefore, perpetual, virginity of Mary.

Doubting Salome

The Doubting Salome story was the first of three sections of material that were attached in succession by the Redactor to the original Birth story of the *GenMar*.[205] The Redactor thus co-opted the ending of his source document and created his distinctive grand finale by substituting his own materials for whatever may have been the original conclusion. The original Birth story, leading up to the appearance of the divine child, is contained in *ProtJac* 19:08 and 10-11.[206] The Midwife's exclamation follows in *ProtJac* 19:12. At this point in the narrative the Redactor interpolated his Doubting Salome episode in *ProtJac* 19:13-20:04, 7-11, thus fashioning his own version of the conclusion of the Birth story that focused on the interaction between Salome and Mary. The text of the fully redacted Doubting Salome story is presented below. The midwife's original exclamation in *ProtJac* 19:12 is prefixed to this text to emphasize its role as a transitional link between the preceding events of the original Birth story (the dark cloud, the bright light, and the child) and the attached Doubting Salome story in *ProtJac* 19:13-20:11. Thus also is highlighted the Redactor's editorial technique of repeating the words καινον θεαμα from *ProtJac* 19:12 in 19:14 to facilitate his interpolation of his Salome materials:[207]

ProtJac 19:12—The Midwife's original Exclamation of Wonder:

19:12 και ανεβοησεν η μαια ως μεγαλη η σημερον ημερα,
 And the midwife cried out, "today is a great day,
οτι ειδον το <u>καινον θεαμα</u> τουτο.
 for I saw this <u>new spectacle</u>."

ProtJac 19:13-14—The beginning of the Redactor's Doubting Salome Episode:

19:13 και εξηλθεν εκ του σπηλαιου η μαια, και απηντησεν αυτη σαλωμη.
 And the midwife came out of the cave and Salome encountered her.
19:14 και ειπεν αυτη σαλωμη, σαλωμη,
<u>καινον</u> σοι <u>θεαμα</u> εχω εξηγησασθαι
 And she said to her, "Salome, Salome,
 I have a <u>new spectacle</u> to describe to you,
παρθενος εγεννησεν α ου χωρει η φυσις αυτης.
 a virgin gave birth to something that her nature does not allow."

---

205. It would be followed by the Magi story and the Zachariah Apocryphon.
206. P.Bodm V 19:09 is the Redactor's interpolated exclamation of wonder by the midwife.
207. καινον θεαμα is underlined in this text. The latter part of *ProtJac* 20:04 is designated as 20:04b and is indented and italicized to emphasize its problematic nature.

ProtJac 19:15—The Doubting Salome will not believe that a virgin gave birth, unless she physically examines Mary with her finger:

19:15 και ειπεν σαλωμη ζη κυριος ο θεος μου,
    And Salome said to her, "The Lord my God lives,
εαν μη βαλω τον δακτυλον μου ερευνησω την φυσιν αυτης,
    if I do not put my finger [and] examine her nature,
ου μη πιστευσω η παρθενος εγεννησεν.
    I will not believe the virgin gave birth."

ProtJac 20:01-03—Salome enters the cave and physically examines Mary; Salome screams as her hand is burned off:

20:01 και εισηλθεν και εσχηματισεν αυτην.
    And she [σαλωμη] went in and prepared her,
20:02 και ηραυνησε η σαλωμη την φυσιν αυτης,
    And Salome examined her nature.
20:03 και ανηλλαξεν σαλωμη, οτι εξεπειρασεν θεον ζωντα,
    And Salome cried out, "Because it tempted [the] living God,
και ιδου η χειρ μου πυρι αποπιπτει απ εμου.
    behold, my hand falls away from me by fire."

ProtJac 20:07-11—Salome prays, is instructed by an angel to touch the child and is healed by prayer; is instructed to publicize what she has seen:

20:04 και προσηυξατο προς κυριον
    And she prayed to the Lord,
    20:04b *και ιαθη η μαια εν τη ωρα εκεινη*
        and the midwife was healed in that hour.
20:07 και ιδου αγγελος κυριου εστη προς σαλωμην λεγων
    And behold, an angel of the Lord stood towards Salome saying,
εισηκουσθη η δεησις σου ενωπιον κυριου του θεου,
    "Your supplication has been heard before the Lord God,
20:08 προσελθουσα αψαι του παιδιου, και αυτος εσται σοι σωτηρια.
    drawing near, touch the child and he will be salvation for you."
20:09 και εποιησεν ουτω.
    And she did thus.
20:10 και ιαθη σαλωμη καθως προσεκυνησεν,
και εξηλθεν εκ του σπηλαιου.
    and Salome was healed in accordance with her prayer,
    and she came out of the cave.
20:11 ιδου αγγελος κυριου εν φωνη λεγων σαλωμη, σαλωμη,
    Behold, an angel of the Lord with a voice saying, "Salome, Salome,
αναγγειλον οσα ειδες παραδοξα
εως ελθη ο παις εις ιεροσολυμα.
    proclaim all the strange things you saw
    until the child comes to Jerusalem."

The Redactor has already created one serious conflict at the transitional point at which he attached the beginning of the Doubting Salome episode in *ProtJac* 19:13-14 to the culminating event in the original Birth story in *ProtJac* 19:12, the midwife's shout of wonder at the "new spectacle" that she has seen. Now, in *ProtJac* 19:13, the Redactor creates another conflict by placing Salome outside the cave, just as the midwife was exiting the cave and announcing to Salome the Redactor's version of the "new spectacle" that she saw: "a virgin gave birth to something that her nature does not allow." But as noted above,[208] the midwife does not appear to have entered the cave in *ProtJac* 19:08-12; rather she was standing outside the cave as the events of the birth transpired.[209] When the midwife arrived at the cave in *ProtJac* 19:08, it was covered with the dark cloud,[210] and there is no indication in the text that she passed through the cloud into the cave. The only opportune time for the midwife to have entered the cave would have been after the withdrawal of the cloud. But she would have been impeded from entering at that time because of the appearance of a light so "great" as to be "unbearable to the eyes."[211] With the gradual withdrawal of the "great light," the midwife would now have been able to witness the appearance of the remarkable child from her position outside the cave.[212]

The most conspicuous sign of redactional activity in the Doubting Salome story is the contextually incompatible verse, *ProtJac* 20:04b, in which the midwife was healed: και ιαθη η μαια εν τη ωρα εκεινη ("and the midwife was healed in that hour"). But there is no indication in the P.Bodm V text that the midwife had suffered a wound that required healing. Why would the midwife require healing when it was Salome whose hand was burned off in *ProtJac* 20:03? Furthermore, the healing of the midwife produces an incongruous redundancy in the text as Salome herself is healed in *ProtJac* 20:10: και ιαθη σαλωμη καθως προσεκυνησεν ("and Salome was healed in accordance with her prayer"). Without *ProtJac* 20:04b, the text of *ProtJac* 20:04-10 flows smoothly. Salome's hand was burned off in *ProtJac* 20:03; she "prayed to the Lord" in v. 20:04 and was told by an angel in v. 20:07 that her prayer had been heard by the Lord God. In v. 20:08 the angel instructed Salome to touch the child for her salvation, which she did in v. 20:09. The events that began with Salome's prayer in *ProtJac* 20:04 were suitably completed in *ProtJac* 20:10 where she was healed in "accordance with her prayer." Therefore, the healing of the midwife in *ProtJac* 20:04b is clearly incompatible with the context in which it occurs and likely constitutes a remnant of an original *GenMar* Birth story that

---

208. See pp. 104-6, n. 199.

209. *ProtJac* 19:08: "at the place of the cave."

210. νεφελη σκοτεινη επισκιαζουσα το σπηλαιον.

211. ωστε τους οφθαλμους μη φερειν.

212. This is supported by another very early reference to the absence of a midwife at the birth of Jesus, *Odes. Sol.* 19:9. The cave referred in *ProtJac* 19-20 would not necessarily have been a deep cave but a simple overhanging rock that could have provided a rudimentary shelter.

the Redactor inadvertently left in the text of his Doubting Salome story as he was overwriting the original story by interpolating his materials into his source document.[213]

The central event in the Doubting Salome story, and in the entire redacted *ProtJac*, is the physical examination of Mary by Salome to prove that Mary remained a virgin after giving birth to her child. This story represents the culmination of all the efforts of the Redactor in his systematic revision of the CEGM. In *ProtJac* 19:15 Salome responded with disbelief to the midwife's testimony that she had seen a "new spectacle," that "a virgin gave birth to something that her nature does not allow." Salome stated that she would not believe the virgin gave birth unless she herself performed a physical examination of the virgin's "nature" (φυσιν): εαν μη βαλω τον δακτυλον μου ερευνησω την φυσιν αυτης, ου μη πιστευσω η παρθενος εγεννησεν ("if I do not put my finger (and) examine her nature, I will not believe the virgin gave birth").[214] There is a striking similarity between the words spoken by the Doubting Salome in *ProtJac* 19:15 and those spoken by the Doubting Thomas in the canonical Gospel of John 20:25 in which Thomas will not believe that the risen Jesus had appeared to the disciples unless he puts his finger in the nail marks in Jesus's hands. The two parallel texts are presented below with the common verbatim vocabulary underlined for emphasis:

ProtJac 19:15 <u>εαν μη βαλω τον δακτυλον μου</u> ερευνησω την φυσιν αυτης,
<u>If I do not put my finger</u> (and) examine her nature,
<u>ου μη πιστευσω</u> η παρθενος εγεννησεν.
<u>I will not believe</u> the virgin gave birth.

Jn 20:25 <u>Ἐὰν μὴ</u> ἴδω ἐν ταῖς χερσὶν αὐτοῦ τὸν τύπον τῶν ἥλων
<u>If I do not</u> see in his hands the mark of the nails
καὶ <u>βάλω τὸν δάκτυλόν μου</u> εἰς τὸν τύπον τῶν ἥλων
and <u>put my finger</u> into the mark of the nails
καὶ βάλω μου τὴν χεῖρα εἰς τὴν πλευρὰν αὐτοῦ, <u>οὐ μὴ πιστεύσω</u>.
And put my hand into his side, <u>I will not believe</u>.

It has been a consistent editorial modus operandi of the Redactor to interpolate texts from the canonical Gospels into the CEGM. But heretofore, invariably, these texts have derived from Luke and Matthew. *ProtJac* 19:15 represents the unique instance of a close parallel to a Johannine text. The closeness of the parallel, in both the identical vocabulary and the context of a tactile physical examination, makes it difficult to deny the existence of an actual literary relationship between *ProtJac* 19:15 and Jn 20:25. Ordinarily the uniqueness of this single Johannine element in the *ProtJac* would appear to militate against any assumption that the Redactor

---

213. See the discussion in "The Author: *The Genesis Marias*," pp. 166-7.

214. There is great disagreement among the MSS of the *ProtJac* with regard to the text of the digital examination. For the textual evidence and a discussion of the compositional issue, see Zervos, "Caught," 83-94.

knew the Gospel of John as well as Luke and Matthew.[215] Furthermore, the angel's words to Mary in *ProtJac* 11:07 that she would conceive εκ λογου ("from the logos") of God betrays ignorance of the Hymn to the Logos in Jn 1:1-18. If Jesus were the "Logos" of God who existed in the beginning with God as in Jn 1:1, and who was incarnated as the "only-begotten Son of God" in Jn 1:14,[216] it would be unreasonable for this Logos to have conceived himself in *ProtJac* 19:15.

However, the striking similarities between the Doubting Salome story in the *ProtJac* and the Doubting Thomas story in Jn 20:24-29,[217] including their parallel tactile examinations, would not necessarily lead to the conclusion that the entire Gospel of John must have been known to the Redactor. Some scholars have concluded that the Doubting Thomas story may have been a late addition to the Gospel. Ernst Haenchen views Jn 20:24-29 as "a later insertion into the source" that was used by the evangelist to form the Gospel of John.[218] Robert Fortna considers "the all-important and crowning Johannine episode of questioning Thomas (20:24-29)"[219] to be the evangelist's "addition and possibly creation."[220] The possible independent pre-Gospel

---

215. This conclusion will have serious ramifications in the discussion concerning the possible *Sitz im Leben* of the Redactor. See "The Redactor: *The Protevangelium Jacobi*," pp. 133–5 and the following discussion.

216. Καὶ ὁ λόγος σὰρξ ἐγένετο ("and the Logos became flesh").

217. It has been suggested that Salome was Jesus's sister and Thomas Didymus was Jesus's twin brother Judas, cf. R. Bauckham's full discussion of the possibility that one of Jesus's sisters referred in Mk 6:3 was named Salome, *Jude and the Relatives of Jesus in the Early Church* (Edinburgh: T&T Clark, 1990), 37–44; cf. *Gos. Thom.*, "These are the secret sayings which the living Jesus spoke and which Didymus Judas Thomas wrote down"; *Thom. Cont.*, "The secret words that the savior spoke to Judas Thomas ... Brother Thomas ... Now, since it has been said that you are my twin and true companion ..., " Bentley Layton, ed., *Nag Hammadi codex II, 2-7: Together with XIII, 2*, Brit. Lib. Or. 4926(1), and P. OXY. 1, 654, 655*, vol. 20 in *Nag Hammadi Studies*, eds. M. Krause, J. M. Robinson, and F. Wisse (Leiden; New York: E. J. Brill, 1989), vol. 1, 53; vol. 2, 181.

218. *A Commentary on the Gospel of John*, ed. R. W. Funk with Ulrich Busse, trans. R. W. Funk, 2 vols. (Philadelphia, PA: Fortress Press, 1980) 2:60. Haenchen cites Jn 20:24-29 and the *Pericope Adulterae* in Jn 7:53–8:11 as two of his four best examples supporting the composite nature of the Gospel of John; the other two, the opening prologue with its "Hymn to the Logos" and chapter 21, are widely regarded as later accretions to the text, ibid., 1:76-77.

219. *The Fourth Gospel and Its Predecessor: From Narrative Source to Present Gospel* (Philadelphia, PA: Fortress Press, 1988; for T. & T. Clark), 214. Fortna views the Doubting Thomas episode as the "dramatic close," the completion of the "schematic structure," and the culmination of the whole Gospel of John, ibid., 46. The Doubting Salome story performs the same functions in the *ProtJac*.

220. Ibid., 200. Fortna speaks of an independent Passion Source (PQ) and a Signs Source (SQ), which were once separate but joined together and then integrated into the Gospel, 118; it was at some point in this process that the Thomas episode was added by the Evangelist, 187. Rudolf Bultmann seems ambivalent as to the origin of Jn 20:24-29: "We

origins of the Johannine Doubting Thomas story raise intriguing prospects of an earlier source, separate from the complete Gospel of John from which the Redactor may have derived his inspiration for the Doubting Salome episode.

The Magi

ProtJac 21:01-02 appears to have been created by the Redactor as a transitional seam to accommodate his attachment of his revised version of Matthew's Magi story to his Doubting Salome story. And the Redactor has again left traces of his editorial activity. The Salome episode has concluded in *ProtJac* 20:10-11 with Salome exiting the cave after being healed and then receiving instruction from an angel to announce[221] the "strange things" that she has seen "until the child comes to Jerusalem" (εως ελθη ο παις εις ιεροσολυμα). A point of tension occurs with the immediately following verse, *ProtJac* 21:01, in which Joseph is at the cave outside of Bethlehem preparing to "go out into Judea" (ιωσηφ ητοιμασθη του εξελθειν εν τη ιουδαια). But Bethlehem is in Judea. And Joseph and his entourage—including Mary, her child, Joseph's sons, and Salome—have been in Judea since their arrival at the Cave of the Nativity where all the events of the Birth story in *ProtJac* 19-20 took place.[222] It has been customary among scholars—most of whom conform to the de Strycker consensus opinion of the *ProtJac* as a monolithic single-author work—to attribute this confusion to the ignorance of Palestinian geography on the part of the "author" of the *ProtJac*.[223] But our redaction-critical analysis of the *ProtJac* has instead revealed these contradictory geographical references to be indicators of the Redactor's clumsy editorial activity.

must not regard it as impossible that the source [of the Gospel] itself already contained this story. Admittedly it can only have been a secondary appendix, even for the source," *The Gospel of John: A Commentary*, trans. G. R. Beasley-Murray, R. W. N. Hoare, and J. K. Riches (Philadelphia, PA: The Westminster Press, 1971), 693-6. For the case against the independence of this passage, see Raymond Brown, *The Gospel According to John XIII-XXI* (AB 29A; Garden City, New York: Doubleday & Company, 1977), 2:1031-33.

221. In the two most ancient witnesses to this text, P.Bodm V and the eighth-century Sinai 491, the angel tells Salome to announce her experiences in Jerusalem; in the vast majority of later MSS the angel tells her not to publicize them.

222. This is reminiscent of a similar editorial conflict resulting from interpolations into the text of the Gospel of John by its composer(s) who also created seams in the text to accommodate their revisions. In Jn 3:1-21 Jesus is having a discussion with Nicodemus in Jerusalem, but the next verse, Jn 3:22, states that from Jerusalem Jesus and his disciples came into "the Judean land" (τὴν Ἰουδαίαν γῆν). But, as was the case in *ProtJac* 21:01-02 with Bethlehem, in Jn 3 Jerusalem also is in Judea. In both contexts geographical confusion is caused by the work of careless redactors.

223. The opinion that the "author" of the *ProtJac* was ignorant of Palestinian geography has taken on the nature of a repetitive mantra among scholars, cf. Hock, *Infancy Gospels*, 12, n. 30.

The tension in the Redactor's editorial seam further intensifies as the text continues from *ProtJac* 21:01 to 21:02. Following *ProtJac* 21:01—where Joseph is at the cave near Bethlehem preparing to go into Judea—in 21:02 Bethlehem is actually designated as "Bethlehem of Judea" (Βηθλέεμ τῆς Ἰουδαίας).[224] This even more noticeable geographical contradiction, again, is not due to the purported unitary *ProtJac* single author's ignorance of Palestinian geography but to yet another editorial blunder of the Redactor of the *ProtJac*. In addition to being part of the redactional seam linking the Doubting Salome episode to the Matthew-inspired Magi story, *ProtJac* 21:02 also constitutes the actual introduction to the Magi story itself, which follows in *ProtJac* 21:03–22:02. But *ProtJac* 21:02 serves a larger purpose as well in the Redactor's augmentation of the ending of the CEGM with the Matthean Magi story and the Zachariah Apocryphon in *ProtJac* 22:03–24:11. *ProtJac* 21:02 and 25:01 appear to function as a pair of editorial brackets within which the Redactor has enclosed his last two additions in his edited version of the CEGM. Both of these verses contain a reference to a θορυβος ("disturbance") that took place: in Bethlehem in *ProtJac* 21:02 with the arrival of the Magi and in Jerusalem in 25:01 with the death of Herod.[225]

The text of the Magi story in *ProtJac* 21:02–22:02 is presented below followed by a commentary that emphasizes the dependence of the Redactor's interpolated version of the Magi story in P.Bodm V upon the Matthean original. The following literal translations of the texts of both the *ProtJac* and Matthew are my own:

ProtJac 21:02–22:02
02 και θορυβος εγενετο μεγας εν βηθλεεμ της ιουδαιας.
    And there was a great disturbance in Bethlehem of Judea.
03 ηλθωσαν γαρ μαγοι λεγοντες
    For Magi came, saying,
που εστιν ο βασιλευς των ιουδαιων;
    "where is the king of the Jews?
04 ειδομεν γαρ τον αστερα αυτου εν τη ανατολη,
    for we saw his star in the East,
και ηλθαμεν προσκυνησαι αυτω.
    and we came to worship him."
05 και ακουσας ο ηρωδης εταραχθη,
    And hearing, Herod was shaken,
και επεμψεν υπηρετας
    and he sent servants

---

224. See below, p. 116, where it appears that the phrase ἐν Βηθλέεμ τῆς Ἰουδαίας in *ProtJac* 21:02 was probably duplicated by the Redactor from its original setting in Mt. 2:1 and 2:5.

225. See below, pp. 126–7. The references to Jerusalem in *ProtJac* 20:11 and 25:01-02 may also constitute a pair of geographical brackets that enclose the Magi story and the Zachariah Apocryphon.

06 και μετεπεμψατο αυτους
and he summoned them [the Magi]
και διεσαφησαν αυτω περι του αστερος.²²⁶
And they explained to him about the star.
12 και ιδου ειδον αστερας εν τη ανατολη,
And behold they saw stars in the East,
και προηγαν αυτους
εως εισηλθαν εν τω σπηλαιω,
and they [the stars] went before them [the Magi]
until they [the stars] entered into the cave,
και εστη [a single star]²²⁷ επι την κεφαλην του παιδιου.
And stood upon²²⁸ the head of the child.
13 και ιδοντες οι μαγοι εστωτα μετα της μητρος αυτου μαριας,
And the Magi, seeing [the child] standing with its mother Mary,
14 εξεβαλλον απο της πηρας αυτων δωρα,
took gifts out of their bag,
χρυσον και λιβανον και σμυρναν.
gold and frankincense and myrrh.
15 και χρηματισθεντες υπο του αγγελου,
And being warned by the angel,
δια αλλης οδου ανεχωρησαν εις την χωραν.
they departed for [their] country by another road.
22:01 τοτε ηρωδης ιδων οτι ενεπαιχθη υπο των μαγων,
Then Herod, seeing that he had been deceived by the Magi,
οργισθεις επεμψεν αυτου τους φονευτας λεγων αυτοις
becoming angry, sent his executioners, saying to them
ανελειν παντα τα βρεφη απο διετιας και κατω.
to kill all the babies from two years and under.
02 και ακουσασα η μαρια οτι τα βρεφη ανελειται,
And Mary, hearing that the babies were being killed,
φοβηθεισα ελαβεν τον παιδα
becoming afraid, she took the child,
και εσπαργανωσεν αυτον και εβαλεν εν φατνη βοων.
and wrapped him and put him in a cattle-manger.

Lk. 2:7 καὶ ἔτεκεν τὸν υἱὸν αὐτῆς τὸν πρωτότοκον,
καὶ ἐσπαργάνωσεν αὐτὸν καὶ ἀνέκλινεν αὐτὸν ἐν φάτνῃ,
διότι οὐκ ἦν αὐτοῖς τόπος ἐν τῷ καταλύματι.

226. In *ProtJac* 21:07-11 many MSS follow Mt. 2:4-5 but are confused about whom Herod is questioning.

227. Cf. the references to the single star in *ProtJac* 21:04, 06; Mt. 2:2, 9, 10.

228. The preposition επι is translated as "upon" here with respect to the fact that the child itself is standing (εστωτα) in the very next verse, *ProtJac* 21:13, when the Magi see him in the cave with his mother. See the discussion below, pp. 117-20.

The Redactor has followed his standard procedure in the manner with which he modified the Matthean Magi story to create his own version that he interpolated into the *ProtJac*. And, as usual, he has left behind abundant evidence of his redactional process. First, he eliminated the sections of Matthew's text that contained references to the Nativity in Bethlehem, ostensibly to remain consistent with the central element in the *ProtJac* Nativity story, the birth of Mary's child in the cave outside of Bethlehem. As stated above, *ProtJac* 21:02 was an important verse that functioned in several important ways in the Redactor's work: (1) introducing the Redactor's Magi story, (2) as the redactional seam joining his Magi story to his preceding Doubting Salome story, (3) as the first of a pair of brackets enclosing his final two major interpolations into the CEGM, his Magi story and the Zachariah Apocryphon. Consequently, the Redactor did not eliminate the introductory verse in Matthew's Magi story in Mt. 2:1 when he transferred it into his Magi story as its introductory verse. Instead he adjusted the clear statement in Mt. 2:1 that Jesus was born in Bethlehem so that the reference to Bethlehem in *ProtJac* 21:02 was not associated with the birth of Mary's child but rather with the ("disturbance") that occurred in Bethlehem in *ProtJac* 21:02. A comparison of the texts of Mt. 2:1 and *ProtJac* 21:02 reveals the Redactor's editorial work:

Mt. 2:1
Τοῦ δὲ Ἰησοῦ γεννηθέντος <u>ἐν Βηθλέεμ τῆς Ἰουδαίας</u>
   Jesus having been born <u>in Bethlehem of Judea</u>
ProtJac 21:02
και θορυβος εγενετο μεγας <u>εν βηθλεεμ της ιουδαιας</u>.
   And there was a great disturbance <u>in Bethlehem of Judea</u>.

The Redactor also excluded larger tracts in Matthew's text that contained significant references to Bethlehem in Mt. 2:4-6 and 8-9a. Mt. 2:4 describes Herod gathering the high priests and scribes of Israel to inquire specifically about the location of the birth of the "Christ." In Mt. 2:5 the high priests and scribes respond to Herod's query: the "Christ" would be born "in Bethlehem of Judea" (ἐν Βηθλέεμ τῆς Ἰουδαίας). In Mt. 2:6 they justify their response to Herod by quoting the OT prophecy of Mic. 5:2, which identifies Βηθλέεμ γῆ Ἰούδα ("Bethlehem, land of Judea") as the place from which "will come forth a leader who will shepherd my [God's] people of Israel" (ἐξελεύσεται ἡγούμενος ὅστις ποιμανεῖ τὸν λαόν μου τὸν Ἰσραήλ). The remaining texts in Mt. 2:1-3, 9-12, and 16 are those that the Redactor modified and incorporated into his revised version of the Magi story.

The Redactor also eliminated Mt. 2:8-9a from his revised version. In this text Herod sends the Magi to Bethlehem to enquire about the child and to report back to him. But in this instance the Redactor's characteristically careless editorial technique has produced significant irregularities in the continuity between *ProtJac* 21:06 and the immediately following verse in the text of P.Bodm V at *ProtJac* 21:12. Mt. 2:8-9a would have occurred within what appears as a gap in our text of the

Evidence of Redaction of the ProtJac   117

Redactor's revised version of the Magi story between *ProtJac* 21:06 and 21:12, which constitute two consecutive verses in P.Bodm V.[229] Mt. 2:7-9 and its redacted parallel, *ProtJac* 21:06 and 21:12, are presented below in such a way as to display the Redactor's editorial work. The suppressed reference to Herod sending the Magi to Bethlehem in Mt. 2:8-9a is indented; close verbal parallels between the two versions of the Magi story are underlined:

Mt. 2:7-9:

2:7 Τότε Ἡρῴδης λάθρᾳ καλέσας τοὺς μάγους
   Then Herod, in secret calling the Magi
ἠκρίβωσεν παρ᾽ αὐτῶν τὸν χρόνον τοῦ φαινομένου ἀστέρος,
   ascertained exactly from them the time of the appearing star,
2:8 καὶ πέμψας αὐτοὺς εἰς Βηθλέεμ εἶπεν·
   and sending them to Bethlehem, said,
Πορευθέντες ἐξετάσατε ἀκριβῶς περὶ τοῦ παιδίου·
   "Go and investigate exactly about the child,
ἐπὰν δὲ εὕρητε, ἀπαγγείλατέ μοι,
ὅπως κἀγὼ ἐλθὼν προσκυνήσω αὐτῷ.
   and when you find out, report to me,
   so that I can come worship him."
2:9a οἱ δὲ ἀκούσαντες τοῦ βασιλέως ἐπορεύθησαν,
   And having heard the king, they left,
2:9b καὶ ἰδοὺ ὁ ἀστὴρ ὃν εἶδον ἐν τῇ ἀνατολῇ
προῆγεν αὐτούς,
   and behold the star that they saw in the East
   went before them
ἕως ἐλθὼν ἐστάθη ἐπάνω οὗ ἦν τὸ παιδίον.
   until, having arrived, it stood above the place where the child was.

ProtJac 21:06, 12 according to the text of P.Bodm V:

21:06 και μετεπεμψατο αυτους
   and he [Herod] summoned them [the Magi]
και διεσαφησαν αυτω περι του αστερος.
   And they explained to him about the star.
21:12 και ιδου ειδον αστερας εν τη ανατολη,
   And behold they saw stars in the East

229. This gap in the versification of our text has been implemented to accommodate the readings of many of the later MSS of the *ProtJac* that do not occur in the text of P.Bodm V but which are enumerated in our text as *ProtJac* 21:07-11. It is significant that the earliest extant MS that preserves substantial portions of *ProtJac* 21, the eighth-century Sinai 491, follows P.Bodm V in going directly from *ProtJac* 21:06 to 21:12, without the intervening verses 21:07-11. Furthermore, this is also the only MS to follow the text of P.Bodm V in *ProtJac* 21:06.

και προηγαν αυτους
εως εισηλθαν εν τω σπηλαιω,
    and they [the stars] went before them [the Magi]
    until they [the stars] entered into the cave,
και εστη επι την κεφαλην του παιδιου.
    And [a single star] stood upon the head of the child.

In *ProtJac* 21:06 the Magi were explaining to Herod about the star (αστερος) that they had reported seeing in the East in *ProtJac* 21:04: ειδομεν γαρ τον αστερα αυτου εν τη ανατολη ("for we saw his star in the East").[230] The Redactor took *ProtJac* 21:04 verbatim from Mt. 2:2, which also spoke of a single star. But the redacted storyline in P.Bodm V proceeds directly from *ProtJac* 21:06 to *ProtJac* 21:12, which contradicts both *ProtJac* 21:04 and 21:06 regarding the number of stars in the story. In *ProtJac* 21:12 the Redactor introduced multiple stars that the Magi saw in the East (ειδον αστερας εν τη ανατολη) that would now lead them to the cave. The Redactor created this contradiction in his story when he restructured Mt. 2:9b after he had excised Mt. 2:8-9a from his text. Mt. 2:9b had identified the star that the Magi would follow, after meeting with Herod, as the same star that they initially had seen in the East: καὶ ἰδοὺ ὁ ἀστὴρ ὃν εἶδον ἐν τῇ ἀνατολῇ προῆγεν αὐτούς ("and behold the star that they saw in the East went before them"). But in the Redactor's narrative in *ProtJac* 21:12, after the Magi met Herod they would now follow multiple stars (αστερας), which appeared at that moment "in the East," as opposed to the single star that they originally saw in *ProtJac* 21:04 and 21:06.

The Redactor exacerbated the contradiction in the number of the stars seen by the Magi by reverting within the same verse, *ProtJac* 21:12, to a single star that stood (εστη) upon the head of the child.[231] This reversion is part of the general confusion caused by the Redactor's restructuring of Mt. 2:9b with respect to the course that the Magi and the star(s) followed after the meeting between the Magi and Herod. Mt. 2:9b presents these events coherently: the single star that the Magi had seen in the East "went before them" (προῆγεν αὐτούς) until it came and stood above the location where the child was (ἕως ἐλθὼν ἐστάθη ἐπάνω οὗ ἦν τὸ παιδίον). The Redactor's revised version of this verse in *ProtJac* 21:12 is anything but coherent. The now plural "stars" (αστερας) that the Magi suddenly saw "in the East" likewise "went before them" (προηγαν αυτους). But the confusion begins when "they entered into the cave" (εισηλθαν εν τω σπηλαιω) and "it," that is, now again the single star, "stood upon the head of the child" (εστη επι την κεφαλην του παιδιου). The relevant question is to whom the understood "they" refers in the

---

230. This star had prompted the Magi to come to Judea to worship the "king of the Jews." The star will continue to play a role in the Magi story, but it is not clear in the texts of either the *ProtJac* or Matthew that this star followed the Magi to Judea.

231. The singular form of the verb εστη ("stood") is supported almost universally in the MS tradition of the *ProtJac*.

plural forms of the verbs προηγαν ("they went before them") and εισηλθαν ("they entered into the cave").

It is clear that the "stars" in ProtJac 21:12 "went before" (προηγαν) the Magi (αυτους) on the way to the Cave of the Nativity. But the immediately ensuing text is ambiguous with respect to the "they" who actually "entered into the cave" (εισηλθαν εν τω σπηλαιω). The Redactor created this ambiguity by inserting the phrase "into the cave" (εν τω σπηλαιω)[232] into his revised text of Mt. 2:9b in ProtJac 21:12, as he was also simultaneously changing the number of the stars that went before the Magi, from Matthew's consistently single star to his own plural "stars" and then back again to a single star in the same verse. This becomes apparent in a comparative presentation of the parallel verses from Matthew and the ProtJac:[233]

Mt. 2:9b—The single star that the Magi saw in the East:
προῆγεν αὐτούς, ἕως ἐλθὼν
    went before them [the Magi], until having arrived,
ἐστάθη ἐπάνω οὗ ἦν τὸ παιδίον.
    [the star] stood above the place where the child was.

ProtJac 21:12—The plural stars that the Magi saw in the East:
προηγαν αυτους εως εισηλθαν εν τω σπηλαιω
    went before them [the Magi] until they [the stars] entered into the cave,
και εστη επι την κεφαλην του παιδιου.
    and [a single star] stood upon the head of the child.[234]

The most comfortable interpretation initially is that the "they" who entered the cave in ProtJac 21:12 are the same as the "them" before whom the stars went (προηγαν αυτους), that is, the Magi. But, grammatically, the "they" who entered the cave could refer also to the "stars" that "went before" the Magi toward the cave or even to both the Magi and the stars. If one wished to engage in an ultimately futile attempt to bring lucidity to the obvious editorial gaffes of the Redactor, the latter option is to be preferred. Since the stars were going "before" the Magi, the stars in any case would have entered the cave first. The stars would already have been inside the cave when the Magi arrived, whether or not the Magi themselves would have entered the cave. This is confirmed also by the directly ensuing text, which states that one of the stars "stood upon the head of the child." One of the

---

232. The prepositional phrase εν τω σπηλαιω literally means "in the cave." But in the present context this phrase is preceded by the compound verb εισηλθαν, which consists of ἦλθαν, the aorist tense of the verb ἔρχομαι "to come," preceded by the preposition εἰς "into." The preposition εἰς prefixed to the verb ἦλθαν in combination with the preposition εν allows the prepositional phrase εν τω σπηλαιω to be translated as "into the cave."

233. I have added underlining to emphasize the pertinent phrases.

234. The preposition επι is translated as "upon" with reference to the position of the star vis-à-vis the child's head, as the child is described as εστωτα "standing" when the Magi see him with his mother within the context of ProtJac 21:13. See below.

Magi would hardly have "stood upon the head of the child" (εστη επι την κεφαλην του παιδιου).[235]

The Redactor confused himself and his readers when he excised Mt. 2:8-9a from his text and rewrote Mt. 2:9b with multiple stars, forgetting that Mt. 2:7 had spoken of a single star, as did he himself in *ProtJac* 21:04 and 21:06. But he appears to have had a particular motive to insert his problematic phrase εισηλθαν εν τω σπηλαιω into *ProtJac* 21:12 to indicate that the stars—and perhaps the Magi as well—"entered into the cave," and that specifically a single star "stood upon the head of the child." His motive appears in the ensuing text of Matthew that the Redactor is following and revising. In Mt. 2:10 the Magi rejoice at seeing the star that "went before them" in Mt. 2:9b; this star is now standing "above [ἐπάνω] the place where the child was." In Mt. 2:11 the "place where the child was" is shown to be a "house" (οἰκίαν), ostensibly Joseph's house in Bethlehem, into which the Magi enter and see the child: ἐλθόντες εἰς τὴν οἰκίαν εἶδον τὸ παιδίον μετὰ Μαρίας τῆς μητρὸς αὐτοῦ ("entering into the house, [the Magi] saw the child with Mary his mother"). Obviously, the Redactor must eliminate Matthew's reference to Joseph's Bethlehem "house." He does this by replacing the "house" element in Mt. 2:11 with his problematic phrase "they entered into the cave" (εισηλθαν εν τω σπηλαιω), thus indicating that subsequent events would now take place "in the cave" outside of Bethlehem.

The scene, in which the Magi see the child and its mother in the cave, contains significant parallels to the original *GenMar* Birth story. In the Birth scene in *ProtJac* 19:08-12, the midwife witnessed the miraculous birth, or rather appearance, of the baby from outside the cave.[236] This parallel would negate the non-issue of whether or not the Magi entered the cave after the stars in *ProtJac* 21:12, since they also, from outside the cave, could have witnessed the child εστωτα μετα της μητρος αυτου μαριας ("standing with Mary his mother"). The essential term here is εστωτα, which describes the newborn child (παιδίον) as "standing" with its mother. How can a newborn child stand? It stands in the same way that the newly born βρεφος ("baby") in the original Birth scene in *ProtJac* 19:11 "came and took the breast of his mother Mary" (ηλθεν και ελαβε μασθον εκ της μητρος αυτου μαριας). The divine child born to Mary in the cave was truly remarkable. It was born, or rather appeared, already able to stand and walk.[237]

---

235. Once again the Redactor has created a problematic reading with his editorial manipulation of the text.

236. Cf. pp. 110-11 above. It was the Redactor who added the element of the midwife leaving the cave and meeting Salome. According to photographs of the foundations of the Kathisma Church provided to me by Professor J. H. Charlesworth, the terrain of the Kathisma appears flat. Thus the cave may have been a rocky overhang as opposed to a deeper opening in the earth, cf. "Appendix 4: The Kathisma Church," pp. 205-20; images on pp. 219-20.

237. See the discussion in "The Author: *The Genesis Marias*," on the possible Docetic character of the Annunciation and Nativity scenes in the *GenMar*, pp. 160-8.

After the scene in which the Magi saw the child with his mother, the Redactor essentially reproduced the scenes from Matthew's Magi story in which the Magi presented their gifts of gold, frankincense, and myrrh to the child and then, being warned by an angel, avoided returning to Herod.[238] The Redactor omitted almost the entire Matthean signature flight to Egypt episode, including Joseph's angelic dream vision warning him to flee with Mary and her child to Egypt (Mt. 2:13-15), the associated fulfillment citation of Jer. 31:15 (Mt. 2:17-18), and a second angelic dream vision to Joseph, prompting him to return to Judea and ultimately to settle in Nazareth (Mt. 2:19-23). The Redactor's revised Magi story ends with Herod becoming angry at being deceived by the Magi and ordering the slaughter of all babies two-years-old and under in *ProtJac* 22:01 (Mt. 2:16).[239] As we have come to expect, the Redactor omitted Matthew's reference to Herod's slaughter of the children specifically in Bethlehem and "all its surroundings" as is evident in the parallel presentation of the texts below:

Mt. 2:16 Τότε Ἡρῴδης ἰδὼν ὅτι ἐνεπαίχθη ὑπὸ τῶν μάγων
   Then Herod, seeing that he was deceived by the Magi
ἐθυμώθη λίαν, καὶ ἀποστείλας
   became very angry, and sending out [executioners]
ἀνεῖλεν πάντας τοὺς παῖδας τοὺς ἐν Βηθλέεμ καὶ ἐν πᾶσι τοῖς ὁρίοις αὐτῆς
   to execute all the children in Bethlehem and in all its surroundings
ἀπὸ διετοῦς καὶ κατωτέρω,
   from two years and less,

ProtJac 22:01 τοτε ηρωδης ιδων οτι ενεπαιχθη υπο των μαγων,
   Then Herod, seeing that he had been deceived by the Magi,
οργισθεις επεμψεν αυτου τους φονευτας λεγων αυτοις
   becoming angry, sent his executioners, saying to them
ανελειν παντα τα βρεφη
απο διετιας και κατω.
   to kill all the babies
   from two years and under.

In *ProtJac* 22:01 the Redactor had finalized the adjustments that he was compelled to make to Matthew's Magi story in order to accommodate his own

---

238. The Redactor's revised text contains numerous verbatim borrowings from Matthew.

239. The Redactor has also omitted the scene in Mt. 2:8-9 in which Herod sends the Magi to Bethlehem, asking them to report back to him about the child. This omission causes a discrepancy in the Redactor's account in *ProtJac* 22:01 where Herod becomes angry that the Magi deceived him and returned directly to their country. The Redactor obtained this verse from Mt. 2:16 in which Herod's anger is justified because in Matthew Herod did ask the Magi to report back to him. But in the Redactor's account Herod's anger is not justified because he never actually asked the Magi to return to him.

revised version of that story to its new matrix in the Birth narrative of the CEGM.[240] The Redactor then created an idiosyncratic ending to his redacted Birth story in *ProtJac* 22:02, which functioned also as a transition to the Zachariah Apocryphon. Herod's execution of the babies (βρεφη) in *ProtJac* 22:01 segues into 22:02, which begins with "Mary hearing that the babies were being killed" (ακουσασα η μαρια οτι τα βρεφη ανελειται) and "becoming afraid" (φοβηθεισα). The Redactor completed this verse with an insertion taken from Lk. 2:7: Mary "took the child, and wrapped him and put him in a cattle-manger" (ελαβεν τον παιδα και εσπαργανωσεν αυτον και εβαλεν εν φατνη βοων). He adjusted this material as well by omitting elements of Lk. 2:7 that were contrary to his editorial agenda. This becomes evident in the following parallel presentation of the texts from Luke and the *ProtJac*:

Lk. 2:7
καὶ ἔτεκεν τὸν υἱὸν αὐτῆς τὸν πρωτότοκον,
and she gave birth to her first-born son,
<u>καὶ ἐσπαργάνωσεν αὐτὸν καὶ</u> ἀνέκλινεν αὐτὸν <u>ἐν φάτνῃ</u>,
<u>and wrapped him and</u> lay <u>him in a manger</u>,
διότι οὐκ ἦν αὐτοῖς τόπος ἐν τῷ καταλύματι.
because there was no room for them in the shelter.

ProtJac 22:02
<u>και εσπαργανωσεν αυτον και</u> εβαλεν <u>εν φατνη</u> βοων.
<u>and wrapped him and</u> put [him] <u>in a cattle-manger</u>.

The Redactor omitted the reference in Lk. 2:7 to Jesus as Mary's "first-born son" (τὸν υἱὸν αὐτῆς τὸν πρωτότοκον) because this could be interpreted as conflicting with his primary objective of establishing the perpetual virginity of Mary. If Jesus was Mary's "first-born son," then other sons may have followed as indicated in Mk 6:3 where four "brothers" of Jesus are named. The Redactor also eliminated from Lk. 2:7 the statement that "there was no room for them in the shelter" (οὐκ ἦν αὐτοῖς τόπος ἐν τῷ καταλύματι). He seems to have understood the word "shelter" as a place of lodging in the town of Bethlehem itself, which contradicts a central element in the *ProtJac*, the Nativity in a cave outside of Bethlehem. The Redactor's introduction of this element from Luke's Nativity story into *ProtJac* 22:02 suggests that the confusion in his Birth story may stem from his awareness of three separate Nativity accounts as he struggled to integrate his version of the Matthean Magi story into his already radically edited Birth narrative: Matthew, Luke, and the CEGM. The difficulty of the Redactor's task was compounded by the discrepancies in the details between his three sources and in the larger issues of the point of origin of the Journey to Bethlehem and the location of the Nativity itself.[241]

---

240. The Redactor had already extended the Birth story with his interpolated Doubting Salome episode to which he attached his revised Magi story.

241. In Matthew, Joseph and Mary were a betrothed couple living in Joseph's house in Bethlehem, where Jesus was born; in Mt. 2:7-9, the Magi followed the star until it stopped "above the place where the child was." Matthew had no Roman census that prompted Joseph

Evidence of Redaction of the ProtJac 123

The Zachariah Apocryphon[242]

Immediately after his Doubting Salome episode in *ProtJac* 19:13–20:11 and his Matthew-inspired Magi story in *ProtJac* 21:01–22:02, the Redactor attached in *ProtJac* 22:03 what has been labeled as the *Apocryphum Zachariae*.[243] Up to this point the narrative of the *ProtJac* was entirely concerned with Mary and her child. But in the Zachariah materials, the story is abruptly reoriented to an entirely different scenario in which the angry Herod is no longer seeking to kill Mary's child, as in *ProtJac* 22:02, but in 22:03 is now searching for the infant John the Baptist. The Zachariah materials begin with a fanciful story in *ProtJac* 22:03-06 about John's mother Elizabeth who hears that her son is being hunted and flees to the hills looking for a place to hide him. Finding none, she speaks to the mountain and asks it to receive her, a mother and her child. The mountain immediately splits open and receives her. The mountain is described in *ProtJac* 22:06 as "shining light through for her, for an angel of the Lord was with them, protecting them" (ην το ορος εκεινο διαφαινων αυτη φως αγγελος γαρ κυριου ην μετ αυτων ο διαφυλασσων αυτους).[244]

Elizabeth's Flight into the mountain is followed directly in *ProtJac* 23–24 by an account of the murder of the high priest Zachariah. Although it is thematically related to the Elizabeth materials in *ProtJac* 22:03-06—Zachariah is her husband and the father of her child—the story of Zachariah's Death appears to be an independent, self-contained narrative that is not entirely congruent with the

---

and the pregnant Mary to travel toward Bethlehem as in Luke and the *ProtJac*. In Mt. 2:19-23, after their stay in Egypt, Joseph and Mary initially intended to return to their home in Bethlehem but instead chose to settle in Nazareth of the Galilee for fear of Herod Archelaus. In Lk. 2:1-5, Joseph and Mary were residing in Nazareth, from where they departed to register in the census in Joseph's ancestral home town of Bethlehem. In the *ProtJac* Joseph's home was in Jerusalem, where the journey of Joseph and his entourage toward Bethlehem originated and ended "in the middle of the road" between Jerusalem and Bethlehem, three miles outside of Bethlehem. Mary's ancestral home also may have been located in Jerusalem according to the *ProtJac*.

242. See the discussion below regarding the significance of the Zachariah Apocryphon toward identifying the *Sitz im Leben* of the Redactor as a member of the "School" of Justin Martyr in mid-second-century Rome, "The Redactor: *The Protevangelium Jacobi*," pp. 136-8.

243. For the various scholarly opinions on this document, see "The Compositional Problem of the *ProtJac*," pp. 15–21.

244. The presence of an angel in the story of Elizabeth's Flight may suggest the editorial influence of the Redactor or, alternatively, may have derived from the same source as the Baptist materials in Lk. 1:8-19 in which the archangel appears to the high priest Zachariah in the Holy of Holies to announce to him the birth of his son John. The Redactor was aware of the Lukan angelic appearance as indicated by his interpolated text in *ProtJac* 10:08 that referred the silence of Zachariah detailed in Lk. 1:19-20, 64; see pp. 38–9.

preceding story of Elizabeth's Flight. The Zachariah story is introduced in *ProtJac* 23:01 as new subject matter that exhibits no awareness of the preceding Elizabeth material: "And Herod was seeking John" (ο δε ηρωδης εζητει τον ιωαννην). This text appears redundant within its present context after the notice was already given in *ProtJac* 22:03 that Elizabeth had heard that Herod was seeking her son John (η δε ελισαβεδ, ακουσασα οτι ιωαννης ζητειται). The Redactor seems to have patterned *ProtJac* 22:03 after 22:02 to facilitate the sudden transition from his Magi story, which ended in *ProtJac* 22:02 with Herod seeking Mary's son, to *ProtJac* 22:03 with Herod pursuing Elizabeth's son.[245] And since the initial verse of the Zachariah story in *ProtJac* 23:01 is associated thematically with *ProtJac* 22:03, the Redactor has also provided an appropriate, although awkward, segue from his Magi story to the Zachariah materials. The verbal parallels between these verses are illuminating:

ProtJac 22:02
και <u>ακουσασα</u> η μαρια οτι τα βρεφη ανελειται,
    And Mary, <u>hearing</u> that the infants are being killed,
φοβηθεισα <u>ελαβεν</u> τον παιδα και εσπαργανωσεν αυτον
    becoming afraid, <u>took</u> the child and wrapped him
και εβαλεν εν φατνη βοων.
    and put him in a cattle-manger.

ProtJac 22:03
η δε ελισαβεδ, <u>ακουσασα</u> οτι ιωαννης <u>ζητειται</u>,
    And Elizabeth, <u>hearing</u> that John is being sought,
<u>λαβομενη</u> αυτον ανεβη εν τη ορεινη,
    <u>taking</u> him, she went up into the hills,
και περιεβλεπετο που αυτον αποκρυψη
    and looked around for where she might hide him.

ProtJac 23:01
ο δε ηρωδης <u>εζητει</u> τον ιωαννην
    And Herod was seeking John.

However, there exists a viable alternative explanation that may resolve the chronological incongruence between Elizabeth having heard that Herod was seeking John in *ProtJac* 22:03 and the redundant statement in *ProtJac* 23:01 that "Herod was seeking John." It is conceivable that the story of Elizabeth's Flight may have existed as part of the story of Zachariah's death that was detached from its original matrix by the Redactor and inserted as a transitional element between the end of the Birth story in *ProtJac* 22:02 and the beginning of the Zachariah story in *ProtJac* 23:01. The story of the death of Zachariah begins in

---

245. This has been a standard editorial technique used by both the Composer and the Redactor in their respective augmentations of the narrative of the *ProtJac*.

ProtJac 23:01 with Herod seeking John. *ProtJac* 23 describes a dialogue between Herod and Zachariah in which Herod becomes enraged that Zachariah does not know where his son is. In *ProtJac* 23:09 Zachariah is murdered, ostensibly by Herod's servants. *ProtJac* 24 describes the discovery of the crime and a three-day mourning period by the people. The Zachariah story ends in *ProtJac* 24:10 where the priests replace Zachariah with Symeon, who appears only here in the *ProtJac*. This unique reference to Symeon no doubt represents an interpolation by the Redactor that he derived, characteristically, from a canonical Gospel, Lk. 2:25-35, which features the aged Symeon who identified Jesus as the "Messiah of the Lord." This is evident from a comparison of the texts of the description of Symeon in *ProtJac* 24:11 and its parallel in Lk. 2:26. Verbatim connections between the two texts are underlined:

ProtJac 24:11
ουτος γαρ ην ο <u>χρηματισθεις</u> <u>υπο του αγιου πνευματος</u>
for this was he who was <u>prophesied</u> <u>by the Holy Spirit</u>
<u>μη ιδειν θανατον</u> εως <u>αν</u> <u>τον χριστον</u> εν σαρκι <u>ιδη</u>.
<u>not to see death</u> until <u>he would see the Christ</u> in the flesh.[246]

Lk. 2:26
καὶ ἦν αὐτῷ <u>κεχρηματισμένον</u> <u>ὑπὸ τοῦ πνεύματος τοῦ ἁγίου</u>
and it was <u>prophesied</u> to him <u>by the Holy Spirit</u>
<u>μὴ ἰδεῖν θάνατον</u> πρὶν ἢ <u>ἂν ἴδῃ</u> <u>τὸν χριστὸν</u> κυρίου
<u>not to see death</u> before <u>he would see the Christ</u> of the Lord.

In view of the Redactor's contrived ending to the Zachariah materials in *ProtJac* 24:10-11, and the possibility that the Elizabeth story was part of the Zachariah story, we may postulate that the Elizabeth story originally may have been located after *ProtJac* 24:09-10 where it functioned as the conclusion of the Zachariah materials. The Redactor could have detached the Elizabeth story from the end of the Zachariah story and inserted it as a transitional bridge between the ending of his Magi story in *ProtJac* 22:02, with Mary hiding her child from Herod, and the precipitous beginning of the Zachariah story in *ProtJac* 23:01, with Herod seeking John.[247] The contiguous parallel scenarios of two mothers hiding their sons from

---

246. The Redactor's insertion of the prepositional phrase εν σαρκι into his description of Symeon, which does not occur in the text that he derived from Lk. 2:26, most likely betrays an anti-Docetic polemic. See the discussion of the Docetic character of the original *GenMar*, which the Redactor would have opposed, "The Author: *The Genesis Marias*," pp. 161–8.

247. This interpretation is supported by the similarity of the content of what is now the beginning of the Zachariah narrative in *ProtJac* 23:01 that "Herod was seeking John" (ο δε ηρωδης εζητει τον ιωαννην) and what is now the initial verse of the Elizabeth story in *ProtJac* 22:03 where she heard "that John is being sought" (η δε ελισαβεδ, ακουσασα οτι ιωαννης ζητειται).

Herod shift the narrative smoothly from Mary's son in *ProtJac* 22:02 to Elizabeth's son in *ProtJac* 22:03 and the ensuing death of her son's father.[248] This theory is suggested first by the apparent chronological antecedence of the Elizabeth story vis-à-vis the beginning of the Zachariah materials in *ProtJac* 23:01.[249] Furthermore, the story of Elizabeth's Flight would represent an appropriate ending of the Zachariah Apocryphon, bringing to a conclusion the entire narrative of Herod's pursuit of the infant John and explaining how Elizabeth and her son miraculously escaped Herod after he had killed the child's father Zachariah.

The Colophon

The colophon in *ProtJac* 25 attributes this complete document to James: εγω δε ιακωβος ο γραψας την ιστοριαν ταυτην ("I, James, who wrote this history"). Ostensibly this is the James who was named in Mk 6:03 as one of the four brothers of Jesus and who was recognized by Paul and the Acts of the Apostles as the leader of the Jerusalem community after the crucifixion of Jesus.[250] The Redactor provided a clue that supports our conclusion that he did in fact attach the Magi story and the Zachariah materials to his redacted Birth narrative, after his interpolated Doubting Salome story.[251] The Redactor inserted *ProtJac* 21:01-02 as yet another of his characteristically incongruous transitional seams by which he attempted to facilitate his interpolations into his source document. In this case, *ProtJac* 21:01 was intended to enable his attachment of his Magi story and Zachariah materials to his redacted Birth story.[252]

ProtJac 21:01 is a particularly discordant element within its present context in which Mary has just given birth to her child and was physically examined by Salome in the cave just outside of Bethlehem in Judea.[253] And it is in *ProtJac* 21:02 that the Redactor provides us with the clue to the editorial process by which

---

248. In spite of the abruptness with which the Redactor injects the Zachariah materials into his Birth story, one can discern a reasonable, purposeful segue from Mary and her child to Elizabeth and hers in *ProtJac* 22:02-03. Both mothers are concerned with protecting their infant sons from King Herod who is seeking to kill them.

249. See above, pp. 123–6.

250. Gal. 2:11-13; Acts 15:13-20.

251. See above, pp. 108–11. The original Birth story of the Redactor's source document, the CEGM, had ended with the culminating event of the birth of Mary's divine child in *ProtJac* 19:12 into which the Redactor had integrated his Doubting Salome episode in *ProtJac* 19:13–20:11.

252. See above, pp. 113–14.

253. Ibid. Immediately after these events, in *ProtJac* 21:01, Joseph was preparing "to go out into Judea" (ιωσηφ ητοιμασθη του εξελθειν εν τη ιουδαια). But Joseph is already in Judea where all the events involving the midwife, the birth of Mary's child, and Salome have taken place.

he created the ending of the *ProtJac*. The Redactor's Magi story and Zachariah materials appear to be enclosed within two verses, *ProtJac* 21:02 and 25:01, which share very similar terminology, specifically the word θορυβος ("turmoil") that occurs only in these two contexts in the *ProtJac*. *ProtJac* 21:02 reads θορυβος εγενετο μεγας εν βηθλεεμ της ιουδαιας ("there was great turmoil in Bethlehem of Judea"); *ProtJac* 25:01 εν ιεροσολυμοις θορυβου γενομενου ("there being turmoil in Jerusalem").[254] Apparently the Redactor employed the "turmoil" motif as a set of parentheses within which he enclosed his major interpolations of his revised Matthean Magi story and his Zachariah materials. And it is with these materials that the Redactor finalized his editorial work, which resulted in his own apocryphal Gospel, the *ProtJac*.

---

254. In *ProtJac* 21:01 the turmoil was related to the appearance of the Magi; in *ProtJac* 25:01 the turmoil occurred "when Herod died" (οτε ετελευτησεν ηρωδης). Since there is no mention of the death of Herod in the Redactor's Magi story, he must have derived this information from Mt. 2:19-22. This is entirely consistent with the fact that the Redactor's Magi story itself was mostly derived from the original Matthean Magi story that occurs in the preceding verses in Mt. 2:1-18; cf. "The Magi," pp. 113-22 above.

CONCLUSIONS: THE "AUTHORS" OF THE *PROTJAC*

The compositional theory set forth in this publication represents a radical departure from the current scholarly consensus, which continues to follow the major transformation in *ProtJac* studies that was initiated by de Strycker over fifty years ago. But de Strycker's own substantial reinterpretation of the composition of the *ProtJac* itself represented a radical departure from the incisive, critical discussions on this issue that had been carried out by earlier scholars.[1] The critical hypotheses presented in this volume are based upon the tripartite compositional theory of the *ProtJac* that had been espoused by Harnack, Amann, et al., who formulated this theory before the discovery of P.Bodm V. Testuz, the first editor of P.Bodm V, also accepted the multisource theory on the cusp of the revolution in *ProtJac* studies that would be ignited by de Strycker.[2] As opposed to viewing the *ProtJac* as a composition of three originally independent source documents, as was the case with the early investigators, the present study instead understands the *ProtJac* to be the product of a multistage process involving successive authors and editors. This conclusion has necessitated a new dating scheme for the document as a whole and for each of its component elements.[3]

If there were successive writers, composers, and redactors at work to produce the *ProtJac* as we know it today, then the questions of date, provenance, and theological *Sitz im Leben* must be addressed for each of these individuals. The comprehensive theory presented here is general in scope but attempts to account for these principal critical issues. It is intended to provide a basis for further in-depth investigations by scholars who are more expert than I in each of the areas involved. Who was the original Author of the *GenMar*? When and where did he live and write, and what was his purpose for creating such a document? These same questions apply to the Composer, if in fact he was a different person than the

---

1. See "The Compositional Problem of the *ProtJac*," pp. 15–21.

2. For details of the interactions between Testuz and de Strycker, especially de Strycker's questionable presentation of the correspondence between Testuz and himself, see pp. 8–9.

3. In this study I have revised some of my earlier conclusions about the relationship between Justin Martyr and the *ProtJac*, and its significance for the date of the *ProtJac*, cf. "Dating," see below, p. 146, especially n. 59.

GenMar Author. And they apply to the Redactor who essentially transformed his source document, the CEGM, into the final form of the *ProtJac*.[4] It is my hope that the evidence presented here has, at least, revealed the composition of the *ProtJac* to be more complex than the prevailing one-dimensional theory allows and that it will encourage new scholarly investigation of the *ProtJac* as it was in the more fertile pre–de Strycker era.

Of the three individual writers who participated in the composition of the *ProtJac* as it exists today, the one whose work is most clearly identifiable is the Redactor. Therefore, if the Redactor's revisions and canonical interpolations are eliminated from the text of the *ProtJac*, then the text of the Redactor's source, the CEGM, will be visible in its original unredacted state—independent of the canonical Gospels—as it existed before its radical alteration at the hands of the Redactor. Subsequently, the Composer's augmentations of his own source document, the *GenMar*, may likewise be removed to reveal the work of the original Author who began the compositional process that eventually resulted in the final form of the *ProtJac* as it is known today.

---

4. The same questions should also be asked, from the perspective of textual criticism, regarding the generations of later scribes and editors from antiquity to modernity who subjected the text of the *ProtJac* to further manipulation, each according to their own literary or dogmatic agenda.

THE REDACTOR: THE *PROTEVANGELIUM JACOBI*

Most of the extant text of the *GenMar* is preserved in the first seven chapters of the *ProtJac* in a relatively pristine state that is devoid of evidence of later editorial activity by the Redactor or the Composer. The impact of the Redactor on his source, the CEGM, begins to appear in the Joseph Council (*ProtJac* 8:03–9:12), increases exponentially in the Veil Council (*ProtJac* 10:01–12:11),[5] and becomes manifest in the Nativity Complex (*ProtJac* 17:01–24:11). Specific elements in the Redactor's material that bear his distinctive signature are canonical texts, angelic visitations, and references to Zachariah. The Redactor's heavy-handed manipulations of the text of his source document left a trail of conspicuous interruptions in the flow of its narrative, dislocated material, and obvious attempts to reconcile his disruption of the text by using various editorial techniques. The Redactor was unaware of the already heavily revised nature of his source, the CEGM, and thus carried out his editorial revisions in the order in which he found its text after it had left the pen of the Composer.

The confusion in the *ProtJac* text related to the Redactor's editorial revisions is sometimes exacerbated by existing irregularities caused by the Composer's previous redactional activity. The first instance of the Redactor's work occurs at the location in the *ProtJac* in which the Composer had inserted the Joseph Council into the *GenMar*.[6] The Redactor interjected *ProtJac* 8:07 into the scenario in which the high priest sought divine guidance regarding the twelve-year-old Mary in the Holy of Holies: "and behold, an angel of the Lord stood, saying, 'Zachariah, Zachariah, go out and gather together the widowers of the people.'"[7] This verse contains three distinctive elements that betray the influence of the Redactor: (1) the name of the high priest as Zachariah, (2) the appearance of an angel, and (3) the angel's use of the verb εκκλησιασον, which is an echo of a uniquely Matthean term.[8] The second instance of an additional disruptive element inserted by the

---

5. According to our compositional theory, the Veil Council constituted an original part of the *GenMar* that followed directly after chapters 1–7. The Veil Council, now preserved in *ProtJac* 10:01–12:11, was separated from its original context when the Composer inserted the Joseph Council into the *GenMar*. The Veil Council was highly redacted, first by the Composer, and subsequently by the Redactor.

6. Cf. "The Joseph Council," pp. 25–8. *ProtJac* 8:03–9:04 was described as a "fragmented" passage in which the secondary elements of the Composer and the Redactor are so closely intermixed with the original components of the *GenMar* narrative that it "represents a most daunting, and perhaps insurmountable, challenge" to disentangle the conflicting elements in the text.

7. Ibid., p. 26.

8. The noun form of the verb εκκλησιασον ("call out") is ἐκκλησία, which is the word used uniquely in Matthew among the NT Gospels as a designation for the "church." The term ἐκκλησία occurs in only two passages, Mt. 16:18; 18:17, both of which are manifestly insertions by the author of the Gospel of Matthew into the text of his source documents; ἐκκλησία is used assiduously in the letters of Paul and in the Pauline Book of the Acts of the Apostles.

Redactor occurs in *ProtJac* 10:02-09 where the virgins were brought to the temple and assigned colored threads to weave the temple veil. The Composer had altered this text to show that Mary was brought to the temple from her home, to harmonize the text with his previous removal of Mary from the temple in his Joseph Council.[9] The Redactor interrupted the flow of the Composer's revised narrative with the insertion of his own text, *ProtJac* 10:08: "at that time Zachariah became silent, and Samuel took his place, until the time when Zachariah spoke."[10] Typically, the Redactor's text derives from a canonical Gospel, Lk. 1:5-22, 59-64, and includes a reference to Zachariah.

The Redactor's editorial manipulations of the CEGM become more pronounced as the Veil Council progresses and cause even more confusion in the text. Again the Redactor brusquely interpolates his materials into his source document, which already exhibits significant irregularities caused by the Composer's radical recasting of his own source document, the *GenMar*, to remove Mary from the temple before her Annunciation.[11] The essential element in the Veil Council—as it appeared to the Redactor after its enhancement by the Composer—was the Annunciation story as preserved in *ProtJac* 11:01-05 and 12:01-02.[12] The Redactor inserted into this story two consecutive angelic visitations in *ProtJac* 11:06-12, which consist largely of material derived from the Annunciation story of Lk. 1:26-38. The Redactor's purpose was to overwrite the "unorthodox" direct Annunciation and impregnation of Mary by the Voice of God, the *Bath Kol*, with the Lukan version of the Annunciation through mediator angels. To this now twice-augmented version of the Annunciation, the Redactor then attached his revised version of Mary's visit to her relative Elizabeth, which is based upon the canonical Elizabeth story in Lk. 1:39-56.[13] Again the Redactor's activity is betrayed by the presence of materials featuring angels that are derived from the canonical Gospel of Luke.

Significant editorial activity by the Redactor occurs next in the story of the Trial of Mary and Joseph in *ProtJac* 13-16.[14] In the Trial story the narrative returns to and continues the Joseph Council, which had broken off abruptly after Joseph received Mary from the temple priests and left her at his home before returning to his construction work in *ProtJac* 9:10-12. The Composer had separated his Joseph Council (*ProtJac* 8:03-9:12) from its continuation in his Trial story (*ProtJac* 13-16) by inserting his enhanced Veil Council (*ProtJac* 10-12) between these two major

---

9. *ProtJac* 10:03-05, "The Veil Council," pp. 35-7. The Composer's Joseph materials will resume in the Trial story following the Veil Council.

10. Ibid., p. 39; the Redactor's inserted verse follows immediately upon the Composer's own insertion of *ProtJac* 10:07b in the *GenMar* to reflect Mary's presence "in her house" as opposed to her being in the temple: τω δε καιρω εκεινω ζαχαριας εσιγησεν, εγενετο αντι αυτου σαμουηλ, μεχρι οτε ελαλησεν ζαχαριας.

11. Ibid., pp. 44-5.

12. Cf. "The Original *GenMar* Annunciation Story," pp. 39-49.

13. Cf. "Mary's Visit to Elizabeth," pp. 49-54.

14. Cf. "The Trial of Joseph and Mary," pp. 55-76.

sections of his Joseph materials.[15] The Redactor compounded the confusion in these texts by inserting his angelic appearances into the enhanced Annunciation story in which the angels gave Mary details about her conception. He created discord with two texts in the Trial story (*ProtJac* 13:10-12 and 15:10-12) in which Mary expressed uncertainty regarding the circumstances of her conception.[16] Mary's uncertainty in *ProtJac* 13 and 15 is irreconcilable with the details she received from the angels in the Redactor's interpolation in *ProtJac* 11. The Redactor did not redress these anomalies, but he left his signature on the Trial story with a major revision involving yet another interpolated canonical angelic appearance, this time in a dream vision to Joseph in *ProtJac* 14.

Within the Composer's otherwise homogeneous Trial narrative in *ProtJac* 13-16, *ProtJac* 14 constitutes, almost entirely, an interpolation by the Redactor.[17] After returning home from his construction work and finding Mary pregnant in *ProtJac* 13, Joseph had lamented fervently and engaged in a bitter accusatory dispute with her. This dispute ended in *ProtJac* 14:01a with Joseph considering whether to hide her "sin" or expose her. *ProtJac* 14:01b-04a represents a contrived transitional passage by the Redactor that facilitates yet another of his interpolations of canonical Gospel materials into the Composer's document.[18] *ProtJac* 14:04-08 constitutes a characteristic angelic appearance episode created by the Redactor from texts that he derived, some verbatim, from Mt. 1:19-21, 24 in which an angel appears to Joseph in a dream telling him not to put Mary away because her child is from the Holy Spirit.[19] The Redactor further enhanced Mary's virginal status, even beyond that in his canonical source, by replacing two references to Mary as Joseph's γυναῖκα ("wife") in Mt. 1:20 and 24 with the term παῖδα in *ProtJac* 14:06 and 08, which could mean "young girl" or "maiden." He also omitted two verses from Mt. 1:18 and 25 that imply that Mary was a virgin only up to the point at which she gave birth to Jesus.[20]

Significant interpolations by the Redactor continue to occur as the narrative of the *ProtJac* transitions from the Composer's Trial story into the Nativity complex, which includes the Journey to the Cave, the Midwife episode, the Birth story, the Magi story, and the Zachariah materials.[21] The Redactor adjusted the Journey story in *ProtJac* 17:01 with a canonical reference to the name of the king who called for the registration as Aostos, a corruption of the Augustus of Lk. 2:1.

---

15. Ibid., p. 55.

16. Ibid., pp. 57-8. The Redactor had caused the same type of inconsistency previously in his interpolated Elizabeth story in *ProtJac* 12:05-06 where Mary also showed uncertainty about her pregnancy in responding to the blessing of Elizabeth after the double angelic Annunciation in the preceding chapter, "Mary's Visit to Elizabeth," pp. 49-53.

17. Cf. "The Trial of Joseph and Mary," pp. 60-5.

18. Ibid., pp. 63-5.

19. Ibid., pp. 60-1.

20. Ibid., pp. 62-3.

21. Cf. "The Nativity Complex," pp. 77-127.

Similarly, his motif of Joseph's internal dialogue in *ProtJac* 17:02-04 on how to register Mary follows the pattern of his likewise interpolated internal dialogue in *ProtJac* 14:01-04 on what to do about the newly discovered pregnancy of Mary.[22] The Redactor inserted *ProtJac* 17:06-10 into the Journey story to alter the location of the cave between Jerusalem and Bethlehem. With this passage, the Redactor resolved a discrepancy between the point of origin of the Journey in the *ProtJac* and its parallel in canonical Lk. 2:4 but also placed the location of the cave in closer proximity to the shrine of the tomb of Rachel in nearby Bethlehem. *ProtJac* 17:06-10 recalls Rachel's weeping and mourning over her dead children in Mt. 2:17-18 and matches Mary's birth pangs and vision of two nations with the matriarch Rebekah's difficult pregnancy in Gen. 25:19-26.[23]

The Midwife episode and the following Birth story are replete with manipulations by the Redactor. The evidence of redaction in the Midwife episode is exceedingly complex and could be clarified only with reference to the substantial discrepancies in the Greek MS tradition. The very convoluted editorial activity of the Redactor in the Midwife episode in *ProtJac* 18:01-19:07 was designed to eliminate any hints from his source text that Mary was Joseph's wife or had conjugal relations with him at any point.[24] The original *GenMar* Birth story that followed in *ProtJac* 19:08-12 seems to have been preserved intact with the exception of the apparent redundancy in the midwife's two exclamations of wonder in *ProtJac* 19:09 and 19:12. The Redactor inserted *ProtJac* 19:09 into the narrative to facilitate the integration of his Doubting Salome passage into the end of the Birth story in *ProtJac* 19:13-20:11. The birth of Mary's child in *ProtJac* 18:01-19:12 originally served as the culmination and conclusion of the CEGM. But the Redactor seized control of the Composer's document and radically augmented its ending to create his own conclusion featuring his Doubting Salome story, his revised Matthean Magi story, and the Zachariah materials, all of which he attached in *ProtJac* 19:13-24:11.

The Doubting Salome story represents the climactic event of the Redactor's revision of the CEGM in which he clearly displays his prime objective, to substantiate the perpetual virginity of Mary.[25] The Redactor insinuates the previously unknown and unidentified character Salome into the Birth story with a contrived dialogue in *ProtJac* 19:13-15 in which the midwife declares to Salome that "a virgin gave birth to something that her nature does not allow." Salome will not believe that a virgin gave birth unless she herself physically examines Mary, which she does with the result that her hand is burned off. The Redactor introduces two angels into the story; the first instructs Salome that she will be healed if she touches the child, and the second instructs her to publicize "the strange things" she saw. The Redactor's standard angelic elements in his interpolated Doubting Salome episode

---

22. Cf. "The Journey to Bethlehem," pp. 84–8.
23. Cf. "Topographical and Archaeological Factors," pp. 89–92.
24. Cf. "The Midwife," pp. 92–103.
25. Cf. "Doubting Salome," pp. 108–13.

are accompanied by a, likewise standard, canonical reference from the Doubting Thomas story in the Gospel of John. Salome's words in *ProtJac* 19:15—"If I do not put my finger" (Ἐὰν μὴ βάλω τὸν δάκτυλόν μου) and examine her "I will not believe" (οὐ μὴ πιστεύσω)—are taken verbatim from Jn 20:25.[26]

The Redactor's revised Matthean Magi story actually constitutes the end of the *ProtJac* proper as an account of the early life of Mary leading up to the birth of her divine child. At that point, Mary and her child completely disappear, and in the following Zachariah materials the narrative is concerned exclusively with John the Baptist and his parents, Elizabeth and the high priest Zachariah. The Redactor provided an awkward transitional seam in *ProtJac* 21:01-02 from his Doubting Salome story to his Magi story, featuring a geographical inconsistency between the ending of the Doubting Salome story in *ProtJac* 20:10-11 at the cave outside of Bethlehem in Judea and the immediately following passage *ProtJac* 21:01-02 where Joseph is preparing "to go out into Judea."[27] The Redactor's Magi story in *ProtJac* 21:02-22:02 is manifestly dependent upon its parallel in the canonical Nativity story in Mt. 2:1-18, as witnessed by numerous verbatim contacts.[28] The Redactor was compelled to make a number of significant adjustments to Matthew's Magi story to accommodate his own revised version of that story to its new matrix in the Birth narrative of the CEGM.[29] In doing so, he committed a number of characteristic editorial blunders that caused confusion in his text but also provided us with abundant evidence of his redactional activity.[30]

The Redactor's Magi story—and the entire narrative of the *ProtJac* regarding Mary and her child—ends abruptly in *ProtJac* 22:02 with a brief statement that upon hearing that Herod's executioners were killing "all the babies" two-years old and younger, Mary became afraid and "wrapped him [her child] and put him in a cattle-manger." The Redactor derived the relevant terminology in this verse verbatim from Lk. 2:7: "and wrapped him … in a manger."[31] This constitutes an appropriate segue to his Zachariah materials in *ProtJac* 22:03-24:11, which begin

---

26. Ibid., pp. 111–13; cf. scholarly opinions regarding the "intriguing prospects" raised by "the possible independent pre-Gospel origins of the Johannine Doubting Thomas story," pp. 112–13, nn. 218, 219, and 220.

27. Cf. "The Magi," pp. 113–14.

28. Ibid., pp. 114–16.

29. Ibid., pp. 116–22.

30. The proponents of the de Strycker compositional theory attribute this inconsistency to the ignorance of the single "author" of the *ProtJac* with respect to Palestinian geography. Instead it is apparent that this inconsistency is due to the Redactor's deficient editorial skills; ibid., pp. 113–14, especially n. 223.

31. Ibid., pp. 121–2. The Redactor omitted the elements of the Lukan verse that contradicted his theme of Mary's perpetual virginity and the location of the Nativity in the *ProtJac* outside of Bethlehem: the reference to Jesus as her πρωτότοκον ("first born son"), which implied that other sons followed, and the reference that they had sought shelter (ἐν τῷ καταλύματι), ostensibly in the town of Bethlehem in Luke's story.

with the flight of Elizabeth and her infant son John also from Herod's executioners and which continue with the death of Zachariah, Elizabeth's husband and John's father. Thus having Lk. 2:7 before him, and having often alluded to the Nativity materials in Lk. 1-2 in his ongoing revision of the *ProtJac*, the Redactor must have been well aware that the Lukan Nativity story is followed in Lk. 3 by the Baptism of Jesus by John the Baptist, who is named in Lk. 3:2 as "John the son of Zachariah."

The Redactor's awareness of Lk. 3 may be reflected in a noteworthy connection between his Zachariah materials and Lk. 3:15 with respect to the peculiar perception that John the Baptist was the Messiah. According to Lk. 3:15 the people were considering "in their hearts concerning John that perhaps he might be the Messiah" (ἐν ταῖς καρδίαις αὐτῶν περὶ τοῦ Ἰωάννου, μήποτε αὐτὸς εἴη ὁ χριστός). The messianic identification of John is mirrored in the Zachariah materials in *ProtJac* 23:04 where Herod states that the son of Zachariah will rule over Israel as King: ο υιος αυτου μελλει βασιλευειν τω ισραηλ.[32] The reference to John the Baptist as the Messiah in Lk. 3:15 is followed immediately by a strong denial of this possibility by John himself who diminishes the importance of his own baptism "by water" in comparison to the baptism of Jesus "by the Holy Spirit and fire."[33] This confusion over the identity of the King/Messiah in the *ProtJac* has been caused by the Redactor's successive interpolation of texts from various sources: the Magi story from Matthew, the Zachariah materials, and elements from Luke's Nativity story.

The Redactor's precursory access to the Zachariah Apocryphon[34] and his rather extensive knowledge of the Lukan Nativity story allow us to speculate

---

32. Herod's reference to John as King in the Zachariah materials seems to contradict the earlier scenario in the Magi story in which Mary's child is still the central figure and John has yet to appear. Upon their arrival in Bethlehem in *ProtJac* 21:03—in search of Mary's child— the Magi declare: που εστιν ο βασιλευς των ιουδαιων ("where is the King of the Jews?"). This quotation was taken almost verbatim from Mt. 2:2: που εστιν ο τεχθεις βασιλευς των ιουδαιων ("where is he who was born King of the Jews?"). *ProtJac* 21:03 and 23:04 both occur in the text of P.Bodm V; two other similar texts are found only in the later MSS, *ProtJac* 20:09b βασιλευς εγεννηθη μεγας τω ισραηλ, and 21:10 ουτως εγνωμεν οτι βασιλευς εγεννηθη τω ισραηλ.

33. John's self-deprecating attitude vis-à-vis Jesus in Lk. 3:16 as "he who is more powerful than I, the strap of whose sandals I am not worthy to untie" is repeated in Jn 1:26-27 where the Baptist is purported to have described Jesus as "the one coming after me of whom I am not worthy to loosen the strap of his sandals." It was necessary for the second-century church to subjugate the popular rival Messiah figure, John the Baptist, as the "forerunner" of Jesus, their true Messiah.

34. The Redactor inserted references to Zachariah into two previous locations in the *ProtJac*: (1) his becoming silent in the Annunciation story in *ProtJac* 10:08 and (2) his being named as the high priest by an angel in the Holy of Holies in *ProtJac* 8:07. It is tempting to speculate that the Samuel who took Zachariah's place as high priest "until Zachariah spoke" again in *ProtJac* 10:08 may have some connection to the Samuel who was part of Joseph's entourage on their Journey to Bethlehem in *ProtJac* 17:05.

about a possible historical context in which he may have operated. The Zachariah Apocryphon constitutes a self-contained, originally independent block of material that is alien to its host document, the CEGM. Is it mere coincidence that this discrete document, the Zachariah Apocryphon, consists of material that is closely related to likewise discrete materials found in the Lukan Nativity story, which itself may have constituted a self-contained, originally independent block of material that was also alien to its own host document, the Gospel of Luke?[35] And is it coincidence as well that the Zachariah Apocryphon and the distinct elements in Lk. 1:5-25 and 57-80 are grounded in a scenario that is concerned with the birth of John the Baptist and the liturgical functioning of his father, the priest Zachariah, in the temple? Last, but not least, can it be coincidental that the Zachariah materials in the *ProtJac* and the analogous texts in Lk. 1:5-25, 57-80, when viewed together in succession, constitute a coherent chain of events? The angelic Annunciation of John's conception to his father Zachariah in the temple and John's conception and birth in Lk. 1:5-25, 57-80 are followed by the Flight of Elizabeth with her newborn baby John and Zachariah's death in the temple as related in the Zachariah Apocryphon.

Since the materials concerning John the Baptist and his parents in the Lukan Nativity story and the Zachariah Apocryphon, when viewed in succession, constitute a coherent storyline of the Annunciation and birth of John the Baptist and his escape from Herod's slaughter of the infants, it is not unreasonable to postulate that these materials may have derived from the same source. And just such a source is described by Helmut Koester with respect to the discrete material in Lk. 1:5-25, 57-80: "There can be little doubt that it was formed and transmitted by the community of John the Baptist which, in this story, proclaimed the memory and heritage of their great prophetic leader."[36] This preexisting Baptist source must be viewed against the backdrop of scholarly deliberations concerning the compositional history of the Gospel of Luke and most especially vis-à-vis the critical issue of whether the Nativity stories in Lk. 1–2 formed an original part of this Gospel or were a later addition. This question can only be understood within the even larger historical framework of the dispute between Marcion and Justin Martyr in the early to mid-second century CE. Central to this perennial scholarly debate is precisely the problem of the original form of Luke: whether it was best represented by today's Gospel,

---

35. See "The Nativity Complex," pp. 78–80, concerning a hypothetical precursor to canonical Luke; cf. "Appendix 3: The *ProtJac* and the New Testament Gospels," pp. 198–204.

36. Helmut Koester, *Ancient Christian Gospels: Their History and Development* (Philadelphia: Trinity Press International; London: SCM Press Ltd., 1992), 304, cf. 340; ibid., 334, Koester himself opined that the Gospel of Luke "was perhaps written as late as the first decades of the 2d century." Cf. Raymond E. Brown, *The Birth of the Messiah: A Commentary on the Infancy Narratives in Matthew and Luke* (Garden City, NY: Image Books, 1979), 245, n. 34.

including Lk. 1–2; or Marcion's version, without Lk. 1–2; or a "Proto-Luke" or "Ur-Luke," which originally began with Lk. 3:1 and to which Lk. 1–2 were added at a later date.[37]

It is not our purpose here to resolve the exceedingly complex scholarly controversy over the relationship of canonical Luke, with or without Lk. 1–2, to a hypothetical Proto-Luke or to Marcion's Luke. But one important factor within this debate may shed light upon the *Sitz im Leben* of the Redactor of the *ProtJac*. The environment within which the Nativity stories in Luke 1–2 may have been prefixed to an earlier, shorter form of the Gospel has been associated with the School of Justin Martyr, which is reported to have functioned in Rome in the mid-second century CE.[38] It is pertinent for our investigation that canonical Luke may have been augmented in Justin's School with Nativity materials in the same manner that the CEGM was augmented by our Redactor with interpolations derived from the same Nativity materials in Lk. 1–2. And it is extremely significant that in the same setting half of the preexisting Baptist document noted above was included in Lk. 1:5-25, 57-80, while the other half found its way into the Zachariah Apocryphon in *ProtJac* 22–24.[39] These connections between Lk. 1–2 and the *ProtJac* in our view advance the hypothesis that the final redaction of the *ProtJac* could have occurred within the same historical scenario in which Luke may have attained its own final canonical form—in the School of Justin Martyr—and that the Redactor of the *ProtJac* may have been associated with this School.

Since Matthew and Luke were the sources of the texts on the Annunciation and Nativity of Jesus that were interpolated into the CEGM, the Redactor must have acted in an environment in which Matthew and Luke were known and revered as authoritative sources of information about Jesus. Koester describes just such an environment: Justin's "writings permit insights into the work of a school of scriptural exegesis in which careful comparison of written gospels with the prophecies of scripture endeavored to produce an even more comprehensive new gospel text."[40] Arthur Bellinzoni conducted groundbreaking research on the sayings of Jesus in the works of Justin and concluded:

---

37. For a succinct overview of the problem, see Joseph B. Tyson, "The Birth Narratives and the Beginning of Luke's Gospel," *Semeia* 52 (1991), 103–20, esp. 106–9, 116; for more details see above pp. 78–9, n. 133, Tyson, *Marcion*; for a comprehensive presentation up to 1979, Brown, *Birth*, 239–53.

38. H. Gregory Snyder, "'Above the Bath of Myrtinus': Justin Martyr's 'School' in the City of Rome," *HTR* 100 (2007), 335–62; Jörg Ulrich, "What Do We Know about Justin's 'School' in Rome?", *ZAC* 16 (2012), 62–74; Tobias Georges, "Justin's School in Rome–Reflections on Early Christian 'Schools'," *ZAC* 16 (2012), 75–87; Philip Carrington, *The Early Christian Church*, vol. 2 (Cambridge: Cambridge University Press, 1957), 101–2.

39. Could our Redactor have been present when the Baptist document was divided between the Lukan Nativity story and the Zachariah Apocryphon in the *ProtJac*?

40. *Gospels*, 378.

There is evidence in Justin's writings for the use in the school at Rome of catechisms, manuals for instruction against heresies, harmonistic texts of the synoptic gospels ... and that the catechisms and church manuals used in Justin's school at Rome were the compositions of Justin and his pupils.[41]

Among the sources used by Justin, Koester cites a harmony of the Synoptic Gospels: "Justin himself or his 'school' ... was composing the one inclusive new gospel which would make its predecessors, Matthew and Luke (and possibly Mark) obsolete."[42]

The investigations of Koester and Bellinzoni into these harmonized Gospel texts provide a significant piece of evidence supporting the link between Justin's School and the Redactor of the *ProtJac*. At least one of the harmonized Gospel texts spoken of by Koester and Bellinzoni with respect to Justin's school occurs also among the Gospel materials that the Redactor interpolated into the Annunciation story of the CEGM. Koester characterized Justin's 1 *Apol.* 33.5 as a harmonization of two angelic announcements of the birth of Jesus: one from Mt. 1:20-21 in which the angel visits Joseph in a dream,[43] the other from Lk. 1:31-32 in which the archangel Gabriel appears to Mary.[44] The harmonized message of the two announcements in 1 *Apol.* 33.5 contains elements from both Matthew and Luke as becomes clear from the following analysis of the three texts:

1 *Apol.* 33.5

Ἰδοὺ συλλήψῃ ἐν γαστρὶ ἐκ πνεύματος ἁγίου
καὶ τέξῃ υἱόν,
   "Behold you will conceive in your womb from the Holy Spirit
   and will bear a son,
καὶ υἱὸς ὑψίστου κληθήσεται,
   and he will be called the Son of the Most High,
καὶ καλέσεις τὸ ὄνομα αὐτοῦ Ἰησοῦν,
   and you will call his name Jesus,
αὐτὸς γὰρ σώσει τὸν λαὸν αὐτοῦ ἀπὸ τῶν ἁμαρτιῶν αὐτῶν.
   for he will save his people from their sins."

---

41. Arthur J. Bellinzoni, *The Sayings of Jesus in the Writings of Justin Martyr* (Leiden: E. J. Brill, 1967), 140-1.

42. Helmut Koester, "The Text of the Synoptic Gospels in the Second Century," in *Gospel Traditions in the Second Century* (Notre Dame, IN: University of Notre Dame Press, 1989), 29–30. In a subsequent publication Bellinzoni found "very attractive" "Koester's thesis that Justin composed a full harmony of Matthew and Luke (and possibly Mark)," "The Gospel of Luke in the Second Century CE," in *Literary Studies in Luke-Acts* (Macon, GA: Mercer University Press, 1998), 66.

43. Mt. 1:20: ἰδοὺ ἄγγελος κυρίου κατ᾽ ὄναρ ἐφάνη αὐτῷ λέγων· Ἰωσήφ, υἱὸς Δαυίδ ....

44. Lk. 1:26-30: ἀπεστάλη ὁ ἄγγελος Γαβριὴλ ἀπὸ τοῦ θεοῦ ... πρὸς παρθένον ... καὶ τὸ ὄνομα τῆς παρθένου Μαριάμ ... καὶ εἰσελθὼν πρὸς αὐτὴν εἶπεν ....

Justin took from Lk. 1:31 the two phrases Ἰδοὺ συλλήψῃ ἐν γαστρὶ ("Behold you will conceive in your womb") and καὶ τέξῃ υἱόν ("and will bear a son") and inserted between them from Mt. 1:20 the phrase ἐκ πνεύματός ... ἁγίου ("from the Holy Spirit").[45] Justin then seems to have transposed from Lk. 1:32 καὶ υἱὸς ὑψίστου κληθήσεται ("and he will be called the Son of the Most High").[46] The text of καὶ καλέσεις τὸ ὄνομα αὐτοῦ Ἰησοῦν, αὐτὸς γὰρ σώσει τὸν λαὸν αὐτοῦ ἀπὸ τῶν ἁμαρτιῶν αὐτῶν ("and you will call his name Jesus, for he will save his people from their sins") also must have originated from Mt. 1:21, since Lk. 1:31 only has the first half of this verse: καὶ καλέσεις τὸ ὄνομα αὐτοῦ Ἰησοῦν ("and you will call his name Jesus").

A comparison of these harmonized Annunciation texts from Luke and Matthew in 1 *Apol.* 33.5 with the parallel materials interpolated by the Redactor into the Annunciation story in *ProtJac* 11:06-12 provides striking evidence that both Justin and our Redactor seem to have been drawing from the same harmony of Annunciation texts originating from Luke and Matthew, a harmony that must have been produced in the School of Justin Martyr. The same texts shown above in 1 *Apol.* 33.5 and Lk. 1:31-32 are present also in *ProtJac* 11:09-11 and in a form closer to 1 *Apol.* 33.5 than to the corresponding verses of Luke:

ProtJac 11:10b-11
κληθησεται υιος υψιστου
    he will be called the Son of the Most High
11 και καλεσης το ονομα αυτου ιησουν
    and you will call his name Jesus,
αυτος γαρ σωσει λαον αυτου εκ των αμαρτιων αυτων.
    for he will save his people from their sins.

1 *Apol.* 33.5
υἱὸς ὑψίστου κληθήσεται
    he will be called the Son of the Most High
καὶ καλέσεις τὸ ὄνομα αὐτοῦ Ἰησοῦν,
    and you will call his name Jesus,
αὐτὸς γὰρ σώσει τὸν λαὸν αὐτοῦ ἀπὸ τῶν ἁμαρτιῶν αὐτῶν.
    for he will save his people from their sins.

The relevant texts occur in both Justin and the *ProtJac* in the same order but are scattered and in a different order in Lk. 1:31-32. The angel's statement that

---

45. Underlined in the text above. The Matthean text reads in its entirety: ἐκ πνεύματός ἐστιν ἁγίου ("is from the Holy Spirit"). Mt. 1:20 is more likely to have been Justin's source for this phrase than the expanded version present in Lk. 1:35: Πνεῦμα ἅγιον ἐπελεύσεται ἐπὶ σέ ("The Holy Spirit will come upon you").

46. Lk. 1:32 would be a more likely source of this text than the expanded version in Lk. 1:35: τὸ γεννώμενον ἅγιον κληθήσεται, υἱὸς θεοῦ ("that which will be born will be called holy, the Son of God").

Jesus will be called the "Son of the Most High" (υἱὸς ὑψίστου) does not occur in Lk. 1:31 but is found later in Lk. 1:32; also only the first half of Mt. 1:21 is present in Lk. 1:31. The passages in 1 Apol. 33.5 and ProtJac 11:10b-11 contain the υἱὸς ὑψίστου κληθήσεται ("he will be called the Son of the Most High") followed by the full version of Mt. 1:21 almost verbatim. Even the reference to the "power of God" (δύναμις θεοῦ) that "overshadowed" (ἐπεσκίασεν) Mary, which precedes the harmonized texts in ProtJac 11:09-10a, is referenced by Justin in 1 Apol. 33.4 immediately before his own harmonized texts in 1 Apol. 33.5. And it is noteworthy that both Justin and our Redactor refer to the divine "power" as the "power of God" (δύναμις θεοῦ) in their harmonized text, in contrast to Lk. 1:35 in which the power is described as δύναμις Ὑψίστου ("the power of the Most High").

As further evidence that Justin is quoting from a harmony of Matthew and Luke, Koester observes that in 1 Apol. 33.8 Justin repeats the angel's command from Mt. 1:21 that Mary's child be called Jesus, which in Hebrew means "savior": Καὶ καλέσεις τὸ ὄνομα αὐτοῦ Ἰησοῦν· αὐτὸς γὰρ σώσει τὸν λαὸν αὐτοῦ ἀπὸ τῶν ἁμαρτιῶν αὐτῶν ("And you will call his name Jesus, for he will save his people from their sins").[47] The command in Mt. 1:20-21 is given to Joseph by an angel in a dream. But in both Justin's 1 Apol. 33.8 and in our Redactor's interpolation in ProtJac 11:06-12, the command to name the child Jesus is given to Mary, not Joseph, again indicating the use by both writers of a harmony of the Annunciation stories of Luke and Matthew. It is relevant to this discussion that the Redactor also quoted Mt. 1:20-21 a second time in ProtJac 14:05-08 in his revised version of the angelic dream vision to Joseph in Mt. 1:18-21 that he interpolated into the CEGM Trial story.[48] In that context the Redactor did present the angel's command as being given directly to Joseph, thus demonstrating that our Redactor had access to the documents that were available in the School of Justin Martyr, including full texts of Matthew and Luke as well as the Gospel harmonies that were being created in the school.[49]

Noteworthy connections between the Redactor's interpolated canonical texts and Justin's works also exist in shared references to an Eve/Mary typology and to the cave in which Jesus was born. In his later *Dialogue with Trypho* 100.5, Justin again referred Lk. 1:35 in drawing a comparison between Mary's conception and Eve's conception through the latter's interaction with the serpent in the garden of Eden. Justin described Eve as an uncorrupted virgin who conceived by the "logos" of the serpent and gave birth to disobedience and death (παρθένος γὰρ οὖσα Εὔα καὶ ἄφθορος, τὸν λόγον τὸν ἀπὸ τοῦ ὄφεως συλλαβοῦσα, παρακοὴν καὶ θάνατον ἔτεκε). In contrast to Eve, Mary the virgin received the "good news" from Gabriel the angel that the Spirit of the Lord would come upon her and the power of the

---

47. *Gospels*, 380.

48. See "The Trial of Joseph and Mary," pp. 60–1 for the redactional context within which ProtJac 14:05-08 was interpolated by the Redactor into the CEGM directly from Mt. 1:20-21, 24 intact and not as part of a harmony.

49. See above p. 141.

most High would overshadow her so that which would be born from her would be holy, the Son of God.⁵⁰

Through his association with the School of Justin, the Redactor could have been aware of the remarkable parallel between Justin's text in *Dial*. 100.5 and the lamentation of Joseph after he returned from his business trip and found Mary pregnant in the CEGM in *ProtJac* 13:01-06. Joseph compared his own situation with that of Adam in *ProtJac* 13:06:

> μητι εν εμοι ανεκεφαλαιωθη ιστορια;
> "has history not been repeated in me?
> ωσπερ γαρ αδαμ ην εν τη ωρα της δοξολογιας αυτου
> for as Adam was in the time of his prayer
> και ηλθεν ο οφις και ευρεν την ευαν μονην
> and the serpent came and found Eve alone
> και εξηπατησεν αυτην και εμιανεν αυτην.
> and deceived her and defiled her."

The connection between the Mary/Eve typologies in the *ProtJac* and Justin's *Dial*. is supported by a linguistic parallel between the two texts. The phrase χαραν λαβουσα μαρια ("Mary, receiving joy") occurs in both *ProtJac* 12:03, where Mary received joy from the blessing of a priest, and *Dial*. 100.5, where Mary received joy in the Annunciation from being "evangelized by Gabriel the angel" (εὐαγγελιζομένου αὐτῇ Γαβριὴλ ἀγγέλου). It is noteworthy that Mary received joy from the priest's blessing in the CEGM in *ProtJac* 12:03, shortly after her Annunciation by the Redactor's interpolated angels in *ProtJac* 11:06-12.

The Redactor may have expressed his understanding of the parallel Eve/Mary typology in Justin and the *ProtJac* in a significant adjustment that he made to Justin's harmonized text of the Annunciation in 1 *Apol*. 33.5: συλλήμψῃ ἐν γαστρὶ ἐκ πνεύματος ἁγίου ("you will conceive in your womb from the Holy Spirit"). In his parallel to Justin's harmony the Redactor substituted in *ProtJac* 11:07 εκ λογου αυτου ("from his logos") for the ἐκ πνεύματος ἁγίου ("from the Holy Spirit") in Justin's text:

Lk. 1:31/Mt. 1:20
συλλήμψῃ ἐν γαστρὶ ἐκ πνεύματος ἁγίου

ProtJac 11:07
συνλημψη εκ λογου αυτου

The Redactor's version of this harmony echoes a text in Justin's *Dial*. 100.5 according to which Eve "conceived by the logos from the serpent" (τὸν λόγον τὸν ἀπὸ τοῦ ὄφεως συλλαβοῦσα). The parallel between the conception of the Virgin

---

50. Μαρία ἡ παρθένος, εὐαγγελιζομένου αὐτῇ Γαβριὴλ ἀγγέλου ὅτι πνεῦμα κυρίου ἐπ' αὐτὴν ἐπελεύσεται καὶ δύναμις ὑψίστου ἐπισκιάσει αὐτὴν διὸ καὶ τὸ γεννώμενον ἐξ αὐτῆς ἅγιον ἔσται υἱὸς θεοῦ.

Mary by the "logos" of God and the conception of the virgin Eve by the "logos" of the serpent is obvious. Justin himself in another context confirmed that he agreed with the Redactor's understanding that Jesus was incarnated through the "logos of God." In 1 Apol. 66.2 he wrote: διὰ λόγου θεοῦ σαρκοποιηθεῖς Ἰησοῦς Χριστὸς ὁ σωτὴρ ἡμῶν καὶ σάρκα καὶ αἷμα ὑπὲρ σωτηρίας ἡμῶν ἔσχεν ("Jesus Christ our savior was incarnated through the logos of God and had flesh and blood for our salvation").[51]

Another important point of contact between Justin and the Redactor regards the motif of Jesus's birth in a cave near Bethlehem. The location of the Cave of the Nativity midway between Jerusalem and Bethlehem was original to the CEGM, but the Redactor adjusted his source so as to place the cave closer both to Bethlehem and to the shrine of Rachel's tomb. This ancient shrine, which was on the outskirts of Bethlehem on the road to Jerusalem, marked the traditional site where Rachel died in painful childbirth.[52] The Redactor interpolated a scene into the Journey of Mary and Joseph toward Bethlehem in ProtJac 17:06-10 in which Mary appears alternatingly both sad and laughing. Mary's explanation that she saw two nations, one crying and mourning, and the other happy and rejoicing, associates this scene thematically with the tomb of Rachel. Rachel was the wife of Jacob, who struggled with his twin brother in the womb of their mother, Rebekah, causing her to pray to God about her difficult pregnancy. God responded that Rebekah also held two nations in her womb that would vie with each other for power. The Redactor's interpolation thus connected the Cave of the Nativity with Rachel's tomb thematically but also geographically by adjusting the location of the cave closer to Rachel's tomb.[53]

The Redactor's acceptance of the location of the Cave of the Nativity outside of Bethlehem poses a problem; he thereby seems to contradict his otherwise consistent adherence to the Nativity stories of Matthew and Luke, which present Jesus's birth as having taken place in Bethlehem.[54] The Redactor's understanding

---

51. In this context Justin is speaking of the reality of the transformation of bread and wine into the actual flesh and blood of Christ in the Christian Eucharist. He asserts that just as Jesus himself was incarnated "through the logos of God" (διὰ λόγου θεοῦ), the food offerings in the Eucharistic service were changed into Jesus's flesh and blood through the "logos of the prayer" (δι' εὐχῆς λόγου) of the officiant.

52. Cf. Gen. 35:16-20. See the discussion in "Topographical and Archaeological Factors," pp. 89–92. Justin was born in Samaria and therefore may have had knowledge of an early Christian shrine at the traditional location of the Cave of the Nativity outside of Bethlehem.

53. The Redactor's association of the Cave of the Nativity with Rachel's tomb is further supported by the reference in the Nativity story in Mt. 2:17-18 regarding the slaughter of the infants by Herod: Φωνὴ ἐν Ῥαμὰ ἠκούσθη, κλαυθμὸς καὶ ὀδυρμὸς πολύς· Ῥαχὴλ κλαίουσα τὰ τέκνα αὐτῆς, καὶ οὐκ ἤθελεν παρακληθῆναι ὅτι οὐκ εἰσίν ("A voice was heard in Rama, weeping, and much mourning, Rachel crying for her children, and she did not want to be comforted, because they are not").

54. See the discussion in "Topographical/Archaeological Factors," pp. 89–90.

of the geographical proximity of the cave to Rachel's tomb would have incentivized him to retain the location of the cave outside of Bethlehem in his final version of the *ProtJac*. Furthermore, this position was in agreement with the account contained in his source, the CEGM. But the Redactor's knowledge of the location of the Cave of the Nativity is corroborated also through his association with Justin's School. A particularly pertinent text from Justin's writings demonstrates that Justin himself knew of the tradition of Jesus's birth ἐν σπηλαίῳ τινὶ σύνεγγυς τῆς κώμης ("in a cave near the village") of Bethlehem, *Dial*. 78.5:

> γεννηθέντος δὲ τότε τοῦ παιδίου ἐν Βηθλεέμ,
>   the child having been born then in Bethlehem,
> ἐπειδὴ Ἰωσὴφ οὐκ εἶχεν ἐν τῇ κώμῃ ἐκείνῃ που καταλῦσαι,
>   since Joseph did not have in that village a place to stay,
> ἐν σπηλαίῳ τινὶ σύνεγγυς τῆς κώμης κατέλυσε·
>   he stayed in a cave near the village.
> καὶ τότε, αὐτῶν ὄντων ἐκεῖ, ἐτετόκει ἡ Μαρία τὸν Χριστὸν
>   and then, they being there, Mary gave birth to the Christ
> καὶ ἐν φάτνῃ αὐτὸν ἐτεθείκει.
>   and placed him in a manger.

A careful analysis of this passage reveals it to be a conflation of elements from the Nativity stories of Matthew and Luke but also of the *ProtJac*. The first phrase of this text, γεννηθέντος δὲ τότε τοῦ παιδίου ἐν Βηθλεέμ ("the child having been born then in Bethlehem"), shares verbatim vocabulary with Mt. 2:1: Τοῦ δὲ Ἰησοῦ γεννηθέντος ἐν Βηθλέεμ τῆς Ἰουδαίας ("Jesus having been born in Bethlehem of Judea"). The second phrase, ἐπειδὴ Ἰωσὴφ οὐκ εἶχεν ἐν τῇ κώμῃ ἐκείνῃ που καταλῦσαι ("since Joseph did not have in that village a place to stay"), strongly resembles Lk. 2:7: διότι οὐκ ἦν αὐτοῖς τόπος ἐν τῷ καταλύματι ("because there was no room for them in the shelter").[55] The third phrase of *Dial*. 78.5, ἐν σπηλαίῳ τινὶ σύνεγγυς τῆς κώμης κατέλυσε ("he stayed in a cave near the village"), has its parallel in *ProtJac* 18:01: και ευρεν εκει σπηλαιον και εισηγαγεν αυτην ("and he found a cave there and took her in"). The element of the cave from the *ProtJac* represents the complexity of the exact geographical location of the cave with respect to Bethlehem.[56]

The composite character of *Dial*. 78.5 is further verified by incongruities between the first phrase in which Jesus was born in Bethlehem and the remaining text in which Joseph found no lodging in Bethlehem, left the village, and stayed in a nearby cave where Jesus was born a second time. The duplicate terms δὲ τότε in the first phrase and καὶ τότε in phrase four, both of which mean "and then," signify two distinct time periods which Justin is attempting to combine

---

55. See "The Nativity Complex," p. 122.

56. See "Appendix 4: The Kathisma Church," pp. 205–20. In 1 *Apol*. 34.2 Justin provides specific information that Bethlehem was a village thirty-five stades from Jerusalem (ἀπέχουσα σταδίους τριάκοντα πέντε Ἱεροσολύμων).

into one. The first "and then" refers to Jesus's first birth in the first phrase, γεννηθέντος ... τοῦ παιδίου ("the child ... having been born"), while the second "and then" introduces the second birth in the fourth phrase, ἐτετόκει ἡ Μαρία τὸν Χριστὸν ("Mary gave birth to the Christ"). Justin thus presents two discrete births of Jesus; the first ἐν Βηθλεέμ ("in Bethlehem") with Matthew and Luke and the second with the ProtJac, αὐτῶν ὄντων ἐκεῖ ("they [Joseph and Mary] being there"), with "there" referring to the cave near Bethlehem. The αὐτῶν ὄντων ἐκεῖ recalls Lk. 2:6, ἐγένετο δὲ ἐν τῷ εἶναι αὐτοὺς ἐκεῖ ("and it [Jesus's birth] happened while they were there"), "there" in this case designating Bethlehem.[57]

There are additional contacts between the ProtJac and Justin's work leading up to the Birth story in Dial. 78.5. In Dial. 78.3 Joseph considered putting Mary away because he "thought she was pregnant from sexual contact with a man, that is, by fornication" (νομίζων ἐγκυμονεῖν αὐτὴν ἀπὸ συνουσίας ἀνδρός, τοῦτ' ἔστιν ἀπὸ πορνείας). This language is too strong to have originated in Luke or Matthew, which Justin used as sources in Dial. 78. The canonical Nativity stories contain no hint that Mary may have committed fornication. The language of Dial. 78.3 is more likely to have been inspired by the bitter lament of Joseph when he returned home and found Mary pregnant in ProtJac 13. In ProtJac 13:05 Joseph asks: "who did this evil in my house and defiled her" (τις το πονηρον τουτο εποιησεν εν τω οικω μου και εμιανεν αυτην;), and in ProtJac 14:02 even refers to Mary's αμαρτημα ("sin"). In Dial. 78.4 Joseph was frightened (φοβηθεὶς) by his vision of an angel telling him not to put Mary away. But Joseph was not frightened in the corresponding text of Mt. 1:24; he simply awakens from his angelic dream vision and accepts Mary as his wife as the angel had instructed him. It is in ProtJac 14:01 that Joseph was "very frightened" after his heated argument with Mary about her pregnancy (και εφοβηθη ο ιωσηφ σφοδρα).

The composite nature of Justin's Birth story in Dial. 78.5 raises the question of whether he produced this passage from a harmony that had been developed previously in his School or created the text ad hoc from the source documents themselves. However, the incongruities in the passage argue against him having accessed a preexisting harmony. It is pertinent to our discussion that the cluster of elements in Dial. 78.3-5 from the ProtJac derives exclusively from those sections of this document that belonged to the CEGM. This was the case also with the text from ProtJac 13:01-06 that was parallel to the Eve/Mary typology in Dial. 100.5. It appears that Justin created his Birth story in Dial. 78.5 ad hoc by conflating materials from Luke, Matthew, and the CEGM, whether or not he knew the latter as a discrete document before it was embedded into the finished ProtJac by the Redactor. In contrast, the Annunciation texts in ProtJac 11:07-11, which were interpolated by the Redactor into the CEGM and which parallel 1 Apol. 33,[58]

---

57. The last phrase, ἐν φάτνῃ αὐτὸν ἐτεθείκει ("[Mary] placed him in a manger"), recalls Lk. 2:7 ἀνέκλινεν αὐτὸν ἐν φάτνῃ ("laid him in a manger") and ProtJac 22:02 εβαλεν εν φατνη βοων ("put him in a cattle-manger").

58. See pp. 139–41 above; cf. "The Original GenMar Annunciation Story," pp. 44–9.

derive from a harmony to which both Justin and the Redactor had access in Justin's School. Thus both writers made use of individual Gospel texts as well as harmonies of these documents that were available in the School.

The parallels and linguistic affinities between the *ProtJac* and the works of Justin Martyr provide substantial evidence of a literary association between these documents. It is axiomatic among the adherents of the de Strycker consensus that the *ProtJac* was written later than Justin's works, and therefore any parallels between the two should be attributed to the author of the *ProtJac* appropriating Justin's material.[59] But the presence of elements from the *ProtJac* in Justin's harmonies and in a conflation of Gospel sources indicates a more intimate relationship. It cannot be mere coincidence that Justin was compelled to justify both the λόγος relating to the Annunciation and the cave with respect to the Nativity, the two most striking extra-biblical, distinctive features of the *ProtJac*. It is significant also that the connections with Justin's works are concentrated in only a few chapters of the *ProtJac* (11–13 and 17–18), whereas they are dispersed in 1 *Apol.* and the *Dial.* It seems more reasonable for Justin to have derived his parallel material from these concentrated areas in the *ProtJac* than for a hypothetical single author of the unitary *ProtJac* to have gleaned his from references scattered throughout two separate works of Justin.

In 1 *Apol.* and especially in his *Dial.*, Justin often referred to the written sources from which he was quoting as τὰ ἀπομνημονεύματα τῶν ἀποστόλων ("the memoires of the apostles").[60] He never named the memoires, but Matthew and Luke were certainly included among them.[61] Since the analysis above has revealed that Justin appears to have accessed the *ProtJac* along with Matthew and Luke in creating certain harmonies and conflations, the *ProtJac* should also be counted among Justin's "memoires of the apostles." This prospect is illustrated in 1 *Apol.* 33.4-6 by the presence of an element from the *ProtJac* in close proximity to a reference to the memoires. In 1 *Apol.* 33.4-5 Justin cites a harmony of Matthew and Luke that Mary will conceive by the δύναμις θεοῦ ("power of God") and ἐκ πνεύματος ἁγίου ("by the Holy Spirit"), ὡς οἱ ἀπομνημονεύσαντες … ἐδίδαξαν

---

59. Cf. Zervos, "Dating." This was the first article that I wrote in my long process toward understanding the compositional history of the *ProtJac*. At that time, in 1994, I understood the *ProtJac* to have been a document that had been written earlier than Justin and had been used by him as a source in his own works. The present study contains the results of my investigations since then, according to which the *ProtJac*, in its present form, was produced by a member of Justin's School who redacted a document containing an earlier form of the *ProtJac*, the CEGM, using the canonical materials available to him in the School.

60. See Richard Heard, "The Apomnemoneumata in Papias, Justin, and Irenaeus," *NTS* 1 (1954-55), 122-9; Cf. 123-5 for a comprehensive listing of the instances in which Justin used this term.

61. Only once does he refer to the ἀπομνημονεύματα specifically as Gospels, ἃ καλεῖται εὐαγγέλια ("which are called Gospels"), in a disputed passage in 1 *Apol.* 66.3.

("as they who wrote memoires ... taught").⁶² But in 1 *Apol.* 33.6 he equates the "power of God" and the "Holy Spirit" with the λόγος: τὸ πνεῦμα οὖν καὶ τὴν δύναμιν τὴν παρὰ τοῦ θεοῦ οὐδὲν ἄλλο νοῆσαι θέμις ἢ τὸν λόγον ("but there is no appropriate way to understand the Spirit and the power from God other than as the logos"). It is difficult to deny the possibility of a connection between Justin's statement and the element of Mary's conception εκ λογου αυτου ("from his logos") from *ProtJac* 11:07 that the Redactor substituted for ἐκ πνεύματος ἁγίου ("from the Holy Spirit") in his parallel to Justin's harmony in 1 *Apol.* 33.4-5.⁶³

Abundant direct linguistic and ideological evidence has been presented above that links the Redactor of the *ProtJac* to the School of Justin Martyr. The Redactor made use of precisely the documents that have been associated with Justin's School, the Gospels of Matthew and Luke as well as harmonies of these works. The Redactor interpolated elements of these texts into the CEGM in such a way that betrays his theological position as a conservative proto-Orthodox Christian who would have fit very well into the environment of Justin's School with its anti-heretical catechisms and instruction manuals. On numerous occasions in this study it was noted that one of the Redactor's primary objectives was to "Orthodoxize" the CEGM, which he must have considered to have been a heretical document. On the basis of this evidence it is reasonable to identify the Redactor of the *ProtJac* as a member of Justin's School and possibly even as a disciple of Justin himself. One could even speculate that Justin himself may have been the Redactor of the *ProtJac*.

62. See pp. 138-41 above.
63. See pp. 141-3.

THE COMPOSER: THE COMPOSER-ENHANCED *GENMAR*

Once the second-century Redactor's interpolations and disruptions were eliminated from the *ProtJac* text, the underlying source document on which he performed his editorial work came more clearly into focus. In this study the Redactor's source has been labeled as the CEGM, thus indicating that another distinct individual, the Composer, had himself perpetrated a major enhancement of an even earlier document, the *GenMar*, at some point after it had been written by its own original Author. The materials with which the Composer expanded the *GenMar* largely concerned the person of Joseph. These were viewed by early scholars as a discrete document, *The Joseph Apocryphon*, one of several sources of the *ProtJac*. The main difficulty in understanding how the preexisting source materials of the *ProtJac* came together was the problem of whether the Joseph materials were added to the original *GenMar* in a later phase of composition by the same writer who authored the *GenMar* or were inserted by a second writer, the Composer. The preponderance of the evidence indicates the latter to be the case.

It is significant for our compositional-redactional theory that the first seven chapters of the *ProtJac* show no evidence of disruptions in the text on the scale of those that begin to occur in chapter 8. We may thus postulate that the beginning chapters of the *GenMar*, which relate the conception and birth of Mary and the first three years of her life, are preserved in *ProtJac* 1:01–8:02. The Composer's work begins at *ProtJac* 8:03 where the narrative abruptly leaps forward nine years to the first of two consecutive Councils of the temple priests.[64] This first Council, in *ProtJac* 8:03–9:12, is labeled the Joseph Council, as it introduces Joseph and recounts how the now twelve-year-old Mary was assigned to his care. The temple priests decided to remove Mary from the temple, so as not to defile the holy place with the onset of her menstruation. Having gathered the widowers of Israel, the high priest entered the inner sanctum and prayed for a sign showing which widower would receive Mary. The sign fell upon Joseph who took Mary to his home, left her there, and departed to his construction work for six months. The purpose of the Joseph Council was to remove Mary from the temple before her Annunciation and impregnation by the Voice of God. Other than a possible parallel with the reference to Joseph as a carpenter in Mt. 13:55, the Composer's Joseph materials show no relation to, or knowledge of, the information about Joseph contained in the canonical Gospels.

The second priestly council, labeled the Veil Council, now in *ProtJac* 10:01–12:11, formed an original part of the *GenMar* that described Mary's role in weaving a new veil for the Jerusalem temple. Originally, the Veil Council followed directly after *ProtJac* 1:01–8:02 but was separated from its former position by the Composer's interpolation of his Joseph Council, now in *ProtJac* 8:03–9:12.[65] In *ProtJac* 10:01 the priests decided to gather the "undefiled virgins of the tribe of David" to weave the new veil. Servants were sent out, found seven such virgins, and brought them to

---

64. Cf. "The Joseph Council," pp. 23–34 and "The Veil Council," pp. 35–54.
65. Cf. "The Joseph Council," p. 23; "The Veil Council," p. 35.

the temple. Since now—because of his interpolation of the Joseph Council into the *GenMar* narrative—Mary was no longer in the temple, but at home, the Composer had to adjust the text of the Veil Council to account for Mary's presence in the temple to participate in the weaving of the veil. He inserted *ProtJac* 10:04 into the *GenMar* text in which the priest suddenly remembered that Mary also was an undefiled virgin of the tribe of David and sent servants to bring her from home to the temple to help weave the veil.[66] The Composer fulfilled two major goals in these two priestly councils: (1) to prove the Davidic descent of Mary, and therefore also Jesus, and (2) to provide Joseph as a cover for the accusations of adultery against Mary and of illegitimacy against Jesus.

ProtJac 10:05-07, 09 contains an original *GenMar* text in which it was determined by lots which virgins were to weave the various colored threads for the veil. The "true purple" and "red" threads were assigned to Mary. The Composer must also adjust the text describing Mary weaving her threads to reflect the fact that she is now at her home, again as a result of his removal of Mary from the temple in the Joseph Council.[67] The Composer again inserts a phrase, *ProtJac* 10:07b, into the *GenMar* text in which Mary, upon receiving the purple and red threads, takes the threads home to spin them εν τω οικω αυτης ("in her house"). In his two insertions into the original *GenMar* text in *ProtJac* 10:04 and 10:07b, as was the case also with his larger interpolation of the Joseph Council, the Composer exhibited his distinctive modus operandi in revising his source text to allow for his interpolated Joseph Council.[68] The Composer duplicated and modified elements of his source text and then combined them with his own materials to create new versions of the original texts reflecting Mary's location, not in the temple, but "at home."

The central feature of the Veil Council is the original *GenMar* Annunciation story, now in *ProtJac* 11:01-05 and 12:01-02, in which Mary was still residing in the temple and assisted in weaving a new temple veil.[69] Mary was spinning the red thread in the Holy of Holies and went out to draw water when she heard the Annunciation from the *Bath Kol* out of the Holy of Holies and thus conceived her child. The now pregnant Mary reentered the Holy of Holies, sat down upon the throne of God, and spun the royal purple thread. For a third time, the Composer must adjust the *GenMar* text to show that Mary was at home when these events occurred. In *ProtJac* 11:04 Mary was frightened at the sound of the *Bath Kol* and εισηει εις τον οικον αυτης ("entered into her house"), instead of the temple, and spun the purple thread. Thus again the Composer effectively changed the location of these events from the temple to Mary's house but also left a telltale clue that betrayed his actions. He failed to expunge the reference to the "throne" upon which Mary sat (εκαθισεν επι τω θρονω) to spin the purple thread, thus raising the question: did Mary have a throne in her house, or was this the throne of God in the temple?[70]

66. Ibid., pp. 35–7.
67. Ibid., pp. 37–9.
68. Ibid., pp. 38–9.
69. Cf. "The Original *GenMar* Annunciation Story," pp. 39–41.
70. Ibid., p. 41.

After *ProtJac* 11:05, where Mary was spinning the purple thread, the *GenMar* resumes in 12:01-02 in which she completes her task of spinning the purple and red threads, returns them to the priest, and receives his blessing. The priest's blessing in 12:02 and Mary's original response to this blessing, now located in 12:08, were appropriated and modified by the Redactor to fit into his edited version of Mary's visit to Elizabeth, which he interpolated into *ProtJac* 12:03-09a.[71] The *GenMar* resumes in 12:09b-10 where Mary's womb is swelling (η γαστηρ αυτης ωγκουτο) and she returns to the temple and hides from the sons of Israel. For the fourth time in the Veil Council, the Composer again adjusted the *GenMar* text to reflect his removal of Mary from the temple in his interpolated Joseph Council. In *ProtJac* 12:10 he replaced the original phrase ηλθεν εν τω ναω ("she went into the temple") with ηλθεν εν τω οικω αυτης ("she went into her house").[72]

After the Veil Council, any remnants of the original *GenMar* become increasingly difficult to identify and isolate. But *ProtJac* 12:09-10 seems to demand a continuation of the story of this hapless twelve-year-old pregnant virgin girl who was left cowering in fear in the temple at the prospect of being discovered as her womb was swelling "day by day." She was genuinely innocent of any transgression and, having been given no information by the *Bath Kol* that had impregnated her in the temple, was completely unaware of what was happening to her. This image of an increasingly more pregnant virgin Mary presumes that eventually there must be a Nativity, but the preponderance of the following material in the *ProtJac* leading up to the highly redacted Birth story in *ProtJac* 18-20 is assigned to either the Composer or the Redactor. It is significant within this context, however, that the Nativity story of the CEGM in *ProtJac* 19:08-12 seems to share certain ideological characteristics with the original *GenMar* Annunciation story in *ProtJac* 12:13-14. These will be discussed below.

ProtJac 12:11, where Mary again leaps forward abruptly in age, this time to sixteen years, is an editorial insertion by the Redactor to facilitate the transition from the first major redactional section of *ProtJac* 8:03-12:11 to another large section of text comprising *ProtJac* 13:01-16:07.[73] These chapters contain mostly Joseph-related material that was inserted into the original *GenMar* by the Composer, with the exception of an obvious interpolation by the Redactor in *ProtJac* 14:02-08 (the angelic annunciation to Joseph), and certain remnants of the original *GenMar* Trial story.[74] In *ProtJac* 13-14 Joseph returns home from his construction work and finds Mary six months pregnant. He laments over the suspected adultery and

---

71. Cf. "Mary's Visit to Elizabeth" pp. 49–53.

72. Ibid., pp. 53–4.

73. Ibid., p. 54; cf. below, pp. 165–6, n. 141; 200–1, n. 132.

74. This interpretation is based on the premise that the Composer was not familiar with the Gospel of Matthew itself and therefore composed his own idiosyncratic Joseph materials. Direct borrowings from the canonical Gospels of Matthew and Luke, such as the angelic annunciation to Joseph from Mt. 1:19-24, derived from the second-century Redactor who was familiar with the two later Synoptic Gospels through the School of Justin Martyr.

scolds Mary for her transgression, which she fervently denies. Joseph experiences an angelic visitation in a dream (the Redactor's interpolation) that verifies Mary's innocence. In *ProtJac* 15-16 Mary's pregnancy is discovered by the temple priests who accuse Joseph and Mary of adultery and subject them to a trial, as a result of which they are exonerated.[75]

Another major redactional section follows in *ProtJac* 17:01-24:11, which encompasses the events surrounding the birth of Mary's child. The Composer contributed to this section the stories of the Journey of Joseph and Mary to the Cave of the Nativity in *ProtJac* 17:01-18:01, the Midwife episode in *ProtJac* 18:02-19:07, and the birth of Mary's child in the cave in *ProtJac* 19:08-12.[76] Although the bulk of these materials are the work of the Composer, their texts are interspersed with remnants of the original *GenMar* and editorial revisions and interpolations by the Redactor. The CEGM concludes with the original Nativity story in *ProtJac* 19:12. The Redactor significantly augmented the Composer's document with the heavily redacted ending of the Nativity story from *ProtJac* 19:13-22:02 to the Zachariah Apocryphon in the final chapters of the *ProtJac* 22:03-24:11.[77] A colophon in *ProtJac* 25 identifies the author of this "history" as James who was, no doubt, one of the brothers of Jesus named in Mk 6:3.[78] In the *ProtJac* James is characterized as a son of Joseph, ostensibly from a previous marriage, who accompanied Joseph and Mary to the census in Bethlehem and afterward witnessed the turmoil over the death of Herod in Jerusalem. Although evidence exists that points to the Redactor as the creator of the colophon,[79] it cannot be excluded that he may have edited a preexisting ending to the CEGM that named James as the author of that source document.

Joseph in the ProtJac

The primary objective of the Composer seems to have been to fashion out of the *GenMar* a more complete document that narrated Mary's life story from her conception and birth through the conception and birth of her divine child. He systematically augmented the text of the *GenMar* to distance Mary from the temple for the major events that would happen to her at the age of twelve, which in the *GenMar* occurred in the temple: her participation in the weaving of the temple veil, and her Annunciation and conception by the *Bath Kol*. The

---

75. Cf. "The Trial of Joseph and Mary," pp. 55-76, especially pp. 65-76 in which evidence is presented supporting the existence of an original *GenMar* Trial story involving only Mary, and not Joseph.

76. Cf. "The Nativity Complex," pp. 77-127.

77. Ibid., pp. 108-27.

78. Mark's list of Jesus's brothers is reproduced in Mt. 13:55 from where the Redactor would have derived the name of James, being that the Redactor was familiar with Matthew and not Mark.

79. Cf. "The Colophon," pp. 126-7.

Composer's materials are readily distinguishable from those of the Redactor, not only by their independence from any canonical influence but also by the fact that they contain elements that directly contradict the Nativity stories of Matthew and Luke. The Composer's original unredacted Journey story shows no knowledge of the parallel Lukan account, and Mary's child is not born in Bethlehem as in the canonical Gospels, nor in a house as in Matthew, but he is born in a cave outside of Bethlehem.[80] The key, however, to understanding the Composer's *Sitz im Leben* is the person of Joseph. Joseph appears suddenly in the Composer's new material and takes the stage as a central figure in this second major phase of the compositional process that produced the *ProtJac*.[81]

The question of the prominence of Joseph in the CEGM is quite germane to our investigation in view of the uncertain place of Joseph within the early Christian literature. Joseph was entirely absent from the earliest major Christian writings of Paul, Mark, Q, and Thomas. He first appeared in the independent Nativity stories of the second generation of Christian writers, the Synoptic duo of Matthew and Luke.[82] It is significant that both Matthew and Luke added Joseph in their respective redactions of their shared source, Mark, from whom Joseph was absent.[83] It is particularly relevant that the Joseph materials in the *ProtJac* derive from two separate and distinct sources, the Composer and the Redactor, and that the material in each of these sources exhibits no relation to the other. Whereas the Composer appears to have created his own distinctive Joseph materials, the Redactor obtained his from Matthew and Luke. Thus, Joseph first enters the Christian literature in Matthew, Luke, and the CEGM, but these sources present conflicting images of Joseph.

Luke and Matthew present the relationship of Joseph to Jesus quite differently, and Luke's Nativity story contains ambiguity within itself regarding that relationship.[84] In Lk. 1:26-35 the archangel Gabriel informs the virgin Mary, who is betrothed to Joseph, that she will conceive Jesus through the Holy Spirit and the power of God. But this vital information does not occur in Lk. 2:8-20 where the shepherds relay their own angelic revelation to Mary and Joseph, who wonder at the identification of their son as the savior, the Lord Christ. Likewise, when the righteous Simeon refers to Jesus in Lk. 2:25-35 as the Lord's salvation, Joseph and Mary, who are described as "his father and his mother," "marveled at what was said

---

80. Cf. "Topographical and Archaeological Factors," pp. 89–92, also "Appendix 4: The Kathisma Church," pp. 205–20.

81. Cf. "The Joseph Council," pp. 29–32.

82. Cf. "Appendix 1: Mary's Evolving Virginity in Early Christianity," pp. 171–3.

83. See the discussion above, pp. 78–80, on the questionable origins of the Lukan Nativity story in which Joseph appears.

84. In the Gospel of John, Joseph is named twice (Jn 1:45 and 6:42) as the father of Jesus, the "son of Joseph"; it should be noted that the Hymn to the Logos in Jn 1:1-18, which describes Jesus as the preexistent Logos of God, is likely one of the last additions in the progressive, complex compositional development of the Gospel of John.

about him." In the story of the twelve-year-old Jesus in Lk. 2:41-51, Joseph and Mary are twice designated as "his parents," and, in addressing Jesus, Mary refers to herself and Joseph as "your father and I." When Jesus implies to them that God is "my father," Mary and Joseph do not understand his words. Furthermore, both Lk. 3:23 and 4:22 refer to Jesus specifically as "the son of Joseph."[85] Thus, in Luke the relationship of Joseph to Jesus is not clearly defined, and considerable ambiguity exists between the virgin-born Jesus of Lk. 1 and Jesus as son of Joseph in Lk. 2.[86]

Matthew, on the other hand, consistently and repeatedly specifies that Jesus is Mary's son alone, and not Joseph's. In his genealogy at Mt. 1:16 he obscures any paternal relationship of Joseph toward Jesus with the convoluted depiction of Joseph as "the husband of Mary, of whom was born Jesus who is called Christ." By using the feminine gender of the relative pronoun "of whom" (ἐξ ἧς), Matthew refers to Mary alone as the begetter of Jesus, to the exclusion of Joseph, and this in a list of forty-two generations of Joseph's ancestors in which most of the fathers "begot" their own sons.[87] Matthew affirms twice that Joseph had no involvement in Mary's conception of Jesus: Mt. 1:18 "before they came together she was found to be with child of the Holy Spirit," and Mt. 1:25 "Joseph knew her not before she had borne a son." In Mt. 1:20 the angel tells Joseph, "Do not fear to take Mary your wife, for that which is conceived in her is of the Holy Spirit"; and this is followed by the citation from Isa. 7:22-23 that "a Virgin will conceive." In Mt. 2:11 the Magi "saw the child with Mary his mother"; Jesus and Mary are "the child and his mother" four more times, in Matt 2:13, 14, 20, and 21. At the center of this cluster of references to Mary and her son Jesus, excluding Joseph, is a citation of Hos. 11:1 in Mt. 2:15 designating God as Jesus's father: "out of Egypt I called my son."

The differing portraits of Joseph in Matthew, Luke, and the CEGM provide a context within which we may perhaps discern a possible *Sitz im Leben* for the Composer. Matthew and Luke, individually and independently of each other, but also in tandem, introduced Joseph into their common source document, Mark, by most accounts after the Roman destruction of Judea in 70 CE. It seems plausible that the Composer could have done the same to his source document, the *GenMar*, also individually and independently of Matthew and Luke. The incidental concurrence of three documents introducing Joseph into the Christian narrative may represent a juncture in early Christian history when writers within the Jesus movement deemed it necessary to shield Mary against the allegations

---

85. See "Appendix 2: The Apologetic Purpose of the *ProtJac*," p. 184 regarding the description of Jesus in the genealogy in Lk. 3:23 as υἱός, ὡς ἐνομίζετο, Ἰωσήφ. The phrase ὡς ἐνομίζετο ("as was thought") seems to have been inserted into the original reading υἱός Ἰωσήφ ("the son of Joseph") by a later editor for the purpose of clarifying that Joseph was not Jesus's real father; this was to support the virgin birth concept in the Nativity story in Lk. 1 that we view as a later addition to Proto-Luke, which began in what is now Lk. 3:1.

86. It has been noted above that the Composer also displayed considerable ambiguity with respect to the relationship between Joseph and Mary, "The Joseph Council," pp. 32-4.

87. "Appendix 2: The Apologetic Purpose of the *ProtJac*," pp. 182-4.

of adultery and to assuage the stigma of illegitimacy from Jesus, both of which were no doubt circulating at that time.[88] The figure of Joseph as the husband or betrothed of Mary would provide a most effective cover for that purpose. Thus, in this respect, it would be appropriate to assign the Composer to the same general chronological and ideological milieu as Matthew and Luke.

But although the Composer's incorporation of Joseph into his narrative placed him within the same general ideological environment as Matthew and Luke, his distinctive portrayal of Joseph distinguished him from those gospels, as did his apparent acceptance of Mary's Annunciation and conception by the Voice of God directly, instead of through a mediating angel. In this respect the Composer seems to have lived in a theological environment closer to that of the Author of the *GenMar*. But the Composer's alteration of the *GenMar* regarding the location of the Annunciation differentiates him from the Author. These distinguishing characteristics of the Composer vis-à-vis the *GenMar* Author, Matthew, and Luke may shed further light on his *Sitz im Leben*.[89] Since the Composer accepted the character of the *GenMar* Annunciation by the *Bath Kol* while at the same time relocating the Annunciation to Joseph's home, the factor that distinguished the Composer and the Author of the *GenMar* was not their approach to the Annunciation itself, but their respective attitudes toward the temple.[90] The Author of the *GenMar* and the Composer appear therefore to have been two separate individuals who operated within the same, or a similar, ideological matrix, but perhaps at different developmental stages of that matrix.

We thus have before us four individual documents that share certain characteristics with respect to Joseph and Mary's Annunciation and conception but also diverge from each other in other respects. The Composer may be associated with Matthew and Luke chronologically, but not ideologically, while being associated with the Author of the *GenMar* ideologically, but not chronologically. Valuable insights toward ascertaining the *Sitze im Leben* of these documents, but especially of the Author of the *GenMar* and our Composer, may perhaps be found in the work of Andries van Aarde, who applied the principles of social scientific criticism in the search for the historical Jesus.[91] Van Aarde traced two rival trajectories in Israelite history that differed significantly in their perception of

---

88. Ibid., pp. 186–8.

89. Cf. "The Veil Council," pp. 35–9, 43–4.

90. See "The Composer: The Composer-enhanced *GenMar*," pp. 148–50.

91. Andries van Aarde, "Methods and Models in the Quest for the Historical Jesus," *HTS* 58 (2002), 425–6. As innovative as van Aarde's approach was, he still adhered to the consensus opinion of the *ProtJac* as a second-century document, which caused him to fail to consider the *ProtJac* fully in his very insightful assessment of early Christianity and its documents; cf. e.g., Andries van Aarde, "The Earliest Jesus Group in Jerusalem," *Verbum et Ecclesia* 25 (2004), 712, n. 2; Andries van Aarde, "The Carpenter's Son (Mt. 13:55): Joseph and Jesus in the Gospel of Matthew and Other Texts," *Neotestamentica* 34 (2000), e.g., 174, 179, and 180.

Joseph and which thus may provide a viable context for understanding the various approaches to the person of Joseph in the early Christian writings:

1. The northern "Samaritan" Israelites: descended from the biblical Patriarch Joseph, the youngest son of Jacob by Rachel, his second, and beloved, wife (Gen. 35); Jacob favored Joseph, took the birthright from Judah and Reuben, and gave it to Joseph (1 Chron. 5:1-2); Joseph's jealous brothers sold him into slavery in Egypt (Gen. 37) where he married the Egyptian Aseneth (Gen. 42:50) who bore him two sons, Ephraim and Manasseh, the forefathers of the Samaritans; the Samaritans were connected to the Levite priesthood and worshipped at Mt. Gerizim close to Shechem (Judg. 9:6-7), the first capital of the Northern Kingdom of Israel (1 Kgs 12) and Joseph's burial place (Josh. 24:32); their only biblical canon was the Samaritan Pentateuch.
2. The southern Judeans: considered themselves to be the legitimate Israelites; worshipped at Mt. Zion in Jerusalem; were connected to the Zadokite priesthood (Sadducees[92]); had a larger collection of holy writings, the Torah, Prophets, historical books, and Wisdom Literature; disliked Joseph for taking their ancestor Judah's birthright and marrying the Egyptian Aseneth, whom, in spite of being a virgin,[93] they nevertheless considered to be an "impure" non-Israelite, mother of the "bastards" Ephraim and Manasseh.[94]

Van Aarde thus establishes a historical scenario within which the variations between the early Christian documents with respect to the person of Joseph may be understood:

> References to Joseph as the father of Jesus "do not occur in writings originating in the period before the beginning of the separation of the Pharisaic synagogue and the church after the destruction of Jerusalem in 70 CE and the termination of the earliest Jesus movement in Jerusalem."[95]
>
> These include Paul, Mark, Q, Thomas, and I would add the *GenMar*.

Van Aarde continues:

> We meet Joseph for the first time in those documents that dispute the defamatory claims of the opponents of the Jesus movement, Matthew, John, and Luke.[96]
>
> To this list I would add the CEGM.

---

92. The identity of the Sadducees (Σαδδουκαίοι) is much debated among scholars. See the discussion below, pp. 158–60, regarding the possible connection of the *GenMar* to the Sadducees.

93. Aseneth's virginity is not mentioned in the Genesis story of Joseph.

94. "Carpenter's Son," p. 182, "for the puritan Judeans the name 'Samaritan' was equivalent to being a bastard, a people with no right to enter the temple in Jerusalem because they were not the 'true' children of Abraham."

95. Ibid., p. 179.

96. Ibid. At this point in this list van Aarde includes "the dependent *Proto-James*"; cf. n. 91 above regarding van Aarde's adherence to the de Strycker consensus model of a late, unitary *ProtJac*.

Van Aarde describes the antagonistic atmosphere that formed the backdrop of this transitional juncture in the early Christian writings:

> For Greek speaking Israelites Joseph was an ethical paradigm. For Pharisees he was the symbolic adversary of Judah. For them he was the forefather of people who either came from the pagan world or mixed with them. In other words, Joseph-people were regarded by the Judeans as bastards because they were a mixture of the children of God and gentiles, people who should be treated as if they had no parentage.[97]

Just such a hostile atmosphere would explain the characterization of Jesus by the aged Simeon in the temple as a σημεῖον ἀντιλεγόμενον ("sign that is opposed").[98] Jesus, the son of Joseph, with his own reputed legitimacy issues, would certainly be at the center of this dispute between the rival Jewish factions. But Jesus's geographical origins—his being from northern Israel and born in Bethlehem—would further stoke the fires of opposition.

The figure of Joseph is not the only bone of contention in the first century between the northern and southern Israelites, between the earlier and later first-century Christians, and between the post-70 CE Jews and Christians. Van Aarde speaks of a more specific geographical aspect of the ideological "Joseph-Judah" dispute among the Jews and Christians, which he describes as "the Bethlehem-Jerusalem controversy."[99] The appearance of Joseph in the post-70 Christian gospels, especially Matthew and John, may be understood within the context of this Bethlehem-Jerusalem controversy: "Both of these gospels originated against the background of the antagonism of the Pharisaic Academy in Jamnia towards the Jesus-movement during the period after the destruction of the temple in Jerusalem after 70 C.E."[100] Van Aarde appears to have identified the appropriate historical framework of complex ideological and geographical disputations among first-century Christians and Jews, within which the distinguishing features of the Composer and the Author may permit us to identify their distinctive *Sitze im Leben*.

The Composer's introduction of Joseph into the Christian narrative, which was his primary purpose in enhancing the *GenMar*, decisively places him in the camp of the northern Israelites for whom the biblical Joseph was their honored progenitor and ethical paradigm. Likewise, his second objective, the removal of Mary from

---

97. "Carpenter's Son," p. 179.
98. Lk. 2:33-4.
99. "Carpenter's Son," p. 180.
100. Ibid., p. 185 "For the puritans in the Judean tradition it did not take much to use the label 'son of Joseph' for a man of alleged illegitimate background, also known for his association with prostitutes and other outcasts."

the Jerusalem temple ahead of her Annunciation by the *Bath Kol*, betrays the anti-Jerusalem temple bias of the northern Israelites who worshipped at their own temple on Mt. Gerizim close to Shechem. So also the northern Israelite leaning of the Composer is evident in his presentation of the birth of Mary's child near Bethlehem, close to the shrine of the tomb of Rachel; Rachel was the beloved wife of Joseph who bore him Ephraim and Manasseh, the forefathers of the northern Israelites.[101] On the basis of van Aarde's social-scientific elucidation of the two major trajectories in Israelite history that are relevant to our study, the Composer may be assigned to the post-70 CE Christian environment in which the figure of Joseph was introduced as a shield against accusations of adultery by Mary and the consequential stigma of the illegitimacy of Jesus. The association of the New Testament Joseph with the idealized Old Testament Patriarch Joseph lent an air of respectability and legitimacy to the images of Mary and her son.[102]

---

101. The Composer would not have been aware of the canonical tradition of Jesus's birth in the town of Bethlehem itself; cf. Mt. 2:6; Lk. 2:4; Jn 6:41; 7:27, 41. It is possible also that he may have been aware of the traditional site of the Cave of the Nativity outside of Bethlehem; see the discussion in "The Original Cave of the Nativity," pp. 209–11.

102. Van Aarde discusses the positive reflection of the "ethical paradigm" of the biblical Joseph upon Jesus through such documents as *The Testaments of the Twelve Patriarchs* and *Joseph and Aseneth*, which contain "clear parallels between Jesus, recorded in the gospel tradition, and Joseph the Patriarch," cf. "Carpenter's Son," pp. 176–80.

THE AUTHOR: THE *GENESIS MARIAS*

When the Redactor's revisions and canonical interpolations are eliminated from the text of the *ProtJac*, his underlying source document, the CEGM, is liberated from the "orthodox" prison in which it has been confined for nineteen centuries. When the Composer's own voluminous intrusions into the text of the *GenMar* are removed, the truncated, but coherent, narrative that emerges exhibits certain notable features that appear to be quite eccentric; hence, the likely reason for its suppression in later phases of Christianity. But these features may seem to be eccentric only because they possibly bear witness to a primal form of Christianity that reaches back to the earliest decades of the Jesus movement before the proto-Orthodox Christianity represented by the canonical Gospels and the emerging Catholic Church began its millennia-long journey toward becoming the normative version of the religion that constitutes the faith of the Western world. By virtue of its position as an antecedent to the work of the Composer, which seems to have been contemporary with the post-70 canonical gospels, the *GenMar* would have originated in an even earlier, idiosyncratic Judean-Christian milieu that was contemporary with, although independent of, the first generation of Christian sources, Mark, Paul, and Q.

ProtJac 1:01–8:02 essentially coincides with the initial chapters of the *GenMar*, which contain a series of stories centering around Mary's childless parents, Ioachim and Anna, who were wealthy members of the highest society of the Jerusalem elite, including, among others, the high priests of the temple. The story continues with Anna's conception and birth of Mary, certain events in the first three years of the infant Mary's life that authenticated her extreme purity, her dedication to the Jerusalem temple at the age of three, and a brief account of the pre-pubescent Mary's life in the temple. This opening section of the *GenMar* was followed by the unredacted Veil Council, now contained in a heavily edited form in *ProtJac* 10:01–12:11.[103] The central element of the Veil Council is the Annunciation story of the *GenMar* that is preserved in *ProtJac* 11:01-05 and 12:01-02. Any subsequent narrative of the *GenMar* after the Veil Council appears to have been overwritten by the Composer's incorporation of voluminous Joseph material beginning in *ProtJac* 13:01. But traces of the underlying *GenMar* text may be discerned in the Composer's Trial and Nativity stories. The swelling womb of the unmarried virgin Mary predictably would have brought about an enquiry by the temple priests and eventually would have resulted in the birth of her child.[104]

In attempting to identify the *Sitz im Leben* of the *GenMar*, one must first take into account one of its major characteristics, its thoroughgoing partisanship in favor of Jerusalem, the temple, and its priests.[105] In *ProtJac* 5:01-04 Mary's father

---

103. See the detailed analysis of the successive, heavy revisions of the *GenMar* by the Composer and the Redactor in "The Veil Council," pp. 35–54.
104. See the discussion below, pp. 160–1.
105. Cf. pp. 153–7 above.

Ioakeim presented his gifts in the temple and received verification from the petalon (πεταλον) of the priest that the Lord God accepted them and forgave his sins. In *ProtJac* 6:06-11, on her first birthday, Mary's father held a large reception to which he invited the high priests, the priests, and scribes of the temple, as well as the elders (γερουσιαν) and all the people of Israel. The priests asked "the God of our fathers" to bless Mary with a renowned name in all the generations and the people said, "Let it be, amen." Then the high priests asked "the God of heights" to bless Mary with the highest eternal blessing. In *ProtJac* 7:06-12 three-year-old Mary entered the temple in a ritualistic procession and was received by a priest who kissed and blessed her, and said to her that the Lord God had magnified her name in all the generations. He sat her on the third step of the sanctuary and "the Lord God put grace upon her." Mary danced and "all the house of Israel loved her." In 8:02 Mary remained in the temple of the Lord and was fed by the hand of an angel.

In the ensuing unredacted *GenMar* Veil Council, beginning in what is now *ProtJac* 10:01, the pure twelve-year-old virgin Mary has been assigned the red and true purple threads to spin for the new temple veil. In *ProtJac* 11:01 Mary was spinning the red thread in the Holy of Holies, put down the red thread, which symbolized her first menstruation, went out to the temple court to draw water from a laver, which represented her ritual purification, was impregnated by the *Bath Kol*, and was now worthy to reenter the temple, sit upon God's throne in the Holy of Holies, and spin the true purple thread, which was symbolic of the royal child whom she now bore. In *ProtJac* 12:01 Mary finished spinning the red and purple threads, returned them to the priest, and received his blessing. As her womb began to swell, Mary hid herself in the temple. Thus, in the *GenMar*, Mary's entire life is presented within the context of an ongoing series of interactions with the Jerusalem temple and its priests. Even more significantly, the temple and its priesthood are still efficacious as a conduit for operative interaction with the God of Israel. With respect to a possible *Sitz im Leben*, these characteristics situate the *GenMar* generally within the milieu of van Aarde's southern Judean trajectory, although a more specific time and place remain elusive.

The first-year birthday reception hosted by Mary's father in *ProtJac* 6:06-11 may provide further insights into the world of the Author of the *GenMar*. The guest list at Mary's birthday party has the appearance of a "who's who" of Jerusalem's priestly aristocracy, including the high priests, priests, temple scribes, and elders.[106] This catalog of the invitees to Mary's reception coincides largely with most descriptions of the Sadducees, who were one of the major factions reported by Josephus to have been active in first-century Judea.[107] Scholarly opinions regarding the Sadducees

---

106. Although "all the people of Israel" are also included in the list, it would be unreasonable to think that the entire population of Israel would be invited to a private party along with the highest social elites.

107. Josephus, *Wars*, 2, 8, 14; *Ant*. 18, 1, 4; Acts 5:17. See also Anthony J. Saldarini, *Pharisees, Scribes, and Sadducees in Palestinian Society: A Sociological Approach* (Wilmington, DE: Michael Glazer, 1988), 298–308.

differ, but generally: "The Sadducees were aristocrats, wealthy (εὔποροι) and persons of rank (πρῶτοι τοῖς ἀξιώμασι); which is to say that they mostly belonged to, or were associated with, the priesthood."[108] The Sadducees were connected historically to the ancient Zadokites who formed the priestly aristocracy throughout the period of the Second temple.

An important aspect of the *GenMar* that may be illuminated with reference to van Aarde's southern Judean trajectory is the unabashed presentation of Mary's Annunciation by the *Bath Kol* in the temple. Striking parallels exist between this central element in the *GenMar* and Ezekiel's vision of the future temple in which he also hears the *Bath Kol* coming "out of the house [of the Lord]."[109] In Ezek. 43:7 the *Bath Kol* indicates to the prophet that "this is the place of my throne," which is echoed in the *GenMar* Annunciation story, now in *ProtJac* 11:05, where Mary sat on the throne of God in the Holy of Holies after hearing the *Bath Kol*.[110] This parallel highlights the clear distinction between the *GenMar* Author and the Composer. The Author, a southern Judean with the Sadducean pro-temple faction, endorsed the direct impregnation of Mary by the *Bath Kol* in the temple; the Composer, a northern anti-Jerusalem temple Israelite, distanced this event from the temple and relocated it in Mary's home, even at the expense of creating the anomaly of Mary sitting on a throne in her house spinning thread. The Composer thus also avoided identifying the Annunciation with Ezekiel, who was a Zadokite priest descended from Zadok, the chief of the priesthood in the days of David and Solomon.[111] Ezekiel extolled the Zadokite priesthood as alone worthy to discharge their holy office.[112]

Valuable insights into the *Sitz im Leben* of the *GenMar* may be derived also from an analysis of certain possibly discernible traces of the underlying *GenMar* text after the Veil Council. These occur in the Trial and Nativity stories, both of which fall within the Composer's extensive augmentations of the *GenMar*. It would not be unreasonable to assume that the unmarried pregnant girl, who was hiding in the temple with her womb swelling at the end of the *GenMar* Veil Council, would have been discovered and questioned by the priests in a now lost, subsequent *GenMar* story. Vestiges of such a scenario may exist, hidden in the text of the *ProtJac* Trial story, which is composed of individual units that were blended together by the Composer and later edited by the Redactor.[113] In *ProtJac* 13 Joseph returns from his construction work and finds Mary with her womb swollen. He

---

108. Cf. Schürer, *History*, vol. II, 404; Greek citations are from Josephus *Ant.* 18, 1, 4.

109. Ezek. 43. See "The Original *GenMar* Annunciation Story," pp. 41–3. It is relevant to this discussion that Ezekiel is considered to have been a Zadokite priest, a forerunner of the Zadokite Sadducees.

110. Mary had emerged from the Holy of Holies to draw water, heard the *Bath Kol*, reentered the inner sanctum, sat on the throne of God, and spun the purple thread.

111. I Kgs 1:28-48, 2:35; I Chron. 29:21-22.

112. Ezek. 40:46, 43:19, 44:15, 48:11.

113. See "The Trial of Joseph and Mary," pp. 65–76.

laments bitterly and argues with Mary.[114] In *ProtJac* 14, which was heavily edited by the Redactor, Joseph considers what to do about Mary and receives an angelic visitation telling him of the divine origin of Mary's child.

Our analysis of the Trial story appears to have confirmed our premise that the original *GenMar* narrative would not have ended in the Veil Council Annunciation story with Mary hiding in the temple with her womb swollen but likely would have extended to the discovery of, and enquiry into, Mary's pregnancy by the temple priests and even further on to the birth of her child.[115] But even assuming the existence of an original *GenMar* Birth story, the vestiges of such a story have been difficult to isolate in the *ProtJac* Nativity narrative that has been so very heavily redacted by the successive interpolations of the Composer's Joseph materials and the Redactor's Doubting Salome story.[116] Perhaps a different strategy may cast light on this subject and enable us to identify significant elements of the *GenMar* Birth story in the *ProtJac* Nativity texts. A comparison of the ideological character of the original Birth story in *ProtJac* 19:08, 10-12 with that of the *GenMar* Annunciation story in *ProtJac* 11:01-05[117] reveals that core elements of these two stories may derive from a similar ideological matrix.

The ideology in question appears to reflect the understanding of the person of Jesus among some early Christians known as Docetism. Scholarly debate has not resulted in a consensus on the definition of Docetism.[118] Thus, scholars have come to refer to Docetism in more nebulous terms, for example:

> In modern scholarly parlance, "Docetism" does not refer to any clearly definable sect, but rather to an attitude, shared by various individuals and movements at the origins of Christianity. Despite the dearth of evidence, one cannot speak of a single, particular, sect of Docetists. A fortiori, it is impossible to refer to one precise body of Docetic beliefs.[119]

While acknowledging the lack of general agreement among scholars on a definition of Docetism, Guy Stroumsa identifies two major perspectives in the Docetic worldview:

---

114. *ProtJac* 13:06 contains the Eve/Mary typology that is paralleled in Justin's *Dial.* 100.5; cf. "The Redactor: *The Protevangelium Jacobi*," pp. 141-3.

115. There is scant possibility of uncovering any further *GenMar* elements after the abrupt end of the involvement of Mary and her child in *ProtJac* 22:02, where Mary hides her child from the executioners of Herod. At that point the family of John the Baptist replaces Mary and her son as the protagonists until the end of the *ProtJac*.

116. See "The Birth," pp. 104-8.

117. See "The Original *GenMar* Annunciation Story," pp. 39-49.

118. For an overview of early opinions see Michael Slusser, "Docetism: A Historical Definition," *SecCent* 1 (1981), 163-72.

119. Ronnie Goldstein and Guy G. Stroumsa, "The Greek and Jewish Origins of Docetism: A New Proposal," *ZAC* 10 (2007), 423.

The two main approaches relate either to Christ's incarnation or to his passion: either Christ was not really incarnated, as the divine and matter could not have a common ground, so Christ would be totally spiritual in nature; or Christ was indeed incarnated, but did not really suffer on the cross. These two views are not identical. The first, being broader, is inclusive of the second. Most scholars seem to support the first approach.[120]

Docetism is further described as a "theological option revealed in a wide variety of early Christian texts" representing "a series of groups holding similar beliefs" that "flourished mainly in the second and third centuries," but "'Docetic' doctrines probably date from the first Christian century."[121] It would be relevant to our investigation to explore possible Docetic influences in the *GenMar* and the Composer's revision of the *GenMar*, both of which also have been dated to the first century. It is not our purpose to debate the definition of Docetism or its origins, particularly in view of the vagueness expressed by scholars regarding that phenomenon. Rather, we will explore the possibility of a relationship between potential Docetic elements in the *GenMar* Annunciation and Nativity stories and compare these to Docetic elements that have been identified in another early Christian apocryphal document, the Ascension of Isaiah (*Asc. Isa.*). It is of great interest to us that the Docetic elements in the *Asc. Isa.* occur in a section of the work that is thought to be an earlier, independent document, the *Vision of Isaiah*, which dates to the first century CE.[122]

The *Asc. Isa.* is an early second-century Christian apocalypse that is made up of two parts: (1) chapters 1–5, dated to the early second century CE, contain a narrative introduction to the whole work and disclosures of futuristic eschatology; (2) and chapters 6–11, the *Vision of Isaiah*, dated to the first century CE, which describes Isaiah's mystical journey to the seventh heaven where he witnesses the descent, earthly sojourn, and ascent of the heavenly redeemer, followed by a narrative conclusion to the whole document. The final chapter of the *Vision of Isaiah* narrates the birth of the Lord Christ by Mary, his infancy, life, crucifixion, resurrection, and ascension again to the seventh heaven where he takes his place at the right hand of the "Great Glory."[123] *Asc. Isa.* 11:2-14 contains an important witness to Mary and the birth of her son that includes close parallels to material

---

120. "Christ's Laughter: Docetic Origins Reconsidered," *JECS* 12 (2004), 268.

121. Goldstein and Stroumsa, "Greek and Jewish Origins," 423-4.

122. In a recent summary of scholarly opinion regarding the *Asc. Isa.*, the I CE date of *Asc. Isa.*6-11 is described as "the consensus view for scholarship in the present millennium" by Jonathan Knight, "The Origin and Significance of the Angelomorphic Christology in the Ascension of Isaiah," *JTS* 63 (2012), 68-71; cf. 68, nn. 6, 7 for significant earlier publications on the *Asc. Isa.*

123. Zervos, "Seeking," 107-20. This article and Knight's article published in the same volume, "The Portrait of Mary in the Ascension of Isaiah," 91-105, are based on papers read by Knight and myself to the Christian Apocrypha Section at the 2000 Annual Meeting of the Society of Biblical Literature in Nashville, Tenn.

about Mary in the Annunciation and Nativity stories in the CEGM. The existence of an authentic passage containing advanced Mariological material dated to the first century CE raises critical questions pertaining to the sources of this material. Unfortunately, the continued adherence of scholars to the de Strycker model of a second-century, unitary *ProtJac* excludes this crucial Marian witness from consideration as a possible source.[124]

A comparison of the parallel Mariological elements in the *Asc. Isa.*, Matthew, and the CEGM indicates that the Marian section in *Asc. Isa.* 11:2-14 appears to have drawn upon Matthew and the CEGM for its details on Joseph, Mary, and the birth of her child.[125] A number of these details are shared by all three sources, and others only by the *Asc. Isa.* and Matthew. But the most important elements for our investigation of the Docetic elements in the Annunciation and Nativity stories of the CEGM are those that are shared only by the *Asc. Isa.* and the *ProtJac*, and not by Matthew.[126]

Elements shared by the *Asc. Isa.*, Matthew, and the CEGM:

Mary was betrothed to Joseph
  Asc. Isa. 11:2—Matt 1:18/*ProtJac* 19:04[127]
Joseph was a carpenter
  Asc. Isa. 11:2—Matt 13:55/*ProtJac* 9:12, 13:01
Mary was found to be pregnant before marriage
  Asc. Isa. 11:3—Matt 1:18/*ProtJac* 13:01, 15:03
Joseph considered divorcing or exposing Mary
  Asc. Isa. 11:3—Matt 1:19/*ProtJac* 14:01-03

Elements shared by the *Asc. Isa.* and Matthew:

Joseph a descendent of David
  Asc. Isa. 11:2—Matt 1:1-16
An angel convinces Joseph not to put Mary away
  Asc. Isa. 11:4—Matt 1:20-25[128]

---

124. Cf. Zervos, "Seeking," 114-15, where I observed that Knight had ignored the witness of the *ProtJac* in his seminal publications on the *Asc. Isa.*; he has done the same in his most recent publication on this document; see n. 122.

125. Ibid., 115-19. My own position regarding the *ProtJac* as a source of some of the Marian teachings in the *Asc. Isa.* has been modified since my 2002 publication. Whereas in my original article I posited the *GenMar* as the underlying source document in the *ProtJac* that contained these Marian teachings, my most recent research, reflected in the present study, has revealed the CEGM to be the true source.

126. The text and versification of these quotations of the *Asc. Isa.* are based on Michael A. Knibb's, "Martyrdom and Ascension of Isaiah," *OTP* 2 (1985), 143-76.

127. See "The Joseph Council," pp. 32-4 regarding the confusion in the *ProtJac* text with respect to Mary's status vis-à-vis Joseph, i.e., as his betrothed or as his wife.

128. The parallel passage in *ProtJac* 13:05-08 occurs in the Redactor's interpolation of the Matthean dream vision into the CEGM.

Jesus was born in Joseph's house in Jerusalem
Asc. Isa. 11:7—Matt 2:11[129]

Elements shared only by the *Asc. Isa.* and the CEGM:

Mary is a descendent of David
Asc. Isa. 11:2—*ProtJac* 10:04
Joseph came into his "lot"[130]
Asc. Isa. 11:2—*ProtJac* 9:05
There was no midwife present at Mary's delivery
Asc. Isa. 11:14—*ProtJac* 19:08-12[131]
Mary's postpartum virginity is verified
Asc. Isa. 11:9—*ProtJac* 19:13-20:10[132]
A voice told Mary and Joseph not to announce the "vision" of the Birth
Asc. Isa. 11:11—*ProtJac* 11:02[133]
Mary's child was born in an unconventional manner after a short pregnancy
Asc. Isa. 11:7-10, 13-14—*ProtJac* 8:04, 9:12, 13:01

In the all-important final section of the above list—which contains only the non-canonical Marian elements shared by the *Asc. Isa.* and the CEGM—Mary's Davidic descent, Joseph's coming into his "lot," and the absence of a midwife at the birth of Mary's child constitute evidence of a direct relationship between the *Asc. Isa.* and the Composer's work.[134] That these elements are interspersed with unrelated canonical Matthean materials in *Asc. Isa.* 11:2-14 strongly suggests that the CEGM, together with Matthew, served as a source for, and thus preceded chronologically, the Mariological section in *Asc. Isa.* 11. And if, therefore, it is "the consensus view for scholarship in the present millennium" that the *Vision of Isaiah*—including the Marian section—is dated to the first

---

129. See the discussion in "The Magi," pp. 119-20.

130. See the discussion in "The Joseph Council," p. 33.

131. See the discussion in "The Midwife," pp. 92-103.

132. Although Mary's postpartum virginity is verified in the Redactor's interpolated Doubting Salome episode, there is evidence that the Redactor may have overwritten a possible underlying *GenMar* story in which the midwife may have physically verified Mary's postpartum virginity, was punished and subsequently healed for her action; see pp. 166-7 below, and "Doubting Salome," pp. 110-11.

133. An interesting parallel between an unidentified "voice" telling Mary and Joseph not to publicize the miraculous birth in *Asc. Isa.* 11:11, and the unidentified voice (*Bath Kol*) in the *GenMar* Annunciation story speaking to Mary but giving her no information on her conception and the eventual birth of her son. Mary remains completely ignorant of the cause of her pregnancy throughout the CEGM.

134. Zervos, "Seeking," 116-17.

Conclusions: The "Authors" of the ProtJac 165

century CE,[135] then our dating of the CEGM to the first century is confirmed. And since the Composer's revision of the *GenMar* predates the *Vision of Isaiah*, then the *GenMar* itself would necessarily have been written even earlier in the first century CE.

The dating of the *GenMar* to the first century may be corroborated by a comparison of the Docetic elements in the *Asc. Isa.* with their parallels in the *GenMar* Annunciation and Nativity stories.[136] Since Docetism seems to evolve and become intertwined with the burgeoning multifaceted phenomenon of Gnosticism as the second century progresses, our investigation will be limited to the earliest primary witnesses to the manifestation of Docetic concepts, the NT letters of John 1 and 2, dated to the end of the first century CE, and certain letters of Ignatius of Antioch in the early second century CE.[137] 1 Jn 4:3 speaks of those who do not confess "Jesus Christ having come in the flesh" (τὸν Ἰησοῦν Χριστὸν ἐν σαρκὶ ἐληλυθότα)[138]; 2 Jn 7 also refers those who do not confess "Jesus Christ coming in the flesh" (Ἰησοῦν Χριστὸν ἐρχόμενον ἐν σαρκί). Ignatius, who battles deniers of the reality of Jesus's physical existence in Asia Minor,[139] refers to individuals in Smyrn. 5:2 "not confessing him [Jesus] bearing flesh" (μὴ ὁμολογῶν αὐτὸν σαρκοφόρον) and in Trall. 9:1 to those who deny that Jesus "was truly born" (ἀληθῶς ἐγεννήθη) "from Mary" (ἐκ Μαρίας). We must depend on these earliest polemical statements against Docetism to assist us in evaluating the parallel Docetic aspects of the *GenMar* and the *Asc. Isa.*[140]

If our premise is correct that the *GenMar* Annunciation and Nativity stories as preserved in the *ProtJac* contain Docetic elements, then these elements, corroborated by the parallel Docetic materials in the *Asc. Isa.*, should constitute a reasonable representation of the Docetic perspective in the first century regarding the exceptional nature of the birth of Mary's child. This perspective centers around the spontaneous materialization of the child after a short pregnancy by Mary.[141] In *Asc. Isa.* 11:7-9 "after two months of days ... Mary then looked with her eyes and

135. See n. 122 above.

136. Zervos, "Seeking," 118-19.

137. See Carl B. Smith II, *No Longer Jews: The Search for Gnostic Origins* (Peabody, MA: Hendrickson Publishers, 2004), 49-71 for a helpful summary of the theories of gnostic origins with relevant bibliography; 116-17 distinguishes early Docetism from the progressively "negative evaluation of the cosmos and the creator evident in Gnostic works and among Gnostic teachers," cf. 146-7.

138. The MSS are divided on the exact wording of this verse, but this seems to be the best reading with respect to 4:2.

139. E.g., *Trall.* 9-10, *Smyrn.* 2.

140. As far as I know, the *Asc. Isa.* and the *GenMar*, and the enhancement of the *GenMar* by the Composer, are the principle witnesses to first-century Docetism.

141. Whereas it is clear in *Asc. Isa.* 11:7 and 13 that Mary was pregnant for only two months before giving birth to her son, the chronology of Mary's age in the *ProtJac* is confused by an interpolation by the Redactor. Mary's age is given as twelve years in *ProtJac* 8:03-04

saw a small infant, and she was astounded." In *ProtJac* 19:10-11 a blinding bright light appeared in the Cave of the Nativity "and for a little while that light receded until a child appeared" (και προς ολιγον το φως εκεινο υπεστελλετο, εως εφανη βρεφος). The correspondence between these two scenes in the central event of the birth of the child is striking. In the *ProtJac* version the child "appeared" as the blinding light receded. In *Asc. Isa.* 11:8 Mary looked "and saw a small infant." Other subsidiary features of the parallel birth scenarios further reinforce their Docetic character.

Mary is pregnant but does not appear to experience labor pains in either account of the birth itself, in *Asc. Isa.* 11:7-8 or in the *GenMar* version in *ProtJac* 19:11. This seems to be supported by secondary elements in the larger contexts in both narratives. Later, in *Asc. Isa.* 11:14 it is stated that Mary felt no pain in her delivery: "we did not hear (any) cries of pain." This may represent a later elaboration in the *Asc. Isa.* Nativity narrative that preserves an echo of a similar element that may have occurred in the original *GenMar*, given that the *GenMar* Birth story served as one source of *Asc. Isa.* 11:2-14.[142] Also related to Mary's lack of labor pains in the birth of her son is the absence of a midwife. In *Asc. Isa.* 11:14 this element occurs in the same reference as the lack of labor pains and is directly connected to the Docetic concept that Mary's child was not really born in the physical sense: "But many said, 'She did not give birth; the midwife did not go up (to her), and we did not hear (any) cries of pain.'" In the *GenMar* Birth story in *ProtJac* 19:08-11, the midwife also was not present in the Cave of the Nativity when the child appeared. Joseph and the midwife arrived at the cave just in time to see the dark cloud that was covering the cave being replaced immediately by the blinding light out of which the child appeared.

The Docetic Nativity elements of the parallel birth stories in the *GenMar* and the *Asc. Isa.* reach their climax in the authentication of Mary's postpartum virginity. *Asc. Isa.* 11:8-9 clearly states that Mary's womb was not affected by the birth of her

and seems to remain so throughout the text. In *ProtJac* 13:01 Mary was less than six months pregnant when Joseph returned home and discovered her condition. The Trial, Journey to the Cave, and Nativity followed in rapid succession, implying that her child was born after a short pregnancy of not much more than six months. The Redactor caused an irreconcilable contradiction in the chronology of the text by interpolating *ProtJac* 12:11, which stated her age as sixteen years. His purpose most likely was to address the sensitivities of the Romans with respect to a twelve-year-old girl being impregnated by the Jewish God.

142. Such an element also may be reflected in the Composer's Nativity narrative in *ProtJac* 17:11, where Mary tells Joseph to take her down from the donkey "because he who is in me presses me to come forth" (οτι ο εν εμοι επειγει με προελθειν). The verb επειγει, "exert pressure upon," does not necessarily connote the notion of labor pains. See the discussion in "The Journey to Bethlehem," pp. 84–5. In fact, Mary's ambiguous allusion to her fetus as "he who is in me" may refer figuratively to the identity of Mary's divine child as the unnamed Docetic heavenly redeemer figure; see discussion below.

child: "Mary looked with her eyes and saw a small infant, and ... her womb was found as (it was) at first, before she had conceived." Any Docetic elements attesting to Mary's postpartum virginity in the original *GenMar* Birth story have been obscured by the Redactor's interpolated Doubting Salome story, the purpose of which, not coincidentally, was to verify Mary's postpartum virginity.[143] However, a remnant of an original *GenMar* story may survive in the dislocated, contextually incompatible verse *ProtJac* 20:04b in which the absent midwife is healed although there is no hint in the present text that she had been injured. In the *GenMar* story the midwife, not Salome, would have been she who verified Mary's postpartum virginity physically and was punished, then healed, for her transgression.[144] And if the *GenMar* was a source of the *Asc. Isa.* Birth story, the Docetic witness to Mary's postpartum virginity in *Asc. Isa.* 11:9 could be an echo of a preexisting parallel element in the unredacted *GenMar*.

Central to this investigation is the identity of Mary's child, who is not named in the Docetic Mariological section in *Asc. Isa.* 11 nor anywhere in the *GenMar* or the Composer's work.[145] The child is identified in *Asc. Isa.* 9 and 10 as the Lord Christ, the Beloved Son of the Most High God, who will descend through the seven heavens, while progressively changing his form to conceal his identity.[146] *Asc. Isa.* 11 recounts the arrival of the Beloved on earth in his spontaneous appearance to Mary, which is paralleled in his materialization out of the light of the cave in *ProtJac* 19:11. By providing the larger context of Docetic Christology vis-à-vis the "hidden descent" of the Beloved One, *Asc. Isa.* 11 may also validate the Docetic nature of the *GenMar* Annunciation story in *ProtJac* 11:01-05. Mary's surprise at hearing the unidentified voice in the temple evokes the image of her astonishment at the sudden appearance of her child in *Asc. Isa.* 11:7-9. Her obliviousness to the circumstances of her pregnancy in these parallel Docetic birth scenes explains her ignorance when interrogated by the high priest in the probably authentic *GenMar* scenario in *ProtJac* 15:10-12.[147] Mary's denial in *ProtJac* 13:12 of any knowledge of the origins of her child rings true: ου γινωσκω ποθεν εστιν εμοι ("I do not know from where this is in me").

The results of this investigation support our premise that the *GenMar* originally extended beyond its initial text in *ProtJac* 1:01-8:02 and its Annunciation story in

---

143. *ProtJac* 20:02. See "Doubting Salome," pp. 108-13.

144. Ibid., pp. 108-11.

145. Jesus is named earlier in *Asc. Isa.* 9:5 and 10:7, and only in the Redactor's interpolations of canonical Gospel materials in *ProtJac* 11:11 and 14:07.

146. In *Asc. Isa.* 9:13 the prophet is told that the Beloved One will "become like you in form, and they will think that he is flesh and a man." Cf. Knight, "Angelomorphic Christology," 76, regarding the hidden descent of the Beloved One in disguised form, "the deliberate deception of the angel world and humankind in which that identity remains concealed until the ascension."

147. See "The Trial of Joseph and Mary," pp. 67-75.

11:01-05 and included stories of a Trial and a Nativity. But the character of the *GenMar*, as it has been revealed in this study, represents a paradox with respect to its *Sitz im Leben*. On the one hand, the *GenMar* can be located within van Aarde's conservative Judean trajectory, which is identified with Jerusalem and its temple, and with the Zadokite (Sadducean) temple priesthood.[148] But where in the first century would one find a Christian individual, or a community, that would produce a writing that exhibits such a strong partisanship in favor of the priestly aristocracy of the Jerusalem temple, including the high priests, priests, scribes, and elders? These were the very elements in Judea that are depicted in the canonical tradition as being hostile to Jesus and his followers, to the point of being responsible for his crucifixion and their persecution. Further complicating this paradoxical scenario, the *GenMar* seems to have emerged as a rare witness to a pristine, first-century pre-Gnostic form of Docetism, which elucidates certain eccentric aspects of the *GenMar* that are otherwise unfathomable within the ideological context of proto-Orthodox Christianity.

There is much to be said for the idea of an early messianic Jew who authored the *GenMar*, and that this document was augmented shortly afterward by another writer, the Composer, who lived at a time when Christians were introducing Joseph into their message as a cover for Mary's unwed pregnancy.[149] Unfortunately, little insight into the critical issues of the date, provenance, and purpose of the *GenMar*, and its later enhancement, can be gained from scholarly publications on the *ProtJac*, given the dominance of the de Strycker consensus opinion that this document was a unitary, second-century work, thus excluding the existence within it of earlier Jewish sources. It is beyond my purpose, and certainly beyond my expertise, to explore potential associations between these early Jewish sources and other areas of interest in the first century, for example, the Sadducees, Qumran, Pella, Edessa, Eastern Syrian asceticism, *et alia*.

The *GenMar* truly is "a riddle wrapped in a mystery inside an enigma."[150] The "enigma" inside of which the mystery-wrapped "riddle" of the *GenMar* has been secreted is the *ProtJac*, which itself represents an anachronistic puzzle that defies conventional interpretations of the history of Mariology.[151] If scholars have been

---

148. Cf. pp. 154–7 above.

149. Lily C. Vuong provides a comprehensive, analytical survey of scholarly opinions on the provenance and date of the *ProtJac* and its relationship to Judaism, *Gender and Purity in the Protevangelium of James* (Tübingen, Germany: Mohr Siebeck, 2013), *Wissenschaftliche Untersuchungen zum Neuen Testament* 2. Reihe 358, 34–51.

150. Quotation from a radio address by Winston Churchill broadcast by the BBC on October 1, 1939.

151. Interpretations of historical phenomena must be based upon the available evidence. At the very least, the *ProtJac* represents a primary historical source of evidence concerning Mariology. Any conflict between a primary source and secondary, subjective interpretations based on preconceptions of the chronology of "received" doctrines must be resolved at the expense of the subjective interpretations.

perplexed by the *ProtJac*, dating by all accounts to the second century CE, whose principle purpose was to certify what eventually would become the full-blown Catholic dogma of the perpetual virginity of Mary, how much more would they be confounded by its source document, the apparently Jewish *GenMar*, which seems to promote the same objective and dates to a century earlier? The "mystery" inside of the *ProtJac* "enigma," in which the "riddle" of the *GenMar* is wrapped, is the CEGM which contains copious amounts of extraneous materials inserted by the Composer into the *GenMar* in pursuit of his own agenda. The Composer thus contributed an entire level of additional complexity to the overall *ProtJac* puzzle and further obscured the original character of the *GenMar*. It is my hope that this redaction-critical study of the *ProtJac* has provided insights that will form a basis for future scholarly investigations toward the ultimate resolution of the many enigmas, mysteries, and riddles hidden in the pages of this extraordinarily important Apocryphon and its sources.

APPENDICES

APPENDIX 1: MARY'S EVOLVING VIRGINITY IN EARLY CHRISTIANITY

The single most important factor in understanding the compositional complexities of the *ProtJac* is the issue of the evolving perception of the virginity of Mary in this document against the backdrop of the development of Mariology in early Christianity. The clarification of this matter ultimately may prove to be helpful in dating the consecutive stages of the compositional augmentation of the *ProtJac*. The confusing, and sometimes contradictory, depictions of the relationship between Mary and Joseph in our document[1] are comprehensible within this framework. The varying portrayals of Mary's marital status in the successive compositional layers of the *ProtJac* are in essential agreement with what I have described in a previous publication as the progressive development of the perception of Mary's virginal status in early Christian literature.[2] According to that analysis, Jesus's mother was treated "rather indifferently" in the earliest Christian sources: first, in Paul's passing reference in Gal. 4:4 to Mary generically as "(a) woman," without naming her,[3] and second, in the seemingly negative relationship between Jesus and his family, including his brothers, as portrayed in the Gospel of Mark:

In Mk 3:21 "when his family heard [of Jesus's activities], they went out to restrain him, for people were saying, 'He has gone out of his mind'";[4] in 3:31-35 Jesus denies his biological family in favor of those around him who do the will of God, whom he describes as "my brother and sister and mother" (ἀδελφός μου καὶ ἀδελφὴ καὶ μήτηρ). Finally, in Mk 6:4 Jesus includes his relatives and household

---

1. These occur especially in the Composer's work; see "The Joseph Council," pp. 30-4.
2. See "The Developing Mariological Framework," in Zervos, "Christmas," 77-80. For the original complete formulation of this framework, credit must go to Gerd Lüdemann, *Virgin Birth? The Real Story of Mary and Her Son* (Harrisburg, PA: Trinity Press International, 1998), 42-126.
3. ἐξαπέστειλεν ὁ θεὸς τὸν υἱὸν αὐτοῦ, γενόμενον ἐκ γυναικός "God sent his son, born (made) of (a) woman."
4. καὶ ἀκούσαντες οἱ παρ' αὐτοῦ ἐξῆλθον κρατῆσαι αὐτόν, ἔλεγον γὰρ ὅτι ἐξέστη. The phrase οἱ παρ' αὐτοῦ has also been interpreted as Jesus's friends or associates.

in his derogatory statement: "a prophet is not without honor except in his own hometown and among his own relatives and in his own house" (Οὐκ ἔστιν προφήτης ἄτιμος εἰ μὴ ἐν τῇ πατρίδι αὐτοῦ καὶ ἐν τοῖς συγγενεῦσιν αὐτοῦ καὶ ἐν τῇ οἰκίᾳ αὐτοῦ).[5]

The second generation of "Synoptic" Gospel writers, Matthew and Luke, treated Mary with more deference in their respective parallel revisions of Mk 6:4.[6] Both Matthew and Luke tempered the derogatory statement of Jesus regarding his relatives.[7] More importantly, it was Matthew and Luke in tandem that introduced the element of the virginal conception of Jesus in the New Testament canon and thus elevated Jesus's mother to her new, permanent status as the "Virgin Mary."[8] But both of these two canonical "Synoptic" Gospels appear to have been concerned primarily with Mary's virginal status before the birth of Jesus. Matthew and Luke, individually and independently of each other, contain statements in their Nativity stories that seem to imply that Mary and Joseph may have had marital relations after Jesus was born.[9] The amplification of Mary's person from Paul's unnamed "woman" and Mark's unbelieving mother, to the *ante partum* virginal conceiver

---

5. Zervos, "Christmas," 78.

6. According to the prevailing theory regarding the literary relationship between the "Synoptic Gospels"—Matthew, Mark, and Luke—Mark served as a primary source of Matthew and Luke, both of whom, independently of each other, followed Mark's narrative framework as they created their own respective Gospels. Both Matthew and Luke felt compelled to modify those aspects of Mark that they considered to be incompatible with their later theological, Christological, and Mariological sensitivities.

7. Mt. 13:57 omits Mark's reference to Jesus's relatives (ἐν τοῖς συγγενεῦσιν αὐτοῦ); Lk. 4:24 deletes both the reference to Jesus's relatives and to "his house" (ἐν τῇ οἰκίᾳ αὐτοῦ).

8. This assertion is based upon the majority opinion of New Testament scholars who accept the first two chapters of Luke as an original part of his Gospel. In this publication, I adopt the minority position that the original form of the Gospel of Luke, referred to by a number of scholars as Ur-Luke, did not contain the entire text of the Nativity stories now present in canonical Lk. 1–2, which included Mary's virginal conception. See "The Redactor: *The Protevangelium Jacobi*," pp. 135–9.

9. Mt. 1:23 cites Isa. 7:14, which refers only to Mary's virginal conception and birth: Ἰδοὺ ἡ παρθένος ἐν γαστρὶ ἕξει καὶ τέξεται υἱόν. This prophecy is preceded and followed by statements implying that Joseph and Mary may eventually have had marital relations. In Mt. 1:18 Mary was found to be pregnant "before they [Mary and Joseph] came together" (πρὶν ἢ συνελθεῖν αὐτούς); in Mt. 1:24-25 Joseph took Mary to be his wife and did not "know her" until she bore her son (οὐκ ἐγίνωσκεν αὐτὴν ἕως οὗ ἔτεκεν υἱόν). The prepositional phrase ἕως οὗ is generally taken to mean "until" when following a negative verb as it does in this case. Likewise, the reference in Lk. 2:7 to Jesus as Mary's "first born" son (τὸν υἱὸν αὐτῆς τὸν πρωτότοκον) insinuates that other sons followed, as verified in Mk 6:3, which names four brothers of Jesus. Cf. W. D. Davies and Dale C. Allison: "had Matthew held to Mary's perpetual virginity (as did the second-century author of *Prot. Jas.* 19.3-20.2), he

of the Son of God in Matthew and Luke represents only the first phase in the progressive magnification of Jesus's mother in early Christianity.

The CEGM is well suited to this first phase of the augmentation of Mary in first century CE Christianity from being a mere "woman" to being the "Virgin Mary." And it is within this framework that the Composer's concept of the evolving relationship between Mary and Joseph may be understood. Together with Matthew and Luke, the Composer was concerned primarily with demonstrating Mary's virginity up to the time that she gave birth to her divine child. He could thus refer to Mary in the Midwife episode as Joseph's betrothed, and concurrently as his wife, with the understanding that they had no marital relations before the birth of her child.[10] According to the results of this investigation, it seems to have been the Author of the *GenMar*, together with the *Asc. Isa.* who introduced the second phase in the development of Mariology by extending the chronological limits of Mary's sexual inactivity beyond Jesus's conception to the birth process itself (*in partu*) and its aftermath (postpartum).[11] These two Docetic documents quietly engineered the momentous leap in Christian Mariology from Jesus's mother as virgin *ante partum* (before giving birth) to what would eventually become her more elevated status in the Catholicizing churches as Μαρία Ἀειπάρθενος, the Ever-Virgin Mary, virgin before, during, and after giving birth to Jesus.

The Redactor brought this historic transformation in Mariology into the mainstream of Christian thought by his systematic revision of the text of his source document, the CEGM, which we have chronicled above. But the *coup de grâce* of his efforts was delivered in his redaction of the Birth story, specifically when he superimposed his signature "Doubting Salome" episode over the original account of the birth of Mary's divine child. This narrative in *ProtJac* 19–20 constitutes the central core of the Nativity Complex in *ProtJac* 17–21 and represents the climax and conclusion of the redacted CEGM. The redacted Birth story functions as the capstone of the narrative edifice of the events of Mary's life: her own conception, birth, and childhood; her Annunciation and conception of her divine child; and her trial for adultery. By positioning the Doubting Salome episode as the central climactic event, not only of the Birth narrative but also of the *ProtJac* in its entirety, the Redactor produced a document that substantiated the postpartum, perpetual virginity of Mary, which would eventually become an essential element of Christian dogma.

would almost certainly have chosen a less ambiguous expression—just as Luke would have avoided 'first-born son' (2.7)," *A Critical and Exegetical Commentary on the Gospel According to Saint Matthew* (ICC; Edinburgh: T&T Clark, 1988), 1:219. These interpretations are based on a straightforward reading of the original texts. For the immense literature on this subject, much of which is driven by confessional concerns, see Brown, *Birth*.

10. See "The Joseph Council," pp. 30–4.

11. See pp. 158–67 on the limited Docetic environment represented by the *GenMar* and the *Asc. Isa.* On the relationship between the *ProtJac* and the *Asc. Isa.* see Zervos, "Seeking." Whereas the *Asc. Isa.* was virtually forgotten, the *ProtJac* would have a dramatic and lasting effect on subsequent Christian thought and practice.

APPENDIX 2: THE APOLOGETIC PURPOSE OF THE *PROTJAC*

A number of scholars have noted the possibility that the magnification of Jesus's mother in the *ProtJac* may have been in response to disparaging comments about the legitimacy of Jesus's birth in ancient sources. Most scholars have associated these disparaging comments with Celsus, a Greek philosopher of the late second century who published an anti-Christian treatise, *The True Logos*.[12] For example, J. K. Elliott states:

> One motive behind the composition [of the *ProtJac*] seems to have been the defense of aspects of Christianity in the light of attacks on it by such as Celsus. Our author is concerned to tell us that Jesus' parents were not poor: Joseph is a building contractor; Mary spins, but not for payment. Another apologetic motive is to defend the conception of Jesus against charges of sexual irregularity: Mary's virginity is vindicated before Joseph (14. 2 [*ProtJac* 14:05-08]) and the priests (16 [*ProtJac* 16]).[13]

Mary Foskett echoes Elliott's opinion and frames the elevation of Mary in terms of the wide divergence between the portrait of Mary in Luke and that in the *ProtJac*; she attributes this to an apologetic purpose in the *ProtJac* as a response to slanders such as those recorded in Celsus:

> Whereas the Lukan Mary bears little social status, Mary is a figure of elevated standing throughout PJ ... the Jacobean Mary is born into a wealthy family, a great deal is made of her parents' standing within Israel, and the text repeatedly details the circumstances in which she lives and the characters with whom she interacts. Because of these differences from Luke, interpreters have long read the Protevangelium as an apologetic piece that aims to defend Mary against the kind of slander reflected in Celsus' *True Doctrine*. The text implicitly refutes ancient claims that Mary was of little or no social status, that she had to work with her hands at weaving in order to earn a badly needed income, and that she was publically exposed as an adulteress.[14]

---

12. Celsus's book has not survived but quotations from it were preserved by the third-century Christian Bible scholar Origen in his refutation of Celsus's work, *Contra Celsus* 1.28, 32, and 39. See below for further discussion of the hypothetical relationship between Celsus and the *ProtJac*. Cf. John Granger Cook, *The Interpretation of the New Testament in Greco-Roman Paganism* (Peabody, MA: Hendrickson, 2002), for a most helpful discussion of the date of Celsus's *Logos Alethes*; also Michael Frede, "Celsus Philosophus Platonicus," *ANRW* 36, no. 7 (1994), 5188-90, who carefully reevaluates the evidence for the date of Celsus's work and sets a *terminus post quem* as early as 160 CE.

13. James Keith Elliott, *The Apocryphal New Testament* (Oxford: Oxford University Press, 1993), 50.

14. "Miriam/Mariam/Maria: Literary Genealogy and the Genesis of Mary in the Protevangelium of James," 68 in *Mariam, the Magdalen and the Mother*, ed. Deidre Good (Bloomington; Indianapolis: Indiana University Press, 2005), 63-74.

Lily C. Vuong widens the scope of the search for the source of the disparaging comments against Jesus and Mary. She provides a comprehensive overview of scholarship regarding the "scandalous versions of Mary's conception and birth of Jesus in classical rabbinic literature" that indicate an apologetic purpose behind the elevated portrayal of Mary and her family in the *ProtJac*.[15] She cites references to Celsus and rabbinic sources that declared Jesus to have been the product of an adulterous liaison between Mary and the Roman solder Panthera and seemed to contain additional disparaging remarks about Mary and the legitimacy of Jesus. Vuong submits: "we might speculate that the connection between Jesus and Panthera was part of popular oral and/or folkloristic Jewish tradition already in the first century, and that hints about the illegitimacy of Jesus and critique of the virgin birth in later rabbinic writings represent traces of a larger tradition."[16] Vuong, alone in recent scholarship, correctly understands that these derogatory references to Jesus's birth may have originated significantly earlier than Celsus, possibly even in the first century.[17]

Celsus's book has not survived but quotations from it were preserved by the third-century Christian Bible scholar Origen, who in his refutation of Celsus's work, *Contra Celsus* 1.28, wrote that Celsus introduced a Jew who addressed Jesus and disputed with him, accusing him of many things:[18]

(1) inventing his birth from a virgin
 ὡς πλασαμένου αὐτοῦ τὴν ἐκ παρθένου γένεσιν
(2) coming from a Judean village
 and from a poor country spinster woman
 ἐκ κώμης αὐτὸν γεγονέναι Ἰουδαϊκῆς
 καὶ ἀπὸ γυναικὸς ἐγχωρίου καὶ πενιχρᾶς καὶ χερνήτιδος

---

15. Lily C. Vuong, *Gender and Purity in the Protevangelium of James*, Wissenschaftliche Untersuchungen zum Neuen Testament, 2. Reihe 358 (Mohr Siebeck: Tübingen, 2013), 53-4 with bibliography in nn. 93 and 98.

16. Ibid., 53.

17. Those who consider the *ProtJac* to have been written as a direct response to Celsus view the writing of the *True Logos* as the *terminus post quem* for the composition of the *ProtJac* in the latter part of the second century CE; cf. P. A. van Stempvoort, "The Protevangelium Jacobi, the Sources of Its Theme and Style and Their Bearing on Its Date," in *Studia Evangelica III*, ed. F. L. Cross; TUGAL 88 (Berlin: Akademie Verlag, 1964), 415. Cf. Vuong's thorough discussion of van Stempvoort's position, *Gender and Purity*, 35-7.

18. Origen accused Celsus of creating the person of this Jew (προσωποποιεῖ) to dramatize his accusations against Mary and Jesus; in *Contra Celsus* 1.32 Origen refers to "the contrived person of the Jew" (τὴν τοῦ Ἰουδαίου προσωποποιία). Regardless of Origen's apologetic opinion, we assume that Celsus derived this information from Jewish sources.

(3) who was forced out by her husband, a carpenter by trade
having been reproved for having committed adultery,[19]

ὑπὸ τοῦ γήμαντος, τέκτονος τὴν τέχνην ὄντος, ἐξεῶσθαι
ἐλεγχθεῖσαν ὡς μεμοιχευμένην

(4) having been cast out by her husband and wandering dishonorably,
secretly gave birth to Jesus

ὡς ἐκβληθεῖσα ὑπὸ τοῦ ἀνδρὸς καὶ πλανωμένη ἀτίμως,
σκότιον ἐγέννησε τὸν Ἰησοῦν

(5) who because of his poverty, worked for hire in Egypt,

οὗτος διὰ πενίαν εἰς Αἴγυπτον μισθαρνήσας

(6) and having become experienced there in certain powers,
in which the Egyptians take pride,

κἀκεῖ δυνάμεών τινων πειραθείς,
ἐφ' αἷς Αἰγύπτιοι σεμνύνονται,

(7) he returned, arrogant in those powers,

ἐπανῆλθεν ἐν ταῖς δυνάμεσι μέγα φρονῶν,

(8) and because of them proclaimed himself to be a god

καὶ δι' αὐτὰς θεὸν αὐτὸν ἀνηγόρευσε.[20]

In *Contra Celsus* 1.32 Origen returns to the witness of Celsus's "Jew" concerning Jesus's mother:

The mother of Jesus was described

ἀναγέγραπται ἡ τοῦ Ἰησοῦ μήτηρ

(9) as having been cast out by the carpenter, her betrothed,

ὡς ἐξωσθεῖσα ὑπὸ τοῦ μνηστευσαμένου αὐτὴν τέκτονος,

(10) having been reproved for adultery,[21]

ἐλεγχθεῖσα ἐπὶ μοιχείᾳ,

(11) and giving birth by a certain soldier named Panthera.

καὶ τίκτουσα ἀπό τινος στρατιώτου, Πανθήρα τοὔνομα

---

19. I prefer the reading "reproved" from *A Patristic Greek Lexicon*, ed. G. W. H. Lampe (Oxford: Clarendon Press, 1976), 446-7, as opposed to stronger translations such as accusation, conviction, prominent in the classical lexica, which cover a wider range of ancient authors and are difficult to pinpoint as viable translations of early Christian texts.

20. In *Contra Celsus* 1.29 Origen again refers to Jesus being slandered "for being the son of a poor seamstress who left his country and hired himself out in Egypt" (ἐπὶ τῷ πενιχρᾶς καὶ χερνήτιδος υἱὸν εἶναι καὶ διὰ πενίαν καταλιπὼν τὴν πατρίδα ἐν Αἰγύπτῳ μισθαρνῆσαι). Cf. *Contra Celsus* 1.30: φησὶ γὰρ αὐτὸν σκότιον τραφέντα, μισθαρνήσαντα εἰς Αἴγυπτον, δυναμεῶν τινων πειραθέντα ἐκεῖθεν ἐπανελθεῖν, θεὸν δι' ἐκείνας τὰς δυνάμεις ἑαυτὸν ἀναγορεύοντα, and 1.46 τὰ ὑπὸ τοῦ Ἰησοῦ παράδοξα γεγενημένα, ἅτινα διαβάλλων Κέλσος φησὶν αὐτὸν παρ' Αἰγυπτίοις μεμαθηκότα πεποιηκέναι.

21. Ibid.

(12)... the adultery of the virgin and Panthera,
... τὴν μοιχείαν τῆς παρθένου καὶ τοῦ Πανθήρα
(13) and the carpenter who forced her out
καὶ τὸν τέκτονα ἐξωσάμενον αὐτήν.

In *Contra Celsus* 1.33 Origen recapitulates the accusation of Celsus that Jesus was born bodily from:

(14) Panthera the adulterizer and the virgin adulterized.
Πανθήρα μοιχεύσαντος καὶ παρθένου μοιχευθείσης.[22]

In *Contra Celsus* 1.39 Celsus's Jew asserts that Mary was not worthy of intercourse with God because:

(15) she was neither gentile nor of royalty,[23]
οὔσης οὔτ' εὐδαίμονος[24] οὔτε βασιλικῆς,
(16) no one knew her, not even her neighbors,
μηδεὶς αὐτὴν ᾔδει μηδὲ τῶν γειτώνων,
(17) she was hated and cast out by her husband the carpenter.
μισουμένην αὐτὴν ὑπὸ τοῦ τέκτονος καὶ ἐκβαλλομένην.

Another Christian writer of the late second century also may have alluded to deprecatory reports concerning Jesus's birth at that time. Tertullian, who was the most important early Latin Christian apologist, wrote a number of anti-heretical tracts, including *Adversus Judaeos* (*Against the Jews*). In his moral treatise, *De Spectaculis* (*On the Spectacles, or Games*), Tertullian spent the entire work vehemently criticizing the public entertainments of the Romans in the circus, the theaters and amphitheaters, and in the stadiums. He was especially critical of those Christians who participated in these amusements. However, in the closing passage of this treatise, Tertullian abruptly shifted the focus of his comments, apparently toward the Jews, and reproachfully provided a litany of their personal attacks against Jesus:

"This is he," I shall say, "the son of the carpenter or the harlot, the Sabbath-breaker, the Samaritan, who had a devil. This is he whom you bought from

22. I have preferred the translations "adulterizer" and "adulterized" here as an accommodation to the context in which Origen speaks of a causative relationship between a body being born from adultery and a corrupted soul that inhabits it: "from such impure intercourses must come an unintelligent and harmful teacher of licentiousness and injustice and the rest of the evils."
23. Mary is not presented as royalty in the *GenMar*, but she is born to a wealthy family of high social status.
24. The term εὐδαίμων usually describes happiness or blessedness but in close association with βασιλική (royal) in this context may connote being of upper-class or wealthy background.

Judas; this is he, who was struck with reed and fist, defiled with spittle, given gall and vinegar to drink. This is he whom the disciples secretly stole away, that it might be said he had risen—unless it was the gardener who removed him, lest his lettuces should be trampled by the throng of visitors!"[25]

That the Jews were Tertullian's primary target in this passage is evident in his usage of the second person pronoun "you" in the statement, "This is he whom you bought from Judas."[26] Also the description of Jesus as "he whom the disciples secretly stole away, that it might be said he had risen" exhibits knowledge of two passages in Matthew that highlight the duplicity of the Jewish priests in concealing Jesus's alleged resurrection. In Mt. 27:62-66, after Jesus's crucifixion, the high priests and the Pharisees went to Pilate and requested that he secure Jesus's tomb until the third day "in case his disciples might steal him and say to the people, 'He has risen from the dead.'"[27] Pilate granted them some soldiers to secure the tomb and seal the stone.[28] In Mt. 28:11-15, after Jesus's resurrection, some of the soldiers reported to the high priests and the priests the events that had occurred. The priests bribed them with silver to say that "his disciples came at night and stole him, as we were sleeping."[29] The soldiers did as they were told and Matthew states that "this story was publicized among the Jews until this day."[30] The phrase "until this day" implies that this account of the empty tomb was still current among the Jews, at least in Syria, when the Gospel of Matthew was written about fifty years after the crucifixion of Jesus.

Other Gospel references in Tertullian's passage also derive from scenarios in which Jews are criticizing Jesus or attacking him in some way.[31] Jesus "the son

---

25. Translation and Latin text from *Tertullian Apology, de Spectaculis*, trans. T. R. Glover, Loeb edition (Cambridge, MA: Harvard University Press, 1977), 298-9; "Hic est ille, dicam, fabri aut quaestuariae filius, sabbati destructor, Samarites et daemonium habens; hic est quem a Iuda redemistis, hic est ille harundine et colaphis diverberatus, sputamentis dedecoratus, felle et aceto potatus; hic est, quem clam discentes subripuerunt, ut surrexisse dicatur, vel hortulanus detraxit, ne lactucae suae frequentia commeantium adlaederentur."

26. This is a reference to the betrayal of Jesus by Judas to the priests for silver, cf. Mt. 26:14-16, Mk 14:10-11, and Lk. 22:3-6.

27. Mt. 27:64: μήποτε ἐλθόντες οἱ μαθηταὶ αὐτοῦ κλέψωσιν αὐτὸν καὶ εἴπωσιν τῷ λαῷ· Ἠγέρθη ἀπὸ τῶν νεκρῶν.

28. Mt. 27:66: ἠσφαλίσαντο τὸν τάφον σφραγίσαντες τὸν λίθον μετὰ τῆς κουστωδίας.

29. Mt. 28:13: Οἱ μαθηταὶ αὐτοῦ νυκτὸς ἐλθόντες ἔκλεψαν αὐτὸν ἡμῶν κοιμωμένων.

30. Mt. 28:15: Καὶ διεφημίσθη ὁ λόγος οὗτος παρὰ Ἰουδαίοις μέχρι τῆς σήμερον ἡμέρας.

31. The references to Jesus as "he, who was struck with reed and fist, defiled with spittle, given gall and vinegar to drink" all derive from the Gospels. During his trial and crucifixion Jesus was spat upon (ἐμπτύειν) and struck with the fist (κολαφίζειν) by the Jews, cf. Mk 14:65, 15:19; Mt. 26:67; Lk. 22:63; Jn 18:22. The Roman soldiers also spat upon him and

of the carpenter" evokes the scenario in Mt. 13:54-58 in which Jesus's neighbors in Nazareth are scandalized by the "son of the carpenter" teaching them in the Synagogue (ἐσκανδαλίζοντο ἐν αὐτῷ). They recall Jesus as the boy from the neighborhood whose mother was named Mary and who had brothers and sisters.[32] Matthew states that because of their faithlessness, Jesus did not perform many miracles there.[33] Jesus being criticized by Jews as a "Sabbath-breaker" is common in the Gospels. In Jn 5 Jesus incurred the ire of the Jews for healing a paralytic on the Sabbath day. In Jn 5:16 "the Jews persecuted him for doing such things on the Sabbath."[34] A similar story in the Synoptic Gospels relates how Jesus healed a man with a withered hand on the Sabbath day in a Synagogue, resulting in the Pharisees and the Herodians coming together against him "to destroy him."[35]

The one element in Tertullian's passage that is not stated in the Gospels, but which most directly concerns our discussion of the virginal status of Mary, is the reference to Jesus as the "son ... of the harlot." Glover is probably correct in identifying this element as "a piece of Jewish polemic."[36] That this accusation against Jesus's mother as a "harlot" may be associated with a Jewish source is indicated by its inclusion—in Tertullian's text—within the larger Matthean context in which Jesus's neighbors in Nazareth are scandalized by him and derisively call him "the son of the carpenter." Tertullian seems to be aware of a Jewish accusation in his own time and place against Mary as a "harlot" and therefore augments the Matthean text by adding this element, thus labeling Jesus as "the son of the

struck him "with reed" (καλάμῳ), and on Golgotha gave him "gall to drink," cf. Mk 15:19; Mt. 27:30, 34; Jn 19:3. When Jesus was dying, according to Mk 15:35-36 and Mt. 27:48, a Jewish bystander gave him vinegar (ὄξος) to drink; in Lk. 23:36 the Roman soldiers gave him the vinegar; in Jn 19:29-30 unidentified bystanders gave Jesus vinegar with hyssop. The label of Jesus as "the Samaritan, who had a devil" comes verbatim from Jn 8:48 in which the Jews tell Jesus, "Σαμαρίτης εἶ σὺ καὶ δαιμόνιον ἔχεις"; more on this text below.

32. See the discussion of Mk 6:3 below regarding the absence of any reference to Jesus's father, as a derogatory manner of identifying a Jewish man by his mother's name.

33. Mt. 13:58: καὶ οὐκ ἐποίησεν ἐκεῖ δυνάμεις πολλὰς διὰ τὴν ἀπιστίαν αὐτῶν.

34. διὰ τοῦτο ἐδίωκον οἱ Ἰουδαῖοι τὸν Ἰησοῦν ὅτι ταῦτα ἐποίει ἐν σαββάτῳ. Likewise in Jn 9 Jesus is criticized by the Pharisees for healing a blind man on the Sabbath. In Jn 9:16 "some of the Pharisees said, 'This man is not from God because he does not keep the Sabbath'" (ἔλεγον οὖν ἐκ τῶν Φαρισαίων τινές· Οὐκ ἔστιν οὗτος παρὰ θεοῦ ὁ ἄνθρωπος, ὅτι τὸ σάββατον οὐ τηρεῖ).

35. Mk 3:6 and parallels in Mt. 12:14 and Lk. 6:11: καὶ ἐξελθόντες οἱ Φαρισαῖοι εὐθὺς μετὰ τῶν Ἡρῳδιανῶν συμβούλιον ἐδίδουν κατ' αὐτοῦ ὅπως αὐτὸν ἀπολέσωσιν. The Herodians were a religious party in first-century Judea who were allied with the Pharisees in their opposition to Jesus.

36. *De Spectaculis*, 299.

carpenter or the harlot" (fabri aut quaestuariae filius). The two independent witnesses of Celsus and Tertullian, representing the Greco-Roman and Christian perspectives, respectively, in the late second century, cast light on the question of the apologetic purpose of the *ProtJac* with respect to the evolving perceptions of Mary's virginity within the framework of the discussion of the compositional problem.

It is notable that both Tertullian, a fervent Christian apologist, and Celsus, a Greek author of an anti-Christian polemic, present scenarios in which Jews are naming Mary, respectively, as a "harlot" and an "adulteress." Celsus's account of a "Jew" defaming Mary's character and Jesus's legitimacy and Tertullian's litany of Jewish hostility against Jesus suggest that derogatory reports of Jesus's birth were circulating independently of each other in Jewish circles in at least two areas of the Roman Empire in the late second century.[37] Scholars have long linked the single-author compositional theory of the *ProtJac* to Celsus's defamatory description of Jesus's illegitimate birth from a promiscuous mother; that is, the "author" of the *ProtJac* framed his document as a point-by-point response to a demeaning portrayal of Mary and Jesus's birth such as Celsus's.[38] However, the additional complementary witness of Tertullian lessens the prominence of Celsus's story and thus diminishes somewhat the single-author aspect of this theory. If the *ProtJac* was written, in any case, as a response to offensive reports of Jesus's illegitimacy, it would be appropriate to examine other, earlier such reports that may have contributed to the creation of a document with so complex a compositional history.

A generation before Celsus and Tertullian, the Christian apologist Justin Martyr provides information about an initiative by the Jews to send out agents to publicize their criticisms of Jesus and his followers "throughout the entire world." This information is found in Justin's polemical *Dialogue with Trypho the Jew*,[39] which is an account of a conversation between Justin and a Jewish man called Trypho that took place in Ephesus round 135 CE.[40] In *Dial*. 108.2 Justin accuses the Jews, through the person of Trypho, of spreading their anti-Christian propaganda throughout the empire:

---

37. See below where Justin Martyr describes a scenario by which Jewish communities in the Roman Empire were in contact with each other and in certain instances shared derogatory information about Jesus.

38. See above, pp. 174–7.

39. Τοῦ Ἁγίου Ἰουστίνου Φιλοσόφου καὶ Μάρτυρος πρὸς Τρύφωνα Ἰουδαῖον Διάλογος. Justin is critical of the Jews in his first Apology for rejecting and shaming Jesus, and ultimately for crucifying him; also for hating the Christians, and for persecuting them and killing them whenever they have the power to do so.

40. Justin actually published the Dialogue decades later.

You ordained and sent select men throughout all the world, proclaiming that a godless and lawless sect had arisen from a certain Jesus, a Galilean deceiver, whom we crucified; but his disciples, having stolen him from the tomb by night, where he was laid when un-nailed from the cross, deceive the people saying that he arose from the dead and ascended to heaven, and [your agents] accuse him of having taught those things which, against those who confess him to be Christ and teacher and son of God for the whole race of humankind, you say are godless and lawless and unholy.[41]

Justin's illuminating historical witness indicates that the Jewish communities in the Roman Empire may have maintained contact with each other and thus would have been able to achieve a strategic uniformity with regard to their collective position on issues such as the legitimacy of Jesus. A prime example is *Dial.* 69.7 in which Justin validates the witness of Celsus decades later that the Jews defamed Jesus as a "magician."[42] Justin lists the miracles of Jesus that, according to the Gospels, were reported among the Jews; his healings of the maimed, the deaf and the blind, even resurrection of the dead. But the Jews interpreted these as magical deception: Οἱ δὲ καὶ ταῦτα ὁρῶντες γινόμενα φαντασίαν μαγικὴν γίνεσθαι ἔλεγον καὶ γὰρ μάγον εἶναι αὐτὸν ἐτόλμων λέγειν καὶ λαοπλάνον ("But they [the Jews] seeing these happening, were saying that they came about by magical fantasy, for they even dared to say that he was a magician and deceiver of the people").

Receding farther back in time, several elements of the Jewish criticisms of Jesus and Mary referred by Tertullian and Celsus occur a full century before Tertullian in a passage in Jn 8 that narrates a rancorous, name-calling dispute between Jesus and, strangely, τοὺς πεπιστευκότας αὐτῷ Ἰουδαίους ("the Jews who believed in him").[43] Most importantly, the primary accusation against Mary, of "harlotry" in Tertullian and "adultery" in Celsus, occurs in Jn 8:41 where the Jews say to

---

41. Ἄνδρας χειροτονήσαντες ἐκλεκτοὺς εἰς πᾶσαν τὴν οἰκουμένην ἐπέμψατε, κηρύσσοντας ὅτι αἵρεσίς τις ἄθεος καὶ ἄνομος ἐγήγερται ἀπὸ Ἰησοῦ τινος Γαλιλαίου πλάνου, ὃν σταυρωσάντων ἡμῶν οἱ μαθηταὶ αὐτοῦ κλέψαντες αὐτὸν ἀπὸ τοῦ μνήματος νυκτός, ὁπόθι κατετέθη ἀφηλωθεὶς ἀπὸ τοῦ σταυροῦ, πλανῶσι τοὺς ἀνθρώπους λέξοντες ἐγήγερθαι αὐτὸν ἐκ νεκρῶν καὶ εἰς οὐρανὸν ἀνεληλυθέναι, καὶ κατειπόντας δεδιδαχέναι αὐτὸν ταῦτα, ἅπερ κατὰ τῶν ὁμολογούντων Χριστὸν καὶ διδάσκαλον καὶ υἱὸν θεοῦ εἶναι παντὶ γένει ἀνθρώπων ἄθεα καὶ ἄνομα καὶ ἀνόσια λέγετε. See also *Dial.* 17.1 for a similar, shorter statement: "You selected select men from Jerusalem and sent [them] out through all the land, saying that the godless heresy of the Christians had sprung up, and recounting those things, which all they who knew us not say against us; so that not only to yourselves are you the cause of your unrighteousness, but also directly to all other people."
42. See above, pp. 175–6, cf. n. 20 for the Greek texts.
43. Jn 8:31.

Jesus: Ἡμεῖς ἐκ πορνείας οὐ γεγεννήμεθα ("We were not born of fornication"). The implication seems to be that Jesus was.[44] Furthermore, in Jn 8:48 these now hostile Jews[45] level another accusation against Jesus that occurs in Tertullian, even employing the same vocabulary: Οὐ καλῶς λέγομεν ἡμεῖς ὅτι Σαμαρίτης εἶ σὺ καὶ δαιμόνιον ἔχεις; ("Do we not correctly say that you are a Samaritan and you have a demon?"; in Tertullian, Samarites et daemonium habens, "Samaritan, and having a demon").[46] It is perhaps revealing that in Jn 8:49 Jesus denies the allegation of the Jews in Jn 8:48 that he has a demon (Ἐγὼ δαιμόνιον οὐκ ἔχω); but he does not challenge their accusation in Jn 8:41 that he was born of fornication.[47]

The unique status of Celsus, in the view of most scholars, as the hypothetical catalyst for the writing of the *ProtJac* has been diminished further by the witness of John in Ephesus at the end of the first century. Here also the same Jewish accusations against Mary and Jesus that were seen in Celsus and Tertullian are spoken again by Jewish opponents of Jesus. But the witness of John still represents a later stage in a process whose origins may be traced back even earlier in the first century. Two scholars who have investigated this possibility extensively, Jane Schaberg and Gerd Lüdemann, speculate that the Nativity stories of Matthew and Luke themselves may have been created as responses to the earlier tradition—or reality—of the illegitimacy of Jesus.[48] According to Schaberg and Lüdemann,[49] if

---

44. Alternatively, on two occasions in John, Joseph is acknowledged as Jesus's father, and Mary once as his mother; in Jn 1:45 Jesus is called by Philip the "son of Joseph from Nazareth" (Ἰησοῦν υἱὸν τοῦ Ἰωσὴφ τὸν ἀπὸ Ναζαρέτ); and in Jn 6:42 the Jews acknowledge him as the "son of Joseph" but also state that they "know his father and his mother" (Οὐχ οὗτός ἐστιν Ἰησοῦς ὁ υἱὸς Ἰωσὴφ οὗ ἡμεῖς οἴδαμεν τὸν πατέρα καὶ τὴν μητέρα).

45. Jesus says twice in this passage that the Jews want to kill him; in Jn 8:37 ἀλλὰ ζητεῖτέ με ἀποκτεῖναι; and in Jn 8:40 νῦν δὲ ζητεῖτέ με ἀποκτεῖναι; in the end, in Jn 8:59 the Jews took up stones to throw at him, but he escaped, ἦραν οὖν λίθους ἵνα βάλωσιν ἐπ' αὐτόν.

46. In Jn 8:52 the Jews repeat their accusation that Jesus has a demon: Νῦν ἐγνώκαμεν ὅτι δαιμόνιον ἔχεις.

47. See scholarly opinions below on the possibility that the charges of Jesus's illegitimacy may have been accurate.

48. See Schaberg's landmark work *Illegitimacy*; Jane Schaberg, "Feminist Interpretations of the Infancy Narrative of Matthew," in *A Feminist Companion to Mariology*, eds. Amy-Jill Levine and Maria Mayo Robbins (New York: T&T Clark International, Continuum, 2005), 15–36; Lüdemann, *Virgin Birth*? It should be noted that, in spite of their cogent insights on Jesus's illegitimacy, both Lüdemann, *Virgin Birth*, 135, and Schaberg, more recently, "The Infancy of Mary of Nazareth," in *Searching the Scriptures*, vol. 2: *A Feminist Commentary*, ed. Elisabeth S. Fiorenza (New York: Crossroad, 1994), 708–27, adopt the de Strycker consensus opinion of the *ProtJac*.

49. Schaberg, *Illegitimacy*, 177–8; Lüdemann, *Virgin Birth*, 59–60, "In itself the Jewish charge of the illegitimate birth of Jesus cannot be dated to the first century. However, seen along with Mk 6, it might reinforce the fact that Jesus was in fact born illegitimately. In that

their theory holds true, the Jewish denigrations of Mary and Jesus are accurate reports that Christians countered by inventing the virgin birth. But accurate or not, the accusations would explain the sudden appearance of the virgin birth tradition concurrently, and independently, not only in the Gospels of Matthew and Luke[50] but also in the CEGM. The Author of the *GenMar* appears to have had a more theologically oriented motivation for espousing Mary's post-partum virginity.[51]

Schaberg has produced significant publications on the issue of Jesus's legitimacy in the Nativity story in Matthew beginning with the genealogy of Jesus in Mt. 1:2-16.[52] She discusses the unusual feature of this genealogy that out of the list of forty-two generations of Jesus's male ancestors, only five women are mentioned, the last of which is Mary. Schaberg points out that these four previous "foremothers" of Jesus "were each involved in extraordinary or irregular sexual unions that were scandalous to outsiders."[53] By mentioning these four women whose sordid sexual liaisons would have been well known to anyone living in a Jewish biblical

case it possibly becomes clear *why* the Christians developed the notion of the conception of Jesus and the virgin birth at all. It was a reaction to the report, meant as a slander but historically correct, that Jesus was conceived or born outside wedlock"; cf. Zervos, "Caught in the Act: Mary and the Adulteress," *Apocrypha* 15 (2004), 57–114, especially "Was Mary the Adulteress," 110–14.

50. See the discussion above in "Appendix 1: Mary's Evolving Virginity in the *ProtJac*," pp. 171–3 on the lack of any hint of the virgin birth concept in the Christian writings before Matthew and Luke. This assumes that the Birth stories in Lk. 1–2 were an original component of that Gospel.

51. See the discussion regarding the compatibility of Mary's postpartum virginity with the Docetic Christology of the *GenMar* in "The Author: *The Genesis Marias*," pp. 166–7.

52. *Illegitimacy*, 20–34; "The Foremothers and the Mother of Jesus," *Concilium* 206 (1989), 112-19; "Feminist," contains a thorough discussion of the lively conversation regarding this issue among feminist scholars. Schaberg's *Illegitimacy* has been described as "foundational for feminist theology," cf. Luis Schottroff, *Lydia's Impatient Sister: A Feminist Social History of Early Christianity* (Louisville, KY: Westminster John Knox Press, 1995), 200.

53. In Mt. 1:3 the patriarch Judah "begot" two sons ἐκ τῆς Θάμαρ ("by Tamar"), his daughter-in-law according to Gen. 38, who tricked him into having sex with her by dressing as a prostitute; in Mt. 1:5 Salmon "begot" Boaz ἐκ τῆς ῾Ραχάβ ("by Rahab") who, in spite of Matthew's anachronistic error, is considered by most to have been the prostitute of Jericho mentioned in Josh. chs 2, 6; also in Mt. 1:5 Boaz "begot" a son ἐκ τῆς ῾Ρούθ ("by Ruth") after being seduced by her according to Ruth 2–3; in Mt. 1:6 King David "begot" King Solomon ἐκ τῆς τοῦ Οὐρίου ("by the wife of Uriah") whom, according to 2 Sam. 11, David saw bathing naked, then called her to the palace and impregnated her. David arranged for her husband Uriah to be killed and then took her as his wife.

environment, Matthew seems to foster the expectation that the fifth woman in the genealogy, Mary, will also be involved in a dubious sexual situation. And the description of Mary in Mt. 1:16 does not disappoint. Matthew's genealogy reaches its ambiguous conclusion with "Joseph, husband of Mary from whom was born Jesus" (Ἰωσὴφ τὸν ἄνδρα Μαρίας, ἐξ ἧς ἐγεννήθη Ἰησοῦς). Matthew has listed forty-two generations of Joseph's forefathers "begetting" their sons only to suggest in the end that Joseph did not "beget" Jesus.[54] The feminine relative pronoun ἧς ("from whom") specifies that Jesus was born from Mary alone and implies that Joseph was not involved in his conception. How could Matthew's readers not suspect that something about Jesus's conception was not as it should have been?

It is significant that the genealogy of Jesus in Lk. 3:23-38—which is largely incompatible with that in Mt. 1:2-16—does agree with Mt. 1:16 in casting Joseph's fatherhood of Jesus into doubt.[55] Lk. 3:23 reads: Ἰησοῦς ... ὢν υἱός, ὡς ἐνομίζετο, Ἰωσήφ ("Jesus ... being the son, as was thought, of Joseph"). Lüdemann is probably correct in stating that Joseph was Jesus's father in the original genealogy of Luke and that a "redactor" inserted the phrase ὡς ἐνομίζετο ("as was thought"). According to Lüdemann, the redacted Nativity narrative in Lk. 1 was constituted from a preexisting, independent source document that recounted the Annunciation and birth of John the Baptist into which were inserted materials related to the birth of Jesus.[56] Lk. 2 contains "four quite independent traditions about the birth and childhood of Jesus, each in isolation."[57] Three of these stories are in agreement with the original genealogy of Lk. 3:23 in assuming that Joseph was Jesus's father.[58]

---

54. Schaberg states the case perfectly: "the pattern, A begot B, B begot C, which has been used throughout the genealogy, is here broken in dramatic fashion," *Illegitimacy*, 35.

55. The Matthean and Lukan genealogies agree in the earlier generations up to David because they follow the OT, but after David, Matthew traces his genealogy through Solomon, and Luke through Nathan; after Zerubbabel, Luke lists nineteen names, Matthew only ten, and even Jesus's grandfather is uncertain, Lüdemann, *Virgin Birth?*, 121.

56. Ibid., 90-7; inserted materials include the parallel Annunciation story of Jesus in Lk. 1:26-38, the visit of Mary to Elizabeth in Lk. 1:39-56, and two psalms, Mary's song of praise in Lk. 1:46-55 and Zachariah's song of praise in Lk. 1:68-79. Lüdemann states that the source document originated within early, non-Christian, Jewish circles that held John the Baptist in high esteem. This interpretation is based upon the view that the Nativity stories in Lk. 1-2 were later additions to this Gospel, which originally began in what is now Lk. 3, ibid. 90.

57. Ibid., 90-1. The actual Birth story of Jesus is in Lk. 2:1-7. In the stories that follow in Lk. 2:8-52 Mary and Joseph show no knowledge of the angelic Annunciation to Mary about her miraculous conception, which had just occurred in Lk. 1, or of the virgin Birth story, which immediately preceded them.

58. According to Lüdemann's plausible analysis, *Virgin Birth?*, 111-12, the narrative of the angels and shepherds in Lk. 2:8-20 was an originally independent Annunciation story in which Mary and Joseph learned what kind of child they will have; pp. 113-16, in the story of the presentation of Jesus in the temple in Lk. 2:22-40, Mary and Joseph are amazed at Simeon's words to them regarding the future greatness of their son; pp. 116-19, in the story

Prior to the initial appearance of the virginal conception motif in Matthew and Luke, the only literary evidence of derogatory accusations by Jews against Jesus's legitimacy occurs in the Gospel of Mark, which is generally recognized to be the earliest of the New Testament Gospels. It is highly significant, with respect to the origin of the virginal conception theme in Matthew and Luke, that both of these later Gospels are considered to have used Mark as their primary narrative source in the creation of their own Gospels.[59] Therefore, in seeking a motive for Matthew's and Luke's parallel introduction of the virgin birth component into the Gospel tradition, it is reasonable to look for such a cause first in Mark. And indeed such a cause exists in Mk 6:3, where Jesus is teaching in the synagogue in his hometown of Nazareth. Many in the audience were scandalized by him (ἐσκανδαλίζοντο ἐν αὐτῷ) and called him "the carpenter, the son of Mary" (ὁ τέκτων, ὁ υἱὸς τῆς Μαρίας). The fact that Jesus's neighbors in his hometown synagogue identified him by his mother's name has generated intense apologetic controversy, already from the time of Matthew and Luke themselves, and in modern scholarship as well. The issue is whether this description of Jesus was intended by his neighbors in a derogatory sense, reflecting that Jesus's lack of a father was a sign of his illegitimate conception and birth.

Matthew and Luke both appear to have understood Mk 6:3 as carrying with it precisely such a negative connotation. In reproducing this verse of Mark in their own Gospels, both later writers felt the need to remedy the perceived problem by recasting the neighbors' statement so as to refer to Jesus as the son of Joseph. The relevant passages from all three "synoptic" Gospels[60] are presented below in such a way as to emphasize the modification of their Markan source by both Matthew and Luke to show that Jesus did have a father, the carpenter Joseph:

Mk 6:3 οὐχ οὗτός ἐστιν <u>ὁ τέκτων, ὁ υἱὸς τῆς Μαρίας</u>;
      Is this not <u>the carpenter, the son of Mary</u>?
Mt. 13:55 οὐχ οὗτός ἐστιν <u>ὁ τοῦ τέκτονος υἱός</u>;
      Is this not <u>the son of the carpenter</u>?
Lk. 4:22 οὐχὶ <u>υἱός</u> ἐστιν Ἰωσὴφ <u>οὗτος</u>;
      Is this not <u>the son of Joseph</u>?

---

of the twelve-year-old Jesus in the temple in Lk. 2:41-52, Mary and Joseph are described twice as Jesus's "parents" (οἱ γονεῖς αὐτοῦ) and when Mary addresses Jesus she refers to herself and Joseph as "your father and I" (ὁ πατήρ σου κἀγώ), they do not understand when Jesus says to them that he must be about his father's business.

59. The priority of Mark vis-à-vis Matthew and Luke is the lynchpin in the prevailing theoretical solution of the "synoptic problem," i.e., the literary relationship between the first three Gospels in the New Testament. See "Appendix 1: Mary's Evolving Virginity in Early Christianity," p. 172, n. 6. above.

60. As is well exemplified in the present case, scholars are afforded a significant advantage by their ability to view Mark, Matthew, and Luke in parallel columns, "synoptically," and to compare and contrast their respective readings in the passages that they share, and thus to determine the perspectives of each of the synoptic Gospel writers.

Whereas Mark describes Jesus himself specifically as "the carpenter" (ὁ τέκτων), Matthew refers to him as "the son of the carpenter" Joseph (ὁ τοῦ τέκτονος υἱός). Matthew has thus detached the label "carpenter" from Jesus and attached it to Joseph. Luke makes no reference to carpentry but directly names Joseph as Jesus's father.[61] Both Matthew and Luke have deflected the stigma of illegitimacy from Jesus and focused attention on Joseph. But both Matthew and Luke may have had a larger strategy in associating Jesus with Joseph that is related to their coincident creation of their genealogies of Jesus.

In a comprehensive study of men bearing their mothers' names in the time of Jesus, Tal Ilan linked this phenomenon to the greater prominence of the mother's pedigree, that is, her being of royal or priestly descent.[62] Ilan observes: "It is not obvious to presume that Mary was the more prominent of Jesus' parents, as we know nothing historically sound about her background," and "Mark, who designates Jesus 'son of Mary', knew nothing of Joseph's royal lineage."[63] Whereas Mark branded Jesus as the "son of Mary" in the absence of any information relating to Joseph's or of Mary's lineage, "in both Matthew (1:1-17) and Luke (3:23-38) a royal pedigree is attached to Jesus' earthly father, Joseph, relating him to the house of David."[64] Thus, Matthew and Luke both have taken a multifaceted approach toward elevating the person of Jesus by (1) suppressing Mark's designation of Jesus as a carpenter, (2) providing him with a "father" as a shelter against the metronyme "son of Mary," and (3) creating royal genealogies for Jesus that both legitimized him and exonerated him of any stigma of a problematic birth.

Lüdemann acknowledges that the modifications of Mk 6:3 by Matthew and Luke suggest that they understood the phrase "son of Mary" in a disparaging sense. He provides additional arguments in favor of this interpretation: (1) the phrase "son of Mary" is applied to Jesus in his hometown by his neighbors who knew him and his parentage, (2) it is expressed by people who "have not fully understood Jesus or are hostile to him," that is, were scandalized by him, and (3) Mark does not reject the statement in Mk 6:3, but he "tones down the mockery by inserting it into a neutral family catalogue of Jesus' brothers and sisters," who seem to have had normal parentage.[65] But even more significantly, in the following

---

61. Both Matthew and Luke may have had a further motive for suppressing Mark's characterization of Jesus as a carpenter. It may have seemed unbefitting to their target audiences for their prospective Messiah to have been a mere carpenter.

62. "'Man Born of Woman ...' (Job 14:1): The Phenomenon of Men Bearing Metronymes at the Time of Jesus," *NT* 34 (1992), 23-45.

63. Ibid., 45. Ilan, in commenting that Mark "knew nothing of Joseph's royal lineage," does not fully state the case. There is no indication that Mark had any knowledge of the person of Joseph at all since he never appears in his Gospel. Joseph was first introduced into the canonical tradition by Matthew and Luke, and into our apocryphal Gospel by the Composer of the *ProtJac*. See the discussion in "Joseph in the *ProtJac*," pp. 151-4.

64. Ibid.

65. *Virgin Birth*, 53-5; cf. Schaberg, *Illegitimacy*, 160-4.

verse Mk 6:4, Jesus's own response to the statement of his neighbors indicates that he himself understood the phrase "son of Mary" as a derogatory slur against him. He intimates that he has been dishonored in his own hometown: "a prophet is not without honor except in his own hometown and among his own relatives and in his own house" (Οὐκ ἔστιν προφήτης ἄτιμος εἰ μὴ ἐν τῇ πατρίδι αὐτοῦ καὶ ἐν τοῖς συγγενεῦσιν αὐτοῦ καὶ ἐν τῇ οἰκίᾳ αὐτοῦ).[66]

In summary, the principal charge of sexual impropriety against Mary in Celsus (μοιχεία, "adultery"), in Tertullian (quaestuariae, "harlotry"), and in Jn 8:41 (πορνείας, "fornication") is reflected already in the earliest relevant literary source, Mk 6:3 (υἱὸς τῆς Μαρίας, "son of Mary"). It is undeniable that one of the principle concerns of the *ProtJac* was apologetic for the purpose of refuting the accusations of adultery on the part of Mary. But the ultimate question is to whose accusations the *ProtJac* was responding, and in view of the redactional theory presented herein, to whose accusations were the individuals who created the *ProtJac* responding. It would be instructive to present the accusations against Jesus and Mary by Celsus's Jew, individually, alongside the analogous purported responses in the *ProtJac* and then to analyze these pairings with respect to the corresponding reports in the witnesses to Jewish accusations in the first two centuries CE. This analysis will be based upon Schaberg's summary of specific points of contact between Celsus and the *ProtJac* that are seen to support the widely held scholarly opinion that the *ProtJac* was composed in the late second century to counter the accusations against Jesus and Mary such as those made by Celsus's Jew.[67]

According to:

Celsus:	Mary was a poor country woman
ProtJac:	Mary was born of wealthy parents of the noble line of David
Celsus:	She spun to make her living
ProtJac:	She was chosen by the priests for the privilege of spinning the temple curtain
Celsus:	She was from a Jewish village
ProtJac:	She was from Jerusalem or the Jerusalem area
Celsus:	She was an unknown nobody
ProtJac:	She was known and loved by all Israel from her childhood
Celsus:	She was the wife of a lowly carpenter
ProtJac:	She was the wife of a builder

---

66. Jesus's assertion that he has also been dishonored "among his own relatives and in his own house" is a reference to Mk 3:21, "when his family heard [of Jesus's activities], they went out to restrain him, for people were saying, 'He has gone out of his mind'"; in Mk 31-5, Jesus denies his biological family in favor of those around him who do the will of God, whom he describes as "my brother and sister and mother," see "Appendix 1: Mary's Evolving Virginity in Early Christianity," pp. 171–3.

67. "Infancy," 719–20.

Celsus:	Mary's husband accused her of adultery, cast her out[68]
ProtJac:	Mary's husband, or betrothed, was disturbed by her pregnancy, thought she had been defiled and considered divorcing her, was convinced by an angel of the divine origin of her child, did not turn her out but watched over her carefully;[69] she was officially accused of adultery and exonerated by the temple priests
Celsus:	Mary's child was illegitimate
ProtJac:	Mary's child was the son of a virgin, miraculously conceived[70]
Celsus:	She was wandering around in disgrace when she gave birth
ProtJac:	She gave birth on a journey with Joseph and his sons to Bethlehem
Celsus:	She gave birth secretly
ProtJac:	The sons of Joseph were present at the birth; Joseph and the midwife were outside the cave

Most of the items in Schaberg's list can be excluded as proof of a direct connection between the *ProtJac* and Celsus on the grounds that they also occur in Matthew and Luke, which were known to the *ProtJac* Redactor; therefore, the *ProtJac* did not necessarily derive them from Celsus. The motif of Joseph as a carpenter and Jesus's presence in Egypt occur in both Matthew and Celsus. But in contrast to Celsus, Matthew and the *ProtJac*, independently of each other, share the tradition that Mary lived in Jerusalem. Celsus's location of Mary, in a "Jewish village" may be a reflection of Luke, who places her in Nazareth of the Galilee. The *ProtJac* agrees with Luke and Matthew that Mary gives birth to Jesus in the company of Joseph,[71] which contradicts Celsus's charge that she birthed Jesus secretly while wandering around in disgrace after being cast out by Joseph.[72] These examples show that the potential sources of the allegations against Jesus and Mary, to which the *ProtJac* is thought to have been a response, are much more variegated than the simplistic view that they were all derived from Celsus.

Celsus describes Mary generally as a poor countrywoman who worked as a seamstress. According to the prevailing consensus position, it was in response to this demeaning description of the mother of Jesus that the single "author" of

---

68. Mary was only suspected of adultery by Joseph in Matthew but was accused in Mark and John.

69. Joseph's posture toward Mary was the same in Matthew, but not as dramatic.

70. Jesus mother was a virgin also in Matthew and Luke, but Jesus was still technically illegitimate.

71. In the *ProtJac* the midwife and Joseph's sons are present, and in Matthew angels and shepherds are nearby.

72. This also contradicts the birth of Jesus in Joseph's home in Matthew, the Gospel that shares affinities with Celsus. Perhaps Mary's "wandering" in Celsus can be associated with the journey of Mary and Joseph to Bethlehem in the *ProtJac* and Luke.

the unitary *ProtJac* created an image of Mary as being born of wealthy parents of the line of David. But this image of Mary is found in the unredacted sources of the *ProtJac*, the *GenMar* and the Composer's work, so the influence of Celsus upon these documents a century after they were written is impossible. Furthermore, Celsus was not the only source of a lowly image of Mary. Mark, the earliest Gospel and the primary source of Matthew and Luke, portrays Mary as a single mother of five sons and at least two daughters.[73] One of her sons, Jesus, was a lowly carpenter whom their neighbors regarded as being illegitimate and whom they also considered to be "out of his mind." Jesus's mother and brothers were aware of their neighbors' impressions of Jesus and sought to bring him home. This is hardly a respectable family portrait and could have served just as well as Celsus is thought to have served as an incentive for the Author of the *GenMar* and the Composer to rehabilitate and amplify the person of Mary. And although they did not know Mark itself, the Author and the Composer may have been aware of actual historical traditions preserved in Mark concerning the perception of Jesus in his hometown of Nazareth.[74]

An important component in the problem of the Celsus-*ProtJac* connection is an element of Celsus's allegations that does not derive from any earlier sources, that Mary was a seamstress. According to the de Strycker model, the "author" of the *ProtJac* is supposed to have expanded this one-word, cursory comment from Celsus into the elaborate story occupying three full chapters in *ProtJac* 10–12 in which Mary was chosen by the priests for the privilege of spinning the temple curtain. It is difficult to entertain the prospect that Celsus's uncorroborated detail of Mary being a seamstress could be the catalyst for the creation of the very disproportionate scenario of a council of temple priests deciding to gather Hebrew virgins to weave a new temple veil, which constitutes the setting for the Annunciation and conception of Mary's divine child. The likelihood of this causative connection between Celsus and the *ProtJac* becomes even more remote in view of the evidence presented above that the Veil Council in *ProtJac* 10–12 is not the monolithic narrative that it is believed to be but consists of the original unredacted *GenMar* Veil Council, which was comprehensively redacted with extensive interpolations by the Composer and the Redactor to form these three chapters in the present final version of the *ProtJac*. Again, the first-century *GenMar* and CEGM would not have been written as responses to the late second-century Celsus.[75]

The image of Mary spinning thread in the *ProtJac* is best understood within the context of the *GenMar* as a discrete preexisting source document, which,

---

73. Mk 3:20-1; 31-5; 6:3-4.

74. Schaberg and Lüdemann correctly assert that the questions regarding the legitimacy of Jesus may have existed already in earlier pre-Gospel traditions that predated Mark. See above, pp. 182-3, nn. 48, 49.

75. "The Veil Council," pp. 35-54.

according to our analysis above, originally began with what is now *ProtJac* 1:01–8:02 and was followed directly by the unredacted sections of the Veil Council in *ProtJac* 10–12. In the redacted *ProtJac* Veil Council, Mary is one of the Hebrew virgins who were brought into the temple to weave a new veil. But in the original *GenMar* Veil Council, the emphasis is on Mary's identity as a temple virgin, who was living in the temple at that time. It was while she was in the temple spinning thread for the veil, that she received the Annunciation of her conception directly from the Voice of God. This image of Mary's conception in the original *GenMar* is much more compatible with the concept of first-century Docetic Christology according to which the unnamed "Beloved One" will descend from the seventh heaven to Earth and will then become known as Jesus.

The original *GenMar* story of Mary the temple virgin who participated in the weaving of the veil actually finds significant support in early Jewish sources. Tal Ilan investigated the issue of women weaving the temple veil and concluded that "it is quite clear that weavers of the Temple curtain ... was a position held exclusively by women" who "were mentioned in ancient, reliable traditions."[76] Ilan cites the Jewish *Apocalypse of Baruch* (*2 Bar.*), which was written shortly after the destruction of the temple in 70 CE, as evidence in support of her "position to maintain the existence of women as historical members of the Temple staff."[77] *2 Bar.* refers to "virgins who spin fine linen" in close proximity to the priests of the temple cult.[78] Ilan also discusses the evidence of the earliest and most important rabbinical writings such as the *Mishnah* (late second century CE) and its supplement the *Tosefta* (early third century CE). In a list of officials on the payroll of the temple, *Tosefta Shequalim* includes the statement: "The women who wove the (Temple) curtain (פרכת) ... would receive their wages from the contribution (of the) chamber."[79] Furthermore, Ilan makes a strong case that such women were originally mentioned in the seminal rabbinic work, the *Mishnah*, but were subsequently censored out of that document.[80]

More recently Megan Nutzman has reexamined the issue of the young Mary living in the Jerusalem temple and has essentially confirmed Ilan's conclusions.[81]

---

76. *Mine and Yours Are Hers: Retrieving Women's History from Rabbinic Literature*; vol. 41, *Arbeiten zur Geschichte des antiken Judentums und des Urchristentums* (Leiden: Brill, 1997), 142.

77. Ibid., 140, cf. n. 19 where Ilan cites "the extended form of this tradition" in the later Talmuds *Y. Shequalim* 4.3, 48a and *B. Ketubbot* 106a.

78. *2 Bar.* 10:19. A. F. J. Klijn, "2 (Syriac Apocalypse of) Baruch," in *The Old Testament Pseudepigrapha*, vol. 1, ed. J. H. Charlesworth (New York: Doubleday, 1983), 624.

79. *T. Shequalim* 2.6, *Mine and Yours*, 139.

80. *Mine and Yours*, 140–2.

81. "Mary in the Protevangelium of James: A Jewish Woman in the Temple?" *Greek, Roman, and Byzantine Studies* 53 (2013), 551–78, esp. 563–70 concerning "virgin weavers"; 551–2: "In this article I investigate one aspect of *Prot. Jas.* that is among the most frequently cited errors in the text: the depiction of a young Mary living in the temple of Jerusalem."

Nutzman distinguishes herself from the "standard scholarly opinion" concerning the relationship between the *ProtJac* and Celsus by understanding correctly that "Celsus' disparagement of Mary did not originate with him, but rather with Jews."[82] She challenges the conventional interpretation of the *ProtJac*, which, on the basis of "questionable descriptions of Jewish practice and Palestinian Geography," labels it as "the work of a Christian whose knowledge of Judaism was problematic."[83] Nutzman surveys the biblical and rabbinic evidence regarding the experience of women in the temple and concludes that the author of the *ProtJac* "betrays a familiarity with Jewish customs that has been overlooked."[84] She suggests that "the author of *Prot. Jas.* was a Christian who was familiar with contemporary Judaism and that he used Jewish motifs to affirm Mary's purity."[85]

One of the motifs used in the CEGM to demonstrate Mary's purity is a test given to Mary and Joseph by the priests of the temple using τo ὕδωρ της ἐλεγξεως ("the water of reproach").[86] The discrepancies between this story and a parallel biblical account in Num. 5:11-31 are cited as evidence against the historical value and, ultimately, the Jewish character of the *ProtJac*.[87] Tim Horner argues convincingly that the version of the "water of reproach" found in *ProtJac* 16:01-07 "is closer to the Mishnaic discussion on this procedure in the *Sotah*" than it is to that in Num. 5.[88] Horner lists the "striking differences between *Prot. Jas.* and the biblical account":

---

82. Ibid., 558-9.

83. Ibid., 551-2. See "The Magi," pp. 113-4, where the seeming ignorance of the *ProtJac* "author" concerning Palestinian geography is attributed to contradictions in the original text that were caused by the clumsy, heavy-handed revisions and interpolations of the Redactor; cf. 148, n. 315.

84. Ibid., 552-4, esp. the very detail rich n. 8.

85. Ibid., 555-6. It is to Nutzman's credit that she was able to gain these insights regarding the independence and originality of the *ProtJac* while still adhering to the consensus opinion of a single "author" of the document.

86. I prefer the reading "reproach" from Lampe, *Patristic Greek Lexicon*, 446, and Danker, *Greek-English Lexicon*, 315, as opposed to the stronger readings, i.e., accusation, conviction, that are employed in translations of the verb form ἐλεγχθεῖσα found in Celsus's derogatory statements against Mary, see above p. 176, n. 19. The phrase τo ὕδωρ της ἐλεγξεως is also translated as "bitter water," Nutzman, "Mary," 559; Smid, *Protevangelium*, 112-13; Hock calls it the "drink test," *Infancy Gospels*, 61.

87. Elliott, *Apocryphal*, 51. Eve Levavi Feinstein conducts a detailed discussion of the reading מי המרים המאררים in Num. 5:18, 19, and 24 and concludes that the most accurate translation is "the bitter waters that curse"; "The 'Bitter Waters' of Numbers 5: 11-31," *VT* 62 (2012), 305; cf. the LXX translation as "waters of conviction of the cursed one" (τὸ ὕδωρ τοῦ ἐλεγμοῦ τοῦ ἐπικαταρωμένου).

88. "Jewish Aspects of the Protoevangelium of James," *JECS* 12 (2004), 313-35. Horner takes Elliott and Hock to task for "relying upon our assumptions about what constituted normative Judaism" and too readily dismissing any possibility of "Jewish" authorship of the *ProtJac*, 316.

(1) "in *Prot. Jas.* Joseph is made to drink the water, whereas in Numbers the drink is solely for the woman";

(2) "in *Prot. Jas.* Mary is known to be six months pregnant, whereas in Numbers the test seems to act as some sort of abortive device that will reveal an illegitimate pregnancy";

(3) "*Prot. Jas.* does not follow the same procedure described in Numbers, for here Mary's hair is not tussled and no curse formula is mentioned."[89]

On the other hand, Horner points out significant similarities between the versions of the water test in the *ProtJac* and *Sotah* as opposed to that in Numbers: "The emphasis of the text in *Sotah* is not so much on whether the woman is pregnant, rather it is focused on establishing the integrity of the relationship and to determine fidelity. This fits much better with the circumstance of *Prot. Jas.* where the question revolves around truth, not the presence of a baby."[90] Nutzman draws attention to a "unique detail" in the *ProtJac* story of "the water of reproach" that "is often used to establish the author's ignorance of Judaism," but that can serve instead to shed light on his background.[91] Nutzman notes that in *ProtJac* 16:03 Joseph is made to drink the water as well as Mary, which contradicts the biblical account that involves only the woman. Horner also views the participation of the man in the *ProtJac* water test as another element that associates the *ProtJac* story with the Mishnaic account. *Sotah* 5.1 states: "As the water puts her to the proof so does it put the paramour to the proof."[92] Likewise, the water test in the *ProtJac* and *Sotah* is not an abortive device as in Numbers but instead acts to reveal the guilt, not only of the woman but also of her suspected paramour.[93]

The similarities between the *ProtJac* and *Sotah* support Horner's position that "*Prot. Jas.* contains elements that may have been more readily understood by readers who were familiar with contemporary Jewish teaching, perhaps even Jews." Horner recognizes that "the earliest attacks against the person of Jesus—against his family, his suspicious origins, and the claim of divinity placed on him—all come from Jewish sources."[94] And since "the earliest critics of Christianity came from within Judaism, then it is easier to understand the kind of audience that would have responded to *Prot. Jas.*"[95] Horner and Nutzman have successfully detached

---

89. Ibid., 328. Cf. "Mary," 559–62 where Nutzman provides further details on the biblical account and compares it to the versions preserved in Josephus, Philo, and *Sotah*.

90. "Jewish Aspects," 328.

91. "Mary," 562.

92. "Jewish Aspects," 329.

93. Ibid., "In the Mishnah [and in the *ProtJac*] it is a matter of revealing guilt, not of a dropped uterus and permanent sterility as in Numbers."

94. Ibid., 330.

95. Ibid., 332, "Against the backdrop of accusations that Jesus was the bastard son of a Roman soldier, or even that he was just one of the natural sons of Joseph and Mary, *Prot.*

the *ProtJac* from its traditional association with Celsus and have reoriented the quest for its *Sitz im Leben* against the backdrop of an internal debate between Jews and "Christian Judaism."[96] But in so doing, they have posited the question that concerns us in this study: where is the Jewish "audience" located within the first two centuries CE that is addressed by the *ProtJac* and its source documents, the *GenMar* and the CEGM? Unfortunately, as was the case with Schaberg and Lüdemann before, Horner and Nutzman also are impeded from pursuing this question by their understanding of the *ProtJac* as a unitary document written by a single author in the era of Celsus at the end of the second century CE.[97]

The Evidence of Malcom Lowe

Both Horner and Nutzman make reference to the work of Malcolm Lowe to bolster their arguments in favor of the Jewish character of the *ProtJac*. But Lowe's evidence also contains significant ramifications for an early date of the *ProtJac* and for the redactional theory espoused in this study. Lowe "surveyed the occurrence of the Greek word Ἰουδαῖος (and its cognates in other languages) in biblical, classical, and rabbinic literature" for the approximate period 200 BCE–200 CE.[98] He concluded from his comprehensive study that, during that time, the word Ἰουδαῖος primarily signified the inhabitants of the geographical area of ἡ Ἰουδαία, that is, "'Judeans' as dwellers in or emigrants from 'Judea.'"[99] Inside Palestine the Jews referred to themselves as "Israel" and called their country "(the land of) Israel," reserving the name "Judea" for the specific region of Jerusalem and calling the inhabitants of that region "Judeans."[100] Outside Palestine "Judea" usually meant all Palestine, "or at least the kingdom or Roman province of Judea," and "Judeans" meant all of the inhabitants of Palestine "of which Judea in the strict sense was only a part."[101] Lowe

Jas. attempts to address these ideas head on and counter them *en masse*. Perhaps because these arguments against Jesus came from predominantly Jewish sources and voices, *Prot. Jas.* could be said to confront those who would have had the most difficulty with this idea: Christian Jews or simply Jewish critics."

96. Ibid., 333–4. Horner struggles with the "deep and lingering question about the *Prot. Jas.*" and distinguishes the "Christian Judaism" of the *ProtJac* from any "facile categorization" as Jewish-Christian.

97. But Horner, ibid., 333, in an apparent self-contradiction, inadvertently shows the way toward the Jewish scenario that might have catalyzed the creation of a document such as the *ProtJac*, which "defies facile categorization."

98. "Ἰουδαῖοι of the Apocrypha: A Fresh Approach to the Gospels of James, Pseudo-Thomas, Peter and Nicodemus," *NovT* 23 (1981), 56, referring to his original study "Who Were the Ἰουδαῖοι?", *NovT* 18 (1976), 101–30.

99. "Ἰουδαῖοι Apocrypha," 56. Lowe emphasizes the distinction between the use of Ἰουδαῖος as a geographical, as opposed to a religious, designation.

100. Ibid.

101. Ibid., 57–8. Cf. n. 6 in which Lowe cites Josephus as "the most striking (and completely undeniable evidence)" of "the existence of this duality of meaning."

identified several important early Jewish and Christian writings as "the prime representatives" of this insider "Palestinian Jewish literature" that used Israel as a "self-name" and "Judean" only for Jews from around Jerusalem: "I Maccabees, the canonical gospels (as opposed to the remainder of the New Testament), and the Mishnah."[102]

Lowe speculated that "inasmuch as the *apocryphal* New Testament Literature shows the same division into gospels, acts and apocalypses as the canonical literature, a further putative source of 'Palestinian' uses of the terms Ἰουδαῖος and Ἰσραήλ is the *apocryphal gospels*."[103] He thus applied his same methodology as above, to three categories of apocryphal gospel writings, "the nativity, infancy, and passion gospels." The first major conclusion of Lowe's survey of the apocryphal writings was that "the *earliest* representatives of each group—and primary sources for later representatives—did in fact conform to 'Palestinian' usage."[104] The second major conclusion was that "as time went on, the word Ἰουδαῖος increasingly crept into the text." Lowe attributed this phenomenon to "the desire of editors and copyists to give 'explanations' for their readers" or to imitate canonical literature, or "to increasing Christian-Jewish animosity."[105] Both of Lowe's major conclusions are particularly germane to our investigation of the *ProtJac*.

The earliest of Lowe's "nativity" gospels is the *ProtJac* in which he found the Jews to be named as Ἰσραήλ twenty-eight times and as οἱ Ἰουδαῖοι only once, in *ProtJac* 21:03.[106] This single incidence of the word οἱ Ἰουδαῖοι in the *ProtJac* is found in the Magi story in *ProtJac* 21:02-22:02 that was identified in this study as a version of the parallel Magi story in Mt. 2:1-18 that the Redactor revised and interpolated into the CEGM.[107] The question that the Magi posed to Herod in *ProtJac* 21:03 was taken by the Redactor verbatim from Mt 2:1: που εστιν ο βασιλευς των ιουδαιων; ("where is the king of the Jews?").[108] This single exception to Lowe's theory has thus been effectively neutralized by our redaction-critical analysis of the *ProtJac*. He is entirely justified in concluding that "the Protoevanglium of James (PJ), the earliest nativity gospel, makes 'Israel' the self-name of the Jews."[109] The membership of the *ProtJac* in Lowe's elite group of early "insider" Jewish Palestinian documents is thus fully confirmed, and furthermore the validity of Lowe's methodology and

---

102. Ibid., 58. Cf. Lowe, "Ἰουδαῖοι," 113-14.

103. "Ἰουδαῖοι Apocrypha," 58.

104. Ibid., 58-9.

105. Ibid., 59.

106. Ibid., 60. It is significant that Lowe prefers the Greek text of Tischendorf over that of de Strycker. Lowe dates P. Bodm V to "barely a century after the original work."

107. See the full discussion of the secondary nature of the *ProtJac* Magi story as an interpolation of the Redactor, "The Magi," pp. 113-22.

108. See "The Redactor: *The Protevangelium Jacobi*," pp. 135-6, nn. 30, 32.

109. "Ἰουδαῖοι Apocrypha," 59; cf. ibid., 60, "'Israel' is quite manifestly the name of the Jews according to the PJ."

insights into the usage of the terms Ἰουδαῖος and Ἰσραήλ in ancient Judaism is corroborated by the evidence of the ProtJac.

Lowe also refers passages in the ProtJac that seem at first to reflect canonical usage but which he ascribes to later editors and copyists who increasingly introduced the word Ἰουδαῖος into the text. These are found in the later MS tradition and do not occur in the text of P.Bodm V; they also occur within sections of the ProtJac that have been identified as interpolations of the Redactor, that is, the Magi story and the Doubting Salome episode, respectively. In ProtJac 21:03 the Magi asked Herod, "Where is the king of the Jews?" (που εστιν ο βασιλευς των ιουδαιων;), but in ProtJac 21:10 they told him that they knew from the star in the sky that "a king was born in Israel" (βασιλευς εγεννηθη τω ισραηλ). Lowe describes this instance of Ἰσραήλ as "one case of *mistaken* imitation of 'canonical usage'" "which is now falsely put into the mouth of foreigners."[110] Salome's analogous statement in ProtJac 20:09b that "a great king was born in Israel" (βασιλευς εγεννηθη μεγας τω ισραηλ) is "due to somebody who could hardly himself have been a Palestinian Jew."[111] Lowe has thus accurately described the Redactor of the ProtJac.

Unfortunately, as insightful as Lowe's research was, the influence of the de Strycker consensus opinion on the *Sitz im Leben* of the ProtJac impeded him also from exploring fully the ramifications of his evidence. This is most visible in Lowe's posture regarding the relationship between the texts of the ProtJac and the canonical Gospels. For example, Lowe observed correctly that the question of the Magi to Herod in ProtJac 21:01 is an "exact duplicate" of the text and scenario of Mt. 2:2, but he interpreted this and other parallels between the ProtJac and the canonical Nativity stories as proof of an actual literary dependence of the ProtJac upon Matthew and Luke: "The closeness of the narrative, in various places, to the nativity accounts of Matthew and Luke makes it virtually indubitable that the author of the PJ both knew these two canonical gospels and drew heavily upon them."[112] As another parallel "between the ProtJac and the canonical nativity stories" Lowe cites ProtJac 8:09 and suggests that "the text—whether ὅλης τῆς περιχώρου τῆς Ἰουδαίας or merely ὅλης τῆς Ἰουδαίας—echoes Lukan usage."[113]

---

110. "Ἰουδαῖοι Apocrypha," 61. Lowe cites parallels in Lk. 1:80, 2:25, 2:34, 4:25, 4:27, 7:9 and Mt. 2:6, 8:20, 9:33, and 10:23. Cf. Salome's reference "to the sons of Israel" (τοις υιοις ισραηλ) in ProtJac 20:05.

111. Ibid.

112. Ibid., 60–1.

113. The Greek texts, respectively, read: "all the environs of Judea," and "all of Judea." Lowe's citation of the text of ProtJac 8:09 is based on two variant readings found in the later Greek MSS of the ProtJac, as listed in Tischendorf's edition of the ProtJac, Evangelia, 17, which Lowe is using for his article. Lowe mistakenly includes P.Bodm V among the MSS that contain these readings: "(inc. ms Z)." P.Bodm V reads καθ ολου της περιχωρου της ιουδαιας. The masculine form of the adjective ολου ("all") was subsequently adjusted in most of the later MSS to the feminine ὅλης, although eleven MSS follow the masculine

But just as the first parallel between *ProtJac* 21:01 and Mt. 2:2 proved to be a false indicator of dependence of the CEGM on the canonical Gospels,[114] the same is the case also with this second suggested parallel.

ProtJac 8:09 is part of a passage that is fraught with textual difficulties. As was discussed at length above,[115] *ProtJac* 8:03-9:04 occupies the precise point at which the Composer's major interpolation of the Joseph Council into the underlying text of the *GenMar* occurs. This passage was labeled in our analysis as "the fragmented section" of the Joseph Council and was described as "the highly problematic text created successively, and collectively, by the Composer and the Redactor." Furthermore, it represented "a most daunting, and perhaps insurmountable, challenge to any attempt to determine which of the conflicting elements in the text should be attributed to the Author of the *GenMar*, the Composer, or the Redactor, respectively." Thus, the "fragmented section" of the *ProtJac*, including v. 8:09, exists within a major interpolation by the Composer into the original text of the Author's *GenMar* and subsequently suffered additional heavy editorial revision at the hands of the Redactor. Since a basic premise of the compositional theory that resulted from this study is that neither the Author of the *GenMar* nor the Composer who later enhanced it knew of the canonical Gospels, any similarity or association of *ProtJac* 8:09 with the canonical texts of Mark, Matthew, and Luke most likely should be attributed to the work of the Redactor who systematically injected canonical texts throughout the CEGM.

Lowe's research has illuminated a significant aspect of early Jewish and Christian writings, but he has also provided substantial evidentiary support for the findings of this study regarding the compositional history of the *ProtJac*. If the *ProtJac* is now liberated from its assumed dependency on Celsus and the canonical Gospels, researchers are free to seek out the historical and ideological circumstances that prompted the Author, the Composer, and the Redactor to make their respective contributions toward the composition of the *ProtJac*. As did Horner before him, now Lowe also shows the way. Both of these scholars initially paid obeisance to the

reading of P.Bodm V. Later scribes no doubt conformed this reading to the canonical texts that attest the feminine form of ὅλη when it occurs together with the noun περιχωρος, which normally is feminine in gender (Mt. 8:5, 14:35; Mk 1:28; Lk. 8:3, 4:14, 4:37, 7:17, 8:37). Closest to the *ProtJac* reading is Lk. 4:14: καθ' ὅλης τῆς περιχώρου, although the text contains no specific geographical reference. περιχωρος also appears in ancient texts, including the LXX, as masculine and neuter gender, Danker, *Greek-English Lexicon*, 808. It is difficult to determine definitively the original text of this anomalous reading in P.Bodm V.

114. See above; since *ProtJac* 21:01 occurs within an interpolation of Matthean materials into the CEGM by the Redactor, it does not constitute evidence of dependence of the Redactor's source document on the canonical materials.

115. "The Joseph Council," pp. 23-33.

presumed late second-century date for the *ProtJac*. But Horner wrote of "evidence that suggests Justin Martyr knew of *Prot. Jas*," thus placing our document, or at least some of its component materials, in the first half of the second century.[116] Likewise, Lowe also suggested that the early insider "Palestinian" usage of Ἰουδαῖος and Ἰσραήλ in the *ProtJac* indicates that it may have "originated in the (possibly early) 2nd century A.D., when the 'Palestinian' usage had not yet died out."[117] Thus, both Horner and Lowe point toward an earlier date for the *ProtJac*.

As a result of our investigation, the canonical Gospels may be viewed as the *terminus post quem* of the Redactor, who liberally reproduced and inserted them into his source document. But this source document, the CEGM, shows no knowledge of the canonical Gospels and in fact contradicts them in significant ways. Consequently, the canonical Gospels can impose no chronological or ideological limitations on either the Author of the *GenMar* or on the Composer who enhanced his work. Lowe has associated the "Palestinian usage" of Ἰουδαῖος and Ἰσραήλ with the canonical Gospels and with the "original author" of the *ProtJac*, whom he labels as a "Palestinian Jew."[118] In our compositional model of the *ProtJac*, Lowe's "original author" would be identified first with the Author of the *GenMar* and second with the Composer who later enhanced the *GenMar* with his own materials. But Lowe also distinguishes the "original author" from a second writer, whom he describes as "someone unfamiliar personally with 1st-2nd century Palestinian usage,"[119] and "somebody who could hardly himself have been a Palestinian Jew." This non-Palestinian writer is our Redactor, who inserted revisions and interpolations into his source document in the second century. Therefore the *GenMar* and the Composer's additions to it—which predate the Redactor and which exhibit the same "Palestinian usage" as that in the canonical Gospels—may be assigned to the first century CE with the canonical Gospels.

116. "Jewish Aspects," 315; cf. the full treatment of the significant evidence indicating a connection between the *ProtJac* Redactor and the School of Justin Martyr, "The Redactor: *The Protevangelium Jacobi*," pp. 136-47.

117. "Ἰουδαῖοι Apocrypha," 59.

118. It must be kept in mind that Lowe considers the *ProtJac* to be a unitary composition, even though he speaks here of two individuals at work in its composition.

119. Ibid., 61-2, "Its [the *ProtJac*'s] original author may thus have been a Palestinian Jew, who used the term 'Israel'—not merely imitatively—quite often, while certainly at a later stage someone unfamiliar personally with 1st-2nd century Palestinian usage multiplied these occurrences of Ἰσραήλ, thinking thereby to make the PJ sound even more 'canonical.'"

APPENDIX 3: THE *PROTJAC* AND THE NEW TESTAMENT GOSPELS

The most essential factor in the more recent scholarly discussions on the composition of the *ProtJac* is the place of the New Testament materials within its text. Many modern scholars exhibit a high degree of commonality in their view of the secondary nature of the *ProtJac* vis-à-vis the New Testament Gospels to the point of repeating certain key words in their writings. Such key words characterize the *ProtJac* as an "expansion," "embellishment," or "development" of the canonical texts. Scholars almost unanimously refer to "the author" of the *ProtJac*, indicating the "given" that this Apocryphon was the creation of a single author. Such is the mindset of the very well-entrenched de Strycker consensus. J. K. Elliot, for example, in his comprehensive volume on the New Testament Apocrypha, pronounces the *ProtJac* to be "<u>one of the most</u> important and <u>influential</u> of the apocryphal gospels"[120] but then portrays it as "<u>the earliest written elaboration of the canonical infancy narratives</u> that has survived."[121] Pieter W. Van der Horst, likewise labels the *ProtJac* as "<u>one of the earliest written</u> and <u>most influential elaborations</u> of the canonical infancy narratives."[122] Van der Horst speaks of the "<u>author</u> of the *Protevangelium Jacobi*," presupposing that it was this single "<u>author</u>" of the *ProtJac* who <u>elaborated</u> upon the canonical infancy materials in his narrative.

Foskett joins Elliott and Van der Horst in articulating the consensus opinion of "the PJ's <u>literary dependence on the earlier canonical gospels</u>."[123] Foskett considers it to be "obvious that the anonymous <u>author</u> of the Protevangelium of James (hereafter called PJ) <u>drew heavily upon the traditions</u> concerning Mary and the infancy of Jesus narrated in the opening chapters <u>of Matthew and most especially Luke</u>."[124] Ron Hock states that "the Infancy Gospel of James <u>assumes, reworks, or develops both Matthew's and Luke's stories at many points throughout the narrative</u>."[125] Hock provides a summary of the contents of the *ProtJac* "to sort out traditional and new elements." The "traditional" elements in Hock's estimation are the canonical texts, whereas the non-canonical materials in the *ProtJac* are the "new elements" that were added subsequently to the preexisting "traditional" canonical elements by the "author" of the *ProtJac*. Hock claims that his "summary

---

120. I underline the repetitive vocabulary used in the quotations from these scholars for emphasis.

121. *Apocrypha*, 48; Elliott continues: "What has sometimes been described as a midrashic exegesis of Matthew's and Luke's birth narratives finds permanent expression in this document."

122. "Sex, Birth, Purity, and Asceticism in the Protevangelium Jacobi," in *A Feminist Companion to Mariology*, eds. Amy-Jill Levine and Maria Mayo Robbins (New York: T&T Clark International, Continuum, 2005), 56. Van der Horst's article immediately precedes my own contribution in this same volume; "Christmas," 77–98.

123. "Miriam," 67.

124. Ibid., 63.

125. *Infancy Gospels*, 4–5.

of the Infancy Gospel of James has shown various points of contact between this gospel and the canonical accounts, and only literary dependence can explain the similarities ... the Infancy Gospel of James is dependent on the canonical stories."[126]

Stanley E. Porter describes the *ProtJac* thus: "The *Protevangelium of James*—dated to between 150 and 250 (around the last part of the second century would be agreeable to most)—is an unhistorical expansion upon the infancy narratives found in the canonical Gospels of Matthew and Luke."[127] Porter presents the most comprehensive exposition of the case for considering the *ProtJac* to be such an "unhistorical expansion upon the infancy narratives" of Matthew and Luke:

> The *Protevangelium of James* is clearly dependent upon the canonical account in at least three ways: (1) it copies the canonical text word for word, sometimes for relatively extensive lengths; (2) it extensively paraphrases the Greek New Testament, usually including a number of words from the canonical text; and (3) it draws upon the two canonical Gospel infancy accounts, and conflates them in its own ordering and sequence, thus displacing or altering the canonical contexts.[128]

But each of Porter's three arguments could just as readily be explained by assuming the existence of a second-century Redactor who had access to the canonical texts and interpolated portions of these texts into a substantially earlier, preexisting source document that did not know the canonical Gospels. Such a Redactor could have (1) copied "the canonical text word for word, sometimes for relatively extensive lengths," (2) "extensively" paraphrased "the Greek New Testament, usually including a number of words from the canonical text," and (3) drawn "upon the two canonical Gospel infancy accounts," and conflated them in his "own ordering and sequence, thus displacing or altering the canonical contexts." The same would hold true regarding Porter's reasoning that "the fluidity and flexibility" of the Greek New Testament in the *ProtJac* "indicates that the texts of both canonical Gospel accounts were relatively well fixed in wording and order by the time of composition of the *Protevangelium of James*, as phrases regularly recur in the same order in the *Protevangelium of James* as in the Greek New Testament."[129] As an associate of Justin Martyr's School in Rome, the Redactor of the *ProtJac* would have had access to canonical Gospel texts that "were relatively well fixed in wording and order" by the middle of the second century.[130]

126. Ibid., 9.
127. "Early Apocryphal Gospels and the New Testament Text," in *The Early Text of the New Testament*, eds. Charles E. Hill and Michael J. Kruger (Oxford, UK: Oxford University Press, 2012), 366.
128. Ibid., 368.
129. Ibid.
130. Ibid. We would take issue with Porter's statement: "Because the *Protevangelium of James* has felt free to change wording, add scenes, events and details, and transpose contexts of the canonical account, it is difficult to use the text of the *Protevangelium of*

However, some of these scholars, while generally following de Strycker, leave open the possibility of multiple sources in the *ProtJac*. Elliott allows for the existence of such sources:

> É. de Strycker's major study of the PJ argues for the homogeneity of the book on literary, linguistic, and palaeographical grounds. This does not, however, mean that the <u>author</u> did not make use of earlier written material in the composition of his work. The stories of Mary, of Jesus' birth, and of Zachariah' death may all have reached him from separate sources …; the story of the midwife could also have reached the <u>author</u> from another source. Certainly, Salome and the midwife are very suddenly introduced into the narrative.[131]

But "the stories of Mary, of Jesus's birth, and of Zachariah's death" and "the story of the midwife," including Salome, are the principal constitutive components of the *ProtJac*; apart from them only the substantially less extensive canonical materials remain. Elliott's position is self-contradictory. How can he state that "the main inspiration and sources behind PJ have been the birth stories in Matthew and Luke and the Old Testament" and still maintain that the vast majority of the *ProtJac* narrative may have derived from "separate sources" and "another source"?[132]

James to comment on the Greek New Testament." In fact, it would seem that the *ProtJac* would be a valuable witness to a form of the New Testament text dating to the second century CE. How many MSS of the Gospels of Matthew and Luke are extant from a time as early as P.Bodm V? And how many of those preserve texts from the Nativity stories of these Gospels? Cf. "The Redactor: *The Protevangelium Jacobi*," pp. 136-47 on the use in the *ProtJac* of harmonized texts of Matthew and Luke that were also present in Justin Martyr in the mid-second century CE.

131. *Apocrypha*, 50. Elliott states that the "I, Joseph" passage in *ProtJac* 18 "probably came from an earlier written source"; he speaks further of "other arguments for disunity."

132. Ibid., 51, cf. n. 2. Elliott lists a number of "peculiar details" in the *ProtJac* but concludes: "Such details do not necessarily indicate the author's use of variant sources; they may result from his own lack of interest in, or awareness of, such apparent inconsistencies." In fact, many of the "peculiar details" in Elliott's list constitute strong evidence precisely of "variant sources" in the *ProtJac*. The "peculiar details" listed by Elliott are fictitious names of Mary's parents, Reuben, Zachariah, Samuel; Zachariah wrongly identified with Zachariah of Mt. 23:35; Simeon not being a high priest; the water of jealousy not being administered to men; the oracular plate on the forehead unknown outside of the *ProtJac*; the contradiction of the angelic Annunciation in *ProtJac* 11 and 12:2 [12:07 in the present edition]; warning given to the Magi not to go to Judea when they were already there in *ProtJac* 21:4 [21:15]; from n. 2, Mary is twelve in *ProtJac* 8:2-3 [8:03], but 16 in 12:3 [12:11]; Joseph has many sons in *ProtJac* 9:2 [9:06], 17:1 [17:02], 18:3 [should be 18:01], but only one in 17:2 [17:05]. Without citing any justification, Elliott dismisses too arbitrarily his "fictitious names" above. Regarding Elliott's perception of the mistaken identification of Zachariah in the *ProtJac* with the Zachariah of Mt. 23:35, our analysis of *ProtJac* 8:07 ("The Redactor: *The Protevangelium*

Foskett adheres as well to the consensus unitary model of the *ProtJac* and its dependence on the canonical Gospels but, paradoxically, also exhibits a more nuanced appreciation of the substantial thematic "discontinuity" of elements of the *ProtJac* vis-à-vis the canonical Gospels. She provides a very insightful

Jacobi," pp. 131-2); cf. *ProtJac* 10:08 ("The Veil Council," p. 39, n. 45) identified all the incidences of Zachariah in the *ProtJac* as interpolations of the Redactor, who derived this material from Luke. Any confusion is due to the flawed editorial activity of the Redactor, as is the reference to Samuel as a high priest in *ProtJac* 10:08. Concerning the water of jealousy not being administered to men, Tim Horner explains satisfactorily that the story of the water in the *ProtJac* agrees with the Mishnaic version of the text instead of the biblical account in Num. 5:11-31; see "*Jewish Aspects*," 328-9. Horner also mitigates Elliott's rejection of the oracular forehead plate, offering valuable clarification from Josephus, the DSS, and rabbinical sources, ibid., 319-20. Elliott's statement on "the contradiction of the angelic annunciation (12.2, cf. 11)" actually points out one of the most obvious confirmations of redactional activity in the *ProtJac*. *ProtJac* 12:2 [12:07] is a blatant gloss by the Redactor intended to conceal his clumsy interpolation of the two successive angelic Annunciations in *ProtJac* 11, cf. "The Veil Council," pp. 51-2. Elliott's concern over the return of the Magi to Judea when they were already there is a textual issue. He follows the text of Tischendorf in *ProtJac* 21:4 [21:15], which states that the Magi, "having been warned by the angel not to enter into Judea, they traveled to their country"; the reading in P.Bodm V does not contain the phrase "not to enter into Judea" but simply states: "having been warned by the angel [the Magi] departed to the [their] country." This verse is part of the revised Matthean Magi story that the Redactor interpolated into the Birth narrative, which again brings into play the deficient editorial skills of the Redactor; cf. "Magi Story," pp. 113-22. The discrepancy in Mary's age between *ProtJac* 8:2-3 [8:03], where she is twelve, and 12:3 [12:11], where she is sixteen, also displays redactional activity in the *ProtJac*. *ProtJac* 8:03 is the opening verse of the Joseph Council, which was interpolated by the Composer into the *GenMar*, and 12:11 is yet another heavy-handed insertion by the Redactor, attempting to provide an editorial transition from his interpolated Elizabeth story (*ProtJac* 12:03-10) back into the narrative of the CEGM, which resumes in the next verse, 13:01, with the Trial story. Finally, Elliott errs in stating: "Joseph has many sons in 9.2, 17.1, 18.3, but only one in 17.2." The actual plural word for "sons" (υιους) in *ProtJac* 9:2 [9:06], 17:1 [17:02], and 18:3 [a typo which should be 18:01] does not necessarily mean "many sons." It can mean two or more. *ProtJac* 17:2 [17:05] contains another textual disagreement between Tischendorf's text, which Elliott follows, and the text of P.Bodm V, which is supported by a significant portion of the MS tradition. Elliott's text reads: "his son led and Joseph followed." P.Bodm V reads: "his son led and Samuel followed." A possible solution to the textual discrepancy in this verse was suggested in "The Journey to Bethlehem," p. 88, according to which the plural "sons" in *ProtJac* 17:02 actually refers to the singular son, probably James himself, who was leading the donkey in 17:05, and the otherwise unknown Samuel in the same verse, who was following. The textual discrepancy can be resolved by assuming that Samuel was a second son of Joseph, given that the Composer was not aware of the list of four sons of Mary in canonical Mk 6:3 and Mt. 13:55. The presence of two sons of Joseph in the *ProtJac* would fit perfectly with the references to "sons" in *ProtJac* 9:06, 17:02, and 18:01.

discussion of the "discontinuity" between the portrayals of Mary, both within the *ProtJac* itself and in comparison to the Mary in Luke.[133] But her examination of the Marys in the *ProtJac* and in Luke is limited to discerning and analyzing the variations in Mary's name and persona in the two documents. Foskett cannot make the leap toward acknowledging that the diversity of thought that she correctly perceives in the *ProtJac* may derive from earlier writers who may have had a hand in composing its discontinuous parts.[134] She concludes that the single second-century "author" of the *ProtJac* "takes the Lukan Mary's virgin identity and spins it in a new direction."[135]

Perhaps the dilemma of modern scholarship on the *ProtJac* is best epitomized by Vuong. In the first chapter of her impressive volume, Vuong fully engages the complete range of opinions on the critical issues related to the *ProtJac*.[136] Touching upon the compositional problem, Vuong acknowledges the possibility of an earlier source within the *ProtJac* but concludes that since a final determination of this issue is still pending, she will concentrate her efforts upon the *ProtJac* in its latest form: "the focus of this study will fall mainly on evaluating the *Protevangelium of James* in its present form, rather than its possible prehistory."[137] Vuong has thus effectively summarized the current scholarly position vis-à-vis our Apocryphon.

In the absence of an acceptable solution to the compositional problem, recent study of the *ProtJac* has not been stymied by the problematic "disunity" (Elliott), "discontinuity" (Foskett), or "various peculiarities in style, structure, and details" (Hock) that scholars have perceived in its text. Scholarly discourse on the *ProtJac* has centered on the genre and purpose of the present fully redacted form of this document within the historical and theological context of the second-century Redactor. Vuong's volume is fittingly entitled *Gender and Purity in the Protevangelium of James*; it is with these issues that the bulk of her book is concerned. Hock quickly dispenses with the "Questions about [the] Literary

---

133. "Miriam," 67–9.

134. I.e., individuals such as the Author of the *GenMar* and the Composer.

135. Ibid., 72. In the end Foskett defers to Hock, who himself prevaricates on the critical issues regarding the *ProtJac*, ibid., 73, n. 1, "noting the multiple problems raised by the precise dating, authorship, and provenance of the text, Hock observes: 'The question of the provenance for the Infancy Gospel of James is the most difficult to answer, and perhaps only negative answers are possible … it may be best at present to withhold judgment on the matter of provenance, at least until new evidence of arguments are forthcoming,'" cf. *Infancy Gospels*, 12–13. Hock also speaks of "various peculiarities in style, structure, and details that have raised questions about the unity of the work," but he minimizes the significance of this evidence and in the end justifies the de Strycker unitary model, ibid., 20.

136. *Gender and Purity*, 32–59. Vuong's volume is the most important book published on the *ProtJac* since de Strycker's *La Forme*, which was published more than fifty years previously; cf. p. 168, n. 149.

137. Ibid., 39, cf. n. 31.

Unity" of the *ProtJac*[138] in order to arrive again at de Strycker's position. He dedicates much of his introduction to discussing the purpose and genre of the *ProtJac*.[139] Scholarly ruminations about the genre and purpose of the "unitary single-author *ProtJac*" are premature, given that the content of the document derives from several individuals who appear to have been at cross-purposes in their writings. The value of such reflections is limited until the essential critical issues of date, authorship, and provenance are clarified for each of the sources that made up the *ProtJac*.

The stories about Mary and Joseph in the source documents of the *ProtJac* seem to have had little correspondence with the parallel stories in the canonical texts. What appears to have survived of the original *GenMar* has no relation to the canonical Gospels. In fact, not only do these sections of the *ProtJac* show an almost total ignorance of the canonical Gospels but even contradict them in significant ways. Prime examples are the idiosyncratic *GenMar* Annunciation story that featured the direct Annunciation and impregnation of the twelve-year-old virgin Mary by the Voice of God in the temple and the extraordinary Birth story of the remarkable walking newborn child in the cave outside of Bethlehem.[140] The Joseph materials that were added by the Composer to the *GenMar* also were strikingly alien to the Joseph materials of the canonical Gospels;[141] for example, the portions attributed to the Composer in the heavily redacted Joseph Council, the Trial of Joseph and Mary, the Journey toward Bethlehem that stopped short of Bethlehem, and the Midwife story. The contrast between these materials and the canonical stories far exceeds what Porter characterizes as "extensively paraphrasing the Greek New Testament." These blatant divergences may seem to some as "elaboration" but should be viewed more appropriately as exhibiting a complete lack of correlation. One is tempted to question whether this substantial inconsistency in the interpretation of the evidence with respect to the *ProtJac* may perhaps betray a prejudicial viewpoint in favor of the "canonical" versus the "non-canonical" early Christian writings.

The redaction-critical analysis of the *ProtJac* presented in this study suggests a complete inversion of the de Strycker consensus. The *ProtJac* itself was not an "expansion," "elaboration," or "development" of the canonical infancy narratives. Rather, the *ProtJac* appears to have been an "expansion," "elaboration," and "development" of early, non-canonical strata of material, some of which seem

---

138. In contrast to Vuong, who presents a detailed overview and assessment of the scholarly debate regarding the date and provenance of the *ProtJac*, *Gender and Purity*, 31–44, Hock devotes barely a single page to these issues, *Infancy Gospels*, 13–14.

139. Ibid., 14–20.

140. *ProtJac* 1:01–8:02; also, respectively, "The Original *GenMar* Annunciation Story," pp. 39–49; and "The Birth," pp. 104–8.

141. "The Joseph Council," pp. 23–34, "The Trial of Joseph and Mary," pp. 55–76, "The Journey to Bethlehem," pp. 84–8, and "The Midwife," pp. 92–103.

to have existed before the New Testament Gospels, others possibly written concurrently with them, but all demonstrably distinct from, and independent of, the canonical writings. It was the second-century Redactor of the *ProtJac* who "expanded," "elaborated," and "developed" the preexisting CEGM by arbitrarily interpolating canonical materials into its text that disrupted the flow of that text and that were mostly incompatible and incongruous with the motifs presented in the underlying narrative.[142] This Redactor is identical with the individual to whom scholars refer as the second-century "author" of the *ProtJac*. The Redactor's objective was to transform the text of this "heretical" source document into an "orthodox" Gospel in accordance with the criteria of second-century "orthodox" Christianity to which he undoubtedly belonged.[143]

---

142. The Composer had expanded and elaborated the *GenMar*, as did the Redactor to the CEGM.

143. See "The Redactor: *The Protevangelium Jacobi*," pp. 131–47.

APPENDIX 4: THE KATHISMA CHURCH

A fortuitous archaeological discovery in 1992 has provided material evidence that seems to support the account in the *ProtJac* regarding the original location of the Cave of the Nativity in the "middle of the way" between Jerusalem and Bethlehem. Previously unknown ancient ruins were unearthed on the road from Jerusalem to Bethlehem midway between the two cities that were excavated between 1993 and 2000 and identified as the foundation of an ancient church known as the Kathisma ("seat") that was built in the fifth century.[144] R. Avner, the principal archaeologist who excavated the Kathisma church, describes it as a monumental church that was laid out in the form of "three concentric octagons," "precisely at the geometrical centre" of which "a large chunk of bedrock was revealed." Avner surmises that "the rock was the focus of the church and no doubt the *raison d'être* for the construction of the building."[145] According to later Christian tradition it was upon this rock that Mary sat to rest on her journey to Bethlehem. To Avner "it is obvious that both the legend and the holy place developed in association [sic] and as a parallel to the Old Testament story of the pregnant figure of Rachel dying at childbirth and her memorial tomb located further along this road closer to Bethlehem."[146]

Avner recounts the archaeological, literary, and iconographic evidence in the East and West beginning in the fifth century and concludes that the Journey to Bethlehem and the Kathisma church were among the "holiest pilgrimage sites and

---

144. R. Avner, "The Initial Tradition of the Theotokos at the Kathisma: Earliest Celebrations and the Calendar," in *The Cult of the Mother of God in Byzantium: Texts and Images*, vol. 11, eds. L. Brubaker and M. Cunningham (Surrey, England: Ashgate Publishing Ltd., 2011), 9–29; R. Avner et al., "Jerusalem, Mar Elias—the Kathisma Church," *Hadashot Arkheologiyot: Excavations and Surveys in Israel* / ארכיאולוגיות: חדשות וסקרים חפירות בישראל 113 (2001), 89–92; cf. Lipschits et al., "Palace and Village, Paradise and Oblivion: Unraveling the Riddles of Ramat Raḥel," *Near Eastern Archaeology* 74, no. 1 (2011), 5–6, 43–5; B. Andonia, "Kathisma—A Place of Rest on the Way to Bethlehem," *The Jerusalem Post*, January 31, 2013. Y. Aharoni, in his original 1954 excavations at the Kibbutz Ramat Rahel, mistook a church he uncovered in the main site at the top of the tell as the ancient Kathisma church, but he also made mention of the ancient well Bir Qadismu at the foot of the tell which would eventually be identified in the 1990s with the actual location of the Kathisma church, "Excavations at Ramat Rahel," *BA* 24 (1961), 98–9, 113–14. The Muslims also eventually adopted the Kathisma as a holy site and participated in its development, cf. R. Avner, "The Kathisma: A Christian and Muslim Pilgrimage Site," *ARAM* 18–19 (2006–2007). The location of the Kathisma church was lost after the expulsion of the Crusaders from Palestine in the twelfth century, but its existence was well known during the Byzantine era and in pilgrim accounts in the Middle Ages.

145. Avner, "Tradition," 13.

146. Avner et al., "Jerusalem," 542, cf. Avner, *Tradition*, 24–7.

churches commemorating events from the Life of Christ."[147] According to Avner, in the early Byzantine period "the road leading south from Jerusalem to Bethlehem loomed large as a holy itinerary, virtually a Christian Via Sacra, connecting the two most holy cities in the Holy Land":[148]

> The archaeological finds clearly indicate that the Kathisma belonged to a group of [sic] earliest churches built in Jerusalem on sites that were regarded among the holiest places to Christianity, chief of which are the Church of the Ascension of Christ on the Mount of Olives, originally built in the Early Byzantine period as a round structure; likewise the Rotunda of the Church of the Anastasis raised over Christ's sepulcher; as well as the octagonal unit built over the Cave of the Nativity In Bethlehem.[149]

Those mostly anonymous individuals, including the Redactor, over a span of centuries melded together the early traditions preserved among the followers of Jesus into a powerful new world faith complete with awe-inspiring sacred buildings to represent their work. This fusion of traditions was reflected in these later church buildings, in the iconography with which they were lavishly decorated, and in the elaborate rituals that took place within them, all of which collectively represented a vibrant living catechism for the masses of Christians. Avner asserts that "the Kathisma was preconceived and designed to be a pilgrim church."[150] And as such it was granted a position of high esteem amidst the major churches along the Christian "Via Sacra" between Jerusalem and Bethlehem. Included among these was the Basilica of the Nativity in Bethlehem that was built over a cave in which Jesus purportedly was born.[151] The popularity and authority of the *ProtJac* must have been great to have survived this massive canonical reworking of early Christian tradition.

The creators of this liturgically, ritualistically based synthesis of "Orthodox" Christian doctrine succeeded in their task so effectively that an important misperception they produced, apropos of the version of the events at the "middle of the way" in the *ProtJac*, has misled even the primary scholars who are investigating the Kathisma church.[152] Avner leaves no doubt in her seminal archaeological investigations that the site upon which the Kathisma church was

---

147. Avner et al., "Jerusalem," 543.
148. Ibid., 541.
149. Ibid., 544–5.
150. Ibid., 545.
151. The Basilica of the Nativity was one of the first monumental Christian churches built in Judea by Constantine the Great in the fourth century; Michelle Bacci et al., "Historical and Archaeological Analysis of the Church of the Nativity," *Journal of Cultural Heritage* 13 (2012), e5–e26, 2.3.
152. These misperceptions by Avner and others persisted from their earliest to their latest articles.

built was associated with the Journey story in the *ProtJac*.[153] Another scholar who has delved deeply into the mystery posed by the rediscovery of the Kathisma church is Stephen J. Shoemaker who also identifies the Kathisma site with the *ProtJac*.[154] Shoemaker has examined very thoroughly the historical evidence for the substantial Marian elements, including the Kathisma traditions, in the liturgical cycle of Byzantium and the later Western Christian cultures. But both Shoemaker and Avner have fallen victim to the deception of the Redactor and of the subsequent creators of the "Orthodox" Christian tradition vis-à-vis the place of the *ProtJac* and of the CEGM within the Nativity narrative.

In recounting the details of the journey to Bethlehem in the *ProtJac*, Avner states that Mary "asked Joseph to help her down and sat to rest, presumably on a rock by the roadside."[155] Avner later correctly qualifies this statement by noting that there is no mention of a rock in the *ProtJac* text: "The account of Mary's rest on the journey to Bethlehem in the Protevangelium of St. James does not specifically mention a rock on which she sat."[156] But Avner fails to notice that there is also no indication in the text of the *ProtJac* that Mary was taken down from the donkey to rest, nor that she rested at all. Even the redacted text of *ProtJac* 17:11–18:01 clearly states that Joseph took Mary down from the donkey and placed her in the cave specifically because it was time for her to give birth and not to rest. Mary's journey toward Bethlehem in the *ProtJac* stops at the cave where she gives birth to her child. In the *ProtJac* she does not rest and then continues on to Bethlehem to give birth.[157] This persistent misunderstanding among scholars betrays the influence of the later contrived legend of the Kathisma as the place of Mary's rest on her way to the Nativity in Bethlehem, which has effectively supplanted the original tradition of the "middle of the way" as the location of the Cave of the Nativity in both the *ProtJac* and its source, the CEGM.

As noted above, the *ProtJac* Redactor, adhering to the canonical Gospel tradition, may have sought to reduce the distance between the cave in the "middle of the way" and Bethlehem and thus identify the Nativity more closely with the city itself.[158] This process was only begun by the Proto-Orthodox Redactor and was completed by the subsequent architects of the "Orthodox" Christian tradition

---

153. See below, p. 208, n. 159.

154. "The (Re?)Discovery of the Kathisma Church and the Cult of the Virgin in Late Antique Palestine," *Maria: A Journal of Marian Studies* 2 (2001), 21–72.

155. Avner, "Kathisma," 541, cf. reference to the specific *ProtJac* text in n. 2.

156. Ibid., 547, Avner cites Theodosius the pilgrim as the earliest source of this error dating to the sixth century CE.

157. The idea of the Nativity having taken place in Bethlehem was not a matter of concern, nor did it even exist, in the CEGM. I specify the CEGM in this discussion as opposed to the *ProtJac* because the final form of the *ProtJac* represents the Redactor's attempt to relocate the Cave of the Nativity closer to Bethlehem precisely in order to conform the Nativity in the three-mile cave to the stories in Matthew and Luke.

158. See "Topographical and Archaeological Factors," pp. 89–92.

who also engineered the Via Sacra of monumental churches on the pilgrims' path between Bethlehem and Jerusalem. They built the imposing Kathisma church specifically to represent the place where Mary supposedly paused on her journey to rest before continuing on to the monumental church of the Nativity in Bethlehem. In a recent publication Avner reconsiders the "Origins of the Feast and the Cult of the Theotokos at the Kathisma"[159] and reaffirms her original observation that "the site of the Kathisma was hallowed by the legend transmitted by the Protoevangelium (17.2-3), according to which Mary sat to rest on the journey to Bethlehem." Unfortunately, this statement also contains the misperception held so persistently by Avner and others that the *ProtJac* was the source of the "legend" that Mary "rested" in the "middle of the way" on her journey toward Bethlehem.

Shoemaker also accedes to this misperception of the creators of the orthodox tradition: "Generally known as the 'Kathisma of the Theotokos', or the 'Seat of the God-Bearer', as the Greek translates, the church apparently was built to commemorate the spot halfway between Jerusalem and Bethlehem, where, according to the second-century *Protevangelium*, the Virgin rested before giving birth in a nearby Cave."[160] In a subsequent publication Shoemaker, as did Avner, acknowledges that the *ProtJac* was the inspiration for the Kathisma church.[161] He also correctly rejects the idea of a seat, or of Mary sitting in the *ProtJac*, and seems to place much of the responsibility for the legend of Mary's resting place in its proper historical perspective as the creation of later orthodox liturgists, hagiographers, and pilgrim accounts. However, Shoemaker ultimately continues to ascribe to the *ProtJac* the legend that Mary rested at the Kathisma:

> Although the Nativity traditions of the *Protevangelium* were undoubtedly the inspiration for the existence of this important early Christian shrine, there is nothing in the *Protevangelium*'s account that would suggest either a seat or Mary's sitting. The full significance of this church is known only from later Palestinian liturgical, hagiographical, and pilgrimage texts from the sixth and seventh centuries, all of which identify this church with the place where the Virgin Mary sat to rest before giving birth nearby, as is described in the *Protevangelium*.[162]

---

159. "*Presbeia Theotokou, Presbeia Mētros*: Reconsidering the Origins of the Feast and the Cult of the Theotokos at the Kathisma, on the Road to Bethlehem," Oesterreichisches Musiklexikon online (*Verlag der Oesterrichischen Akademie der Wissenschaften*: 2015), 41–8.

160. "(Re?)Discovery," 23-4; cf. Shoemaker's comment on the Russian pilgrim Grethinos's report of seeing a rock "on which the Virgin Mary had once supposedly sat, when she paused to rest before giving birth nearby, as the apocryphal *Protevangelium of James* describes the events of the Nativity," ibid., 23.

161. *Ancient Traditions of the Virgin Mary's Dormition and Assumption* (Oxford: Oxford University Press, 2002), 82.

162. Stephen J. Shoemaker, "Christmas in the *Qur'an*: The Qur'anic Account of Jesus' Nativity and Palestinian Local Tradition," *Jerusalem Studies in Arabic and Islam* 28 (2003), 23.

The Original Cave of the Nativity

It is significant that the canonical Nativity stories were not able to usurp entirely the position of the traditions contained in the *ProtJac*. This suggests that the CEGM must have circulated among the earliest followers of Jesus, before or alongside the canonical Gospels, and therefore accrued substantial respectability in the ancient Judean-Christian community. The fact remains that as late as the fifth century CE the Kathisma church, even with its new identity as Mary's resting place, was built at the precise location that was described in the CEGM. It seems odd at first that the builders of the Kathisma did not take into account the Redactor's alteration of the site of the cave and build the Kathisma closer to Bethlehem. But this suggests that they may have been dependent upon a tenacious, local oral tradition that had been preserved, neither in the redacted *ProtJac* nor in the canonical Gospels, but that predated both the canonical tradition and the Redactor's editorial machinations. This ancient local tradition could have been none other than that which had been preserved in the CEGM and in all likelihood in the *GenMar* itself.[163]

It is certainly not outside the realm of possibility that there may have existed a memory in the earliest Judean-Christian circles, of an important event such as the Nativity of Jesus in a cave halfway between Jerusalem and Bethlehem. And it is entirely conceivable that the local Judean followers of Jesus could have perpetuated the memory of this event, as well as the location of the cave in which it occurred. These early Judean Christians could have recorded their memories in a written document such as the *GenMar* and later enhanced this document with materials centering on Joseph. Even later, in the second century, a third individual who was not part of the original Judean-Christian scenario could have refashioned this enhanced *GenMar* document in accord with the prevailing canonical orthodox beliefs in his own theological environment. Although the canonical Gospels eventually superseded the enhanced *GenMar* and its subsequent incarnation, the *ProtJac*, the enduring traditions preserved in the "non-canonical" texts were so thoroughly engrained in the consciousness of the local Christians that eventually they were materialized in the monumental Kathisma church.

The above scenario has been derived from an internal redaction-critical analysis of the text of the *ProtJac* as preserved in its most ancient witness, P.Bodm V. Unfortunately there are only two early external witnesses who mention Jesus's birth in a cave, Justin Martyr in the second century[164] and Origen in the third.[165] It is revealing that the earlier writer, Justin Martyr, describes the location of the Cave of the Nativity ambiguously but in such a way that may be interpreted as supporting the version in the redacted *ProtJac*. Justin first states the canonical position of the birth of Jesus in Bethlehem (γεννηθέντος δὲ τότε τοῦ παιδίου ἐν Βηθλεέμ). He exhibits direct dependence on Lk. 2:7 by stating that Joseph did not have a place

163. "The Birth," pp. 104–8.
164. *Dial.* 78.
165. *Contra Cels.*, 1, 51.

to stay in that town (Ἰωσὴφ οὐκ εἶχεν ἐν τῇ κώμῃ ἐκείνῃ ποῦ καταλῦσαι).¹⁶⁶ But at this point Justin begins to equivocate. He contradicts his earlier position that Jesus was born "in Bethlehem" by stating that Joseph stayed (κατέλυσε) in a certain cave near the town (ἐν σπηλαίῳ τινὶ σύνεγγυς τῆς κώμης). It was there, according to Justin, that Mary gave birth to Jesus and, again as in Luke, placed him in a manger (ἐτετόκει ἡ Μαρία τὸν Χριστὸν καὶ ἐν φάτνῃ αὐτὸν ἐτεθείκει).¹⁶⁷

The pertinent point in Justin's account of the Nativity is his statement that Jesus was born "in a certain cave near the town" (ἐν σπηλαίῳ τινὶ σύνεγγυς τῆς κώμης), "near" Bethlehem. Justin's use of the preposition σύνεγγυς to describe the Cave of the Nativity as being "near" Bethlehem finds a parallel in Shoemaker's repeated references to the cave in *ProtJac* 18:01 as being "nearby" the place that he took Mary down from the donkey on which she was seated. Actually, the *ProtJac* is very specific about the location of the cave with respect to the stopping place at the "middle of the way." In both of the two relevant consecutive verses, *ProtJac* 17:12 and 18:01, the adverb of place ἐκεῖ, meaning "there" or "at that place," is used to specify that Joseph found the cave at the same place at which he took Mary down from the donkey. In *ProtJac* 17:11 at the "middle of the way," Mary asked Joseph to take her down from the donkey because the child in her was pressing her to come out. In *ProtJac* 17:12 Joseph took her down from the donkey ἐκεῖ, "at that place." In *ProtJac* 18:01 Joseph found the Cave of the Nativity again ἐκεῖ, "there" at that same place where he took Mary down from the donkey at the "middle of the way," not "nearby" or "near" the "middle of the way," but ἐκεῖ, "there" at the "middle of the way." That location would eventually become identified with the Kathisma.

If Justin's words are read literally, he may be exhibiting knowledge of the Redactor's adjusted version of the Nativity in a cave one-and-a-half miles outside of Bethlehem.¹⁶⁸ The phrase "near the town" could apply to a location one-fourth of the way from Bethlehem to Jerusalem, one-and-a-half miles outside of Bethlehem, but it would not relate as well to the midpoint between the two cities, which is the same distance from both and therefore just as "near" to Jerusalem as it is to Bethlehem. In any case Justin's statement that Jesus was born outside of Bethlehem contradicts the genitive absolute phrase, which he prefixed to this sentence stating that Jesus was born "in Bethlehem" (ἐν Βηθλεέμ). The fact that Justin qualifies the original Lukan location of the Nativity "in Bethlehem"—where no cave is mentioned—as now occurring "in a certain cave near the town," could very well

---

166. Note that Justin uses the verb form, καταλῦσαι, of the same word that occurs in its nominal form in Luke's statement that there was no place for Joseph and Mary to stay in the καταλύματι ("shelter"): διότι οὐκ ἦν αὐτοῖς τόπος ἐν τῷ καταλύματι. See Carlson, "Accommodations," 326–42.

167. Justin derived his reference to a manger (φάτνη) from Lk. 2:7 as there was no reference to a manger in the *ProtJac* Nativity scene.

168. For the evidence connecting the Redactor to the School of Justin Martyr, see "The Redactor: *The Protevangelium Jacobi*," pp. 136–47, especially as regards the Nativity, pp. 141–4.

indicate that Justin may have had before him both the Gospel of Luke and the redacted *ProtJac* and was attempting to merge the two accounts.[169]

This interpretation of Justin's witness to the Nativity raises an important question: why would Justin, who regularly cites texts from Matthew and Luke as authentic information about Jesus, place the witness of an apocryphal Gospel on the same level of authority as Luke?[170] Two factors may illuminate this paradox. First, at the time Justin was writing in the middle of the second century CE, the Christian communities had not yet conceived the idea of a Christian canon, or of a New Testament, as an authoritative collection of books. Justin holds Matthew and Luke in high esteem and often quotes their texts, but he does not name them or refer to them as Gospels.[171] Instead he consistently describes them as the "memoires of the Apostles."[172] A second relevant factor is that Justin himself was born and lived in Samaria where he also converted to Christianity. He therefore may have been aware of, or personally visited, the traditional local Christian holy sites in the environs of Jerusalem and Bethlehem, including no doubt the location of the Cave of the Nativity.

In contrast to Justin's witness to the very fluid state of the early Christian traditions and their sources in the mid-second century, only a century later another major Christian personality, Origen, represented a church that had advanced significantly toward consolidating its theology and its perception of the authoritative sources of its teachings about Jesus. Origen was very well integrated into the orthodox Christian ecclesiastical organization in Alexandria and mingled comfortably with the church hierarchy; he himself was ordained as a priest. Known for his literal interpretation of the Gospels, Origen adhered closely to the canonical version of the Nativity in Bethlehem. Having lived for a time in Palestine he, like Justin, also must have enjoyed firsthand experience of the Christian holy places. As proof of the Nativity story in the Gospel (εὐαγγελίῳ) Origen described "a cave in Bethlehem" with a manger that was well known to the Christians and non-Christians alike as the place where Jesus was born:

169. Ibid., pp. 143-4.
170. Ibid., pp. 144-7.
171. Only in *I Apol* 66:3 does Justin refer to the "memoires of the apostles" as εὐαγγέλια: οἱ γὰρ ἀπόστολοι ἐν τοῖς γενομένοις ὑπ' αὐτῶν ἀπομνημονεύμασιν, ἃ καλεῖται εὐαγγέλια ..., but his choice of words, ἃ καλεῖται εὐαγγέλια, i.e., "which are called Gospels," indicates that he himself may not consider them to be such.
172. *I Apol* 66:3, 67:3; *Dial.* 100:4, 101:3,102:4, 103:6, 8, 104:1, 105:1, 5, 6, 106:1, 4, 107:1; cf. also ἀπομνημονεύει in *I Apol* 33:5; *Dial*, 130:1. See Zervos, "Dating," 432-4 where, given Justin's reference to the cave in *Dial*. 78, he may have included the *ProtJac* among the "memoires of the Apostles" along with Matthew and Luke. It should be noted that heretofore Justin was thought to have been the first early Christian writer to demonstrate knowledge of, and to cite substantial passages from, canonical Matthew and Luke. But if the Redactor was indeed one of Justin's disciples, then the "author" of the *ProtJac* can now lay equal claim to this distinction.

ἀκολούθως τῇ ἐν τῷ εὐαγγελίῳ περὶ τῆς γενέσεως αὐτοῦ ἱστορίᾳ
"Following the story about the Nativity in the Gospel,
δείκνυται <u>τὸ ἐν Βηθλεὲμ σπήλαιον</u>, ἔνθα ἐγεννήθη,
there is shown <u>in Bethlehem the cave</u> in which he was born,
καὶ ἡ ἐν τῷ σπηλαίῳ φάτνη, ἔνθα ἐσπαργανώθη.
and in the cave the manger in which he was wrapped.
Καὶ τὸ δεικνύμενον τοῦτο διαβόητόν ἐστιν ἐν τοῖς τόποις
And that which is shown is famous in these places
καὶ παρὰ τοῖς τῆς πίστεως ἀλλοτρίοις,
and among those who are foreign to the faith,
ὡς ἄρα <u>ἐν τῷ σπηλαίῳ τούτῳ</u> ὁ ὑπὸ Χριστιανῶν
as it was <u>in this cave</u> that he who by the Christians
προσκυνούμενος καὶ θαυμαζόμενος <u>γεγέννηται Ἰησοῦς</u>.
is worshipped and revered, <u>Jesus, was born.</u>

Much had changed in the century that had passed from Justin to Origen with respect to their perception of the Cave of the Nativity. Origen represents an intermediate stage between the earlier ambiguity regarding the location of the cave in Justin and the Redactor on the one hand, and the creation of the Via Sacra, which followed a century after Origen on the other. With the passage of time the influence of the canonical Gospels spread and the traditions contained in them became accepted in the church as the authoritative truth of the events of the life of Jesus.[173] Origen himself represents a primary witness to the completion of that process. The traditions preserved in the CEGM were amalgamated with those of the canonical Gospels in the formation of the developing "Orthodox Tradition."[174] Within the framework of the "Via Sacra," the Cave of the Nativity, of which the *ProtJac* was the original source, was relocated to its present canonical setting in Bethlehem and was supplanted by a holy rock at its original location in the "middle of the way" between the two holiest cities in the Christian faith. And the rock came to represent a temporary resting place upon which Mary supposedly sat on her way to the new location of the Nativity in Bethlehem.

---

173. Recall for example the consternation caused by Luke's erroneous reference to the Quirinian census of 6 CE, "The Nativity Complex," pp. 78–84.

174. In the Christian East the *ProtJac* was widely accepted as an authoritative, although not canonical, source of information on Mary and the Nativity of Jesus. The canonical Nativity stories were combined with those in the Composer's document: Jesus was born in a cave in Bethlehem. Western Christianity has accepted nothing directly from the *ProtJac* itself because of its condemnation in the so-called Gelasian Decree of the fifth or sixth century CE. Traditions originating in the *ProtJac* did make their way into Western theology through later apocryphal documents whose primary source was the *ProtJac*, such as the Gospel of *Pseudo-Matthew*. The West has retained the canonical version of Jesus's Nativity in Bethlehem but preferred Luke's manger motif, including a stable with animals, over Matthew's scenario, which took place in a house.

All the investigators of the Kathisma Church have worked under the influence of the de Strycker consensus opinion of the *ProtJac* as a unitary, single-author, second-century document. Consequently, they have consistently misinterpreted the witness of the *ProtJac* regarding the events that transpired halfway between Jerusalem and Bethlehem, stating repeatedly, almost as a mantra, the erroneous opinion that the *ProtJac* spoke of this location as the place where Mary rested before giving birth, rather than as the setting of the Nativity itself. But the researchers are divided into two camps with respect to the significance of the *ProtJac* as a witness to the early veneration of Mary at the scene of the Kathisma church and especially to the possible existence of early celebrations of the Nativity at that site before the church was built.

Avner persistently rejects this possibility on the basis of her *argumentum ex silentio* of the absence of "material evidence" that would support the existence of any such veneration. She cites the work of Joan Taylor to bolster her position.

In fact the text of the *Protevangelion*, preserving the legend of Mary's rest on the road to Bethlehem before Christ's birth, contradicts the possibility that the Kathisma could have been the site of the Nativity outside Bethlehem. This may be concluded from the details of the account of Mary's rest after she and Joseph passed the third milestone halfway along the road to Bethlehem. By this account the event that took place at the third mile was Mary's vision of the two people. This incongruity was noticed and discussed by Joan Taylor, who investigated other important early Christian sites, including those established by Constantine.[175]

Not only is Avner's position regarding the *ProtJac* inaccurate, but Taylor's treatment of our document contains numerous glaring errors as well. She refers to the *ProtJac* as a third-century work and states that it "shows an acute ignorance of Palestinian geography and Jewish customs." Taylor judges that the *ProtJac* "clearly arose in a Gentile environment far from the Middle East" and that "its reliability as an historical source for information about the actual location of Jesus' birth is, therefore, very limited."[176] Taylor cites dated information from Cullman's 1963 article as her only source of information on the *ProtJac*.[177]

---

175. *Tradition*, 18; Avner's n. 47, citing J. E. Taylor, *Christians and the Holy Places: The Myth of Jewish-Christian Origins* (Oxford; New York: Clarendon Press, 1993), 99–103, 336, esp. 103. One wonders what "material evidence" could have existed that has not been wiped clean by the successive builders on the Kathisma site.

176. *Christians*, 101.

177. Oscar Cullman, "The Protevangelium of James," trans. A. J. B. Higgins in Edgar Hennecke, ed., W. Schneemelcher, Eng. trans. ed. R. McL Wilson, *New Testament Apocrypha* (Philadelphia: Westminster Press, 1963), vol. I, 370–88. Even Avner does not accept the ignorance of Palestinian Geography in the *ProtJac*. Taylor relies too heavily on the symbology of the cave in her assessment of Justin and the *ProtJac*.

However, Taylor does offer some valuable insights that are pertinent to our discussion. In taking up the issue of "literary evidence from the second and third centuries that would appear at first sight to connect the birth of Jesus with a cave somewhere in the vicinity of Bethlehem," she correctly references Justin Martyr's *Dial.* 78 as "the earliest of the texts."[178] Noting that Justin does not give the source of his information, Taylor speculates that Justin's source (1) "may have been Church tradition" or (2) "may also have been from an apocryphal story."[179] Taylor favors option 2:

> There is some reason to suppose that Justin is employing some sort of apocryphal story as a basis for his explanation, for he gives us three details which are not found in the Gospels: the stable was a cave, the cave was outside the village, and the Magi were Arabs. These details are more than romantic additions, and come from somewhere other than the New Testament nativity stories as know them. But Justin does not give his source, and indeed this may have been oral.[180]

Because of her flawed understanding of the date and multilevel compositional character of the *ProtJac*, Taylor misses the obvious: the *ProtJac* is, in fact, the only viable candidate to be the "apocryphal story" that was the source of Justin Martyr's information about the birth of Jesus in a cave nearby, but outside of, Bethlehem and farther away than the Tomb of Rachel. This is the exact location of the Cave of the Nativity in the *ProtJac*. But even after completely nullifying the *ProtJac* story as a viable source for Justin's information, in the midst of her error Taylor does speak truth: "It may have been an archaic form of this story that was known by Justin, [i.e., our CEGM]." And, Taylor opines, although the "legendary" *ProtJac* should not be used as evidence for the early Christian veneration of the grotto inside Bethlehem, "even if it were to be used as an historical source, it could only tell us of a cave in the Wilderness of Judea over three kilometers distant from Bethlehem."[181] Taylor has thus validated the *ProtJac*.

Although adhering as well to the consensus model of a unitary, single-author, second-century *ProtJac*, some scholars rightly perceive the importance of the *ProtJac* as the primary witness to a tradition among the earliest followers of Jesus specifically related to his birth in a cave at the three-mile site between Jerusalem and Bethlehem. Both Shoemaker and Walter D. Ray[182] conducted extensive studies of the ancient liturgical evidence, especially the Armenian Lectionary and the Georgian Calendar, and recognized the great significance of the *ProtJac* as a

---

178. *Christians*, 99.
179. Ibid., 99–100.
180. Ibid., 100. Taylor notes that Justin was born in Neapolis in Samaria.
181. Ibid., 102.
182. *August 15 and the Development of the Jerusalem Calendar* (PhD Dissertation, University of Notre Dame, 2000).

witness to the early veneration of Mary at the scene of the Kathisma church and to the possible existence of early celebrations of the Nativity at that site before the church was built. Shoemaker and Ray found that both of these sources "mention the 'Feast of the Theotokos' [the Birth-giver of God] celebrated at the Kathisma in the month of August." Avner herself makes reference to the witness of the ancient Armenian Lectionary and associates it with

> architectural remains that pre-date the construction of the octagonal church in c. 456 CE. These remains were ascribed to the period of the Armenian Lectionary (i.e., 417–439 CE). The Armenian lectionary, which reflects the liturgy of Jerusalem in the early fifth century mentions the feast of the Theotokos celebrated on August 15th in the Kathisma, which it describes as situated on the road halfway from Jerusalem to Bethlehem.[183]

Ray presents a convincing cumulative argument for the intensely incarnational character of the August 15 Feast of the Theotokos in the ancient Armenian and slightly later Georgian lectionaries. He conducts a comprehensive survey and analysis of the OT (Isa. 7:10-16a and Ps. 109) and NT (Lk. 2:1-7 and Gal. 3:29–4:7) readings, as well as the hymnological elements of the antiphon (Ps. 131:8), and alleluias. These readings and hymns were recorded in these lectionaries for the August 15 Marian feast in the Jerusalem church and were found as well in the Christmas Eve vigil in Constantinople, in early Syria proper and East Syria, in Rome, and as far afield as the churches in Spain and Gaul. Ray further brings to bear the significant evidence of the early Christian writers, Justin Martyr, Melito of Sardis, Tertullian, Irenaeus, Clement of Alexandria, and Eusebius; as well as patristic homilies by Hesychius, Chrysippus, Epiphanius, Athanasius, Gregory Nazianzen, Pope Leo I, and Asterius the Sophist that contained incarnational elements and were delivered on various liturgical observations related to the Nativity.[184]

Shoemaker also understands the importance of the non-narrative liturgical history as a witness to the early history of the ancient Marian traditions and that liturgical history can often help to date and better understand certain early narratives. In chapter 2 of his seminal book,[185] he undertakes an exhaustive reassessment of the ancient Marian shrines of Jerusalem and their related liturgies, considering first the material evidence of Marian veneration, including the Kathisma as one of two primary Marian churches. He then examines the Marian liturgies of ancient Jerusalem as witnesses to the earliest development of the cult of the Virgin and its relationship to the early Marian shrines in late ancient Jerusalem. Shoemaker states:

183. "*Presbeia Theotokou*," 42.
184. *August 15*, 41–4, 58–94.
185. "*Ancient Traditions*," 78–141.

[The Kathisma] church is the first known centre of organized Marian cult in the Holy Land. Our earliest sources indicate that the Kathisma church was built to commemorate the spot where, according to the *Protevangelium of James*, the Virgin descended from an ass and rested before giving birth to Christ. Although it appears from this and other indicators that the site of the Kathisma was originally associated with the celebration of the Nativity, by the beginning of the fifth century this church had become an important centre of Marian cult.[186]

Shoemaker weaves together the material and literary evidence to fashion a strong argument for the original character of the liturgical setting at the "middle of the way" as an observation of the Nativity of Jesus. He focuses on the ancient Jerusalem Armenian Lectionary, which he describes as a calendar of the liturgical practices in Jerusalem dated 420–440 CE, and as the first text to draw attention to the "middle of the way" site other than the *ProtJac*. He notes that the Lectionary does not name or even indicate the existence of a church at the site and does not associate the location with the tradition from the *ProtJac* but only describes a "Feast of the Theotokos" celebrated at the "mid-point of the Jerusalem-Bethlehem road."[187] But Shoemaker does consider the *ProtJac* to have been the original source of the location of the "three-mile" site of the Kathisma:

Since the site of the Kathisma church itself appears to derive its initial significance from the events of the Nativity as described in the second-century *Protevangelium of James*, it is not at all surprising to find that its primary liturgical celebration was originally linked with the birth of Christ.[188]

Shoemaker notes that the actual readings from the August 15 "Feast of the Theotokos" in the Armenian Lectionary attest to the feast's association with the Nativity:

- The lection from the Hebrew scriptures is Isaiah 7:10-16 ("Behold, a virgin shall conceive", as the Christians were reading it);
- The Epistle reading is Galatians 3:29-4:7, in which Paul emphasizes redemption by God's son, "born of a woman";
- And the Gospel text is the beginning of Luke's birth narrative, which describes Mary's birthing of Christ.[189]

---

186. Ibid., 79–80. Note that Shoemaker still erroneously includes the element of Mary's "rest" in the *ProtJac* story.
187. *Ancient Traditions*, 82, 96.
188. Ibid., 117.
189. Ibid.

Shoemaker also finds that the common theme from the scriptural readings centering upon the birth of Christ by Mary is confirmed by homilies delivered by the priest Hesychius of Jerusalem in the first half of the fifth century. Hesychius's Homily 5, which, according to Shoemaker, was probably delivered on August 15 in the Kathisma church, concerns the role of the virgin Mary in the Nativity and refers to the Nativity-oriented biblical readings in the Armenian Lectionary four times.[190]

Shoemaker and Ray have thus demonstrated that the evidence indicates that the three-mile Kathisma site was originally identified with the Nativity of Jesus and the motherhood of Mary, and not with the legendary concept of Mary resting on her way to a secondary Nativity in Bethlehem. The obvious question arises: what could have happened to change the character of the Kathisma location from being the actual site of the Nativity to its later manifestation as the location where Mary merely paused to rest on her way to giving birth in Bethlehem? Where then, and when, did this legend of Mary's rest originate? Ray provides an appropriate answer to these questions:

> What we see, then, is a progressive reconfiguration of the tradition concerning the station at the third mile. What starts out as the place of Christ's birth becomes the place where Mary rested on her way to Bethlehem, and ends up as the place where she rested as the holy family fled to Egypt.[191] Such an [sic] transformation could be anticipated after the location of Christ's birth had been fixed at the cave in Bethlehem by Constantine's construction and the Jerusalem liturgy.[192]

In spite of viewing the *ProtJac* as a second-century writing, Ray suggests that the three-mile location of the Nativity in the *ProtJac* may reflect an earlier, local, "received" Jerusalem tradition: "The precision and accuracy with which the *Protevangelium* locates this spot—the third mile is indeed the middle of the

---

190. Ibid.

191. Avner, *Tradition*, 27–8, records a later, confused tradition that identified the Kathisma site as the place where Mary rested after the Nativity during her flight to Egypt with Joseph and her newly born child. Shoemaker, *Ancient Traditions*, 90–5, 97–8, identifies the sixth-century apocryphal Latin Gospel of Pseudo-Matthew as the source of the tradition of the flight to Egypt by Joseph, Mary, and the infant Jesus that was confused and conflated with the *ProtJac* story. The conflated story even found its way into the Quran when the Kathisma was later converted into a mosque in which Mary continued to be venerated by Muslims.

192. *August 15*, 58; cf. William S. Abruzzi, "The Birth of Jesus: A Critical Analysis of the Infancy Narratives," 15–16. See the numerous references to the "grotto" of the Nativity in the detailed study of Constantine's Church of the Nativity in Bacci, "Historical and Archaeological Analysis," cf. pp. 206–7, n. 151 above.

journey from Jerusalem to Bethlehem as the narrative says—suggests that this is a tradition local to Jerusalem."[193] The information revealed in our investigation supports this possibility. If the tradition of the Nativity in the three-mile cave that is contained in the *GenMar*, or at least in the CEGM, was current among at least some first-century Judean-Christians, this could very well have been the source of Ray's suggested "tradition local to Jerusalem."

In any case, the authority of the early tradition of the Nativity cave in the *GenMar* and the CEGM was so great that when the site of the Nativity was transferred from three miles outside of Bethlehem to Bethlehem itself in the fourth century, this cave motif was retained and imposed upon the canonical Gospel tradition, which had no mention of the cave. In fact, the "Grotto," or Cave of the Nativity as it is called, represents the central feature of the Constantinian basilica in Bethlehem and is maintained to be the precise spot at which Jesus was born.[194] It remained only for the Kathisma church to be built a century later at the three-mile setting and for this church to be reinvented as the place where Mary simply rested on her way to give birth in Bethlehem. And the reconfigured Kathisma church would now take its place as part of the new Christian Via Sacra as the halfway point between the new basilica of the Nativity in Bethlehem and the church of the Resurrection in Jerusalem.

The following pages contain images of the actual site of the Kathisma church taken personally by Professor James H. Charlesworth. Image 1 shows the octagonal foundations of the ancient church from a wider angle and Image 2 from a narrower angle. In both images the modern Jerusalem-Bethlehem road is clearly visible close by the foundations. This accurately represents the scenario described in the *ProtJac* according to which Joseph and Mary stopped on their journey "in the middle of the way" between Jerusalem to Bethlehem because Mary's child was "pressing" her to come forth (*ProtJac* 17:11). Joseph took Mary down from the donkey "there" (*ProtJac* 17:12) "and found a cave there and took her into [the cave]" (*ProtJac* 18:01). Image 3 is a close-up view of the stone in the middle of the Kathisma Church upon which later tradition claimed that Mary sat to rest. Image 4 depicts a cave nearby that exemplifies the type of rocky overhang that Joseph could have found as a shelter for Mary.

---

193. *August 15*, 56–57; cf. 57, n. 51, where Ray cites the early pilgrim accounts that "always locate Bethlehem six miles from Jerusalem, so that the third mile marker would have been halfway between Jerusalem and Bethlehem, and the text clearly intends to equate these two spatial indicators. Such precision can hardly be pure fantasy. It is more likely that the author was using some kind of received tradition."

194. Bacci, "Historical and Archaeological Analysis," especially e9.

ILLUSTRATIONS

Image 1 Wide angle view of the foundations of the ancient church.

Image 2 Narrower angle view of the foundations of the church.

Image 3 Close-up view of the stone in the middle of the church.

Image 4 Nearby rocky overhang possibly exemplifying the cave in the *ProtJac*.

www.ingramcontent.com/pod-product-compliance
Lightning Source LLC
Chambersburg PA
CBHW052037300426
44117CB00012B/1863